Seeing is understanding: The effect of visualisation in understanding programming concepts

by

Dr Jason Zagami
B.Sc., Grad.Dip.Ed., M.Ed., PhD
Griffith University, Australia
jason.zagami.info

2012

Version 2.0
Copyright 2012 EduTechPress
All rights reserved.
ISBN: 978-1-62154-682-5

Published by EduTechPress

Zagami, J. (2012). Seeing Is Understanding: The Effect of Visualisation in Understanding Programming Concepts. Brisbane, QLD: EduTechPress.

Preface

How and why visualisations support learning was the subject of this qualitative instrumental collective case study. Five computer programming languages (PHP, Visual Basic, Alice, GameMaker, and RoboLab) supporting differing degrees of visualisation were used as cases to explore the effectiveness of software visualisation to develop fundamental computer programming concepts (sequence, iteration, selection, and modularity). Cognitive theories of visual and auditory processing, cognitive load, and mental models provided a framework in which student cognitive development was tracked and measured by thirty-one 15-17 year old students drawn from a Queensland metropolitan secondary private girls' school, as active participants in the research. Seventeen findings in three sections increase our understanding of the effects of visualisation on the learning process. The study extended the use of mental model theory to track the learning process, and demonstrated application of student research based metacognitive analysis on individual and peer cognitive development as a means to support research and as an approach to teaching. The findings also forward an explanation for failures in previous software visualisation studies, in particular the study has demonstrated that for the cases examined, where complex concepts are being developed, the mixing of auditory (or text) and visual elements can result in excessive cognitive load and impede learning. This finding provides a framework for selecting the most appropriate instructional programming language based on the cognitive complexity of the concepts under study.

Keywords

Learning, Visualisation, Mental Model, Programming, Cognitive Load

Contents

Chapter 1

INTRODUCTION 1

    1.1   Background 1

    1.2   Aims of the study 6

    1.3   Significance of the research 7

    1.4   Overview of this study 10

    1.5   Overview of the text 11

    1.6   Terminology 13

Chapter 2

LITERATURE REVIEW 15

    2.1   Visual and auditory processing theory 16

    2.2   Visualisation to support visual processing 26

    2.3   Development of cognitive mental models 29

    2.4   Identification of cognitive levels 36

    2.5   Theoretical models of memory 41

    2.6   Synthesis of the literature 53

Chapter 3   58

CASES: VISUALISATION TOOLS..

    3.1   Unconstrained text.. 61

    3.2   Constrained text.. 64

    3.3   Constrained icons... 65

    3.4   Unconstrained icons... 67

Chapter 4

RESEARCH METHODOLOGY.. 69

    4.1   Collective case studies and narratives................... 70

    4.2   Subjects.. 72

    4.3   Phases of the study.. 75

        4.3.1 Phase 1... 78

        4.3.2 Phase 2... 79

        4.3.3 Phase 3... 80

            4.3.3.1 Problem set completion........................ 80

            4.3.3.2 Final concept map............................... 82

            4.3.3.3 Trace development with stimulated recall........... 82

            4.3.3.4 Verification of student generated traces.............. 83

        4.3.4 Phase 4... 83

        4.3.5 Phase 5... 83

        4.3.6 Phase 6... 84

        4.3.7 Phase 7... 85

4.4	**Data Collection**		85
	4.4.1 Concept Maps		85
	4.4.2 Stimulated Recall		86
		4.4.2.1 Video Recording	87
		4.4.2.2 Screen Recording	89
		4.4.2.3 Speak Aloud	89
		4.4.2.4 Peer Discussion	89
		4.4.2.5 Student Journals	90
		4.4.2.6 Researcher Journal	90
	4.4.3 Surveys		90
		4.4.3.1 Survey 1	90
		4.4.3.2 Survey 2	91
	4.4.4 Trace Analysis		91
	4.4.5 Narrative development		93
4.5	**Data Analysis**		93
	4.5.1 Concept development		93
		4.5.1.1 Level 1 coding	95
		4.5.1.2 Level 2 coding	95
		4.5.1.3 Level 3 coding	96
		4.5.1.4 Level 4 coding	96
		4.5.1.5 Level 5 coding	97
		4.5.1.6 Level 6 coding	97
		4.5.1.7 Level 7 coding	98
		4.5.1.8 Level 8 coding	99
	4.5.2 Trace analysis		99

	4.5.3	Narrative development	100
4.6	**Trustworthiness**		100
4.7	**Role of the researcher**		103
4.8	**Limitations of the study**		105
4.9	**Graphs used in the study**		107
	4.9.1	3D Line Graph	107
	4.9.2	Stacked Column Graph	109
	4.9.3	Standard Bar Graph	109
	4.9.4	Radar Plot Graphs	110

Chapter 5

FINDINGS OF THE STUDY 112

5.1	**Concept development by individual students**		113
	5.1.1	Cohort A	114
		5.1.1.1 Student A1a	115
		5.1.1.2 Student A1b	116
		5.1.1.3 Student A2a	117
		5.1.1.4 Student A2b	118
		5.1.1.5 Student A3a	119
		5.1.1.6 Student A3b	121
		5.1.1.7 Student A4a	122
		5.1.1.8 Student A4b	123
		5.1.1.9 Student A4c	124
	5.1.2	Cohort B	125

5.1.2.1 Student B1a 125

5.1.2.2 Student B1b 127

5.1.2.3 Student B2a 128

5.1.2.4 Student B2b 129

5.1.2.5 Student B3a 130

5.1.2.6 Student B3b 131

5.1.2.7 Student B4a 132

5.1.2.8 Student B4b 133

5.1.2.9 Student B5a 134

5.1.2.10 Student B5b 135

5.1.2.11 Student B6a 136

5.1.2.12 Student B6b 137

5.1.3 Cohort C 138

5.1.3.1 Student C1a 138

5.1.3.2 Student C1b 139

5.1.3.3 Student C2a 140

5.1.3.4 Student C2b 141

5.1.3.5 Student C3a 142

5.1.3.6 Student C3b 143

5.1.3.7 Student C4a 144

5.1.3.8 Student C4b 145

5.1.4 Cohort D 146

5.1.4.1 Student D1a 146

5.1.4.2 Student D2a 148

5.1.5 Concept development comparison 149

		5.1.6 Visualisation tool comparison	151
5.2	**Effectiveness surveys**		157
	5.2.1	Survey 1	157
	5.2.2	Survey 2	174
5.3	**Mental model traces**		182
	5.3.1	Student A1a	184
	5.3.2	Student A2b	186
	5.3.3	Student A3a	187
	5.3.4	Student A4a	188
	5.3.5	Student A4c	189
	5.3.6	Student B1b	191
	5.3.7	Student B2a	193
	5.3.8	Student B2b	194
	5.3.9	Student B3a	195
	5.3.10	Student B4a	196
	5.3.11	Student B4b	197
	5.3.12	Student B5b	198
	5.3.13	Student B6a	199
	5.3.14	Student B6b	200
	5.3.15	Student C1b	201
	5.3.16	Student C2a	202
	5.3.17	Student C3a	203
	5.3.18	Student C4b	204
	5.3.19	Student D1a	205
	5.3.20	Student D2a	206

Chapter 6

NARRATIVES 208

- **6.1 Frodo** 209
- **6.2 Sam** 212
- **6.3 Legolas** 214
- **6.4 Gimli** 217
- **6.5 Gandalf** 220
- **6.6 Aragorn** 222
- **6.7 Boromir** 224
- **6.8 Pippin** 226
- **6.9 Merry** 229

Chapter 7

DISCUSSION 233

- **7.1 Everyman – the archetypical response** 234
- **7.2 Plateauing** 236
- **7.3 Effect of prior learning** 241
- **7.4 Effect of degree of visualisation (different tools)** 244
- **7.5 Effect of degree of visualisation (same tool)** 245

Chapter 8

CONCLUSIONS ... 253

    8.1   The effect of visualisation on the learning process   254

    8.2   Mental model theory to track the learning process.   257

    8.3   Reasons for the failure of previous studies ... 258

    8.4   Summary of contributions ... 259

    8.5   Future research ... 261

REFERENCES ... 264

APPENDICES ... 287

List of Appendices

APPENDIX A	Survey 1: Effectiveness survey (Visualisation tool)	287
APPENDIX B	Survey 2: Effectiveness survey (Multiple tools)	288
APPENDIX C	Mental Model Development Rubric	290
APPENDIX D	Student Workbook – Sequence (Alice)	295
APPENDIX E	Student Workbook (Part) – Iteration (Alice)	306
APPENDIX F	Student Workbook (Part) – Selection (Alice)	308

List of Tables

Table 4.1	Allocation of cohorts to visualisation tools and concepts	74
Table 4.2	Cohort- Participation Level	77

List of Figures

Figure 2.1	Pre-attention causes the oblique line to be detected effortlessly (Crapo, 2002)...	17
Figure 2.2	Lack of pre-attentive features causes difficulties (Crapo, 2002)..........	18
Figure 2.3	EPIC model of cognition...	19
Figure 2.4	Model Human Processor (MHP) model of cognition (complex).........	20
Figure 2.5	Model Human Processor (MHP) model of cognition (simplified).......	21
Figure 2.6	Proximity (Ware, 2000)...	23
Figure 2.7	Similarity (Ware, 2000)...	23
Figure 2.8	Continuity (Ware, 2000)..	24
Figure 2.9	Connectedness (Ware, 2000)..	24
Figure 2.10	Closure (Ware, 2000)...	25
Figure 2.11	Mental Models, views, and visualisations (Waisel, 1998)...................	31
Figure 2.12	Elements of visualisation in model formation (Waisel, 1998).............	32
Figure 2.13	The process of model formation with visualisation within Johnson-Laird's phase of Description (Waisel, 1998)..	34
Figure 2.14	Pirie Kieren pictorial representation of understanding........................	37
Figure 2.15	ACT model (Anderson, 1983)..	43
Figure 2.16	Dual coding theory (Paivio, 1986)..	44
Figure 2.17	Model of multimedia learning (Mayer, 2001)....................................	46
Figure 2.18	An integrated model of text and picture comprehension (Schnotz & Bannert, 2003)..	47
Figure 2.19	Mental models formed by neural linkages...	56
Figure 3.1	Visualisation constraint continua..	60
Figure 3.2	PHP environment..	61

xiii

Figure 3.3	Visual Basic programming environment	63
Figure 3.4	Alice programming environment	64
Figure 3.5	GameMaker programming environment	66
Figure 3.6	RoboLab programming environment	67
Figure 4.1	Student screen capture with inline video capture	81
Figure 4.2	Trace development on Pirie-Kieren model	92
Figure 4.3	Example 3D line graph	108
Figure 4.4	Example stacked column graph	109
Figure 4.5	Example standard bar graph	110
Figure 4.6	Example radar plot graph	111
Figure 5.1	Student A1a	115
Figure 5.2	Student A1b	116
Figure 5.3	Student A2a	117
Figure 5.4	Student A2b	118
Figure 5.5	Student A3a	120
Figure 5.6	Student A3b	121
Figure 5.7	Student A4a	122
Figure 5.8	Student A4b	123
Figure 5.9	Student A4c	124
Figure 5.10	Student B1a	126
Figure 5.11	Student B1b	127
Figure 5.12	Student B2a	128
Figure 5.13	Student B2b	129
Figure 5.14	Student B3a	130
Figure 5.15	Student B3b	131

Figure 5.16	Student B4a	132
Figure 5.17	Student B4b	133
Figure 5.18	Student B5a	134
Figure 5.19	Student B5b	135
Figure 5.20	Student B6a	136
Figure 5.21	Student B6b	137
Figure 5.22	Student C1a	138
Figure 5.23	Student C1b	139
Figure 5.24	Student C2a	140
Figure 5.25	Student C2b	141
Figure 5.26	Student C3a	142
Figure 5.27	Student C3b	143
Figure 5.28	Student C4a	144
Figure 5.29	Student C4b	145
Figure 5.30	Student D1a	147
Figure 5.31	Student D2a	148
Figure 5.32	Overall concept development effectiveness	150
Figure 5.33	Overall visualisation tool effectiveness – Sequence	152
Figure 5.34	Overall visualisation tool effectiveness – Iteration	153
Figure 5.35	Overall visualisation tool effectiveness – Selection	154
Figure 5.36	Overall visualisation tool effectiveness – Modularity	155
Figure 5.37	Overall visualisation tool effectiveness – Combined	156
Figure 5.38	Student perception of tool effectiveness in learning – Sequence	158
Figure 5.49	Student perception of tool effectiveness in learning – Iteration	159
Figure 5.40	Student perception of tool effectiveness in learning – Selection	160

Figure 5.41	Student perception of tool effectiveness in learning – Modularity......	161
Figure 5.42	Student perception of enjoyment – Sequence.....................................	162
Figure 5.43	Student perception of enjoyment – Iteration.......................................	163
Figure 5.44	Student perception of enjoyment – Selection......................................	164
Figure 5.45	Student perception of enjoyment – Modularity...................................	165
Figure 5.46	Student perception of speed of learning – Sequence...........................	166
Figure 5.47	Student perception of speed of learning – Iteration.............................	167
Figure 5.48	Student perception of speed of learning – Selection............................	168
Figure 5.49	Student perception of speed of learning – Modularity.........................	169
Figure 5.50	Student perception overall – Sequence..	170
Figure 5.51	Student perception overall – Iteration..	171
Figure 3.52	Student perception overall – Selection..	172
Figure 5.53	Student perception overall – Modularity...	173
Figure 5.54	Effectiveness of GameMaker over Alice – Sequence..........................	174
Figure 5.55	Effectiveness of GameMaker over Alice – Iteration...........................	175
Figure 5.56	Effectiveness of GameMaker over Alice – Selection..........................	175
Figure 5.57	Effectiveness of GameMaker over Alice – Modularity.......................	176
Figure 5.58	Enjoyment of GameMaker over Alice – Sequence.............................	176
Figure 5.59	Enjoyment of GameMaker over Alice – Iteration...............................	177
Figure 5.60	Enjoyment of GameMaker over Alice – Selection..............................	177
Figure 5.61	Enjoyment of GameMaker over Alice – Modularity...........................	178
Figure 5.62	Learning speed of GameMaker over Alice – Sequence.......................	178
Figure 5.63	Learning speed of GameMaker over Alice – Iteration........................	179
Figure 5.64	Learning speed of GameMaker over Alice – Selection.......................	179
Figure 5.65	Learning speed of GameMaker over Alice – Modularity....................	180

Figure 5.66	Overall effectiveness of GameMaker over Alice – Sequence...............	180
Figure 5.67	Overall effectiveness of GameMaker over Alice – Iteration................	181
Figure 5.68	Overall effectiveness of GameMaker over Alice – Selection..............	181
Figure 5.69	Overall effectiveness of GameMaker over Alice – Modularity............	182
Figure 5.70	Collective Trace..	184
Figure 5.71	A1a Trace...	185
Figure 5.72	A2b Trace...	186
Figure 5.73	A3a Trace...	187
Figure 5.74	A4a Trace...	188
Figure 5.75	A4c Trace...	190
Figure 5.76	B1b Trace...	192
Figure 5.77	B2a Trace...	193
Figure 5.78	B2b Trace...	194
Figure 5.79	B3a Trace...	195
Figure 5.80	B4a Trace...	196
Figure 5.81	B4b Trace...	197
Figure 5.82	B5b Trace...	198
Figure 5.83	B6a Trace...	199
Figure 5.84	B6b Trace...	200
Figure 5.85	C1b Trace...	201
Figure 5.86	C2a Trace...	202
Figure 5.87	C3a Trace...	203
Figure 5.88	C4b Trace...	204
Figure 5.89	D1a Trace...	206
Figure 5.90	D2a Trace...	207

Figure 6.1	Narratives summary by degree of visualisation	208
Figure 6.2	Frodo Trace (repeated from Figure 5.9)	211
Figure 6.3	Frodo Trace (repeated from Figure 5.75)	211
Figure 6.4	Sam Trace (repeated from Figure 5.5)	213
Figure 6.5	Sam Trace (repeated from Figure 5.73)	214
Figure 6.6	Legolas Trace (repeated from Figure 5.20)	216
Figure 6.7	Legolas Trace (repeated from Figure 5.83)	217
Figure 6.8	Gimli Trace (repeated from Figure 5.11)	219
Figure 6.9	Gimli Trace (repeated from Figure 5.76)	220
Figure 6.10	Gandalf Trace (repeated from Figure 5.16)	221
Figure 6.11	Gandalf Trace (repeated from Figure 5.80)	222
Figure 6.12	Aragorn Trace (repeated from Figure 5.29)	223
Figure 6.13	Aragorn Trace (repeated from Figure 5.88)	224
Figure 6.14	Boromir Trace (repeated from Figure 5.26)	225
Figure 6.15	Boromir Trace (repeated from Figure 5.87)	226
Figure 6.16	Pippin Trace (repeated from Figure 5.30)	228
Figure 6.17	Pippin Trace (repeated from Figure 5.89)	228
Figure 6.18	Merry Trace (repeated from Figure 5.31)	230
Figure 6.19	Merry Trace (repeated from Figure 5.90)	231
Figure 6.20	Narratives summary by tool	232
Figure 7.1	Frodo Trace (repeated from Figure 5.9)	235
Figure 7.2	Overall concept development effectiveness	236
Figure 7.3	Gimli Trace (repeated from Figure 5.11)	238
Figure 7.4	Legolas Trace (repeated from Figure 5.20)	240
Figure 7.5	Gandalf Trace (repeated from Figure 5.16)	243

Figure 7.6	Aragorn Trace (repeated from Figure 5.29)	243
Figure 7.7	Boromir Trace (repeated from Figure 5.26)	243
Figure 7.8	Sam Trace (repeated from Figure 5.5)	244
Figure 7.9	Processing continuum	245
Figure 7.10	Programming language continuum	245
Figure 7.11	Visualisation continuum	246
Figure 7.12	Overall visualisation tool effectiveness – Combined	246
Figure 7.13	Overall visualisation tool effectiveness – Sequence	248
Figure 7.14	Overall visualisation tool effectiveness – Iteration	249
Figure 7.15	Overall visualisation tool effectiveness – Selection	250
Figure 7.16	Overall visualisation tool effectiveness – Modularity	251
Figure 7.17	Overall effectiveness	252

Chapter 1

INTRODUCTION

My particular ability does not lie in mathematical calculation, but rather in visualizing effects, possibilities, and consequences

Albert Einstein (as cited in Pinker, 1997, p. 285)

1.1 Background to the study

The focus of this study is on the effect of visualisation on the learning process and, in particular, the effect of software visualisation on learning within the domain of computer programming. The study is a qualitative collective case study, based on mental model theory (Henderson, Putt, & Coombs, 2002; Hundhausen, Douglas, & Stasko, 2002; Johnson-Laird, 1983; Pirie & Kieren, 1992) which tracks the learning processes occurring and the degree to which visualisations support these processes within a population of female secondary school students.

In computer education, the use of visualisations has existed from the beginning of von Neumann computing (Goldstine & Goldstine, 1946). Starting with flowcharts, visualisation tools have migrated from the paper-based through to on-screen environments in which concepts are explained, elaborated, and more recently, generated automatically in response to student actions (Roy & St. Denis, 1976).

Software visualisation is defined as combining of the crafts of typography, graphic design, animation, and cinematography with contemporary human-computer interaction technology to facilitate both human understanding and the effective use of computer software (Price, Baecker, & Small, 1992). While software visualisation promises much as a means of supporting learning in computer education and significant research has been conducted in the field, there has been a marked lack of positive research results and a similarly low uptake of significant software visualisation techniques in computer education courses (Price, Baecker, & Small, 1992). Software visualisation systems for the study of programming concepts pose two additional challenges over those of other educational domains (Petre, Blackwell, & Green, 1996). Firstly, a challenge lies in trying to find simplicity in a complex artefact, namely computer code, to produce a selective representation of a complex abstraction. This means that code is presenting a logical rather than a physical construction. Secondly, and in contrast to the visualisation or graphic representation of a mathematical function, most software visualisation has no simple generating function. The complexity lies not just in the information to be visualised but also in the information's context of use.

There is a generally unchallenged acceptance that software visualisations can improve student learning and research such as this study continues to develop and test the effectiveness of software applications to provide students with visualisations that will aid comprehension of cognitive concepts. It can be argued that the technology to provide visualisation of concepts has advanced faster than our understanding of how such technology impacts on student learning (Grissom, McNally, & Naps, 2003).

Many claims are made on behalf of Information and Communication Technology (ICT) in education. These include improvements in student higher order thinking (Jonassen & Reeves, 1996), reduced learning retention time (Kulik, 1994), increased motivation (Wang, Haertel, & Walberg, 1993), and equity for the disadvantaged (Hsi & Hoadley, 1997) though to the wholesale democratisation of education and subsequently, society (Trow, 2000). An area in which ICT has staked a claim to general educational objectives is in supporting the development of problem-solving skills and the learning of a programming language has long been encouraged as a means of developing problem-solving ability (Kushan, 1994).

There is, however, some dispute that programming develops problem-solving skills and, in particular, the difficulties of transferring ability between domains, for example, Latin and general thinking skills (Mayer, Dyck & Vilberg, 1986). Despite this, changes to the way programming is taught have occurred. The most common response has been to change the way students learn to program with an emphasis on general problem-solving processes and less on syntax and language constructs (Soloway, 1986). Mini-languages (Brusilovsky, et al., 1997) and visual languages (Green & Petre, 1996) have developed to support this approach.

Mental model theory (see Section 2.3) is used by a number of cognitive scientists to develop cognitive representations of knowledge. In this theory, conceptual models are the tool a teacher uses to teach a concept, mental models are an understanding an individual student constructs, and this may be in variance to the conceptual model presented by the teacher (Götschi, Sanders, & Galpin, 2003).

If the adage "a picture is worth a thousand words" is applicable to education, then the use of pictures, diagrams, animations, video and multimedia should logically have an educational use in students' development of mental models of cognitive concepts. Research is conducted on visualisation as a means of supporting learning in a variety of educational domains, primarily mathematics, science, art and literature (Dimopoulos, Koulaidis, & Sklaveniti, 2003; Klotz, 1991; Presmeg, 1997; Reiber, 1995; Ursyn & Sung, 2007). In most cases, it is producing positive research results which support the use of visualisation in general and, in some instances, software visualisation to support learning in these domains. Research into visualisation in non-computer education domains has generally focused on fundamental concepts and skills in these domains further supporting the focus of this study on the concepts of computer programming.

Current research in the field of software visualisation can generally be placed into two broad categories which are elaborated in the literature review (Chapter 2). These broad categorisations are specific studies and general studies. The specific studies involve the validation of author-developed software applications aimed at improving student learning of programming languages through the application of software visualisation techniques. Such studies are predominantly conducted in undergraduate computer science courses and have focused on the most complex of concepts facing their students, in the main, recursion (Hundhausen et al., 2002; Naps et al. 2003). The results of such studies, while enthusiastic in support of software visualisation to teach programming, show minimal if any improvement and generally conclude by advocating further research. The more general studies are concerned with the use of software visualisation techniques for the learning of programming languages. The results of these general studies show very little evidence for, and in some cases against, the use of software visualisation for the learning of programming languages (Stasko & Lawrence, 1998). Much of this research is focused on complex concepts.

For the current study, in order to increase understanding of how visualisations can support the learning of computer programming, four programming concepts were selected to form the subject matter in this study (see Section 4.4.1). To provide manipulable software visualisation environments, five programming languages were selected which provided varying degrees of visualisation support (see Chapter 3) and categorised into four software visualisation tools to form the cases of study (Section 4.1). The programming concepts were selected as fundamental to the field of computer programming but not so complex that they could not effectively be studied and compared (see Section 4.4.1). From this context, the aims of this study (Section 1.2) and the significance of the research (see Section 1.3) are detailed, describing what the study sought to achieve and why. An overview of the study is provided (Section 1.4) along with an overview of the study as a whole (see Section 1.5).

1.2 Aims of the study

Within this study, three aims were addressed. These were:

1. to increase understanding of the effect of visualisation on the learning process with a focus on the effect of software visualisations on learning in the domain of programming;

2. to extend the use of mental model theory to track learning processes and incorporate metacognitive self analysis; and

3. to forward an explanation of the failure of software visualisation to improve educational outcomes in quantitative research studies through the use of a qualitative approach.

The first aim provided a general research direction, overall guidance throughout the study and broader scope to the findings. The second, while operational in nature, allowed the contextualisation and modification of mental model theory that was the study's primary analytic tool. The third aim emerged from the literature and directed greater focus to the research methodology.

1.3 Significance of the research

There is a widespread belief that visualisation technology should impact positively on learning, however, the results of quantitative experimental studies do not unequivocally support this belief (Hundhausen et al., 2002; Naps et al. 2003; Stasko & Lawrence, 1998). The emphasis of current research in this field is focused on the use of software visualisation to teach complex programming concepts and most research studies have reported inconclusive or negative educational benefit. This clear need to reconceptualise research into software visualisation became a driver of this study. An alternative approach was enacted - to conduct research into the learning of less complex and more generalised concepts, supported by a practical theoretical model, in order to better understand the processes occurring.

The inconclusive and negative results of previous quantitative research into the use of software visualisation for the teaching of programming languages suggested the application of a qualitative research study to explore the interactions involved in greater detail. Yehezkel (2003), supported by a meta-study (Hundhausen et al., 2002) suggested that ethnographic field techniques and observational studies may be more useful in understanding the *how* and *why* of software visualisation and that these would have a greater impact on the effectiveness of software visualisation research than the *what* studied by quantitative researchers in this field. Thus, a qualitative approach to determining the effectiveness of visualisation software to support learning was adopted.

The study described in this text bases its understandings on mental model theory (Hundhausen et al., 2002) with the definition of mental models being adopted that:

> Mental models are deeply ingrained assumptions or generalisations that are continuously being processed for each situation. The roots of success or failure are linked to mental models which profoundly influence how and why we act. Yet there is insubstantial research concerning the use of mental models in teaching and learning.
>
> (Henderson, Putt, & Coombs, 2002, p. 44)

By examining the effectiveness of software visualisation to teach programming concepts in this manner, a detailed understanding of the strengths and weaknesses of software visualisation to support learning was achieved. It has drawn from visualisation theories and cognitive theories of memory to produce a greater understanding of both sets of theory on the learning processes involved (see Chapter 8 - Contribution 1).

This necessitated a detailed investigation of a range of programming languages and has resulted in a categorised framework suitable for identifying the most effective programming language to teach a particular concept based on the complexity of the concept and the degree of visualisation supported by the programming language (see Chapter 8 – Contribution 2). The study has provided an explanation, for the lack of positive educational outcomes from previous studies into the use of software visualisations to teach computer programming (see Sections 2.2 and Chapter 8 – Contribution 3) supported by cognitive load theory.

In conducting this study, the researcher was also the classroom teacher of the students involved. As such, every opportunity to educate them in the PhD process, the theories involved in the study, and the research process, was taken. This quickly developed and student involvement became integral to the study. Students were taught how to track their own cognitive development using the theories supplied. They learnt to identify their current mental model level for a concept and carry out learning tasks to develop this mental model and progress their understanding to the next mental model level (see Section 2.3). They learnt how to estimate their working memory usage and the means of reducing cognitive load to improve their learning (see Section 2.5), and they learnt how to collect data (see Section 4.3) to enable them to accurate track and verify their cognitive development. In addition, students actively participated in verifying and analysing the data collected and the process built into the methodology (see Section 4.4) and significantly improved the trustworthiness of the study (see Section 4.5). This has resulted in the development of the methodology used in the study as a pedagogical framework to support student metacognitive development, self directed learning, and a classroom research culture (see Chapter 8 – Contribution 4).

1.4 Overview of the study

The study described in this text has adopted a qualitative approach to counter the limitations noted in previous studies (see Section 1.3 and 2.2). A collective case study methodology (Section 4.1) was used with each case being each of the selected visualisation tools described in Chapter 3. The collective case study was instrumental in nature, making use of the cases to investigate the broader question of the effect of visualisation on the learning process (see Section 1.2).

The participants of the study were adolescent females ($N=31$), aged 15-17 years, who were studying information and communication technology (ICT) by choice at an Australian private girls' secondary school in a metropolitan location. For the purposes of the study, they are grouped into four cohorts (A-D) which matches the organisational structures of the school and the differing courses they were studying.

The study was conducted through seven sequential steps (see Chapter 4) and made use of a range of research instruments including concept maps, video recording of "speak aloud" and peer discussions. These were combined with screen activity recordings and student journals to assist stimulated recall processes at interview and used to analyse traces of student progression through Pirie and Kieren's eight level scale (Pirie & Kieren, 1992). Two supporting survey instruments were used to measure student engagement with the software visualisation tool and, where students had experience of more than one of the four available tools, a comparison between tools was made. The first stages of the study involved all participants ($N=31$) which was later reduced, by a selective process, to a smaller group for interview and trace analysis ($n=20$).

The final stage of the study focused on a small selection of subjects ($n=9$) to develop narratives to describe the development of student mental models, the use of visualisations in this development, and the effectiveness of software visualisations to support the learning of simple programming concepts.

1.5 Overview of the text

This study presents its findings in seven chapters with supporting evidence provided in appendices to the main document. The introduction presented in this chapter defines the research problem, provides an overview of current research, discusses the aims and significance of the research and how it provides an original contribution to the existing body of knowledge in terms of visualisation and mental model theory.

The second chapter of the study, the literature review, begins by defining and describing research on (a) visual and auditory processing theory, and (b) several models linking auditory and visual processing with cognitive processing. The research concerning visualisations developed to support visualisation theory and the various uses to which software visualisation can be applied is also discussed.

The third chapter of the study presents the individual cases in this collective case study. Each case includes a description and categorisation of a software visualisation tool. These are (1) the PHP programming language representing unconstrained text, (2) the Visual Basic programming language also representing unconstrained text, (3) the *Alice* programming language representing constrained text, (4) the *GameMaker* programming language representing constrained icons, and (5) the *RoboLab* programming language representing unconstrained icons.

The methodology of the study is the collective case study; it is introduced in Section 1.4 and described in Chapter 4, detailing the subjects, phases, data collection processes, and data analysis processes of the study. It concludes with an examination of the trustworthiness of the study, the role of the researcher in the study, and limitations of the study. The findings of the study are presented progressively through Chapters 5 and 6, with a respective focus on student concept development, perceptions of effectiveness, and mental model traces annotated by selected student commentary (Chapter 5) which is developed into narratives (Chapter 6). The study concludes with discussion of the results from Chapters 5 and 6 which develop into conclusions in Chapter 7, resulting in a summary of the contributions this study makes and directions for future research.

1.6 Terminology

The following terms have been used in this study and are presented in the order that they appear in the text - full definitions are provided with detailed contextual reference in their associated sections.

Auditory Processing

Sequential and sentential, sound waves arrive over time at the ear and then to the areas of the brain responsible for language processing. Written language follows a similar process, and while passing through the optic nerve, processing again occurs in the language areas of the brain (see Section 2.1).

Visual Processing

Parallel processing with millions of photoreceptors leading to each optic nerve, visual representations are indexed spatially by location in two or three dimensions and processed in the visual areas of the brain (see Section 2.1).

Software visualisations

The means of simplifying complex artefacts such as computer code by selective visual representation of complex abstractions (see Section 2.2).

Software visualisation tools

Use display-based reasoning to provide symbolic representation of software processes in order to reduce the user's cognitive load (see Chapter 3).

Mental models

Comprise mental representations of reality used to understand phenomena, permit reasoning, and can be modified by an educative process (see Section 2.3).

Cognitive levels

Used to delineate the complexity and capacity of various stages of a mental model, eight levels are developed in this study to measure and track the development of concepts (see Section 2.4).

Short term or working memory

Comprises a temporary working space of limited capacity for auditory and visual material, material from long term memory, and for cognitive processing of this material (see Section 2.5).

Long term memory

Near permanent and essentially unlimited storage for material that includes mental models which can be modified through cognitive processing (see Section 2.5).

Dual coding

The representation and processing of auditory and visual material by separate areas of the brain (see Section 2.5).

Cognitive Load

Where working memory capacity is exceeded and this impedes learning (see Section 2.5).

Chapter 2

LITERATURE REVIEW

The literature needed to support the study described in this text is founded in computer science and psychology, particularly the sub branch of cognitive science. Attention is given to the psychological domains of (a) visual and auditory processing theory which necessarily underpins study of visualisation as a tool in learning, (b) the models which link auditory and visual processing with cognitive processing (Section 2.1), (c) the use of visualisation to support visual processing (Section 2.2), and (d) cognitive load theory (Section 2.5). The cognitive models which have been used to inform both the methodology and the findings of the study are discussed in terms of (a) their development within the individual (Section 2.3), and (b) their identification in terms of cognitive levels and level changes (Section 2.3). The methodological model adopted by this study is the eight level mental model (Pirie & Kieren, 1992). This model is described in detail in Section 2.4 through a discussion which (a) highlights the linkages between visualisations and mental model development, and (b) links it to Johnson-Laird's (1983) description of internal representations namely, mental models, propositional representations, and images.

Finally, Section 2.4 draws together theoretical models of memory and provides an explanatory framework to support findings of this study. This chapter begins by outlining the background to the research problem, that is, the efficacy of visualisations in learning (Section 2.1). It concludes with a synthesis (Section 2.6) of the contributions of the literature to the present study.

2.1 Visual and auditory processing theory

An understanding of visual and auditory processing theory is critical to the study described in this text. This section provides a foundation to understanding the processes occurring in the use of visualisations and in how mental model theory can be used to describe these processes.

Auditory processing can be differentiated from visual processing. Crapo (2002) described auditory processing as sentential, primarily sequential and almost one dimensional with sound waves arriving over time at the ear and then to the areas of the brain responsible for language processing. Spoken language is processed in this manner and generally only one conversation can be processed at a time even if multiple conversations are arriving at the ears. Written language follows a similar process, and while passing through the optic nerve, processing again occurs in the language areas of the brain. Written symbols are usually associated with sounds and form strings of symbols which have meaning and can be easily converted back into audio sequences (read aloud). What is sequenced by time in spoken language is sequenced spatially when written.

Vision, by contrast, is not one-dimensional. The retina is a two-dimensional surface and by use of various methods of determining distance to objects can produce a third spatial dimension. Time-dependent processing in our brains can add the fourth dimension of time to visual perception, for example, in motion detection. When we read a two-dimensional page of text, we do not read from any direction, we read sequentially, word by word, line by line and this is processed in the language areas of the brain. Diagrammatic representations are indexed spatially by location in two or three dimensions and processed in the visual areas of the brain.

Visual processing requires parallel processing with millions of photoreceptors leading to each optic nerve (Wade & Swanston, 1991). Numerous features including motion, colour, intensity, size, intersection, orientation, and distance can be extracted within milliseconds "pre-attentively", that is, without conscious effort. Such features seem to 'pop out' of the visual scene (Healey, Booth, & Enns, 1996). Figure 2.1 demonstrates pre-attention to orientation (Crapo, 2002) in which the eye can quickly distinguish the one line segment that is not oriented the same as the others, that is, the one oblique line in the field of vertical lines.

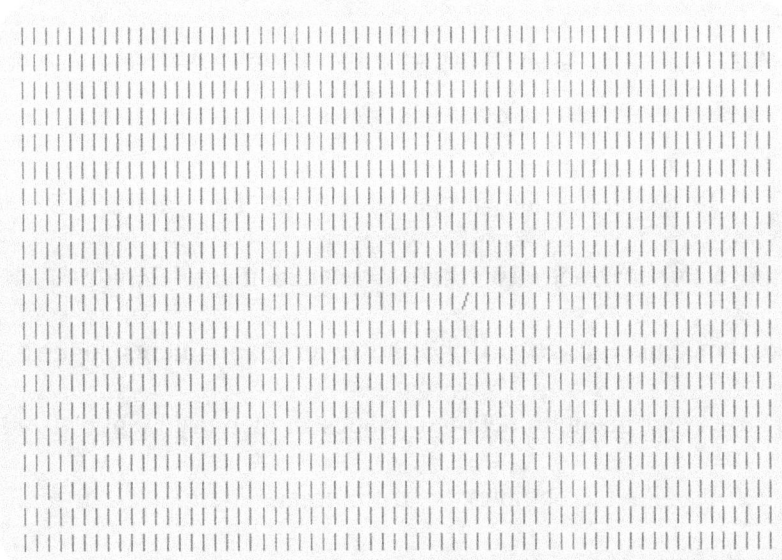

Figure 2.1   Pre-attention causes the oblique line to be detected effortlessly

(Crapo, 2002)

In contrast, it is difficult in Figure 2.2 to detect the unique numeral (an "8"), that is the only one which differs from the others. If the field size (number of objects) for Figure 2.2 was increased, it would take longer to find the "8" but if the field size for Figure 2.1 was increased, as long as it could be seen as a whole, the oblique line would still 'pop out' (Ware, 2000).

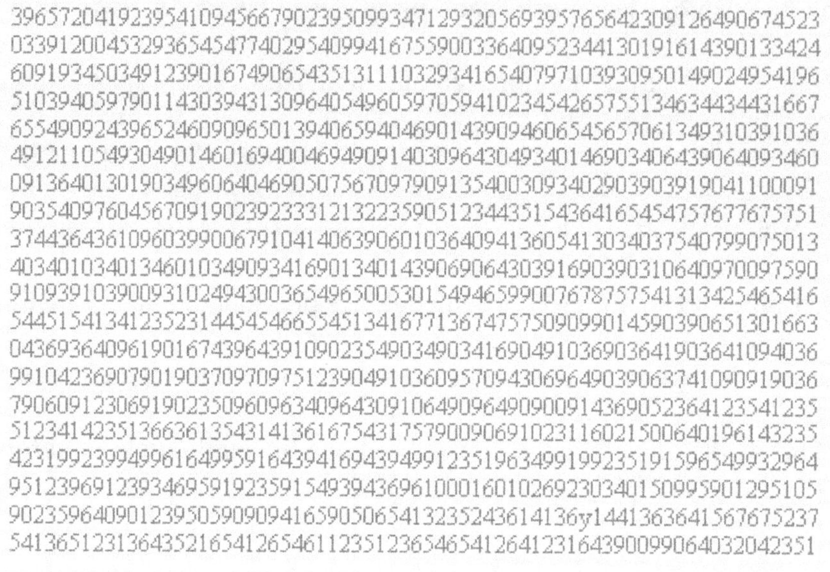

```
39657204192395410945667902395099347129320569395765642309126490674523
03391200453293654547740295409941675590033640952344130191614390133424
60919345034912390167490654351311103293416540797103930950149024954196
51039405979011430394313096405496059705941023454265755134634434431667
65549092439652460909650139406594046901439094606545657061349310391036
49121105493049014601694004694909140309643049340146903406439064093460
09136401301903496064046905075670979091354003093402903903919041100091
90354097604567091902392333121322359051234435154364165454757677675751
37443643610960399006791041406390601036409413605413034037540799075013
40340103401346010349093416901340143906906430391690390310640970097590
91093910390093102494300365496500530154946599007678757541313425465416
54451541341235231445454665545134167713674757509099014590390651301663
04369364096190167439643910902354903490341690491036903641903641094036
99104236907901903709709751239049103609570943069649039063741090919036
79060912306919023509609634096430910649096490900914369052364123541235
51234142351366361354314136167543175790090691023116021500640196143235
42319923994996164995916439416943949912351963499199235191596549932964
95123969123934695919235915493943696100016010269230340150995901295105
90235964090123950590909416590506541323524361413 6y1441363641567675237
54136512313643521654126546112351236546541264123164390099064032042351
```

Figure 2.2   Lack of pre-attentive features causes difficulties (Crapo, 2002).

Research has shown that areas of the brain active when looking at a physical scene also show activity when a detailed mental image is created and examined (Kosslyn, Sukel, & Bly, 1999), however, experiments suggest that it is difficult to construct and maintain detailed images in memory (Finke, 1990; Kosslyn, Sukel, & Bly, 1999). As the complexity of the image increases, our ability to make effective use of the image to solve problems decreases (Reisburt & Logie, 1993). It is difficult to notice things in a mental image that are not normally part of the same context as the indexing mechanisms used to retrieve the image are linked to the context of the image (Finke, 1990).

Research also suggests that problem-solving ability can be improved through the use of appropriate visualisations (Pinker, 1997; Roskos-Ewoldsen, Intons-Peterson, & Anderson, 1993; Waisel, 1998). Two main explanations are offered, that is that visualisation (a) extends working memory and (b) limits expressiveness. By reducing freedoms of expression, interpretation becomes easier making spatial visualisations such as diagrams more effective than sentential representations such as text with its inherent ambiguities. Several models have been developed to describe this cognitive process (see, for example, Gathercole & Baddeley, 1993; Kieras & Myer, 1999; Newell, 1990). The EPIC (Executive-Process/Interactive Control) model is shown in Figure 2.3 for the EPIC model (Kieras & Myer, 1999) while the Model Human Processor (MHP) model (Card, Moran & Newell, 1983) is shown in detail in Figure 2.4 and again in simplified form, Figure 2.5.

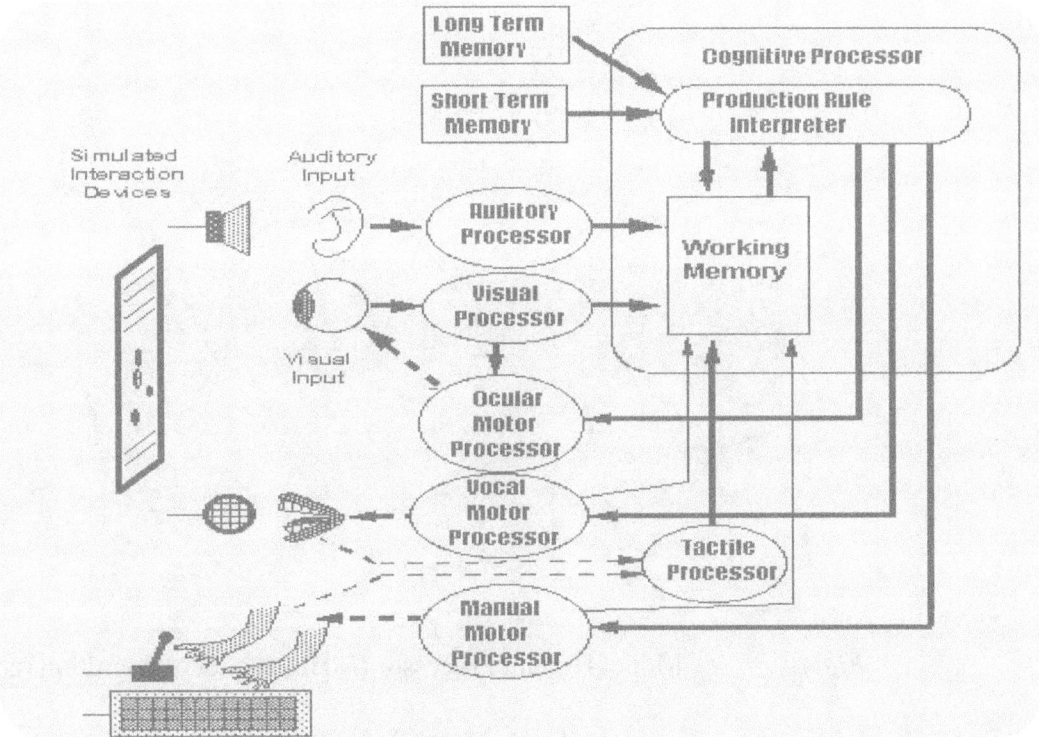

Figure 2.3   EPIC model of cognition (The Brain, Cognition, and Action Laboratory: EPIC, 2005)

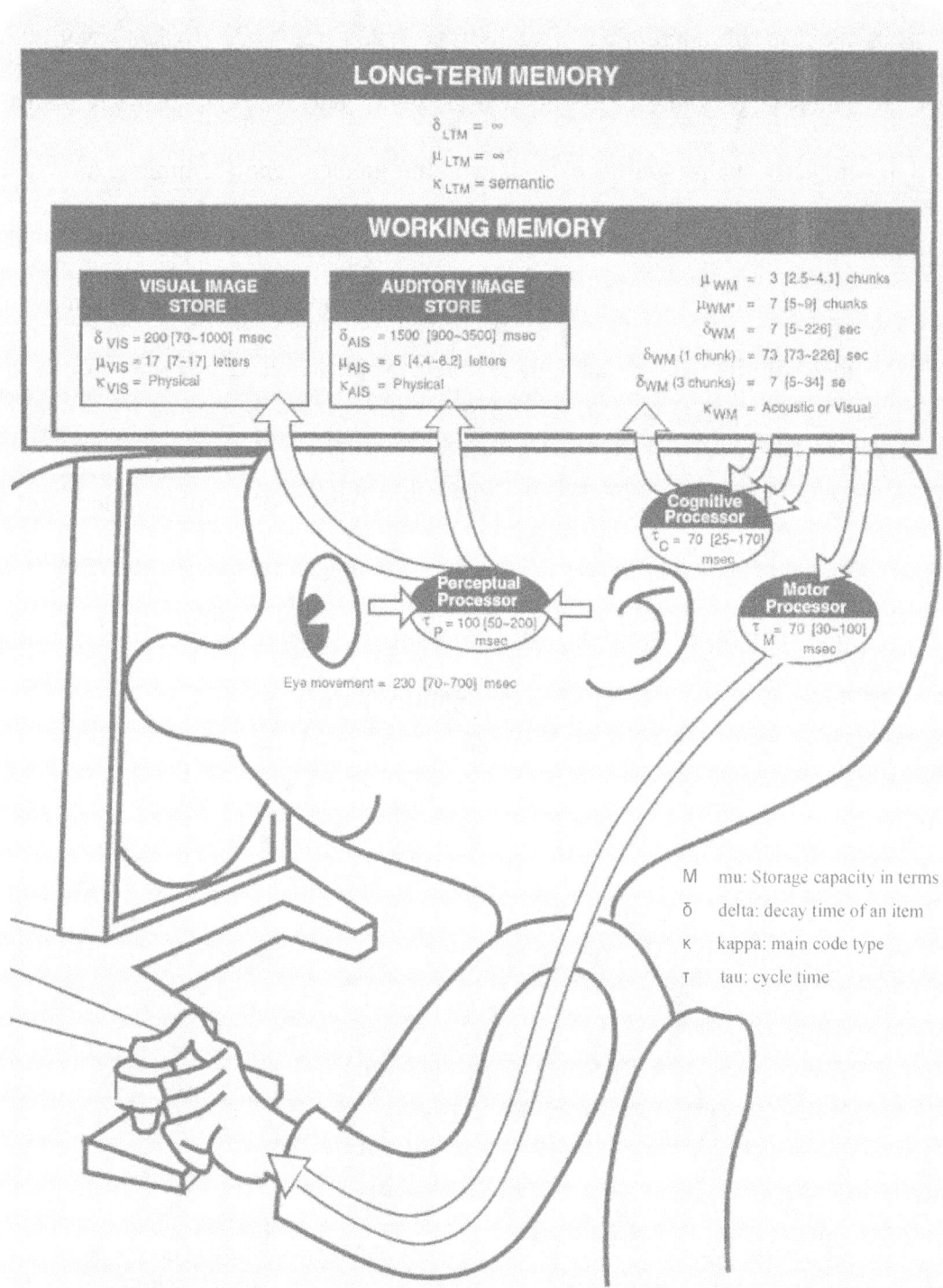

Figure 2.4   Model Human Processor (MHP) model of cognition (complex)

(Card, Moran & Newell, 1983)

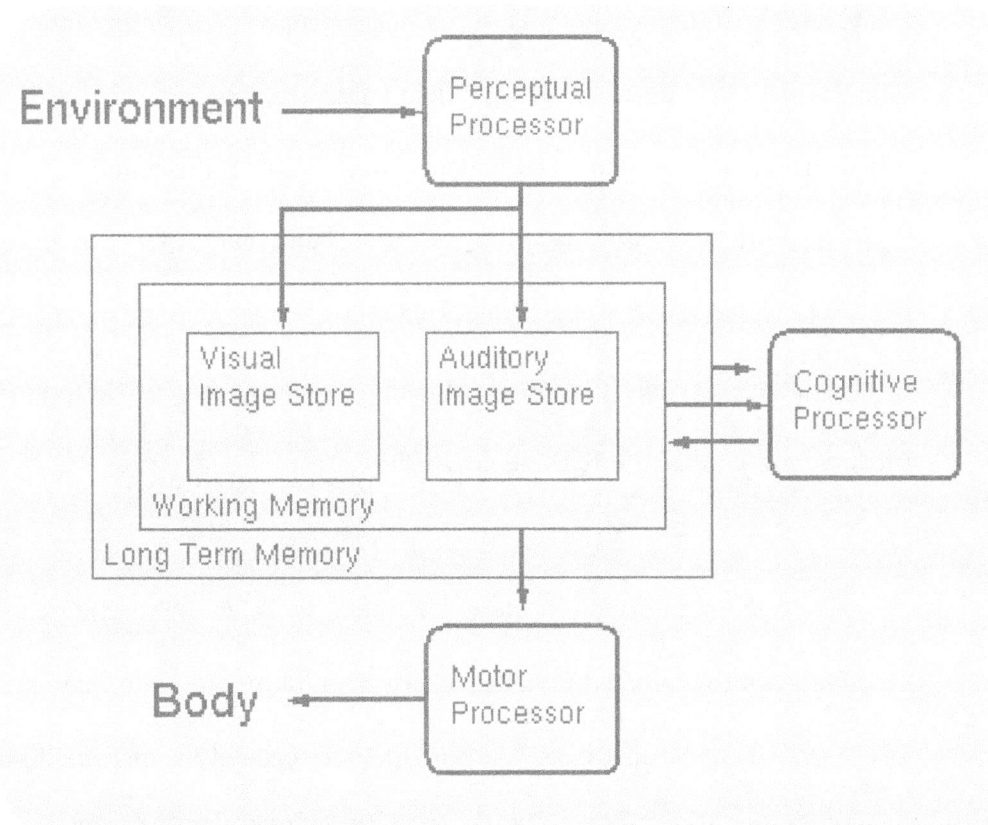

Figure 2.5 Model Human Processor (MHP) model of cognition (simplified) (Card, Moran & Newell, 1983)

The MHP model identifies three kinds of memory, namely, sensory, working, and long-term. The cognitive processor takes input from long-term and working memory, including sensory image stores, and returns results to working memory. The perceptual processors work in parallel with the main cognitive processor. In the case of vision, this gives rise to the previously discussed pre-attentive effects (Crapo, 2002).

The MHP model characterises each memory by storage type, capacity, and decay rate and each processor by cycle time. Long-term memory is essentially unlimited capacity but has a slow access time (~100 milliseconds) and a very slow decay rate. Working memory is of limited capacity (7 plus or minus 2 "chunks") which will be discussed in greater detail later in this section, faster access (~70 milliseconds), and a much faster decay rate (~200 milliseconds). Sensory image stores likewise have very rapid decay rates. Sub-vocalisation can refresh auditory sensory image stores seen, for instance when we repeat a phone number until we dial it. This increases cycle times by reducing reading speed (processing of sentential information) (Gathercole & Baddeley, 1993).

Access to information stored in memory is an important requirement for effective cognitive processing and the organisation of this information is critical to how readily it can be accessed. Working memory capacity is measured in *chunks* and quantified as "seven plus or minus two" (Miller, 1956). For example, asked to repeat the sequence "X O F V T M C B N," most will miss some letters since nine is the limit of working memory capacity. However, through the use of familiar acronyms "N B C M T V F O X" the effective load on working memory has been reduced from nine to three (Newell, 1990). Through efficient organisation of information in long term memory, increasingly larger chunks of this memory can be returned to working memory and result in greater cognitive processing capacity.

Individuals also use organising strategies to deal with visual stimuli. This most commonly occurs through the use of Gestalt principles of organisation namely, simplicity, proximity, similarity, continuity, connectedness, motion, familiarity, symmetry, closure and relative size (Card, Mackinlay, & Shneidermann, 1999; Ware, 2000): In the following section, simple definitions and illustrations are offered of these Gestalt principles.

Simplicity   Every stimulus pattern is seen so as to simplify the resulting structure.

Proximity   Objects near one another tend to be grouped together into a perceptual unit. Figure 2.6 demonstrates how proximity causes a matrix of dots to be perceived as rows or columns.

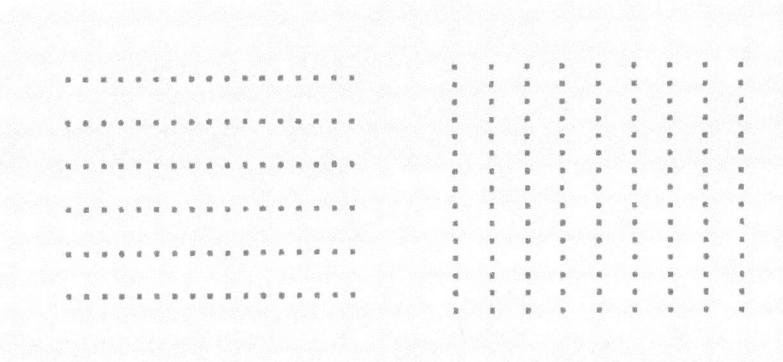

Figure 2.6   Proximity (Ware, 2000)

Similarity   When several stimuli are presented together, similar items tend to be grouped together. Figure 2.7 shows how similarity overrides proximity with the symbols being seen as rows even though proximity favours columns.

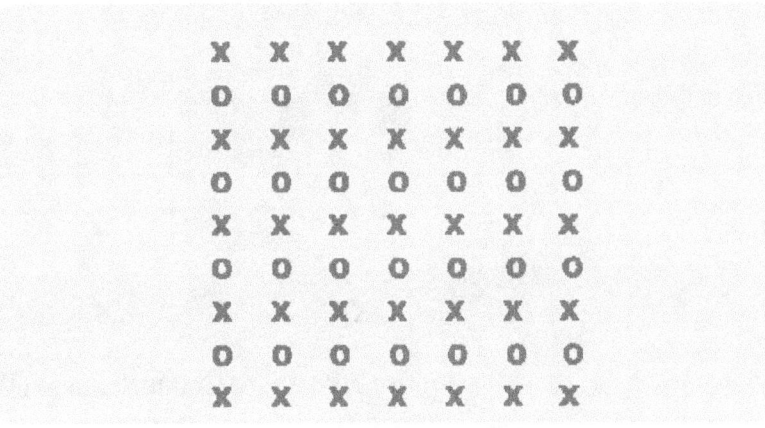

Figure 2.7   Similarity (Ware, 2000)

Continuity	Figure 2.8 shows how it is easier to perceive visual entities that are smooth and continuous. The presence of the first (left-hand) form makes the second form easier to perceive.

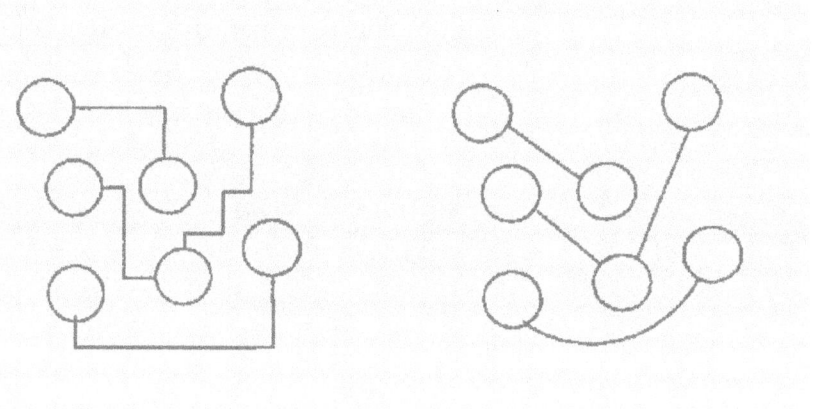

Figure 2.8   Continuity (Ware, 2000)

Connectedness	Figure 2.9 shows neighbouring elements grouped together when straight or smoothly curved lines potentially connect them. This demonstrates that connectedness overpowers (a) proximity, (b) colour, (c) size, and (d) shape.

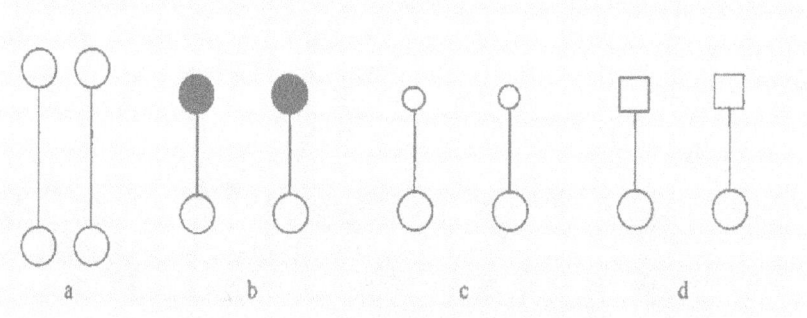

Figure 2.9   Connectedness (Ware, 2000)

Motion   Elements moving in the same direction tend to be grouped together.

Familiarity   Elements are more likely to be perceived as a group if the group is familiar or meaningful.

Symmetry   Elements are perceived much more strongly as a visual whole if there is symmetry in the whole.

Closure   Figure 2.10 shows how a closed contour tends to be seen as an object. In this case it is more likely to be perceived as a circle than an open arc (3/4 of a circle)

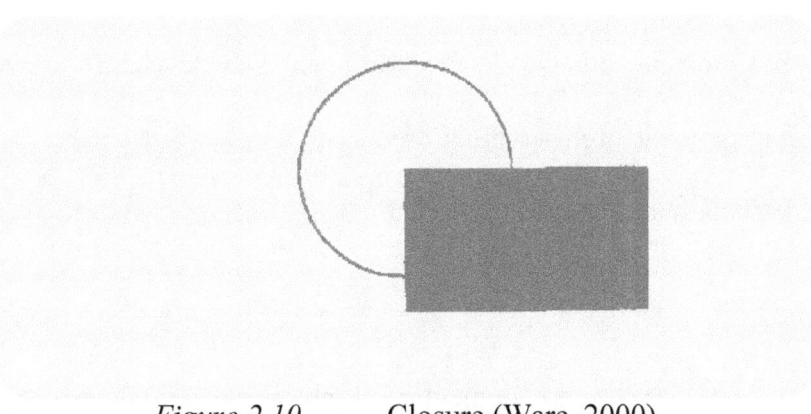

Figure 2.10   Closure (Ware, 2000)

Relative size   Elements in a pattern that are smaller tend to be seen as objects.

Gestalt principles provide a basis on which to examine in further detail, the influence of visualisation on cognitive processes. In particular, the application of Gestalt principles to a greater understanding of software visualisation is developed.

2.2 Visualisation to support visual processing

The use of visualisations to support learning has been developed in a range of domains and visualisation as an aid to understanding computer programs began soon after the development of computers. Starting with flowcharts in 1947 (Goldstein & von Neumann, 1947) an automatic system for producing these from programming code was developed in 1959 (Haibt, 1959; Knuth, 1963). Animated films were developed in 1966 (Baecker, 1975; Knowlton, 1966) to assist in explaining algorithmic processes and flowcharting was further developed in 1973 (Nassi & Shneiderman, 1973) with an automatic generation system produced in 1976 (Roy & St. Denis, 1976). "Pretty-printing" - the use of spacing, indentation, and layout to make textual source code easier to read - was devised (Ledgard, 1975) and systems for automatic pretty-printing produced (Baecker & Marcus, 1990; Conrow & Smith, 1970; Knuth, 1984).

With the development of graphical user interfaces, systems were developed (Brown & Sedgewick, 1984) to allow students to interact with visualisations. Over one hundred software visualisation prototypes have since been built yet very few of these were systematically evaluated to determine their effectiveness and the number that have seen any kind of production use particularly in the domain of tools for professional programmers, is small (Price, Baecker & Small, 1992).

Software Visualisation Systems are a means of finding simplicity in a complex artefact such as computer code by selective representation of a complex abstraction (Petre, Blackwell, & Green, 1996). Software visualisation is used to show different types of information (relating respectively to source code, data, data structures, and execution) in different forms. These include:

i) presenting large data sets such as in radiography and meteorology. This form of visualisation attempts to make data available for interpretation by presenting a data picture and so capitalising on perceptual effects such as foreground/background effects, 'pop out' and detection of discontinuities;

ii) demonstrating the virtual machine to create a visible, dynamic, machine model, often relying on kinematic or mechanical metaphors;

iii) changing the perspective to bring large software engineering problems within the scope of a single view so that a user can grasp particular tasks or functions in relation to the software as a whole;

iv) display-based reasoning to provide a symbolic re-presentation of software processes. The notion is that an effective display can assist in reducing the user cognitive load. The display becomes a focus for reasoning, for example, by replacing some internal representations with external ones allowing the user to use different tactics in finding, recalling, examining, or comparing information;

(Petre, Blackwell, & Green, 1996)

The majority of research into software visualisation is on complex cognitive concepts in computer science such as recursion and linked lists (Bassil & Keller, 2001). Such studies are generally the first exposure students have had to this form of learning and visualisation is used as a replacement to existing methodologies not developed to support an independent methodology.

The capacity of computer-based visualisations to support learning is surprisingly and counter-intuitively not supported by research. Research into software visualisation appears to form two broad groupings. The first includes those that aim to support researcher-developed software applications produced to teach concepts using computer-based visualisations (Reiss & Renieris, 2002). In these cases, support is ambiguous (Tudoreanu, 2003) and generally suggestive of needing further research (Rader, Brand & Lewis, 1997) with very few studies providing positive results and a number showing negative results (Reiss, 2005; Stasko, 1997). The second group studies visualisation independent of a specific software application and is generally negative and does not support the educational use of computer visualisation (Stasko, Badre & Lewis, 1993).

Despite a lack of experimental and empirical support, research in software visualisation has expanded (Baker, Cruz, Liotta & Tamassia, 1995, 1996; Boroni, Goosey, Grinder & Ross, 1998; Kienle & Muller, 2001; Naps, 1996; Naps, Eagan & Norton, 2000; Pareja-Flores & Velázquez-Iturbide, 2003; Sensalire & Ogao, 2007) often refocused on web-based implementations of the software visualisation tool. A problem remains that however developed the visualisations may be there is a lack of understanding of the cognitive processes involved. To date, software visualisation research continues to be inconclusive in support of software visualisation as a means of improving student learning of computer programming languages.

2.3 Development of cognitive mental models

Mental models are representations of reality that people use to understand specific phenomena. Gentner and Stevens (1983) described them as providing predictive and explanatory power for understanding such interaction. Johnson-Laird (1983) proposed mental models as the basic structure of cognition, and Holland et al. (1986) suggest that mental models are the basis for all reasoning processes. Bucciarelli (2007) explores the cognitive processes of non symbolic gestures and Buckner and Carroll (2007) examples integration of mental model theory to neuroscience.

The study of mental models has involved the detailed analysis of small knowledge domains (for example, motion, ocean navigation, electricity, calculators) and the development of computer representations (Gentner & Stevens, 1983). For example, DeKleer and Brown (1981) described how the mental model of a doorbell is formed and how the model is useful in solving problems for mechanical devices. Kieras and Bovair (1984) discussed the role of mental models in understanding electronics and mental models have been applied in the domain of troubleshooting (White & Frederiksen, 1985).

Johnson-Laird (1983) described three kinds of internal representations, namely mental models, propositional representations, and images. Mental models are defined as a model that exists in the mind while propositional representations comprise sets of natural language formulations, that is, a sentential representation. Images reside in the visual portion of the brain and can be created either from information flowing "up" from the eyes or from information flowing "down" from memory or cognitive areas of the brain, including from mental models (Gardner, 1985; Pinker, 1997).

According to mental model theory, each entity perceived or imagined is represented by a token in the model. The properties of the entities are represented by properties of their tokens, and relations among the tokens represent relations among entities.

To perform a deduction, the cognitive system generates one or more models that represent states of affairs or situations compatible with the premises and 'reads' the conclusion from the model(s). If a conclusion is successfully read, a falsification phase follows which seeks to construct a mental model that violates the proposed conclusion. When this fails, the conclusion is accepted and the mental model updated (Johnson-Laird, 1983).

The rendering of a mental model, whether sentential or diagrammatic, for cognitive processing can be referred to as a view (Johnson-Laird, 1983). Visualisation is the external realisation of these views in terms of text or diagrams as shown in Figure 2.11.

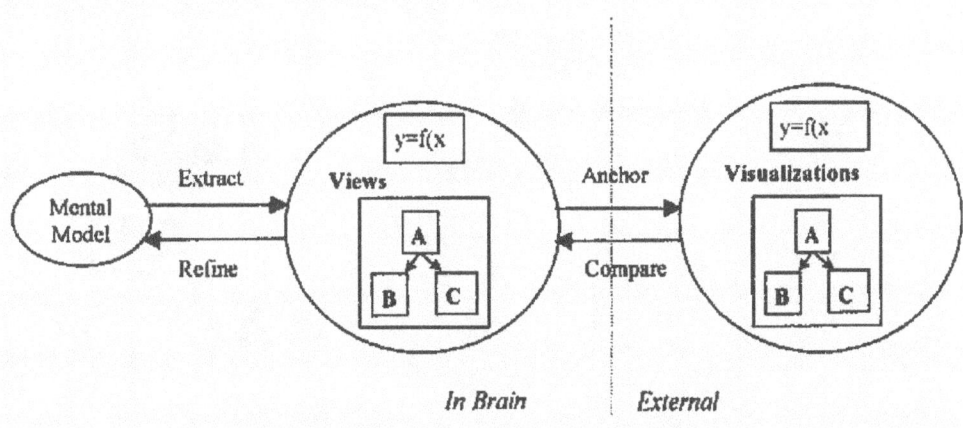

Figure 2.11:   Mental Models, views, and visualisations (Waisel, 1998)

Views are less flexible than visualisations and less supportive of complex problem solving because of the limitations of holding complex views in working memory. The manipulation of mental images is a complex task that stretches the limits of working memory and can be enhanced through the use of external memory aids such as visualisation (Reisburt & Logie, 1993). The learner can translate views into visualisations through drawing, writing or visualisation software. Such visualisations may contain both text representing "propositional views" and pictures representing "imagistic" views. A solution is to anchor aspects of our mental models as visualisations (Reisburt & Logie, 1993) as demonstrated in Figure 2.12.

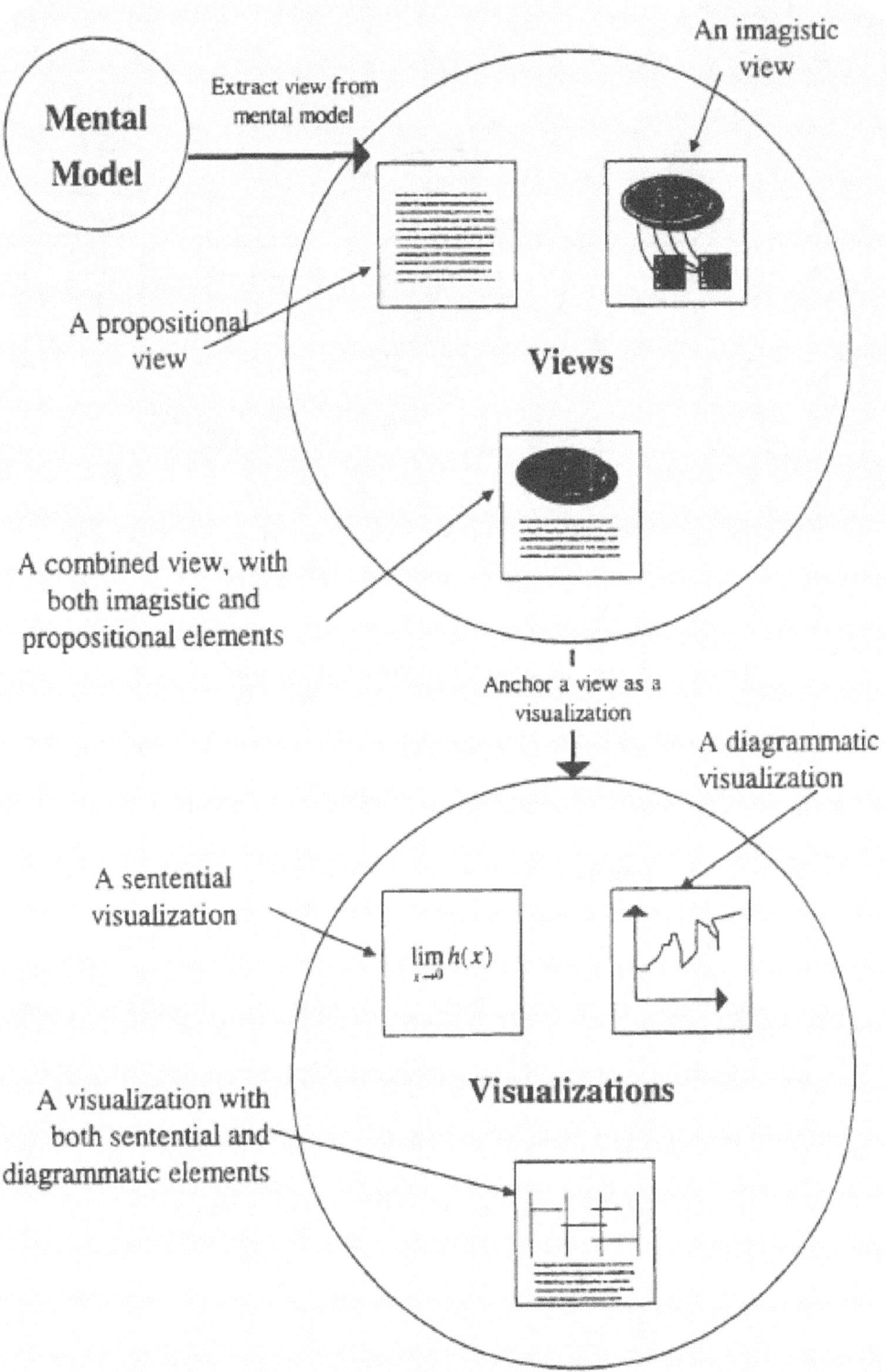

Figure 2.12 Elements of visualisation in model formation (Waisel, 1998)

Visualisations comprised mainly of text are considered "sentential," and visualisations comprised mainly of pictures are considered "diagrammatic" (Larkin & Simon, 1987). Diagrammatic visualisations are those whose meaning depends on the location of marks on a two-dimensional plane.

The views and visualisations are used for both within-model testing during description and between-model testing during validation. During within-model testing, the learner tests the mental model for internal consistency and for consistency with what they know about the concept. To do this a series of views are generated from a mental model. These views are then anchored by using a visualisation tool to create a visualisation.

Comparing visualisation with the generated views, checks for correspondence and contradiction can be made. If a series of views, generated by the learner's mental model of the concept, are non contradictory and correspond to their visualisations, then the learner concludes that the model is satisfactory in comparison with itself and the description phase ends.

If a contradiction or non-correspondence occurs, then the learner checks whether:
i. the visualisation has been inaccurately transcribed;
ii. the view has been incorrectly extracted from the mental model; or
iii. the mental model is incorrect.

When determined, the learner responds accordingly, modifying visualisation, view, or mental model as needed.

The validation phase involves the generation of alternative mental models with their attendant views and visualisations. If the alternative mental models cannot explain the data any better than the original mental model, and if none of the mental models contradict what is already accepted, then the original model is deemed to be satisfactory in comparison with other models and retained. Figure 2.13 describes this model formulation process.

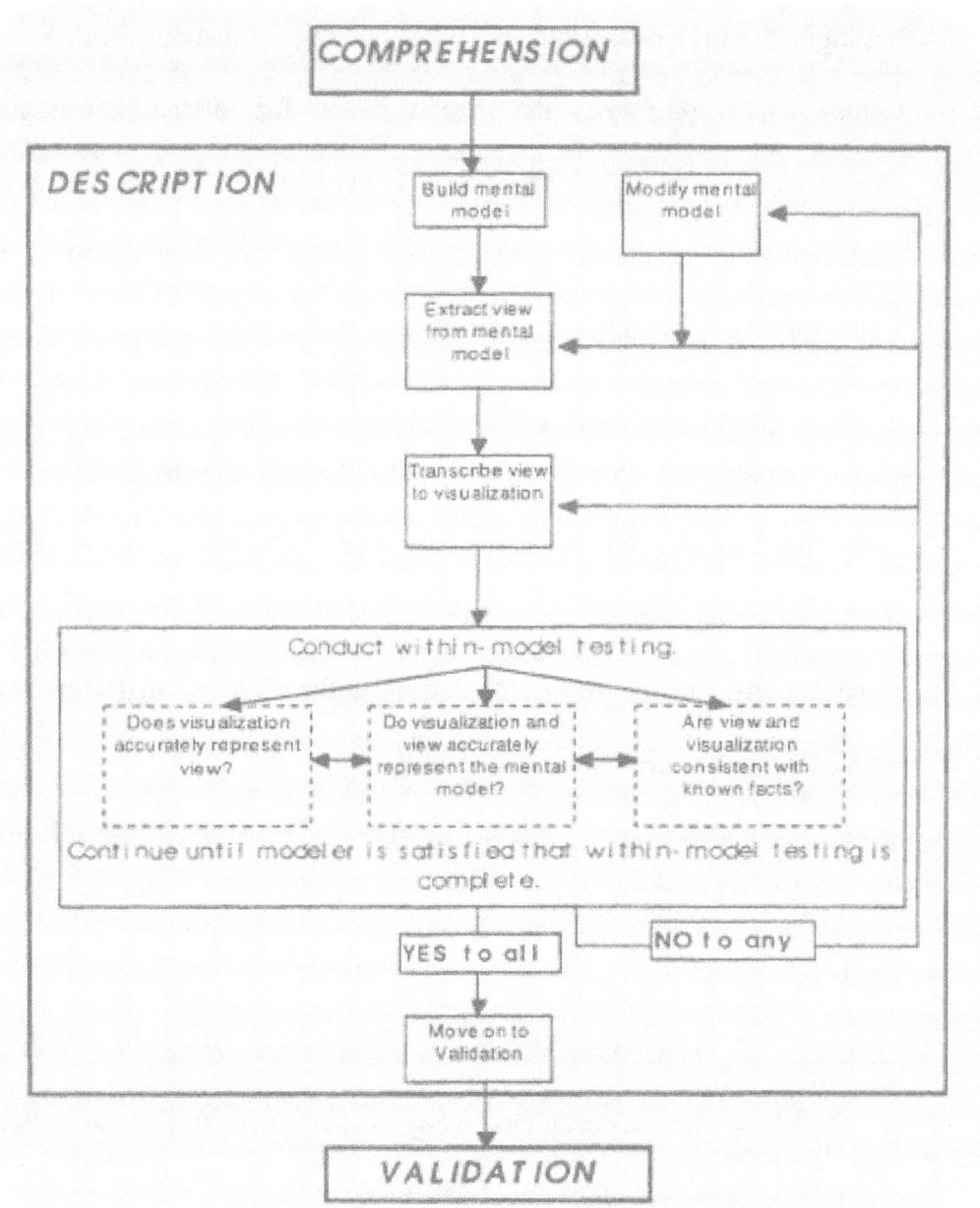

Figure 2.13 The process of model formation with visualisation within Johnson and Laird's phase of Description (Waisel, 1998)

Both the within-model testing, which occurs during Johnson-Laird's description phase, and the between-model testing, which takes place during Johnson-Laird's validation phase, are iterative processes, continuing until the learner is satisfied that the model has been sufficiently validated.

The use of visualisation increases understanding. By comparing the view extracted from the mental model with the view created from the visualisation, the learner is able to identify if anything of importance is missing or if extraneous elements have been included. This may then result in modification of the mental model to more closely resemble the visualisation or manipulation of the visualisation to verify the mental model.

This process of comparison and modification continues until a satisfactory model is obtained. In addition to extending working memory, anchoring a view as a visualisation can be effective in communicating a model to others.

The social aspects of learning can also assist mental model development. Several theories suggest that almost all learning requires interaction with other people to contextualise what is being taught (Norman, 1993). Each learner begins with a different perspective – a different mental model. As these models are made explicit in external representations, common elements can be identified and the discussion that is focused on understanding and resolving differences (Massey & Wallace, 1996) can facilitate the development of increasingly complex mental models.

Due to increasing loads on visual and cognitive processors, especially working memory, the complexity of the visualisations can be a significant factor. Johnson-Laird (1993) argued that a model's effectiveness is maximised by "representing as little as possible explicitly" while still supporting the solution to the problem at hand. Unnecessary representation makes it more difficult to focus on important aspects. Alabastro, Beckmann, Gifford, Massey, and Wallace (1995) described how visual models significantly increase speed and quality of model development by focusing attention on what is absent and important (and should therefore be added) or what is present and unimportant (and should therefore be eliminated) from the representation.

2.4 Identification of cognitive levels

The Pirie and Kieren's (1989) mental model theory provided the basis for a cognitive model of the learning process that permits detailed tracking of student cognitive development. Developed as a recursive theory of mathematical understanding in which they describe a theory of understanding and illustrate how the theory can be used to explain the development of a students' understanding of a mathematical concept. Their theory has been adopted as a foundation to the methodology of this study. The pictorial representation (Figure 2.14) of their theory highlights the eight levels in the process of the growth of understanding which will be described later in this section. The eight levels are (1) primitive knowing, (2) image making, (3) image having, (4) property noticing, (5) formalising, (6) observing, (7) structuring, and (8) inventing.

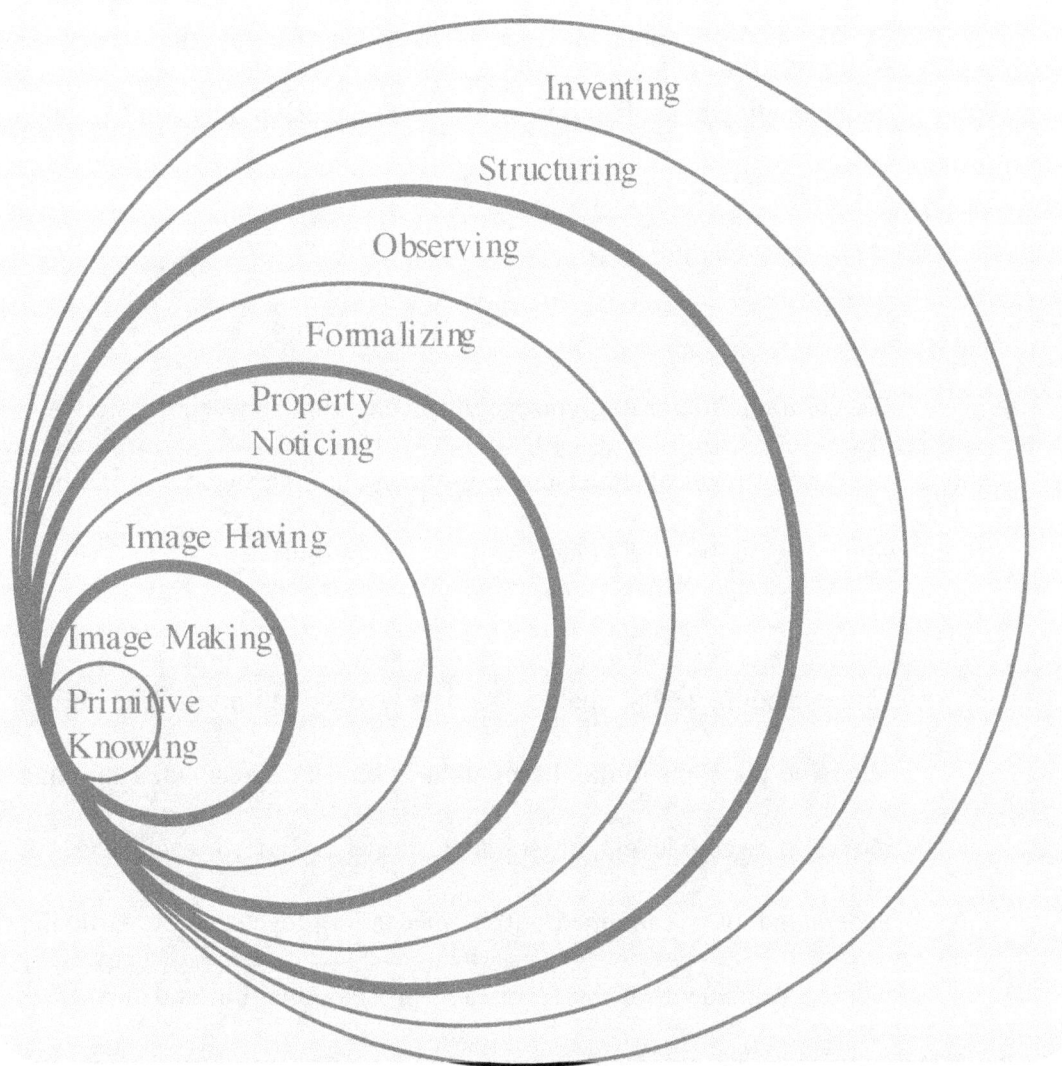

Figure 2.14: Pirie and Kieren pictorial representation of understanding

(Pirie & Kieren, 1992)

Used as tool to map the dynamic growth of understanding in a developing mental model, a significant aspect of the Pirie and Kieren (1992) model is that development is one of *transcendent recursion* (Kastburg, 2001).

It is transcendent in that each level, while compatible with prior levels, transcends those levels in sophistication. It is recursive in that, the structure of the understanding at one level is similar to the structure of the understanding at another and one level of understanding can call into action a previous understanding.

(Kastburg, 2001, p. 4)

If a contradiction or non-correspondence occurs between the students' mental model at a current level of understanding, the student has access to previous "ways of knowing" that can be used to help resolve the conflict:

Understanding can be characterised as levelled but non-linear. It is a recursive phenomenon and recursion is seen to occur when thinking moves between levels of sophistication. ... Indeed each level of understanding is contained within succeeding levels. Any particular level is dependent on the forms and processes within and further, is constrained by those without.

(Pirie & Kieren, 1989, p. 8)

The process of "folding back" to an inner level of understanding when unable to proceed is not simply a return to a previous mental model but is informed and shaped by both the outer level intervention which prompted the folding back and by the existing outer levels of understanding. This suggests that a mental model is built up progressively from the levels described by Pirie and Kieren (1989, 1992) with views generally produced from the highest developed levels.

Although the representation in Figure 2.14 itself was static, it can be used as a tool for mapping a student's development of a mental model of a concept over time. When such a map is completed it represents the student's process of understanding. In general, the inner levels of understanding leading up to formalising are context dependent. The particular problems that the student undertakes and actions they take will enable and constrain the properties that they abstract from them. The formalising stage marks the beginning of reflections on mental objects, concepts that are free of the context from which they were derived and the development and proof of theorems regarding these mental objects (Pirie & Kieren, 1992).

In this study it is argued that the Pirie-Kieren model can be combined with the Johnson-Laird model by equating the development of understanding to the development of a mental model. The following describes the eight levels in greater detail.

1. The process of coming to an understanding of a concept starts at what Pirie and Kieren (1992) called **primitive knowing**. This is a student's basis of understanding. It can equate to an undeveloped mental model of a new concept but can include constructs from related mental models. For example it may include terminology of related concepts.

2. At the second level, **image making**, the learner is asked, through specific tasks, to make distinctions in his/her previous abilities using them under new conditions or to new ends. While Pirie and Kieren (1992) referred to this level as image making, it more readily equates to the ability to develop alternative views of physical representations from the mental model and can contain propositional as well as imagistic representations.

3. The third level, **image having**, involves refining the mental model to enable creation of views that can be manipulated, a "mental object" distinct from physical representations.

4. The fourth level, **property noticing**, involves examining views for specific properties. By noting distinctions, combinations or connections between views, predictions of how they might be achieved can be made and such relationships recorded.

5. The fifth level, **formalising**, involves consciously thinking about the noted properties and abstracting commonalities. The mental model should now be class like and not dependent on example views.

6. The sixth level, **observing**, involves formalising and organising observations to an extent that they are considering and referencing their own formal thinking.

7. The seventh level, **structuring**, involves being able to explain their formal thinking in terms of a logical structure and being aware of assumptions. An example would be the creation of formal proofs.

8. The eighth and final level, **inventising**, is going "freely and imaginatively" (Pirie & Kieren, 1992) beyond structured understanding to create totally new questions that might develop into new concepts.

An example of how these levels have been adapted for use in this study is provided in Appendices C, D and E.

2.5 Theoretical Models of Memory

Memory is a fundamental component of visualisation and mental model theories. While both fields have developed a similar model of short-term, working and long-term memory, a fuller understanding of the history and theories of the function of memory in the learning process is necessary in this study. Memory theories and paradigms of learning (Adams, 1967; Bartlett, 1932; Klatzky, 1980; Loftus & Loftus, 1976; Tulving & Donaldson, 1972) have long been contentious, for example, recall versus recognition, interference versus decay, the structure of memory, and intentional versus incidental learning.

Early behaviourist theories (Thorndike, 1913; Guthrie, 1935; & Hull, 1943) understood memory as a function of Stimulus-Response pairings that acquired strength due to contiguity or reinforcement. Cognitive theories (Tolman, 1922) showed that meaning (semantic factors) played an important role in remembering. In particular, Miller (1956) suggested that information was organised into "chunks" according to some commonality. The idea that memory is always an active reconstruction of existing knowledge was developed by Bruner (1960) and is elaborated in the theories of Ausubel (1963) and Schank (1975, 1982).

Bartlett (1932, 1958) proposed the concept of schema, suggesting that memory takes the form of schema which provide a mental framework for understanding and remembering information. Mandler (1984) and Rumelhart (1980) have further developed the schema concept.

Baddeley and Hitch (1974) developed an early model of working memory and Paivio (1986) suggested a dual coding scheme for verbal and visual information. Craik and Lockhart (1972) proposed that information can be processed to different levels of understanding, and Rumelhart and Norman (1978) delineated three modes of memory (accretion, structuring and tuning) to account for different kinds of learning.

Other theories have focused on the representation of information in memory. Anderson's (1983) ACT model (see Figure 2.15) assumes three types of structures: declarative, procedural, and working memory. Merrill and & Tennyson (1977) proposed two forms: associative and algorithmic, while Laird, Newell, and Rosenbloom's (1987) SOAR model postulated that all information is stored in procedural form. Kintsch (1974) suggested that memory is propositional in nature and it is the relationship among propositions that gives rise to meaning.

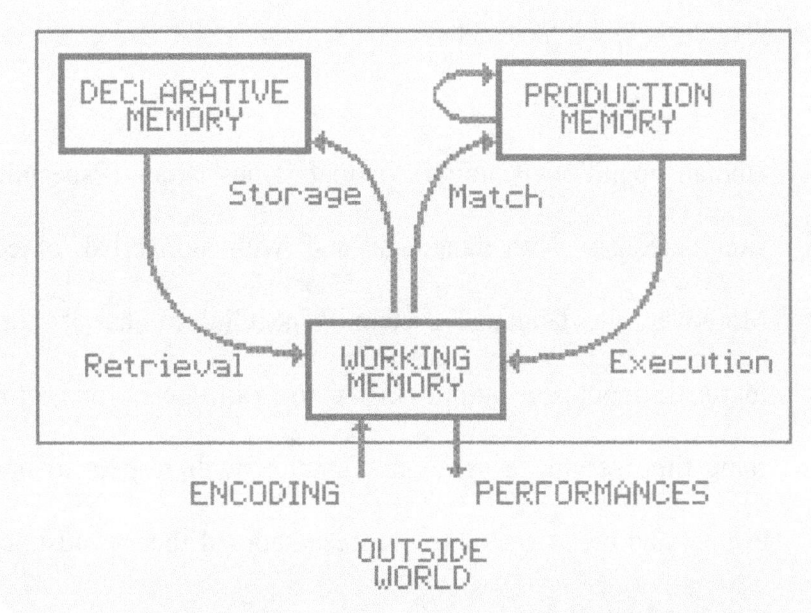

Figure 2.15   ACT model (Anderson, 1983)

Miller's (1956) limit to the amount of information that can be maintained in short-term memory, Paivio's (1986) dual-coding storage hypothesis, and Sweller's (1988) cognitive load theory, form the foundations of a theory of memory used in this study. This theory is also informed by 'subjecting' in which information can be processed to different levels of understanding (Craik & Lockhart, 1972) and delineated into different modes of memory (accretion, structuring and tuning) to account for different kinds of learning (Rumelhart & Norman, 1978).

The concept of 'chunking' (see Section 2.2) introduced by Miller (1956) presented the idea that short-term memory could only hold 5-9 chunks of information (seven plus or minus two) where a chunk is any meaningful unit. A chunk could refer to digits, words, chess positions, or people's faces. The concept of chunking and the limited capacity of short term memory became a basic element of all subsequent theories of memory. Dual coding theory attempts to differentiate verbal and non-verbal processing.

> Human cognition is unique in that it has become specialised for dealing simultaneously with language and with nonverbal objects and events. Moreover, the language system is peculiar in that it deals directly with linguistic input and output (in the form of speech or writing) while at the same time serving a symbolic function with respect to nonverbal objects, events, and behaviours. Any representational theory must accommodate this dual functionality.
>
> (Pavio, 1986, p.53).

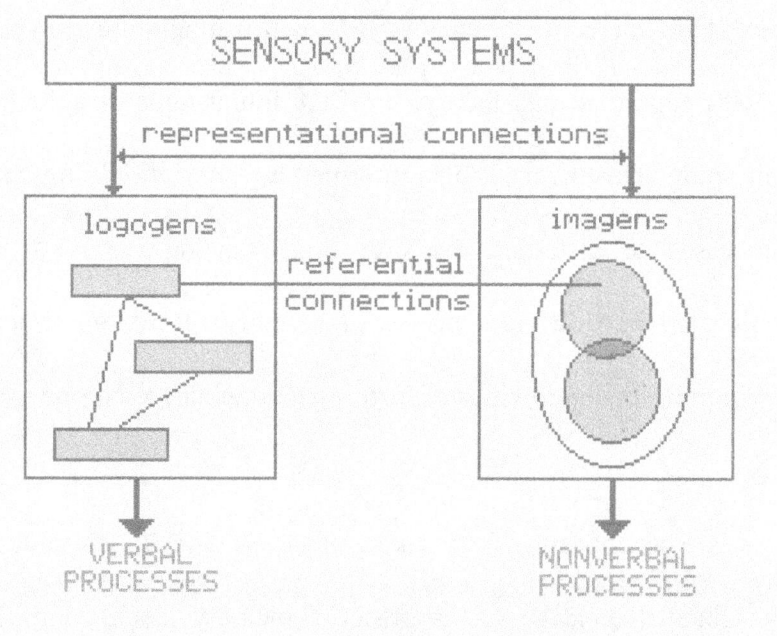

Figure 2.16 Dual Coding Theory (Paivio, 1986)

As with the EPIC and MHP models (see Section 2.2), this theory has two parallel cognitive subsystems, one for the representation and processing of the nonverbal (i.e., imagery), and the other verbal. Paivio (1986) postulates two different types of representational units: "imagens" for mental images and "logogens" for verbal entities which he describes as being similar to "chunks" as described by Miller (1956). Logogens are organised in terms of associations and hierarchies while imagens are organised in terms of part-whole relationships.

Dual Coding theory identifies three types of processing: (1) representational, the direct activation of verbal or non-verbal representations, (2) referential, the activation of the verbal system by the nonverbal system or vice-versa, and (3) associative processing, the activation of representations within the same verbal or nonverbal system. A given task may require any or all of the three kinds of processing. Within this theory recall/recognition is enhanced by presenting information in both visual and verbal form. With similarities to mental model theory (see Section 2.4) Tennyson and Cocchiarella (1986) presented a model for concept development that has three stages: (1) establishing a connection in memory between the concept to be learned and existing knowledge, (2) improving the formation of concepts in terms of relations, and (3) facilitating the development of classification rules.

*Cognitive theory of Multimedia Learning (CTML) (*Moreno & Duran, 2004) consists of the following main ideas:

1. *dual coding* - in which the representation and processing of information concerning verbal and nonverbal materials are handled cognitively by separate subsystems (Clark & Paivio, 1991; Paivio, 1986);

2. *dual processing* - in which working memory includes independent auditory and visual working memories (Baddeley, 1992);

3. *limited capacity* - in which the processing capacities of learners are restricted (Chandler & Sweller, 1991);

4. *active learning* - in which meaningful learning occurs when learners select, organise, and build coherent connections of new information with prior knowledge (Mayer, 2001; Mayer & Moreno, 2003; Mayer & Wittrock, 1996).

The dual coding theory formulated by Pavio (1986) supports the separate processing of verbal and non-verbal (or visual) information. Suggesting that a word encoded verbally will be better recalled if also encoded visually. Mayer (2001) presents an iterative, three phases information processing model (see Figure 2.17) selection, organisation and integration to a prior mental model.

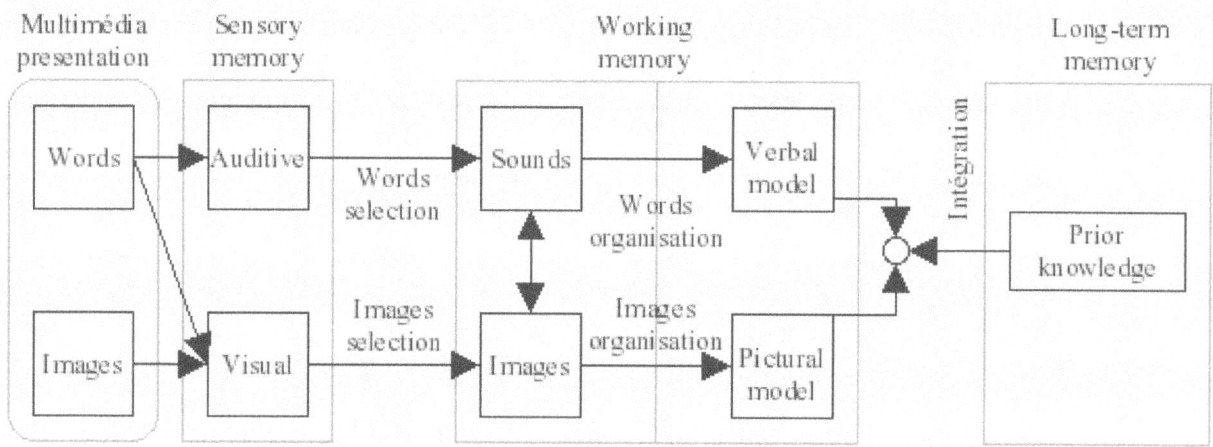

Figure 2.17 Model of multimedia learning (Mayer, 2001)

Schnotz and Bannert (2003) presented a model where auditory-textual and visual information are conjointly and interactively processed in order to form both a mental model and a propositional representation of a concept (see Figure 2.18). In their model, a propositional representation is produced by semantic elements, in a symbolic structure. Meanwhile, a mental model is formed from visualisation of different elements in an analogical form, but also drawing from semantic elements. Subsequently, both representations are interrelated and have similar structures, but are based on different sign systems and different principles of representation.

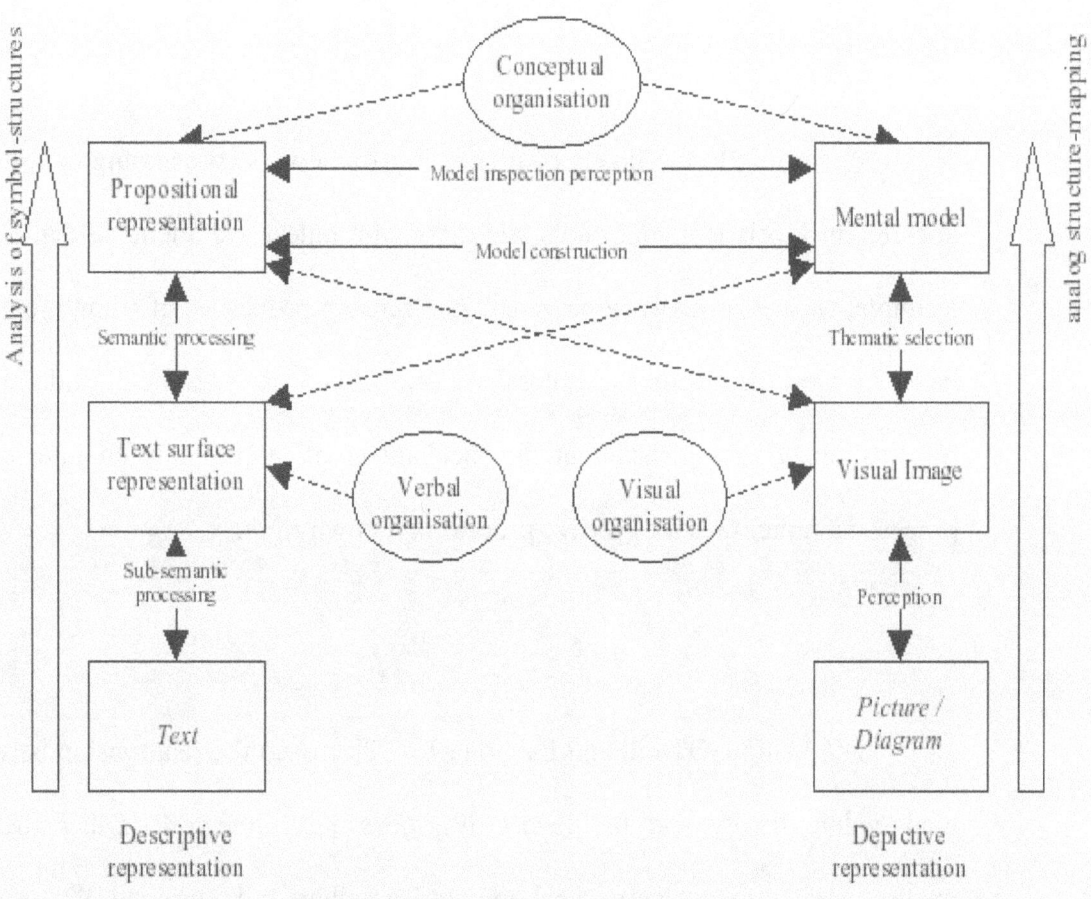

Figure 2.18 Integrated model of cognitive development

(Schnotz & Bannert, 2003)

The Levels of Processing Framework (Craik & Lockhart, 1972) does not have separate stages for sensory, working and long-term memory. In this model, stimulus information is processed at multiple levels simultaneously depending upon its characteristics and the "deeper" the processing, the more that will be remembered, for example, information that involves strong visual images or many associations with existing knowledge will be processed at a deeper level. Similarly, information that is being attended to receives more processing than other stimuli/events, with things that are meaningful to us being remembered because they require more processing than meaningless stimuli.

According to the levels of processing framework, processing of information at different levels is unconscious and automatic unless we attend to that level. For example, we are normally not aware of the sensory properties of stimuli, or what we have in working memory, unless we are asked to specifically identify such information. This suggests that the mechanism of attention is an interruption in processing rather than a cognitive process in its own right.

D'Agostino, O'Neill and Paivio (1977) discussed the relationship between the dual coding theory and the levels of processing framework. Other theories of memory related to levels of processing are Rumelhart and Norman (1978) and Laird, Newell and Rosenbloom's (1987) SOAR model.

Sweller (1988) built a mental model theory that treats schemas, or combinations of elements, as the cognitive structures that make up an individual's knowledge base. The contents of long term memory are sophisticated structures that permit us to perceive, think, and solve problems, rather than a group of rote learned facts. These structures, known as schemas, are what permit us to treat multiple elements as a single element and are the cognitive structures that make up our knowledge base (Sweller, 1988).

Within this model, schemas are progressively developed and may have other schemas contained within themselves. The difference between an expert and a novice is that a novice has not developed the mental model schemas of an expert. Learning requires a change in the schematic structures of long term memory and is demonstrated by performance that progresses from clumsy, error-prone, slow and difficult to smooth and effortless. The change in performance occurs because as the learner becomes increasingly familiar with the material, the cognitive characteristics associated with the material are altered so that it can be handled more efficiently by working memory.

Cognitive load theory (Sweller & Chandler, 1994) described the development of such schemas in terms of an information processing mechanism for storing to long term memory after processing by working memory. Working memory, however, is limited in both capacity and duration and these limitations will, under some conditions, impede learning. Sweller and Chandler (1994) differentiated between three subtypes of cognitive load: intrinsic, germane, and extraneous. **Intrinsic load** relates to the difficulty of concepts, the integral complexity of an idea or set of concepts. For example, in programming, learning to program 'Hello' with PHP is much easier than with Java. **Extraneous load** (irrelevant) is due to the design of the instructional materials. Inefficient instructional designs add unnecessary load. For example, an audio-visual presentation format usually has lower extraneous load than a visual plus text format. **Germane load** (relevant) relates to the processing, construction and automation of schemas that represent some aspect of the world. Germane load is sometimes associated with motivation and interest insomuch as it relates to improved development of schemata. Intrinsic load is unchangeable, whereas the teacher can manipulate extraneous and germane load.

Sweller (1994) identified two mechanisms to circumvent the limits of working memory. (a) Schema acquisition that allows chunking of information into meaningful units, and (b) Automation of procedural knowledge and primary skills. The model is based upon the following concepts:

1. Limited working memories make it difficult to assimilate multiple elements of information simultaneously.
2. Multiple information elements interact and must be processed simultaneously.
3. High levels of element 'interactivity' and their resulting cognitive load can be inherent in content, for example, learning language grammar inherently involves more element interactivity than simple vocabulary learning.

The visualisation tool may also influence cognitive load, such as a complex diagram (for example, Figure 2.18) whose understanding requires repeated consultation of the text. The extra work required in decoding and translating the diagram competes with working-memory resources as the learner attempts to comprehend the material. Cognitive load theory leads to some specific predictions for student learning:

1. Simple content, for example, content with relatively few intrinsic interactive elements, is not impacted by the visualisation tool. Learners can cope with complex and multiple sources (visual and auditory) of information within their working memories in such cases.
2. Content containing high levels of interactivity among its elements cannot be learned effectively if these exceed cognitive processing capacity. Methods that require extra processing by learners make demands that exceed the limits of the learner's working memory and learning is impeded.

Rumelhart and Norman (1978) developed a mental model theory with three modes of learning: accretion, structuring and tuning. Accretion involves addition of new knowledge to existing memory, structuring involves the formation of new conceptual structures or schema, and tuning is the refinement of a model task through practice. The model includes a process whereby restructuring of an existing mental model involves active reflection on the metacognitive processes involved and may correspond to a plateau in cognitive development. Rumelhart and Norman (1981) extended their model to include analogical processes in which new schemas are created by modelling them on existing schema and then modified based upon further experiences. The Soar group (Laird, Newell & Rosenbloom, 1987) developed a unified theory of cognition which includes the concept of a problem space in which all cognitive acts are some form of search task. Memory is unitary and procedural with no distinction between procedural and declarative memory. Within this model, chunking is the primary mechanism for learning and represents the conversion of problem-solving acts into long-term memory. Soar (Newell, 1990) differentiates types or levels of learning: operators (create, call), search control (operator selection, plans), declarative data (recognition/recall), and tasks (identify problem spaces, initial/goal states).

2.6 Synthesis of the literature

The literature review has addressed five key areas, (a) theoretical depth – through an investigation of human cognitive development, specifically visual and auditory processing (Section 2.1); (b) a specific focus – that is, visualisation (Section 2.2); (c) a practical methodology – through mental model theory (Section 2.3); (d) a relationship between theoretical models and research methodology - by identifying cognitive levels and level changes (Section 2.4); and (e) an explanatory framework - through research models of memory and learning (Section 2.5). In addition, it has explained and defended the significance of the research and the original contribution this study makes to the existing bodies of knowledge in these areas.

As noted, cognitive development theory provides foundation theory to the study. Research on visual and auditory processing theory demonstrates the differences between auditory and visual processing with several models describing the links between visual processing and cognitive processing, and the impact of visual stimuli. Visualisation theory provides a specific focus for the study. Visualisation research demonstrates clearly the various uses to which software visualisation can be applied but a lack of positive research outcomes is highlighted as justification for further research. Mental model theory provides a basis on which a practical link between visualisation theory and cognitive development theory can be established. The ability of mental model theory to track cognitive development on an eight level scale provides a foundation for the study's methodology with research into this theory providing additional justification to the study.

This chapter presents the theoretical model, that is, Pirie and Kieren's (1989) representation of understanding, which has been adapted for use as an analytical tool in this study to identify cognitive levels and level changes. Finally, research models of memory and learning are detailed and form a foundation on which the results of the study can be explained and supported. The following chapter of this study (Chapter 3) provides further background to the study. It presents a description of the software visualisation tools which will form the cases for the study and, in consequence, create the digital environments in which subject's skill and use of visualisation will be observed.

In synthesising the literature reviewed by this study, a computational model of the learning emerges and a simplified overview is presented. This model uses a computational metaphor and draws upon terminology of computer processing. Data inputs into this computational model include auditory and visual data packets that are stored for a short time in volatile or transitory memory (see Section 2.1). Volatile memory includes stores of auditory and visual inputs as well as short term memory registers that equate to a computational scratch pads of random access memory that when used for the processing of information equate to working memory and are of fixed capacity (see Section 2.5). Within a traditional computational model of memory, long term memory forms the equivalent of non volatile computational storage that contains addressable data that is stored and retrieved as required into volatile memory for processing through working memory registers (Fernandez & Mackie, 2006). With short term memory containing approximately seven registers (see Section 2.1), this presents a storage problem for the required volatile memory to store auditory and visual inputs, and material retrieved from long term memory.

The traditional storage-retrieval model (Fernandez & Mackie, 2006) is that memories are retrieved in response to the processing of information in working memory registers. For example, a data input of an image of a bee will be stored in a visual image store of volatile memory (see Figure 2.4), processed through working memory registers that identify an aspect as equivalent to some stored information, this information will then be recalled from where it is stored in long term memory, and this will form a resulting mental model of a bee. As each new element of information is recalled it provides addressable links to further elements of information, such as the memory of being stung that has been associated with a bee. While the processing registers have a very limited capacity, the required information is drawn into short term memory and forms a mental model of the concept, in this example, of a bee.

In very general and simplified terms, instead of this information being transferred from long term memory to short term memory as occurs in computer processing with the attendant issues of volatile storage capacity, an alternative process of activated linkages to form a neural network of associated nodes of information is possible. In this model, information stored in various nodes is not moved or copied, but the access to this information is improved for a short time. Through a process of chemically activating linkages between nodes, a temporary network of linkages forms the mental model of a concept (see Figure 2.19). Addressable data comprises this mental model of a concept, the storage of which is distributed throughout long term memory and accessed through addressed links between nodes. The greater the number of nodes contained in this network, the greater the complexity of the mental model that can subsequently form.

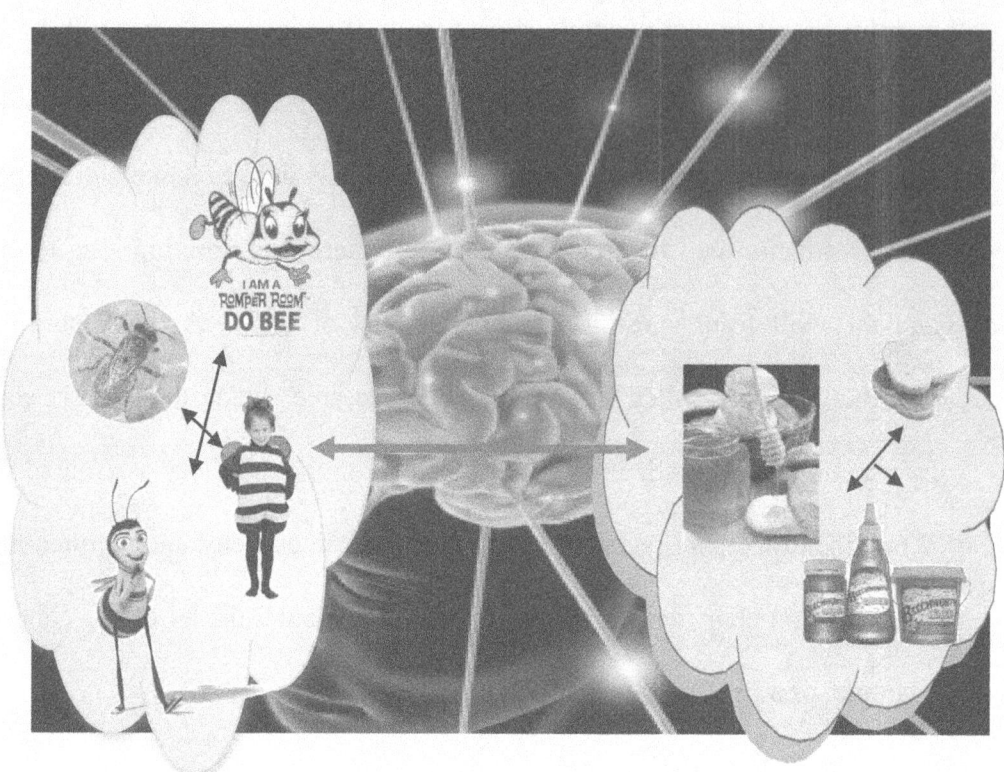

Figure 2.19   Mental models formed by neural linkages

While remaining limited to the processing capacity of the short term memory register, this simplified model permits the chunking process to expand to entire mental models, where only the initial address is required for processing and permits the processing of disparate concepts within the constraints of working memory registers. The model also contextualises pre-attentive effects (Section 2.1) in which cues can be used to quickly retrieve complex stored information, and the differences between visual and auditory processing with regard to the speed and quantity of data provided. The richness of information contained in an image, as detailed by Gestalt principles (Section 2.1), permits visual processing to provide a greater number of possible addresses to stored information and through the use of mental visualisation, generate a more complex mental model.

This simplified model of cognitive processing supports a model of the learning process in which existing linkages between stored elements are modified or additional links created between memory elements. As links are used to form mental models, the neural pathways strengthen and become more efficient in the transmission of signals. This process would not generally occur as discrete nodes, but through a complex interrelationship between concepts, where a mental model is extended to include two or more existing concepts (Fuster, 1995). For example, taking an existing concept of a bee and associating it with an existing concept of honey on learning that bees produce honey (see Figure 2.19). The generated linkage between nodes of these two concepts then permits a mental model to be generated that now includes stored information about bees and about honey. Using a validation process (see Section 2.3) that may be predominately subconscious and occurring during sleep (Hasselmo & McClelland, 1999), the resulting changes will be strengthened with each succeeding use of the new model. This iterative process of improvement and validation based upon increasing the complexity of the generated mental model forms the model of learning adopted by this study.

By breaking down concepts into eight discrete levels of complexity (see Section 2.4), a measurable means of tracking concept development by analysis of the capabilities of the resulting mental model was produced. This model of the learning process was then applied to examining the effectiveness of a set of software programming languages that relied upon varying degrees of textual (auditory) to visual inputs and is described in detail in the next chapter (Chapter 3).

Chapter 3

CASES: VISUALISATION TOOLS

Forming the instrumental cases of this collective case study, the visualisation tools used in this study are categorised as either unconstrained text, constrained text, constrained icon, or unconstrained icon. They represent a subset of cognitive tools that can encompass a wide range of devices to support learning (Lajoie & Derry, 1993; Shim & Lee, 2006) by:

1. supporting cognitive processes, such as memory and metacognition;
2. sharing cognitive load by providing support for lower level cognition so that resources are left over for higher order thinking;
3. allowing the learner to engage in cognitive activities that would otherwise be out of reach; and,
4. allowing learners to generate and test hypotheses in the context of problem solving.

The application of cognitive tools to learning is refined in theories of distributed cognition (Salomon, Perkins & Globerson, 1991) in which learner, tool, and activity form a joint learning system (Kim & Reeves, 2007).

This study focuses on a set of cognitive tools that use differing degrees of visualisation to support learning, which are referred to as visualisation tools. Visualisation tools have been further delineated in this study (see Section 2.2) as software visualisation tools that use display-based reasoning to provide symbolic representation of software processes in order to reduce the user cognitive load.

Differing software visualisation tools can be used by students from the passive viewing of diagrams and animations through to the use of visualisation environments in which students can modify, construct and present their own visualisations of the processes occurring in the concepts under study. Software visualisation tools relevant to this study have been categorised through the literature review (Chapter 2) as being tools that:

1. are predominantly sentential (textual) representations;
2. make use of text but with spatial representation of that text;
3. make use of diagrammatic (pictorial) representations to represent sentential (textual) representations; or,
4. are predominantly diagrammatic (pictorial) representations.

Because of the processing differences between sentential and diagrammatic representations, specific property distinctions relating to the use of visual and auditory memory stores in working memory can be made (see Figure 3.1). These are:

1. *unconstrained text* which makes use of sentential (textual) representations, for example, the PHP (Pre-Hypertext Programming) programming language and the Visual Basic programming language (see Section 3.2);
2. *constrained text* which makes spatial representation of text, for example, the *Alice* programming language (see Section 3.3);

3. *constrained icons* which makes use of diagrammatic (pictorial) representations to represent sentential (textual) representations, for example, the *GameMaker* programming language (see Section 3.4);

4. *unconstrained icons* which predominantly use diagrammatic (pictorial) representations, for example, the *RoboLab* programming language (see Section 3.5).

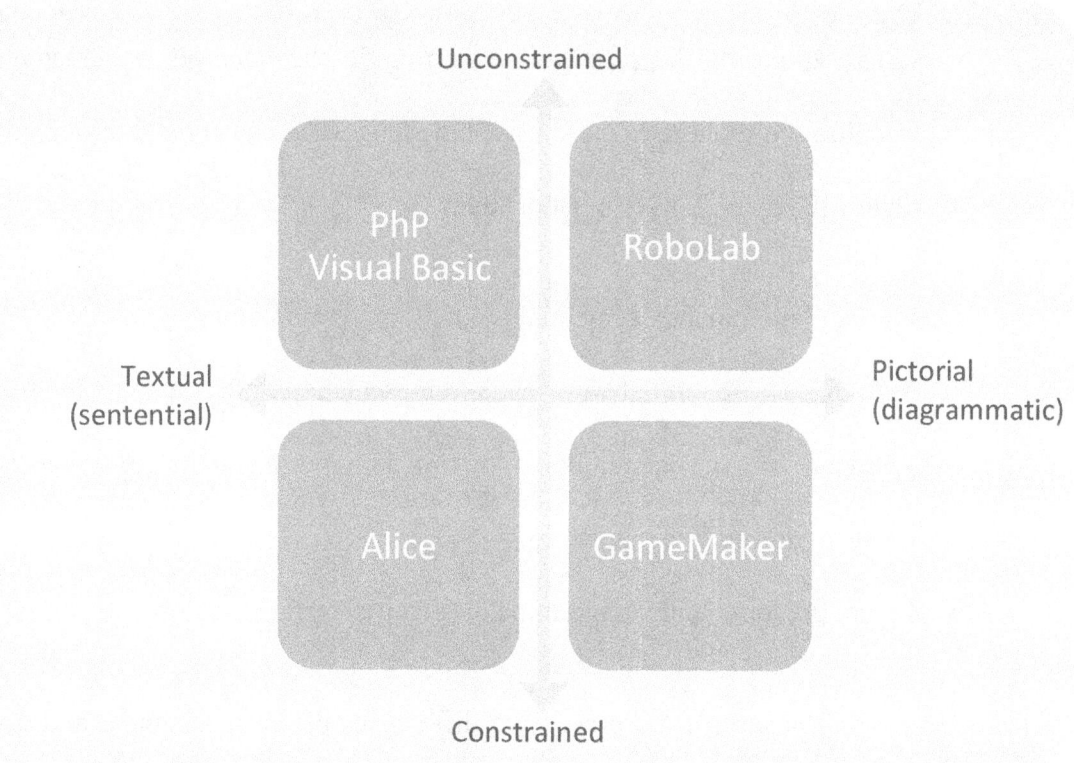

Figure 3.1   Visualisation constraint continua

Within this context, constrained is defined as providing a necessary graphical structure to the text or necessary textual component to icons for these to be effectively used. Unconstrained is defined as text without any relationships or structures beyond sentential, or icons without any text to provide additional explanation.

3.1 Unconstrained text

Two software visualisation tools were chosen for this study as an example of unconstrained text, the PHP programming language and the Visual Basic programming language. Self-referentially short for PHP: Hypertext Preprocessor, PHP is an open source, server-side, HTML embedded scripting language used to create dynamic Web pages. In this language, segments of text representing program code instructions are manipulated in a textual list. In this study it is defined as using *unconstrained text* which makes use of sentential (textual) representations. Figure 3.2 shows a screen grab of the PHP environment.

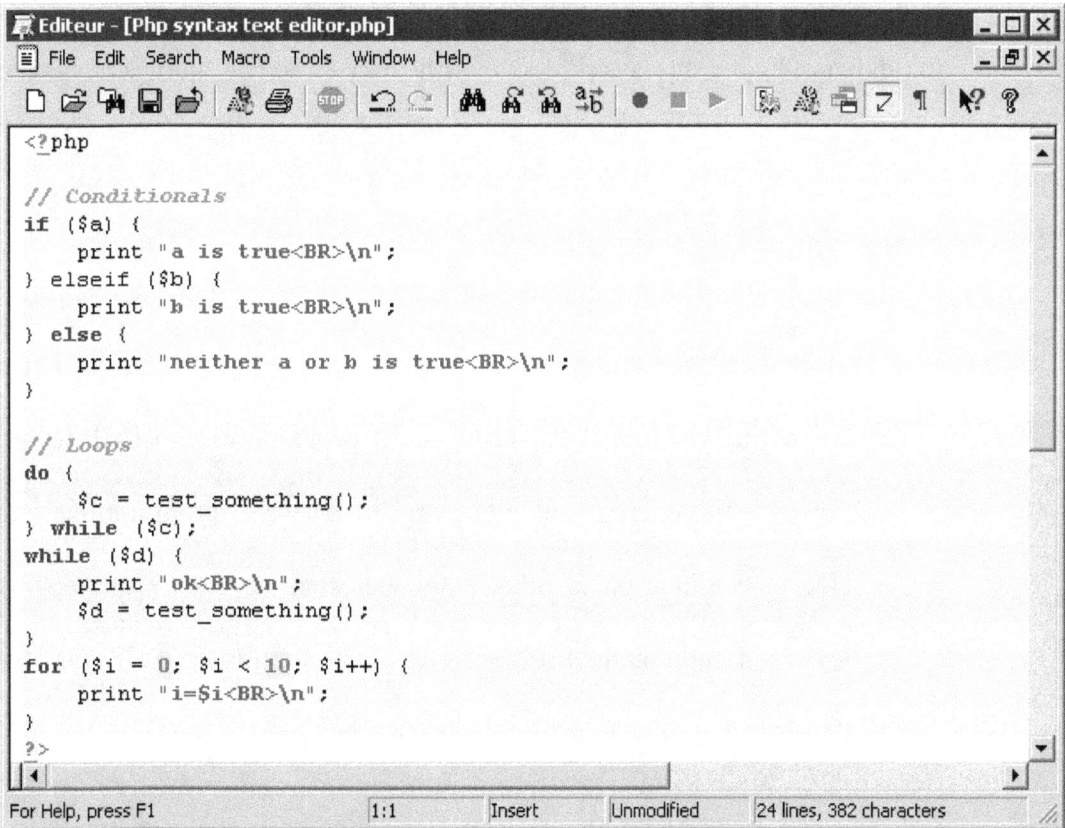

Figure 3.2   PHP environment

PHP, while initially a server-side scripting language for dynamic web content, has evolved into an established mainstream programming language. As a result it has only recently become popular for teaching introductory programming concepts and there is little documented research into its use in the teaching of programming concepts.

Although the language has limitations, most notably around the concept of modularity where the integration with HTML complicates matters, it has become popular because it is a very 'loose' language, that is, it is dynamically typed. The syntax is more flexible, for example, variables do not have to be declared and they can hold any type of object. Although this is arguably an advantage for those using the language, it causes problems with transferability between languages. For example:

> … many PHP programmers have reported having had trouble trying to learn other languages in the past and ultimately giving up after each attempt until attempting to learn PHP. The ease of programming in PHP has made it so these programmers are able to learn the basics of programming and are then able to continue on to other languages such as C/C++ or Perl/Python/Java and then finding themselves back programming in PHP for its speed of development in comparison to other languages.
>
> (PHP, 2005)

Visual Basic (VB) is a programming environment in which a programmer uses a graphical user interface (see Figure 3.3) to choose and modify preselected sections of code written in the BASIC programming language. Visual Basic was one of the first products to provide a graphical programming environment and a paint metaphor for developing user interfaces. Visual Basic programmers can add a substantial amount of code by dragging and dropping controls, such as buttons and dialog boxes, and then defining their appearance and behaviour. They must however resort to textual code for fundamental programming constructs and it is within this context that the language is defined for this study as *unconstrained text* which makes use of sentential (textual) representations.

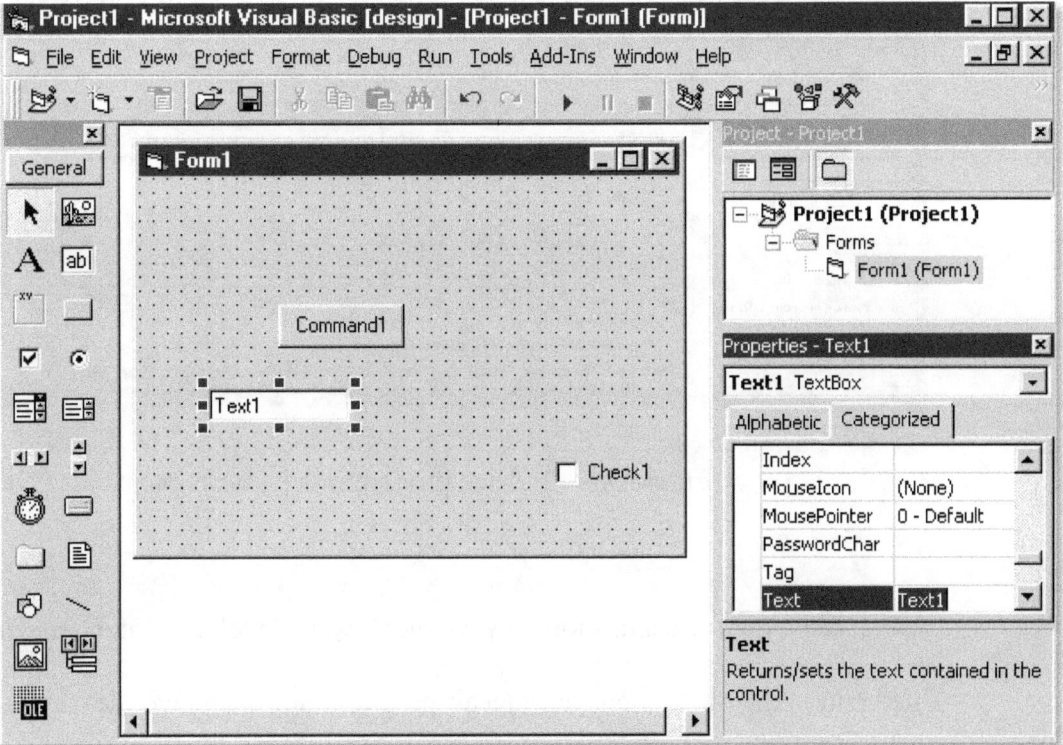

Figure 3.3   Visual Basic GUI

3.2 Constrained text

The *Alice* programming language (see Figure 3.4) uses text segments to represent program code instructions, manipulated in a one dimensional graphical list with program flow represented by spatial placement. It was chosen as a visualisation tool to represent the property of constrained text. Figure 3.4 presents a screen grab of the Alice programming environment displaying the means by which text can be represented and manipulated to create a program.

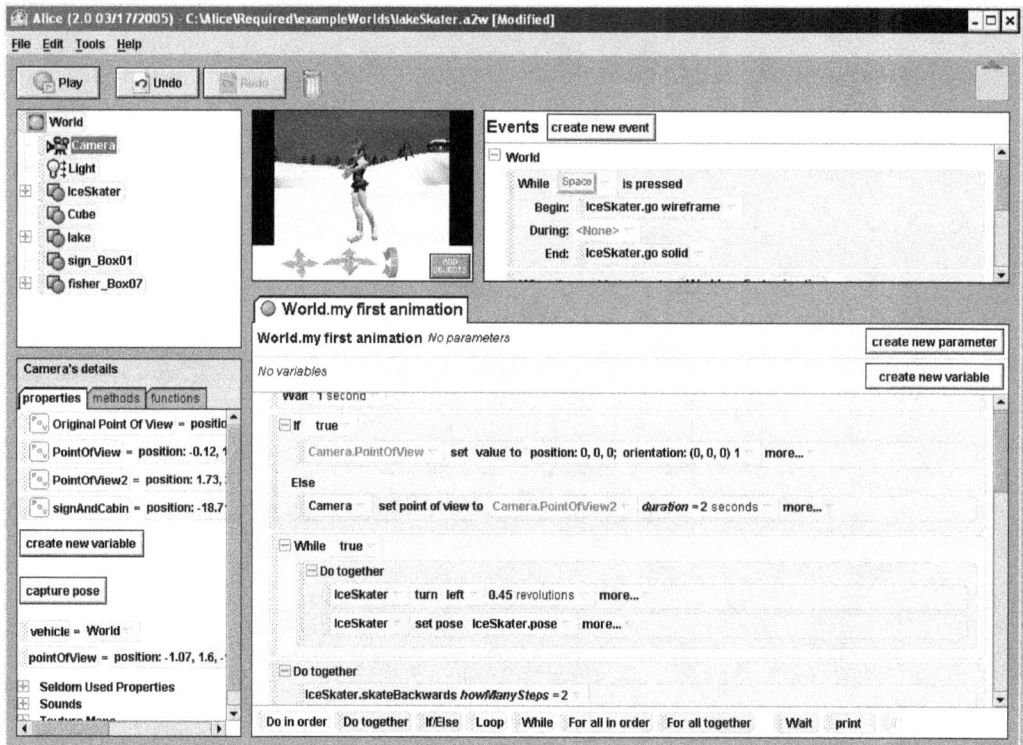

Figure 3.4   Alice programming environment

The Alice visualisation environment was developed at Carnegie Mellon University. Alice builds on the Squeak programming language, developed by Alan Kay (Senior Fellow at Hewlett Packard) and an open-source community of colleagues. Its main advantage lies in its:

> ... address[ing] the mechanical barriers to programming ... [thus] making it much easier for students to create programs. Rather than having to correctly type commands according to obscure rules of syntax, students drag-and-drop words in a direct manipulation interface. This user interface ensures that programs are always well-formed.

(Alice, 2005)

Alice is increasingly under study as an introductory programming language for knowledge construction (Horwitz, 2005; Jonassen, 1999; Kirriemuir & McFarlane, 2004), engagement (Jonassen, 1999; Jonassen et al., 1993; Papert, 1990; Pausch & Conway, 2000; Rieber, 2005) and to facilitate "learners as designers" (Becker, 2007; Cooper et al., 2003; Dann et al., 2005; Jonassen, 1994; Pausch & Conway, 2000; Robertson & Good, 2004). For the present study it will represent *constrained text* making spatial representations of text.

3.3 Constrained icons

The GameMaker programming language has icons representing textual code elements, manipulated in a one dimensional graphical list with program flow represented by spatial placement. It is therefore an appropriate selection to represent the property of constrained icons. Although access is possible in this programming language to textual representation of icons, use will not be made of this during the study.

The GameMaker visualisation environment was developed in 2005 by Mark Overmars from the Institute of Information and Computing Sciences at Utrecht University. It is increasingly being used as an introductory programming environment; however, there is little documented research into its use in the teaching of programming concepts. In this study the language represents *constrained icons* using diagrammatic (pictorial) representations to represent sentential (textual) representations of programming code. Figure 3.5 shows a screen grab of the GameMaker environment.

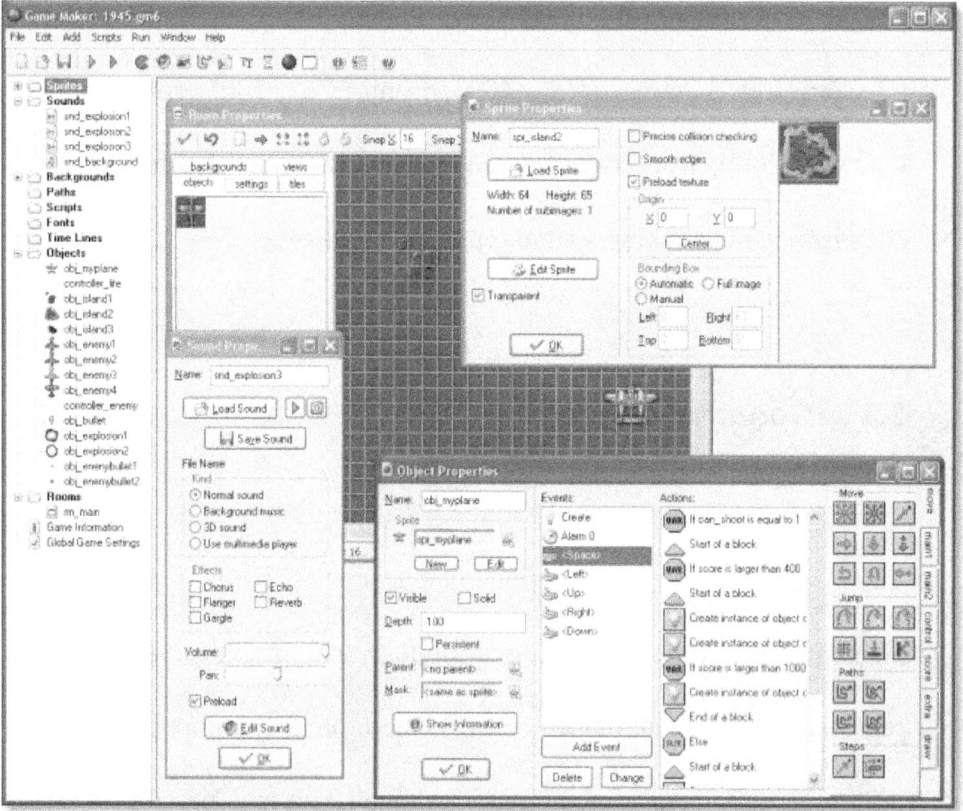

Figure 3.5   GameMaker programming environment

3.4 Unconstrained icons

The RoboLab programming language is one in which unconstrained icons are manipulated in a two-dimensional plane and program flow 'wired' between icons. No textual representation is available. The RoboLab environment is shown in Figure 3.6.

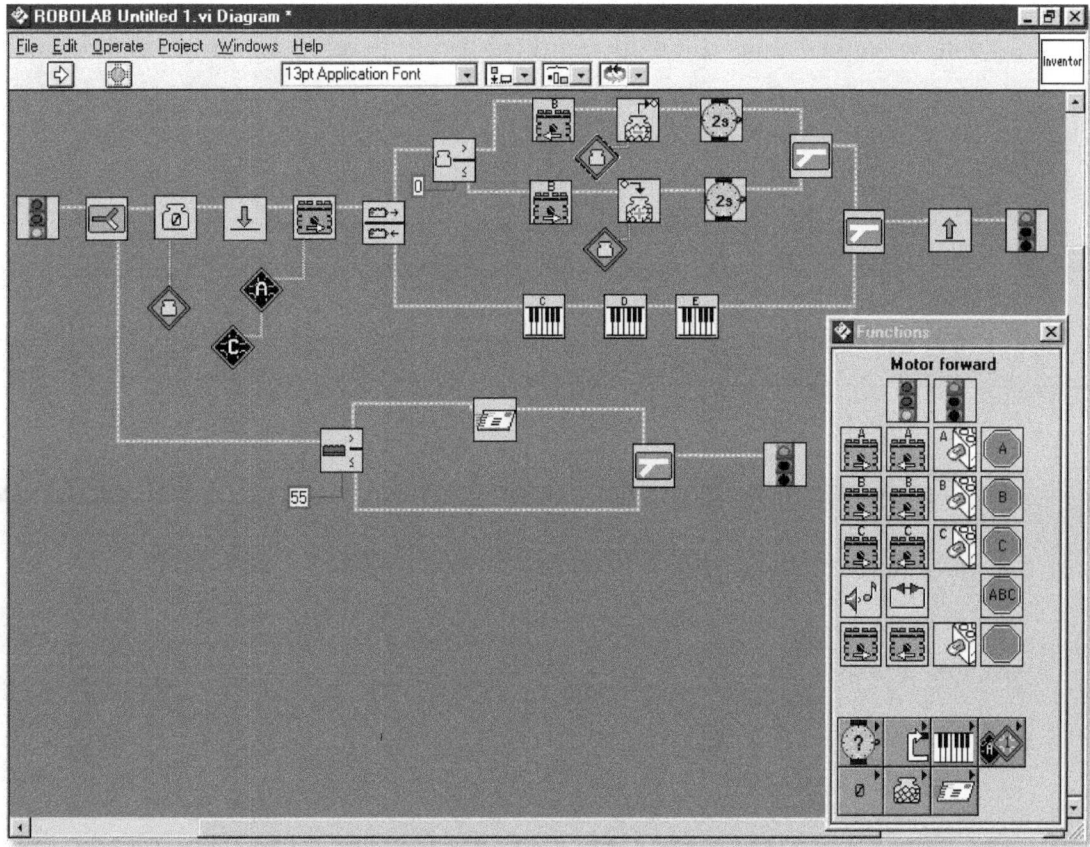

Figure 3.6   RoboLab programming environment

The RoboLab Software Visualisation System was developed by Capozolli and Rogers (2005) from the Department of Mechanical Engineering at Tufts University in collaboration with LEGO DACTA and National Instruments. RoboLab is a modification of National Instruments' LabVIEW Software Visualisation System and has been widely used in educational settings for the teaching of fundamental engineering and scientific concepts. There is little documented research into its use in the teaching of programming concepts. In this study the language represents *unconstrained icons* using diagrams (pictorial) to represent programming code.

These four software visualisation tools comprise the cases of a collective case study (see Section 4.1) used to increase understanding of the effect of visualisation on the learning process with a focus on software visualisations in the domain of programming. The following chapter describes in greater detail the methodology used to develop the cases into an instrumental collective case study.

Chapter 4

RESEARCH METHODOLOGY

The first and over-arching of the three aims of the study (see Section 1.2), was to increase understanding of the effect of visualisation on the learning process with a focus on the effect of software visualisations on the learning of programming languages. In this, the collective cases (see Section 4.1) of the visualisation tools studied – with an emphasis on underlying concepts – were instrumental in achieving this aim.

The specific context for this study was a metropolitan girls' school with the subjects in four student cohorts (see Section 4.2) and the programming concepts tested being (a) sequence, (b) selection, (c) iteration, and (d) modularity. These concepts are fundamental to the study of structured algorithmic computer programming and explain the order of instructions given to the computer (sequence), how computers respond to user input or specific conditions (selection or branching), how particular instructions are repeated until a particular condition is met (iteration or repetition), and how patterns of actions are reduced to repeatable blocks (modularity). These four concepts are fundamental building blocks in students' understanding of software programming and misconceptions at this stage of their cognitive understanding can impact greatly on their understanding of subsequent software programming concepts (Pea & Kurland, 1983).

This chapter will present a description of the methodology and the research methods adopted by this study. The research design will be presented in three separate sections, that is, collective case studies and subsequent narrative development will be outlined in Section 4.1, the participants of the study will be described in detail in Section 4.2 and the phases of the study will be presented in Section 4.3. The methodology is further detailed over five separate sections, that is, the data collection methods will be presented in section 4.4. Data analysis is presented in Section 4.5. The trustworthiness of the study is detailed in Section 4.6, the role of the researcher is described in Section 4.7, and the limitations of the study in Section 4.8.

4.1 Collective case studies and narratives

Analysis of the literature in this study identified a significant research gap in the field, that previous quantitative research into the use of software visualisations to support the learning of computer programming has shown negative learning outcomes from the use of software visualisations (Section 2.2). An emerging aim (Section 1.2) developed to provide an explanation of the failure of software visualisation to improve educational outcomes in quantitative research studies through the use of a qualitative approach.

To address the requirements of the original and emerging aims, a collective case study methodology was selected to provide an explanation of visualisation systems bounded over time through detailed, in-depth data collection involving multiple sources of information rich in context (Creswell, 1998). The cases defined

(Stake, 1995) for the present study are the differing software visualisation tools described in Chapter 3.

The cases are situated within the context of software visualisation (Section 2.2) and comprise four categories of programming languages (see Figure 3.1) depending on the degree of sentential and diagrammatic representation and the level of constraint exhibited by the programming languages interface. Within this framework, the cases were selected for maximum variation (Patton, 1990) in their use of visualisation. The focus of this study is an instrumental collective case study (Stake, 1995), comparing and contrasting visualisation tools against their effectiveness in supporting the learning of computer programming concepts (Section 4.5.1).

In addressing the failure of existing studies and seeking to increase understanding of the effect of visualisation on the learning process, an instrumental collective case study methodology has been used to better understand the substantive issues involved and advance visualisation theory (Stake, 1995). Using four categories of software visualisation tool as the cases for the study, extensive data collection drawing on multiple sources of information (Section 4.4) culminated in the development of a series of nine narratives. The narratives used a theoretical-analytical style and a mix of sequential-focused and category-focused narrative reports (She☐edi, 2005). Sequential-focused narratives were employed to explain what occurred in an understandable manner (McQuillan, 2000) while category-focused narrative elements were aimed at presenting the data (Merriam, 1998) in a manner that detailed the theoretical propositions arising from the study.

Validation was increased through the triangulation of multiple research methods including pre and post test concept mapping, structured interviews based on stimulated recall, participant surveys, trace analysis, narrative analysis, and participant observation (Section 4.4). Similarly, the trustworthiness of the study is detailed in Section 4.6. While it is the nature of case studies not to be representative of entire populations, the use of collective cases examining a range of visualisation tools and drawing upon a rich set of analysable data, provided a degree of generalisability (Jensen & Rodgers, 2001) to visualisation theory based on the cases selected to represent dimensions of that theory. This has resulted in the conclusions (Chapter 8) and contributions (Section 8.4) of the study.

4.2 Subjects

The research subjects for the study, as noted, were students ($N=31$), aged 15-17 years, who were studying ICT by choice at an Australian private girls' secondary school in a metropolitan location. Students were drawn from four ICT cohorts in which studies of fundamental programming concepts occurred. For most students (92%) the course was their first experience with computer programming, some students (8%) had previous experience with programming in primary school, none of which equated to the level of concept development addressed in this study. The cohorts and their allocation to visualisation tools and programming concepts (summarised in Table 4.1) were:

1. **Cohort A.** Nine students (*n*=9) enrolled in *Advanced Information Technology*, an extension ICT course for 15-16 year olds that included the use of the Alice (see Section 3.2) and Gamemaker (see Section 3.3) programming languages. This cohort was focused on the concepts of sequence (Alice), iteration (Alice), selection (Gamemaker) and modularity (Gamemaker). The cohort was made up of four pairs and one group of three.

2. **Cohort B.** Twelve students (*n*=12) enrolled in *Space Sciences and Robotics*, an extension science course for 15-16 year olds that included the use of the RoboLab (see Section 3.4) programming language. This cohort focused on the concepts of sequence (RoboLab), selection (RoboLab) and iteration (RoboLab). This cohort was made up of six pairs.

3. **Cohort C.** Six students (*n*=8) enrolled in Information Technology Systems (ITS), a computer applications course for 16-17 year olds that included the use of the PHP (see Section 3.1) programming language. This cohort covered one concept, that of sequence (PHP). This cohort was made up of four pairs.

4. **Cohort D.** Two students (*n*=2) enrolled in Information Processing and Technology (IPT), a computer science course for 16-17 year olds that included the use of the Alice or the Visual Basic (see Section 3.1) programming languages. This cohort covered all four concepts, that is, of sequence (Alice or Visual Basic), selection (Alice or Visual Basic), iteration (Alice or Visual Basic) and modularity (Alice or Visual Basic). The students in this cohort worked independently.

This allocation provided the opportunity to observe and investigate the selected visualisation tools which represented, as described in Chapter 3, the property distinctions between sentential and diagrammatic representations and which form the cases in this study. The involvement of each of the cohorts, indicating the coverage of all concepts and the overlap in the use of the visualisation tools, is summarised in Table 4.1.

Table 4.1

Allocation of cohorts to visualisation tools and programming concepts

Cohort	n	Visualisation Tools	Programming concepts			
			sequence	*selection*	*iteration*	*modularity*
A	9	Alice	✓		✓	
		GameMaker		✓		✓
B	12	RoboLab	✓	✓	✓	
C	8	PHP	✓			
D	2	Alice	✓	✓	✓	✓
		Visual Basic	✓	✓	✓	✓

Subjects are initially referred to in this study by codes (A1a to D2a), with the first letter indicating cohort membership (see also Section 4.4), the number indicating small group membership (random numbering), and the final lowercase letter providing a personal identifier. For example, B1a is a member of the Group 1, Cohort B who worked in a pair with B1b. Where subjects worked individually, they were also allocated the identifier "a." For subjects selected from narrative development, pseudonyms drawn from popular literature are used (Chapter 6). Participation in the study was voluntary and all students were welcome to take part provided that appropriate consent was given. Similarly, participating students were able to withdraw from the study at any time though none did so.

As noted in Section 1.3, all students were taught the metacognitive processes underpinning the study and provided with the research tools (video recording and screen recording equipment) to conduct their own investigation into the development and tracking of their mental models of the concepts.

No aspect of the study was used for the summative assessment of students. The problem solving sets, however, reflected tasks historically assessed in the courses and were completed by all students irrespective of their participation in the study.

4.3 Phases of the study

As noted in Section 1.3, the study was conducted in seven sequential steps. This research design was informed by the literature in this field presented in Chapter 2 which indicated the essential elements required of a study of visualisations supporting learning. These steps, organised by phases (which are described in greater detail in Sections 4.3.1-4.3.6), were:

Phase 1: a description of the initial mental model (understanding) a student holds of a concept as described by the Pirie-Kieren model (Pirie & Kieren, 1992) (Section 2.5);

Phase 2: the use of visualisations of varying sentential-diagrammatic properties in the learning of a concept as detailed in Chapter 3;

Phase 3: the tracking of changes to a student's mental model (understanding) of a concept as described by the Pirie-Kieren model (Pirie & Kieren, 1992) (Section 2.5);

Phase 4: a description of the role of the visualisation tool in the learning of the concept;

Phase 5: a comparison of visualisation tools used in the learning of concepts;

Phase 6: a determination if tools with differing sentential-diagrammatic properties supported movement in the Pirie-Kieren model (Pirie & Kieren, 1992) (Section 2.5);

Phase 7: a development of narratives which comprise the key research outcomes of this qualitative study.

As noted, thirty one students ($N=31$) grouped in four cohorts (A-D) participated in this study (see Section 4.2.1, Table 4.1). The focused nature of this study, however, required selection of a progressively smaller sample from this group on which to focus available resources, primarily interview time. The selection for Cohorts A-C was based on the richness of data produced in preceding stages and the need for attention to all visualisation tools and programming concepts. Both students from Cohort D were included in all phases of the study. The selection was as follows:

1. In each of the four cohorts, students working individually or in groups of two or three undertook Phases 1-2 ($N=31$).

2. From this group of 31 students, 20 were selected for Phases 3-6, that is, interview and trace development ($n=20$). The selected students were A1a, A2b, A3a, A4a, A4c, B1b, B2a, B2b, B3a, B4a, B4b, B5b, B6a, B6b, C1b, C2a, C3a, C4b, D1a and D1b. Selection was based on cohort representation and randomised within cohorts.

3. From this group of 20, nine were selected for Phase 7, narrative development ($n=9$). The selected students were A3a, A4c, B1b, B4a, B6a, C3a, C4b, D1a, and D2a. For the purposes of this study, they were given pseudonyms from fiction (see Chapter 6). Selection was based on the narratives potential to articulate initial findings identified from analysis (Chapter 5), when they were revelatory, unusual, or extreme cases (Yin, 1984).

A summary of student participation is presented in Table 4.2.

Table 4.2

Cohort- Participation Level

	Cohort A	Cohort B	Cohort C	Cohort D	Total
Participating	$N=9$	$N=12$	$N=8$	$N=2$	$N=31$
Interview/Trace	$n=5$	$n=9$	$n=4$	$n=2$	$n=20$
Narratives	$n=2$	$n=3$	$n=2$	$n=2$	$n=9$

4.3.1 Phase 1

Phase 1 was concerned with the description of the initial mental model (understanding) students hold of a concept. In this phase, all subjects ($N=31$) completed an initial concept map to determine their "primitive knowing" (Pirie & Kieren, 1992) about the concept they were learning, that is, one of the fundamental programming concepts of sequence, selection, iteration and modularity.

"Primitive knowing" of the concept may be based on previous experience with programming languages, reader-directed books, and computer games. Ideally, each of these concepts involved the development of a new mental model, particularly for use in the software programming domain. The concept of sequence initially draws upon sufficient "primitive knowing" of related concepts so that no prerequisites were required. The concepts are however progressive and mental models developed subsequent to the sequence model required models developed of preceding concepts to at least the "property noticing" level in order to provide sufficient "primitive knowing" for their subsequent development. This phase allowed an initial placement of the students' understanding of the concept in the Pirie and Kieren (1992) model (see Section 4.4.1).

4.3.2 Phase 2

Phase 2 was effectively a teaching phase where students were introduced to and made use of visualisation tools of varying sentential-diagrammatic properties, that is, PHP, Visual Basic, Alice, GameMaker and Robolab (as described in Chapter 3) in the learning of the fundamental programming concepts, that is, sequence, selection, iteration and modularity, of interest to this study. Students were presented with a set of programming problems of increasing difficulty which progressively used and developed an increasing understanding of the concept. Specific levels of the Pirie and Kieren (Pirie & Kieren, 1992) model were systematically included in the problem sets to permit development to all levels of the model. Care was needed that students did not progress unobserved through the "inventising" level to develop models of subsequent concepts (see Section 2.5).

Problem sets were developed for each of the four visualisation tools. Each tool developed up to four concepts, and each concept required nine problem sets to enable students to progress through the mental model levels of that concept. This resulted in the development of over 900 problem sets to enable students to work through each mental model level and self identify progression against student identifiable outcomes. These were grouped into 88 booklets (see Appendix C, D and E) which were also used by students to journal their engagement with the tool and trace a progressive record of their mental model development for each concept (see Section 4.4.2.5).

4.3.3 Phase 3

Phase 3 was concerned with tracking changes to the subjects' mental model (understanding) of a concept as described by the Pirie and Kieren (1992) model. This model is fundamentally metacognitive, particularly at the formalising, observing, structuring and inventising levels. Given the nature of the observations required, student participation in identifying "folding back" events and self-determination of their placement in the Pirie and Kieren model is supported by scrutable learner modelling theory (Lum, 2003; Bull, Brna, & Pain, 1995), providing strong learner control of the research process. The tracking of events occurred over time and using the differing methods of observation and data collection which are described in the following sub-sections (Section 4.3.31 – 4.3.3.4). It is in this phase that the first reduction in subject numbers occurs, that is, from 31 to 20 students.

4.3.3.1   Problem set completion with speak-aloud and peer discussion

Students made video recordings (see Section 4.4.2.1) of their comments during problem solving and discussion with peers. Students also made screen recordings (see Section 4.4.2.2) of their interaction with visualisation software to assist in solving the problems (see Figure 4.1).

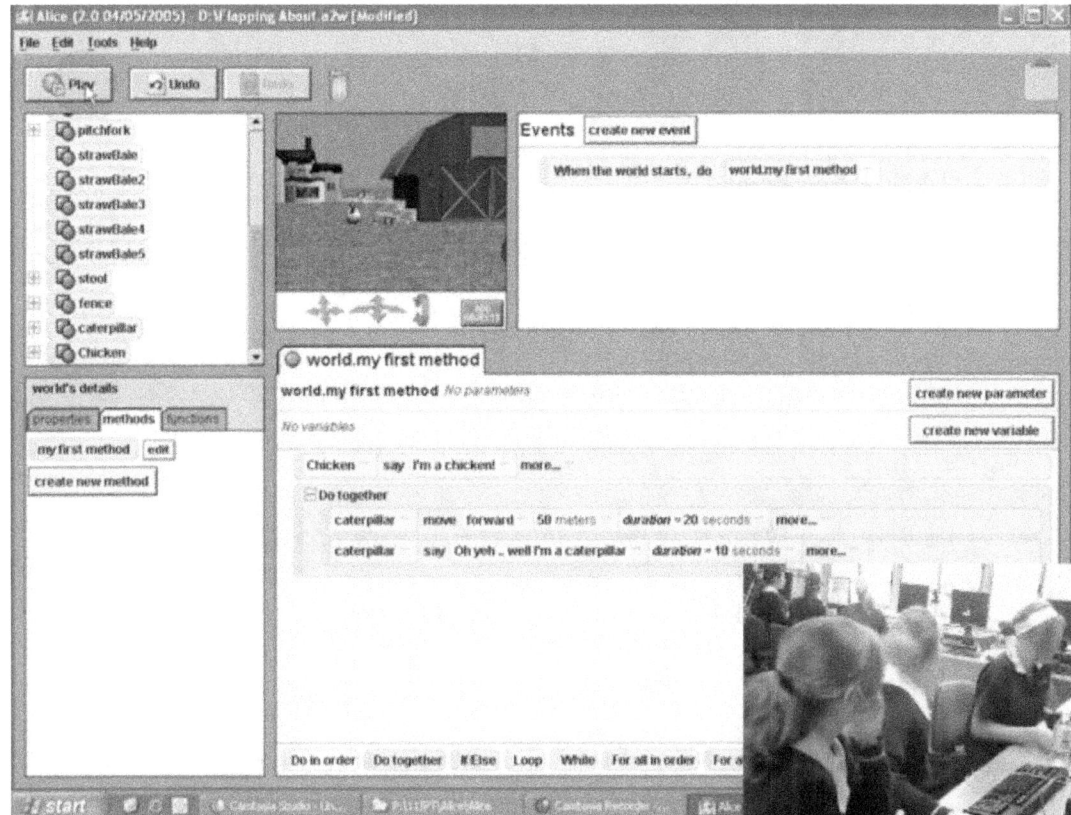

Figure 4.1   Student screen capture with inline video capture

Student control of data recording was aimed at emphasising the metacognitive development aspects of the task. Students from cohorts (A-C) worked in pairs or small groups and used a combination of the speak-aloud (see Section 4.4.2.3) method during individual problem solving attempts and peer discussion (see Section 4.4.2.4) at the completion of each problem to generate and record a description of their thinking process in terms of the Pirie and Kieren model, focusing on folding back events, and generated and recorded a description of their mental model of the concept, focusing on describing level placement on their model, in student journals (see Section 4.4.2.5). Further details of the data instruments are provided in Section 4.4. The detailed results of student problem sets for all subjects (N=31) are presented in Section 5.1.

4.3.3.2   Determination of Final Mental Model using Concept Mapping

All subjects completed a final concept map to assist in determining final placement in the Pirie and Kieren (1992) model for the concept under investigation. The results of this concept mapping are detailed in Section 4.5.1 where, as previously noted, they are compared to the results of the initial concept map (see Section 4.3.1).

4.3.3.3   Trace development interview with stimulated recall

On completion of the problem set for the concept, individually selected students (n=20) were interviewed by the researcher (see Section 4.4.4) and initially asked to provide (a) a description of their thinking in developing their mental model, and (b) an explanation of what they knew of the concept, that is, their mental model.

Prompts, as described by the Pirie and Kieren (1992) model, were provided to assist students in their descriptions and a trace (see Section 4.4.1.1) was constructed of the development of the mental models. Stimulated recall (see Section 4.4.8) using video recordings of the students speak-aloud and peer comments, screen recording of interactions with the visualisation software, concept maps, and individual journals, were used to assist students in describing their learning processes and constructing as accurate a trace as possible (see Section 5.3).

4.3.3.4   Verification of student generated traces

From student generated traces and elaborations, the researcher reviewed video recordings, screen recordings, concept maps, student journals, and observational notes (see Section 4.4.2) to verify and add detail to traces. Three identified elements were specifically noted: These were the:

1.   time taken to complete the problem sets and develop the mental model;

2.   level of development as described by the Pirie and Kieren (1992) model, and

3.   degree of folding back that had occurred.

Students were provided with verified traces and provided with the opportunity to comment on variation to student generated traces.

4.3.4   Phase 4

Phase 4 was concerned with the description of the role of the visualisation tool in the learning of the concept. At the completion of the development of a mental model for each concept, students were surveyed (see Section 4.4.10) on the effectiveness of the visualisations provided by the visualisation tools to support their learning of the concept. The results of these surveys are summarised in Section 5.2.1.

4.3.5   Phase 5

Phase 5 was concerned with the comparison of visualisation tools used in the learning of concepts. At the completion of the development of mental models, where subjects across the four cohorts had used different visualisation tools, they were surveyed on the differences they found in the visualisation tools to support their learning of the concepts. The results of these surveys are summarised in Section 5.2.2.

4.3.6 Phase 6

Phase 6 was concerned with determining if tools with differing sentential-diagrammatic properties supported movement in the Pirie and Kieren (1992) model across various boundaries in the model. Analysis of traces (see Section 4.4.4 and Section 4.5.2) regarding the speed of mental model development, level of development as described by the Pirie and Kieren (1992) model, and degree of folding-back was compared to the sentential-diagrammatic properties of the visualisation tool used (see Section 5.1).

4.3.7 Phase 7

Phase 7, the final step in the conduct of the study, was concerned with the development of narratives to describe the processes of concept development investigated in this study. A set of selected narratives ($N=9$) (see Section 4.4.12) describe the development of (a) student mental models of concepts, (b) use of visualisations in the development of these mental models; and, (c) effectiveness of software visualisations to support the learning of simple programming concepts (see Chapter 6). Pseudonyms drawn from popular fiction were used as cognitive aids in comparing and contrasting the developed narratives.

4.4 Data collection

As mentioned incidentally in Section 4.3, a wide variety of instruments was used to provide a rich collection of data in order to assist students in tracking their cognitive level changes, assist the researcher in verifying student tracking, and allowing the development of narratives that provided detailed and insightful descriptions of the processes that occurred. These were:

a. concept maps in Phases 1 and 3 (Section 4.4.1);

b. stimulated recall (Section 4.4.2) which, through interviews in Phase 3, made use of video recording (Section 4.4.2.1), screen recording (Section 4.4.2.2), speak-aloud protocols (Section 4.4.2.3), peer discussions (Section 4.4.2.4), student journals (Section 4.4.2.5), and researcher (observation) journal (Section 4.4.2.6);

c. surveys (Section 4.4.3);

d. trace analyses (Section 4.4.4); and,

e. narratives (Section 4.4.5).

4.4.1 Concept maps

Concepts maps, used in Phases 1 and 3 of this study, are a tool for externalising learner conceptions of a concept domain. Concept mapping has strong foundations in theories of learning and in empirical studies of brain activity particularly as a mechanism for determining the way that a learner understands a concept (Cimolino & Kay, 2002; Cimolino, Kay & Miller, 2002, 2004). A concept map allows individuals to build accurate and detailed visual models of their mental models of concepts. Analysis can be focused on verification of the described mental model against an establish model of the concept (Cimolino, Kay & Miller, 2002).

In this study, concept maps were constructed of each of the four programming concepts, namely, sequence, selection, iteration, and modularity. Students constructed their own concept maps before and after each concept was developed. Constructing concept maps guided students towards the development of mental models consistent with an established model while recording inconsistencies and misconceptions students made in comparison to the established model. This assisted in determining students initial "primitive knowing" of the concept and in verifying student final placement in the Pirie and Kieren (1992) model.

In this study, concepts maps were incorporated into initial mental model determination (see Section 4.3.1) and in the determination of a final mental model for a concept (see Section 4.3.3.2). Because the development of concept maps was not timed and used a different scaling to the other measures used to record student mental model development, this was not included in mental model traces (see Sections 5.1 and 5.3). Concept maps were used in narrative development (see Chapter 6) to assist in describing the overall effectiveness of concept development.

4.4.2 Stimulated recall

Stimulated recall is being increasingly used in various domains to support interview based research. It acts as a trigger to assist participants notice events and increase their awareness (Jokinen, Pelkonen, Voutilainen, & Meriläinen, 1998; Lindgren & Sullivan, 2003). In this study (Phase 3), stimulated recall, used in interviews, made use of the results of a variety of supporting techniques including video recordings (Section 4.4.2.1), screen activity recordings (Section 4.4.2.2.), "speak-aloud" recordings (Section 4.4.2.3), peer discussions (Section 4.4.2.4), student journals

(Student 4.4.2.5), and observational notes (Section 4.4.2.6) to stimulate student recall of events. Preparation, sequencing and structuring of this material was used to highlight identified key events but the aim was not to influence subjects' observations. It was, rather, to assist subjects in clarifying and elaborating points indicated, but not made explicit, in supporting techniques.

4.4.2.1 Video recording

Videotapes of student "speak-aloud" activity (Section 4.4.2.3) and peer discussions (Section 4.4.2.4) were used in this study primarily to support stimulated recall of folding-back events. Video recording is useful in research in capturing:

> ... events [which] are rare or fleeting in duration or when the distinctive shape and character of ... events unfolds moment by moment, during which it is important to have accurate information on the speech and nonverbal behavior of particular participants in the scene.
> (Erickson, 1992, pp. 204–205)

The methodological issues raised in the use of video recording in data collection, analysis and interpretation have been widely documented in the literature (Cobb & Whitenack, 1996; Davis, 1989; Davis, Maher, & Martino, 1992; Hall, 2000; Lesh & Lehrer, 2000; Pirie, 1996a, 2001; Powell, Francisco, & Maher, 2003; Roschelle, 2000). By allowing subjects to control the use of videotaping for clear task-oriented metacognitive goals, many of the concerns raised over the effective use of videotaping were mitigated.

Methodologically, video recording lends itself to variety of approaches in both data collection and analysis. Pirie (1996) observed that videotaping a classroom is likely to be "the least intrusive, yet most inclusive, way of studying the phenomenon" (p. 554). Bottorff (1994) noted two main advantages of video recordings in research: density and permanence. Density reflects the advantage of video recordings in monitoring different and simultaneous details of ongoing behaviour. Furthermore, from the perspective of density, video recordings capture two data streams — audio and visual — in real time. The second advantage is permanence. Unlike live observations, video recordings can be viewed as frequently as necessary and in flexible ways – real time, slow motion, frame by frame, forwards and backwards. They also allow for participants to assist in providing interpretations (Bottorff, 1994) and this was used in this study to facilitate stimulated recall (see Section 4.4.2).

Powell, Francisco, and Mayer (2003) suggested that a critical prerequisite for using video to capture data is to have clear criteria for its use and analysis. For use in their study of the development of thinking, they mapped an analytical model comprising of seven interacting, non-linear actions: These are (a) viewing the video data attentively; (b) describing the video data; (c) identifying critical events; (d) transcribing; (e) coding; (f) constructing storyline; and (g) composing narrative.

The first three actions of this sequence, that is, viewing, describing and identifying, were used in this study by (a) the participants in the isolating of folding-back events (see Section 2.4) and level identification; and, (b) the researcher as a means of confirming and detecting events not noted by participants. As required, the remaining actions described by Powell, Francisco, and Mayer (2003), were used to analyse and clarify specific folding-back events and level progressions and to build descriptions of the learning processes occurring.

4.4.2.2   Screen recording

In conjunction with videotape data, analysis of screen recordings of student activity were made using the same analytical model and matched to video analysis.

4.4.2.3   Speak aloud

A "speak aloud" or "think aloud," protocol is a technique to record descriptions of subjects' thought processes as they complete problem solving tasks. The technique is well established particularly in research on problem solving (Turner, McGregor, Turner, & Carroll, 2003).

4.4.2.4   Peer discussion

Peer discussions in this study involved video transcript analysis of constructive interaction (Miyake, 1986) in which groups were videotaped as they interacted with software, that is, the visualisation tools described in Chapter 3, to complete a given exercise (Douglas, 1993). As groups collaborated to construct shared meaning - both of the procedures by which they interacted with the software, and of the underlying concepts conveyed through that interaction - they made their understanding or misunderstanding of a particular task or concept inferable if not explicit.

4.4.2.5   Student journals

Student journals were maintained by all subjects in the study to record a variety of items or events of note, their engagement with each task and visualisation tool, and as a progressive record of their mental model development recorded on diagrammatic traces and elaborated with student comments to assist in identifying boundary changes (see Section 2.4).

4.4.2.6   Researcher journal

An observation journal was maintained by the researcher. Its contents were comprised of unstructured field notes recorded by the researcher on participants during each set of problem solving activities and interviews.

4.4.3 Surveys

Two survey instruments (Survey 1 and Survey 2) were developed and administered as Phases 4 and 5 respectively. These are described in Sections 4.3.3.1 and 4.3.3.2. The surveys are presented in full in Appendix A. The surveys were used to supplement data collected through verified measures and provided an additional measure of the effectiveness of the visualisation tool.

4.4.3.1   Survey 1

At the completion of the development of a mental model for each concept, all subjects were surveyed on the effectiveness of the visualisations provided by the visualisation tools to support their learning of the concept. The instrument (Survey 1) was generic for use with each of the four concepts developed. The instrument targeted specific needs fulfilment provided by the visualisations generated by the visualisation tools. It identified:

1. the concept developed;

2. the visualisation tool used;

3. a scaled ranking of the perceived effectiveness of the tool by needs fulfilment;

4. an overall scaled ranking of the perceived effectiveness of the tool; and

5. an opportunity to provide an open ended response.

4.4.3.2   Survey 2

At the completion of the development of mental models for all four concepts, where subjects experienced different visualisation tools, students were surveyed on the differences they found in the effectiveness of visualisation tools to support their learning of the concepts. The instrument (Survey 2) was specifically targeted at the differences learners noted in the needs fulfilment provided by the visualisation tools to support their learning. It identified:

1. the visualisation tools used;

2. a scaled ranking of the perceived effectiveness of each tool by needs fulfilment; and

3. an overall scaled ranking of the perceived effectiveness of each tool.

4.4.4   Trace analysis

A trace can be constructed of the understanding a student has of a concept using the eight levels of the Pirie and Kieren's (1992) model which are: primitive knowing, image making, image having, property noticing formalising, observing, structuring, and inventising (see Section 2.4). Movement forward and backward through the levels, that is, folding back, can be recorded and key events noted as exampled in Figure 4.2. The traces developed in this study were subsequently triangulated to the results of other research tools to verify and elaborate on such movements (see Section 4.5).

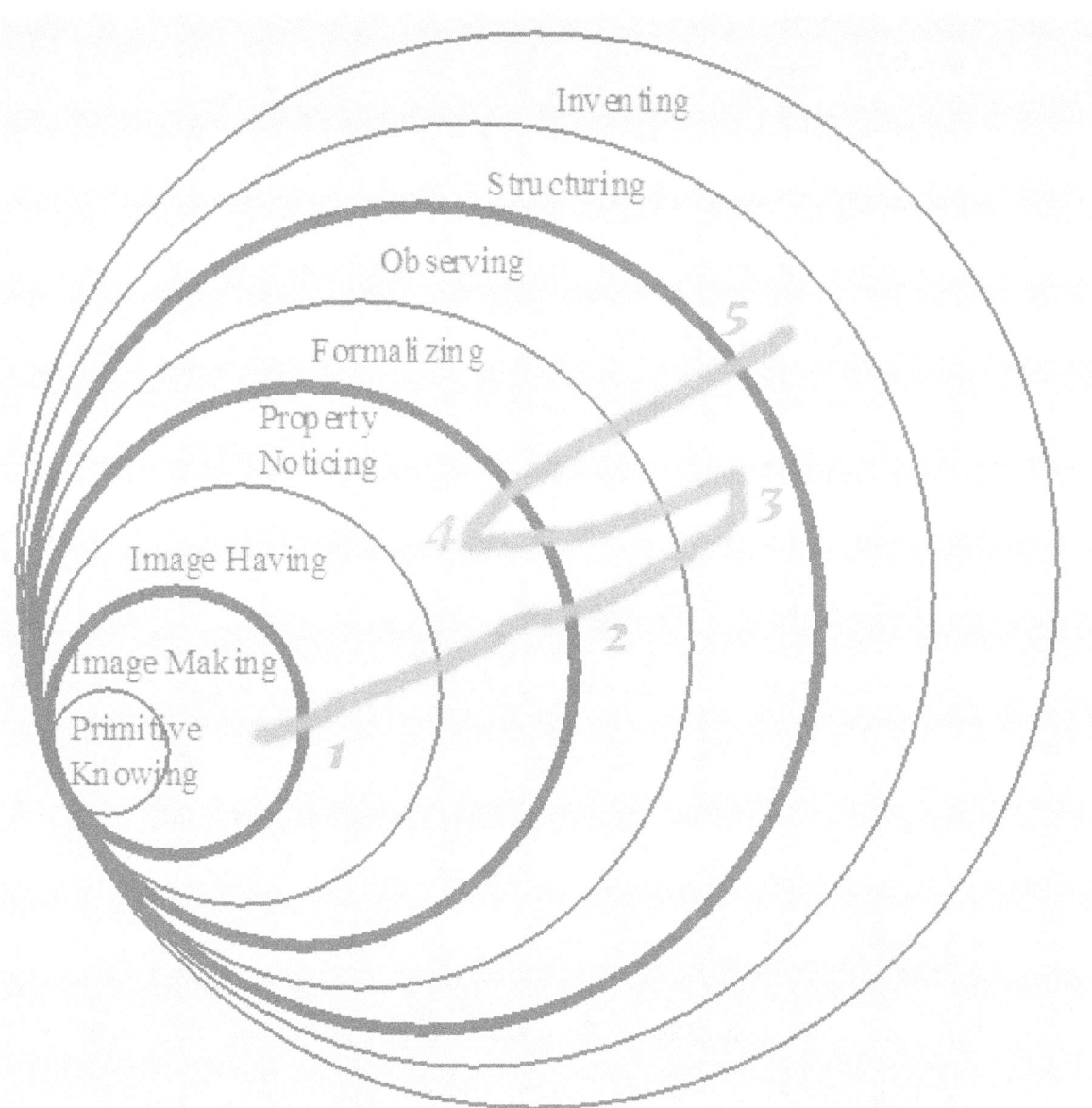

Figure 4.2   Trace development on Pirie-Kieren model

4.4.5 Narrative development

This research tool involved the development of a set of selected narratives to describe the development of (a) student mental models of concepts, (b) use of visualisations in the development of these mental models, and (c) effectiveness of software visualisations to support the learning of simple programming concepts.

4.5 Data Analysis

The data collected for the study comprised 422 hours of video and screen recordings, 183 stimulated recall interviews, 124 trace analysis interviews, and 67 survey responses. In order to facilitate the analysis of this data, a simplified legend was developed. This comprised:

1. Each subject ($N=31$) was identified by a code (A1a-D2a) (see Section 4.2).
2. Each visualisation tool, which represented the cases in this study, was identified by a single letter (PHP (P), Visual Basic (V), Alice (A), Gamemaker (G), Robolab (R)) (see Chapter 3).
3. The programming concepts were identified by a single letter, that is, sequence (S), iteration (I), selection (D), modularity (M).
4. The property distinctions were represented by their acronyms, that is, Unconstrained Text (UT), Constrained Text (CT), Unconstrained Icons (UI), and Constrained Icons (CI).

4.5.1 Concept development

Initial focus was on subjects concept development. The concepts were sequence (S), iteration (I), selection (D), modularity (M) with measurements made across four aspects (see Appendix B for full measurement schema) against Levels 1-8 of the Pirie and Kieren (1992) model (see Section 2.3). The aspects were:

1. the time required for the concept to be developed to the next level;
2. the degree of concept development;
3. the degree of concept refinement; and,
4. the degree of concept complexity.

Time measurement was made from when the task sets related to the concept level were commenced to when the student self-identified that they had met the criteria for the next level of cognitive understanding. For example, from Level 1 (Primitive Knowing) to Level 2 (Image Making), measurement was taken from the start of the provided task set to when the student was confident they could develop a physical storyboard from the concept map of the concept they were developing

At each level and for each concept, the degree of concept development was recorded by measuring the number of concept components identified or transferred to other situations. The degree of concept refinement was recorded by measuring the number of intermediary steps developed or references made to formal thinking processes while the degree of concept complexity was recorded by various measures based on the processes involved in that level of the students' mental model.

A rating was given (from "5" to "1") against performance on each aspect which was customised for each level. This is summarised in the following sections (4.5.1.1-4.5.1.8) and described in full in Appendix C. A detailed analysis of all subjects' concept development is presented in Section 5.1.

4.5.1.1   Level 1 coding

This level, "primitive knowing," was measured through subjects' initial concept map (Phase 1). The relevant aspects, also to be applied to the final concept map (Phase 1), were measured as follows:

- no time was reported at this level;

- the degree of concept development measured from ≥5 concepts (rated as "5") to ≤1 concept (rated as "1");

- the degree of concept refinement ranging from comprehensive (≥5) linkage between concepts to no linkage between concepts; and,

- the degree of concept complexity in terms of the structured grouping of concepts.

4.5.1.2   Level 2 coding

"Image Making" (Level 2) was measured through physical representations, that is, the subjects' storyboards of the mental model, in Phase 2. The relevant aspects were measured as follows:

- a rating was allocated for time taken to develop the storyboards of the mental model– ranging from <10 minutes (rated as "5") to ≥30 minutes (rated as "1");

- the degree of concept development from concept map into a storyboard measured from ≥5 concepts (rated as "5") to ≤1 concept (rated as "1");

- the degree of concept refinement in terms of physical representation ranging from comprehensive (≥5 concepts) representation (rated as "5") to no physical representation (storyboard) of mental model (rated as "1"); and,

- the degree of concept complexity in terms of the alternative development ranging from several (>3) physical representations of the same concept (rated as "5") to no alternative physical representations of the same concept (rated as "1").

4.5.1.3   Level 3 coding

"Image having" (Level 3) was measured through the mental models (Mental Storyboards). The relevant aspects were measured as follows:

- a rating was allocated for time taken to develop the storyboards of the mental model– ranging from <10 minutes (rated as "5") to ≥30 minutes (rated as "1");

- the degree of concept development into a mental storyboard measured from ≥5 concepts (rated as "5") to ≤1 concept (rated as "1");

- the degree of concept refinement through the manipulation of mental objects to develop intermediary steps from ≥4 concepts (rated as "5") to no manipulation (rated as "1"); and,

- the degree of concept complexity in terms of the number of mental steps developed between initial and final scenes ranging from ≥5 (rated as "5") to one step (rated as "1").

4.5.1.4   Level 4 coding

"Property Noticing" (Level 4) was measured through the mental storyboarding. The relevant aspects were measured as follows:

- a rating was allocated for time taken to transfer known properties and abstracting commonalities to similar situations– ranging from <10 minutes (rated as "5") to ≥30 minutes (rated as "1");

- the degree of concept transference to similar situations, ranging from ≥5 properties (rated as "5") to ≤1 property (rated as "1");

- the degree of concept refinement through the manipulation of mental objects to develop intermediary steps from ≥4 concepts (rated as "5") to no manipulation (rated as "1"); and,

- the degree of concept complexity in terms of the number of mental steps developed between initial and final scenes ranging from ≥5 (rated as "5") to one step (rated as "1").

4.5.1.5   Level 5 coding

"Formalising" (Level 5) was also measured through the mental storyboarding. The relevant aspects were measured as follows:

- a rating was allocated for time taken to transfer known properties and abstracting commonalities to non-similar situations – ranging from <10 minutes (rated as "5") to ≥30 minutes (rated as "1");

- the degree of concept transference to non-similar situations, ranging from ≥5 properties (rated as "5") to ≤1 property (rated as "1");

- the degree of concept refinement through the manipulation of mental objects to develop intermediary steps from ≥4 concepts (rated as "5") to no manipulation (rated as "1"); and,

- the degree of concept complexity in terms of the number of mental steps developed between initial and final scenes ranging from ≥5 (rated as "5") to one step (rated as "1").

4.5.1.6   Level 6 coding

"Observing" (Level 6) was also measured through storyboarding or narrative. The relevant aspects were measured as follows:

- a rating was allocated for time taken to formalise and organise observations – ranging from <10 minutes (rated as "5") to ≥30 minutes (rated as "1");
- the degree of concept development into a formal response, ranging from ≥5 properties (rated as "5") to ≤1 property (rated as "1");
- the degree of concept refinement through the consideration of references to formal thinking from ≥4 considerations (rated as "5") to no consideration (rated as "1"); and,
- the degree of concept complexity in terms of the interaction of considerations or references to formal thinking, ranging from ≥5 (rated as "5") to one step (rated as "1").

4.5.1.7   Level 7 coding

"Structuring" (Level 7) was measured through flowcharts. The relevant aspects were measured as follows:

- a rating was allocated for time taken to develop an explanation of formal thinking in terms of a logical structure – ranging from <10 minutes (rated as "5") to ≥30 minutes (rated as "1");
- the degree (number) of concepts included into a logical structure, ranging from ≥5 concepts (rated as "5") to ≤1 concept (rated as "1");
- the degree of concept refinement through the considerations or references to formal thinking, from ≥5 concepts (rated as "5") to no consideration (rated as "1"); and,
- the degree of concept complexity in terms of assumptions made to logical structure, ranging from ≥4 (rated as "5") to no assumptions (rated as "1").

4.5.1.8   Level 8 coding

"Inventising" (Level 8) was measured through student identification of new concepts. The relevant aspects were measured as follows:

- a rating was allocated for time taken before going beyond structured understanding to generate new questions – ranging from <10 minutes (rated as "5") to ≥30 minutes (rated as "1");

- the degree (number) of concepts in terms of the number of questions generated from existing concepts, ranging from ≥5 concepts (rated as "5") to ≤1 concept (rated as "1");

- the degree of concept refinement through the considerations or references to formal thinking, from ≥5 concepts (rated as "5") to no consideration (rated as "1"); and,

- the degree of concept complexity in terms of the number of representations offered of the same question, ranging from ≥3 (rated as "5") to no alternative representations (rated as "1").

4.5.2 Trace analysis

For each level (1-9) of concept complexity, the four measured ratings (time, development, refinement, complexity) were averaged to produce a score for that mental model level. Once a coded representation of the concept development of each subject was available, graphs (see Section 4.9) were produced to assist in the analysis of this data. Particular attention was given to trace the subjects' mental model development at differing levels of concept complexity and to trace movement across boundary points using data drawn from stimulated recall interviews (Phases 3 and 6) and this was facilitated by the use of radar plot graphs (see Section 4.9.4) that closely reflected the traces students created (see Section 4.4.4). Trace analyses using these graphs were subsequently developed for selected students ($n=20$) (see Section 5.3) to show the effectiveness of each visualisation tool in developing each of the concepts studied, at each level of concept complexity.

4.5.3 Narrative Development

Drawing on concept development graphs, trace analysis, student verification interviews, student perception surveys, and researcher observations, a series of nine narratives were then developed to provide a foundational basis on which to base discussion and conclusions for the study (Phase 7).

4.6 Trustworthiness

A measure of trustworthiness is provided by a set of measures that parallel traditional quantitative validity measures, credibility, triangulation, transferability, and dependability. Credibility (internal validity) is supported by techniques of prolonged engagement, persistent observations, peer debriefing, negative case analysis, and progressive subjectivity.

a. This study had a *prolonged engagement* with the subjects for approximately five hours per week over a 12 -24 month period. During this span, active data collection periods averaged eight weeks at a time with an additional two to six weeks of interviews.

b. *Persistent observation* of subjects was facilitated by intensive video and screen recordings, recorded speak-aloud self reflection, recorded peer discussion, subject written observations, and researcher observation (see Section 4.3.2.6).

c. Subjects were included in the research process as active participants and contributed to an ongoing process of *peer debriefing* as assumptions and conclusions were constantly tested and verified.

d. *Negative case analysis* was achieved through an iterative phased design in which working hypotheses were challenged and modified as a result of preceding phases.

e. *Progressive subjectivity* was traced in a researcher's journal (see Section 4.4.2.6) and finally, informal member checks were built into the metacognitive processes subjects engaged with during the study (see Section 1.3) with formal member checks built into the student trace verification process (see Section 4.5.2).

Triangulation was facilitated by student trace verification interviews (see Section 4.3.3.3), research verification of student traces (see Section 4.3.3.4), and through the use of several instruments – traces, concept map comparisons, subject observations, peer observations, researcher observations, and surveys.

Transferability (external validity) is not high for this study. The study is not easily generalisable with specific conditions, subjects and researcher involvement. As complete a description of the study, subjects and instruments is provided within ethical and physical size constraints to enable a degree of transferability. Dependability (reliability) was maintained by methodological comparisons between cohorts, cross checking that cohorts were not diverging due to untracked influences. In addition to those criteria which parallel traditional quantitative validity measures, Guba and Lincoln (1981) introduced an *authenticity* criterion that comprises measures of fairness, and educative, catalytic and tactical authenticity.

a. *Fairness* was achieved by subject involvement in the research process and their involvement in verified trace interviews. Students were expected to argue and defend their observations against available evidence and only where clear evidence existed, and was agreed to exist, was their contributions overruled (see Section 4.2.3.4).

b. *Educative authenticity* was achieved through a peer discussion process in which students not only assisted each other in conducting their observations, but actively worked to develop each other's metacognitive understanding of the processes involved (see Section 1.3).

c. *Catalytic* and *tactical authenticity* are again built into the design study, development of student metacognitive understanding of their learning processes and the ways in which these can be developed, forms not only a core methodology of this study, but an educational outcome for the students involved.

4.7 Role of the researcher

In this study, the researcher's role was that of classroom teacher for all of the cohorts studied (Cohorts A-D). While this provided extensive access to the students and an opportunity to collect data with minimal intrusion, the situation did shape the design of the study.

In most aspects of the study, opportunities were taken to provide educational opportunities for the students involved. They were included fully in the data collection process in all phases of the study. This resulted in some development of their metacognitive understanding of their learning processes. While integral to the success of the study, this was initially introduced as a means of extending the learning opportunities for the students from simple data collection processes to active participation in the analysis and evaluation of their cognitive development.

The involvement of the researcher as the teacher in the study introduced unavoidable elements of subjectivity. Wherever possible, however, processes have been included to reduce the potential for subjectivity. These processes included:

a. *Speak aloud* processes required students to formulate and articulate their thoughts as they developed solutions to problem sets, reducing subsequent subjectivity to their own observations.

b. *Peer discussions* reduced individual subjectivity in initial observations, while video and screen recording promoted honest feedback.

c. *Verification interviews* reduced both subject and researcher subjectivity as each point was argued and justified before included in the data set.

Finally, the structured nature of the data collection process lent itself to reducing subjectivity. Individual student observations were verified by the students themselves, then their peers, then the researcher. In most cases, this occurred for several concepts. From these observations, the results generated concept development graphs (see Section 5.1), effectiveness perception graphs (see Section 5.2), and mental model traces (see Section 5.3). These were then used to develop narratives that were decontextualised as far as possible while still providing a sufficient description of the processes involved to permit effective analysis. While researcher involvement must increase the subjectivity of a study, through considered approaches to reducing its impact, the study has aimed to ensure the involvement of the researcher and the involvement of students in the research process make a net positive contribution to the study.

4.8 Limitations of the study

This was a small scale study conducted on a selected non-representative population, with a methodology that would be difficult if not impossible to replicate because of the particular population and location of this study. The general aim of this study was to understand the effect of visualisations on the learning process. This aim, however, was not necessarily dependent on the scale of the study, the population, or in constraining the methodology to conditions that afforded replication.

As a qualitative collective case study, this study may not seem to be able to meet the rigorous standards traditionally associated with a quantitative study. The choice of a qualitative study was a considered one, however, and was based on the noted inability of previous quantitative studies to explain negative educational outcomes in the use of software visualisations (see Section 1.4 and Section 2.2). To provide an evaluative framework for this study, it addressed the evaluation criteria set down by Guba and Lincoln (1981) (see Section 4.6).

The context for the study was the learning of computer programming as this has been the subject of previous unsuccessful studies into the use of visualisation to promote learning and was readily available to the researcher. The intention in this study was to create the conditions in which the learning processes involved in the use of visualisations would become apparent. The role of the researcher, with its inherent potential for subjectivity has been discussed in this chapter (see Section 4.7).

While the cohort composition provided a rich mix of possible visualisation combinations, it was not comprehensive. A larger population with an even spread in their use of visualisation tools may have improved the study. The distribution of students who studied using more than one visualisation tool also limited some areas of analysis, with only a single cohort using more than one visualisation tool, comparison was limited to the tools used and those concepts developed with these tools.

An area that was not factored into the study was students' intrinsic ability. Differences in student natural or previously-acquired capacity to make mental visualisation, preference to visual or auditory processing, their capacity to develop metacognitive understanding of the learning process, and possible natural aptitudes to various aspects of learning programming, may have limited the effectiveness of some aspects of the study.

Previous programming experience was considered in the initial design of the study. Students were identified through initial concept maps and steps were taken during analysis (see Section 5.3.1) to determine if their prior learning had an effect on subsequent mental model development. For example, one student who had missed development of some concepts was able to catch up in part due to her previous experience with programming (see Section 5.1.2.7).

Overall, the limitations in this study did not impact on the research to an extent of invalidating the findings made. The design of the study, as a qualitative collective case study, permitted a degree of flexibility compared to traditional quantitative studies. This flexibility was used to generate a rich data set from which to draw conclusions and develop findings that satisfy the study's aims. Where limitations had been expected, they were countered with deliberate strategies.

4.9 Graphs used in the study

Four main types of graphs have been used in this study to display results and discuss findings, 3D line graphs (Section 4.9.1), stacked column graphs (Section 4.9.2), standard bar graphs (Section 4.9.3), and radar plot graphs (Section 4.9.4). Each type was selected to permit effective analysis of the data and best represent the resulting findings.

4.9.1 3D Line Graph

A three-dimensional line graph (Figure 4.3) has been used to show mental model development trends at increasing levels of cognitive difficulty for a range of concepts. The vertical scale is derived from four measures: time taken for concept development, degree of concept development, degree of concept refinement, and degree of concept complexity (Section 4.5.1 and Appendix C), averaged and applied to a five point rating. The horizontal scale records this rating at each level of mental model development (Section 2.4 and Appendix D), while the depth scale records this for each of the concepts studied by the student.

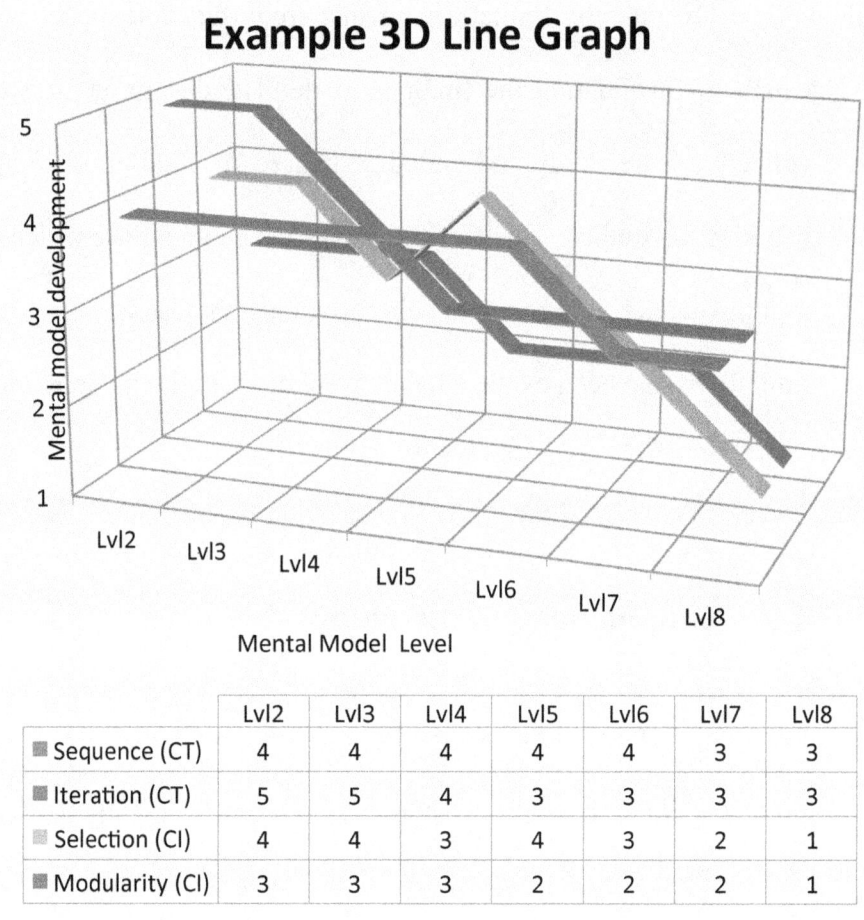

Figure 4.3   Example 3D line graph

4.9.2 Stacked Column Graph

Student perceptions on the effectiveness of the visualisation tool used for the development of each concept was measured by a survey instrument (Section 4.4.3.1 and Appendix A). A stacked column graph (Figure 4.4) was used to display a perceived effectiveness histogram for each concept. Within this overall histogram, the distribution of each individual tool perceived effectiveness resulted in a rough histogram for each tool. The vertical scale records the percentage of participants that responded with a particular rating with each tool displayed in a different colour, for example, 10% of students responded with a rating of 3 for the PHP tool, 5% of students responded with a rating of 3 for the Alice tool, and 15% of students responded with a rating of 3 for the RoboLab tool. For the PHP tool in this example shown in Figure 4.4, there is a visually estimated mean of 3, while for the other three tools, the visually estimated mean is 4.

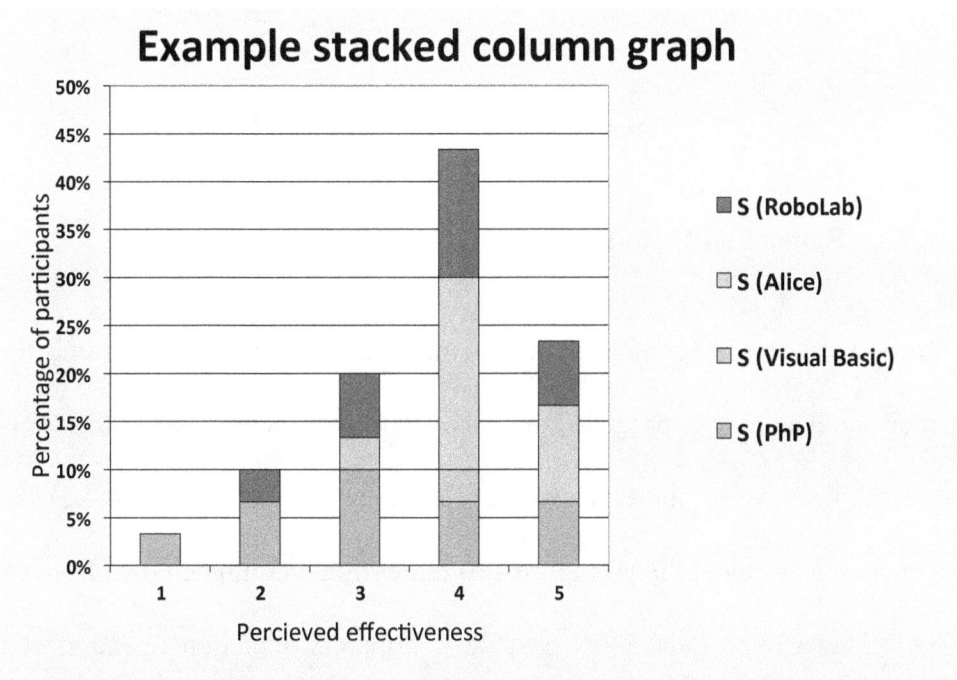

Figure 4.4   Example stacked column graph

4.9.3 Standard Bar Graph

Where student perceptions of visualisation tools could be compared, this was measured by a survey instrument (Section 4.4.3.2 and Appendix B) and a standard bar graph (Figure 4.5) was used to display results.

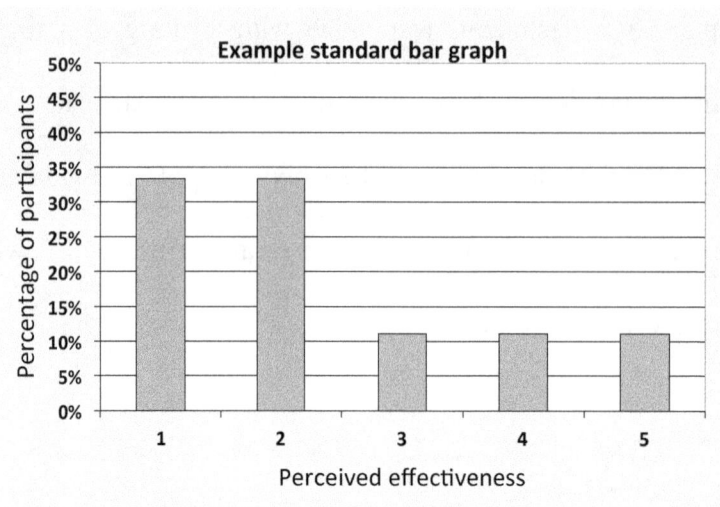

Figure 4.5   Example standard bar graph

4.9.4 Radar Plot Graph

During the study, students generated mental model traces, recording their mental model development progress for each concept (Section 4.4.4 and Appendix D). These traces were subsequently verified (Section 4.3.3.4 and 4.4.2) and used to generate radar plot graphs (Figure 4.6) representing combined data from each mental model trace. The radar plots provide a graphical depiction of the effectiveness of mental model development. Seven points are plotted for each concept (mental model levels from 2 to 8) and points are plotted in a counter clockwise direction. The placement of each point in relation to the centre of the radar plot represent the effectiveness of mental model development at that level, the further from the centre the more effective. This value was derived by combining time taken for concept development, degree of concept development, degree of concept refinement, and degree of concept complexity (Section 4.5.1 and Appendix C), averaged and applied to a five point rating. The shape of the resulting radar plots graphically represents the rate of change in mental model development effectiveness as cognitive difficulty increases. The radar plots also provide an overview of concept development for the students with visual comparison possible between the general trends displayed in the development of each concept.

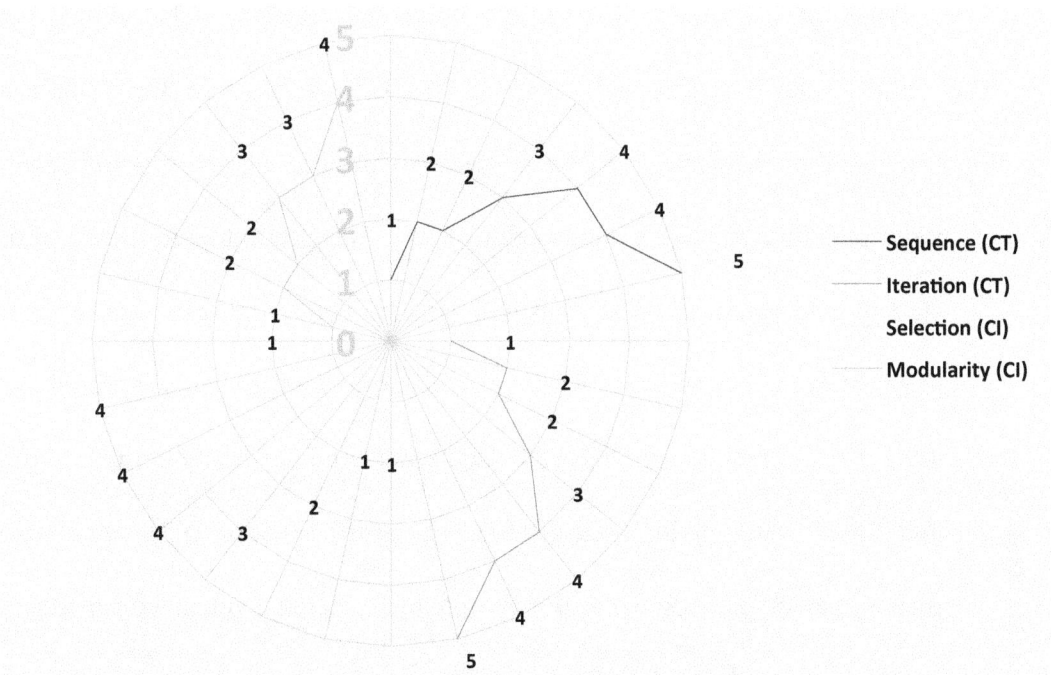

Figure 4.6   Example radar plot graph

The following chapter details the findings of the study through the presentation of three sets of data, summaries of participant cognitive development comparing the effectiveness of the visualisation tools (Section 5.1), summaries of student perceptions of the visualisation tools (Section 5.2), and summaries of student mental model development and selected quotations provided that are relevant to subsequent analysis and narrative development (Section 5.3).

Chapter 5

FINDINGS OF THE STUDY

The purpose of this chapter is to present the three components that comprise the findings of the study. The first component (Section 5.1) summarises student cognitive development and compares the effectiveness of the visualisation tools described in Chapter 3. 3D line graphs were used in the analysis of the visualisation tools and this is detailed in section 4.9.1. The second (Section 5.2) summarises student perceptions of these tools with stacked column graphs used in the analysis of the perceived effectiveness of the visualisation tool and this is detailed in section 4.9.2. In addition, bar graphs were used when students could compare multiple tools and this is detailed in section 4.9.3. The third (Section 5.3) summarises student mental model development illuminated by selected student comments, radar plot graphs were used to aid analysis and these are detailed in section 4.9.4.

The collected data for this study included 422 hours of video and screen captures, recording students' peer discussions as they worked through problem sets, and supplemented by student journals and trace annotations (see Section 4.4.2). For each concept studied, all students ($N=31$) completed a survey on how effective they perceived the visualisation tool (see Section 5.2.1), and where students had used more than one tool ($n=9$), they completed a survey comparing the two tools (see Section 5.2.2). From the students in the study ($N=31$), twenty were selected for stimulated recall interviews and speak-aloud analysis of their video and screen captures (see Section 4.4.2).

This resulted in 46 hours of interviews followed by video and screen capture verification of the students' self-identified progress. The process of stimulated recall and speak-aloud analysis with students enabled variations between self-identified progress and recorded evidence to be discussed and adjustments made through mutual agreement supported by the available evidence. Nine of the twenty students required minor adjustments to their trace analysis based on discussions during interview though no significant variations were identified that would have invalidated a self identified trace.

In total, 26 minor variations were identified from 675 self identified decisions in 75 traces. Subsequent researcher analysis of video and screen recordings, speak-aloud interviews, and student journals and trace annotations did not identify any additional variations between self-identified traces and recorded evidence. From the twenty students selected for interview, nine were subsequently selected for development into narratives based on their representation of various groups within the study.

5.1 Concept development by Individual students

Each student ($N=31$) produced a mental model trace (see Section 5.3) of each concept they developed. The following summarises this development for each student and provides a comparison of student progress at various levels of mental model complexity and a comparison of the effectiveness of the visualisation tools used based on the concept for which they were used.

For each student, grouped by cohort (A-D) (see Sections 5.1.1-5.1.4), a graph (see Section 4.9.1) was produced that summarises their mental model development for each concept the student studied. A rating was derived (from "1" to "5") for each level (1-9) of concept complexity by averaging four measured ratings (time, development, refinement, complexity) (see Section 4.5.1 and Appendix 2). In each case, the higher the number, the more effective the student was at developing that level of her mental model.

5.1.1 Cohort A

During the study, the students in Cohort A ($n=9$) developed mental models of four concepts: sequence, iteration, selection and modularity. They studied sequence and iteration using a Constrained Text visualisation tool (*Alice*) and selection and modularity using a Constrained Icon visualisation tool (*GameMaker*). The students in Cohort A, organised in three pairs and one triad, were A1a and A1b; A2a and A2b; A3a and A3b; and, A4a, A4b, and A4c. Their concept development is discussed respectively in Sections 5.1.1.1-5.1.1.9.

5.1.1.1   Student A1a

A1a developed each concept with a gradually increasing difficulty as the degree of conceptual difficulty (Level) increased. She had increasing difficulty as the complexity of the concept (sequence to modularity) increased. A1a was one of the students (*n*=20) who were interviewed and whose mental model tracing is presented (see Section 5.3.1). Figure 5.1 shows A1a's concept development from Level 2 to Level 8.

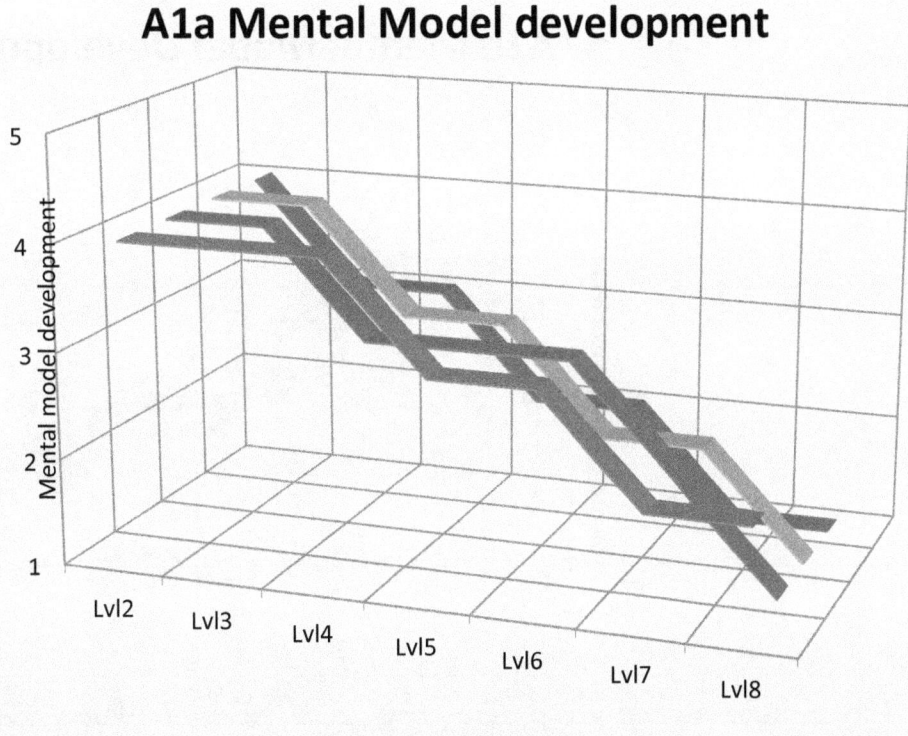

	Lvl2	Lvl3	Lvl4	Lvl5	Lvl6	Lvl7	Lvl8
Sequence (CT)	4	4	4	3	3	2	2
Iteration (CT)	4	4	3	3	3	2	1
Selection (CI)	4	4	3	3	2	2	1
Modularity (CI)	4	3	3	2	2	1	1

Figure 5.1   Student A1a concept development

5.1.1.2   Student A1b

A1b initially developed each concept with increasing difficulty as the complexity of the concept (sequence to modularity) increased. With all four concepts, she experienced significant difficulty in developing beyond observing (Level 6) to structuring (Level 7) that involved the formal use of flowcharting to develop a logical structure to her programming. Figure 5.2 shows A1b's concept development from Level 2 to Level 8.

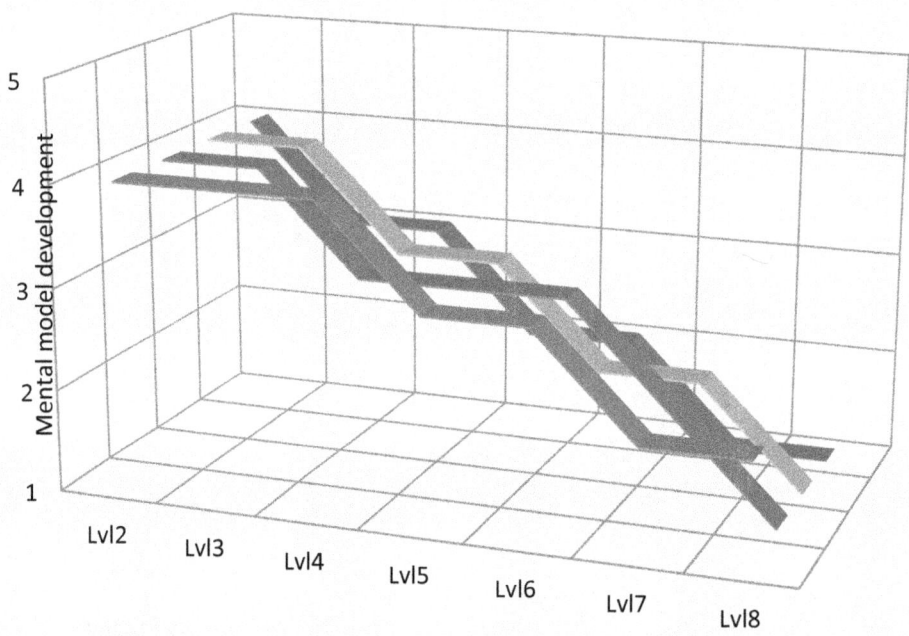

	Mental Model Level						
	Lvl2	Lvl3	Lvl4	Lvl5	Lvl6	Lvl7	Lvl8
Sequence (CT)	4	4	4	3	3	2	2
Iteration (CT)	4	4	3	3	3	2	1
Selection (CI)	4	4	3	3	2	2	1
Modularity (CI)	4	3	3	2	2	1	1

Figure 5.2   Student A1b concept development

5.1.1.3   Student A2a

A2a, as for A1a and A1b, had increasing difficulty as the complexity of the concept (sequence to modularity) increased. Figure 5.3 shows A2a's increasing difficulty as the degree of conceptual difficulty (Level) increased.

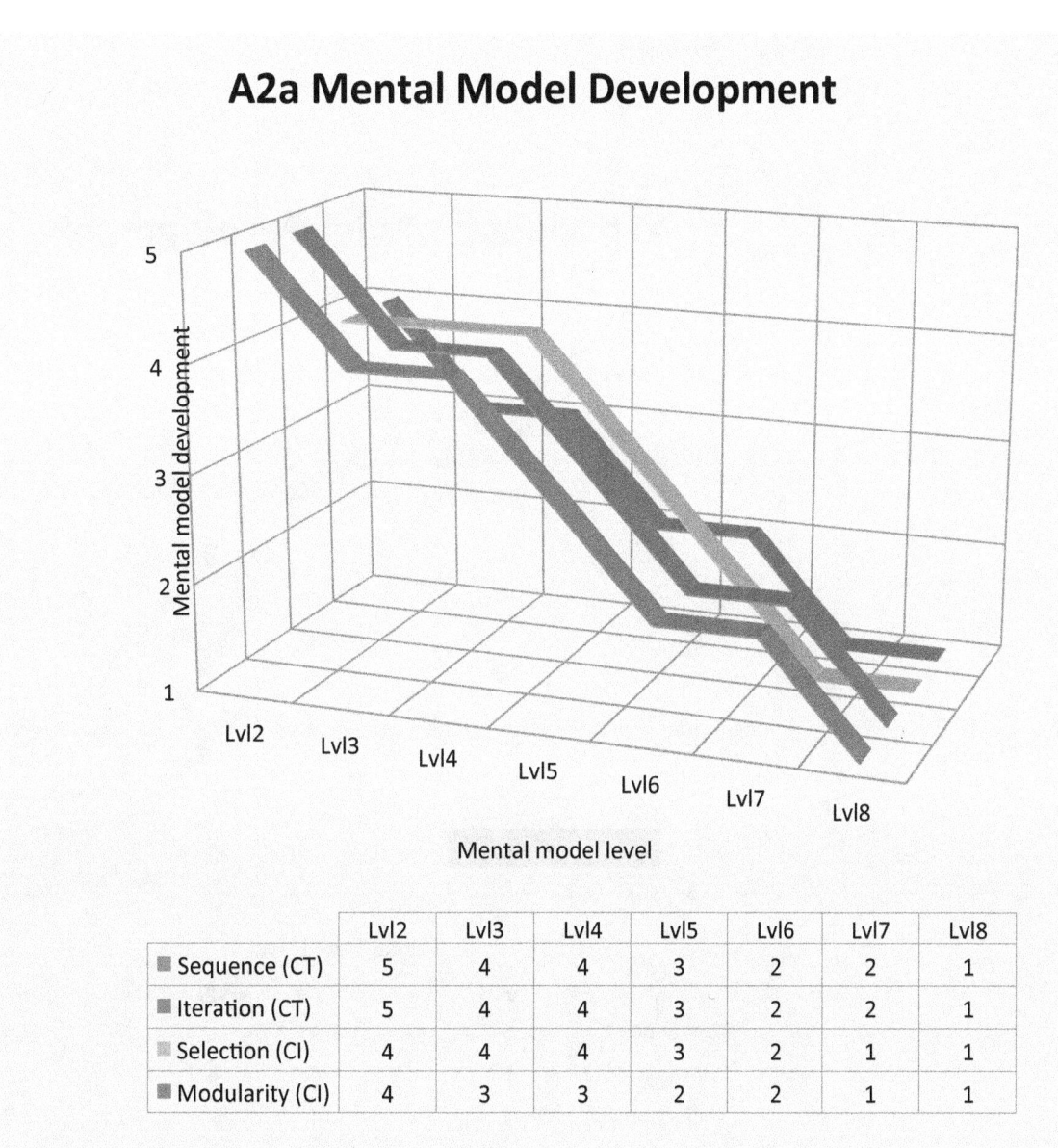

	Lvl2	Lvl3	Lvl4	Lvl5	Lvl6	Lvl7	Lvl8
Sequence (CT)	5	4	4	3	2	2	1
Iteration (CT)	5	4	4	3	2	2	1
Selection (CI)	4	4	4	3	2	1	1
Modularity (CI)	4	3	3	2	2	1	1

Figure 5.3   Student A2a concept development

5.1.1.4   Student A2b

Figure 5.4 shows the rapidly increasing difficulty experienced by A2b as the degree of conceptual difficulty (Level) increased. She also showed increasing difficulty as the complexity of the concept (sequence to modularity) increased. A2b was one of the students (*n*=20) who were interviewed and whose mental model tracing is presented (see Section 5.3.2).

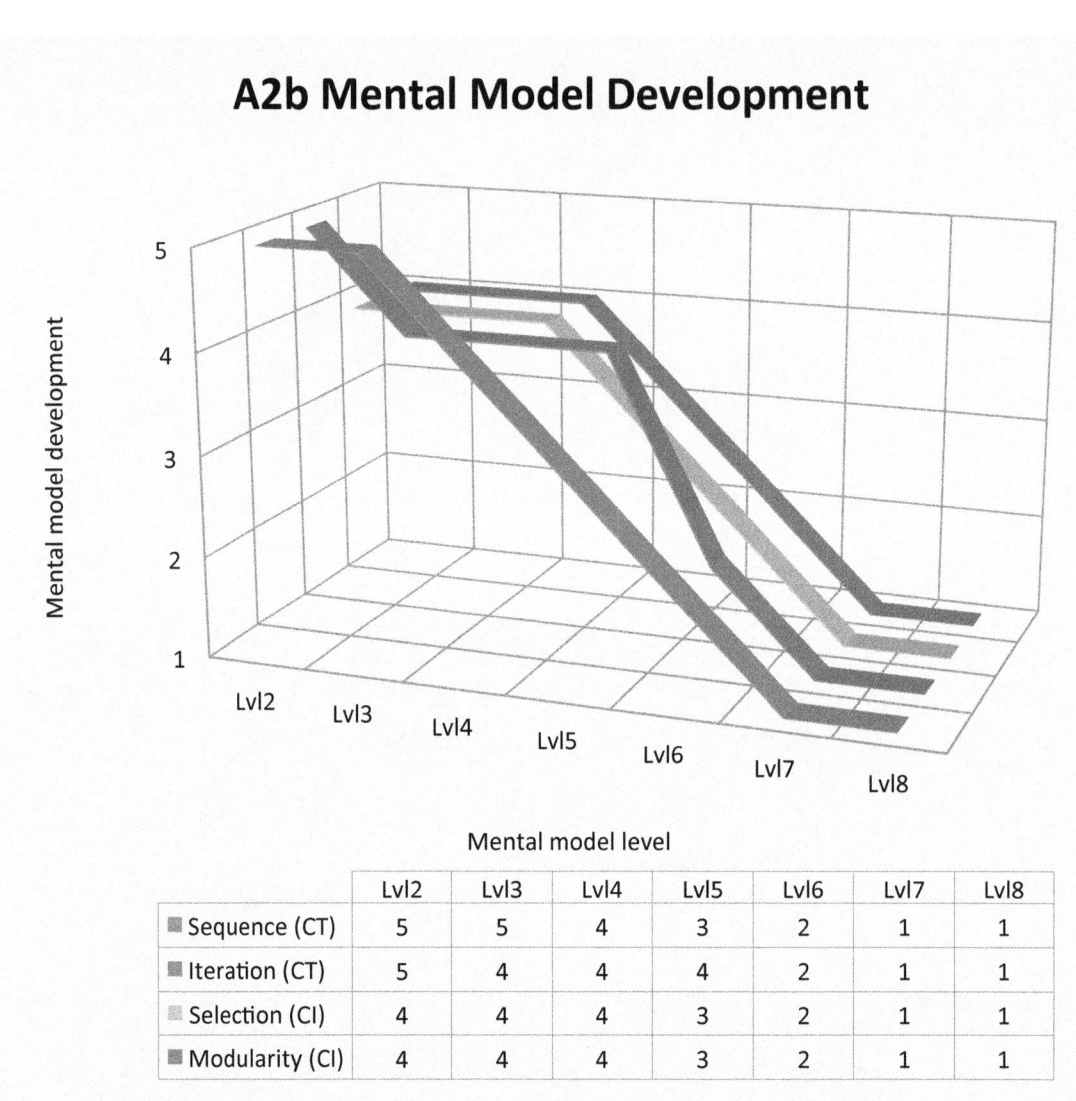

	Lvl2	Lvl3	Lvl4	Lvl5	Lvl6	Lvl7	Lvl8
■ Sequence (CT)	5	5	4	3	2	1	1
■ Iteration (CT)	5	4	4	4	2	1	1
■ Selection (CI)	4	4	4	3	2	1	1
■ Modularity (CI)	4	4	4	3	2	1	1

Figure 5.4   Student A2b concept development

5.1.1.5   Student A3a

A3a initially developed each concept with minimal difficulty but as the complexity of the concept increased, she experienced significant difficulty developing the concepts of sequence and iteration beyond observing (Level 6) to structuring (Level 7) that involved the formal use of flowcharting to develop a logical structure to her programming. She was, however, able to develop the concepts of selection and modularity with relatively little difficulty through to Inventising (Level 8). A3a was one of the students ($n=20$) who was interviewed and whose mental model tracing is presented (see Section 5.3.3). She was also one of nine students included as a narrative (*Sam*, Section 6.2). Figure 5.5 shows A3a's concept development from Level 2 to Level 8.

A3a Mental Model Development

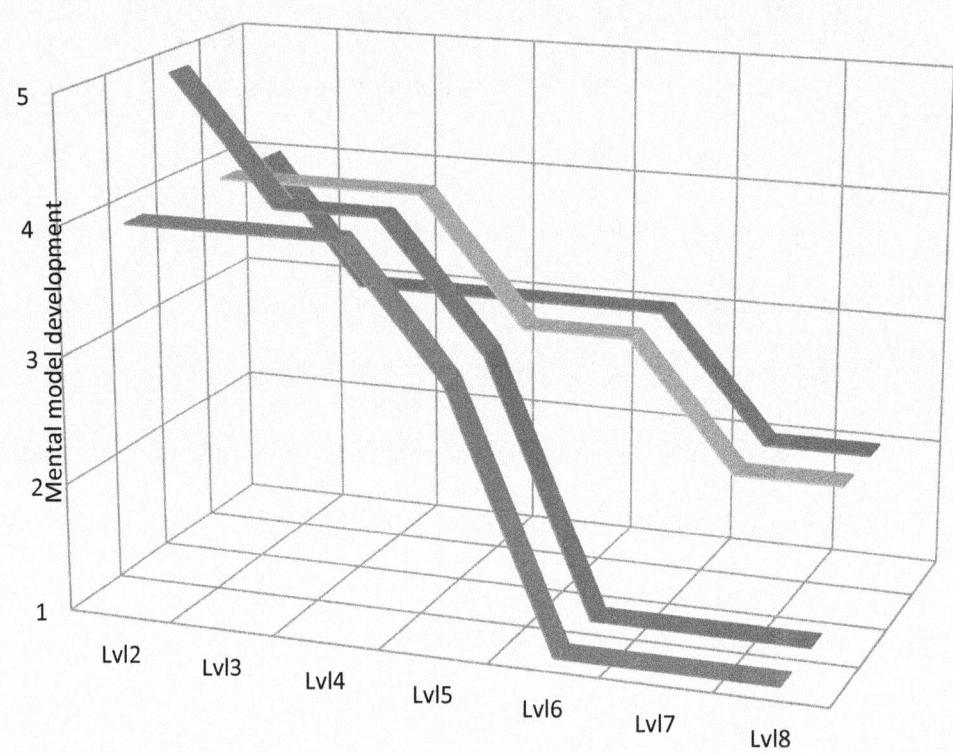

Mental model level

	Lvl2	Lvl3	Lvl4	Lvl5	Lvl6	Lvl7	Lvl8
Sequence (CT)	4	4	4	3	1	1	1
Iteration (CT)	5	4	4	3	1	1	1
Selection (CI)	4	4	4	3	3	2	2
Modularity (CI)	4	3	3	3	3	2	2

Figure 5.5   Student A3a concept development

5.1.1.6   Student A3b

A3b initially had significant difficulty in developing the concept of sequence. She was, however, able to subsequently develop remaining concepts with a general increasing difficulty as the degree of conceptual difficulty (Level) increased. Excluding the difficulties experiences with her initial concept, she also showed increasing difficulty as the complexity of the concept (sequence to modularity) increased. Figure 5.6 shows concept development from Level 2 to Level 8.

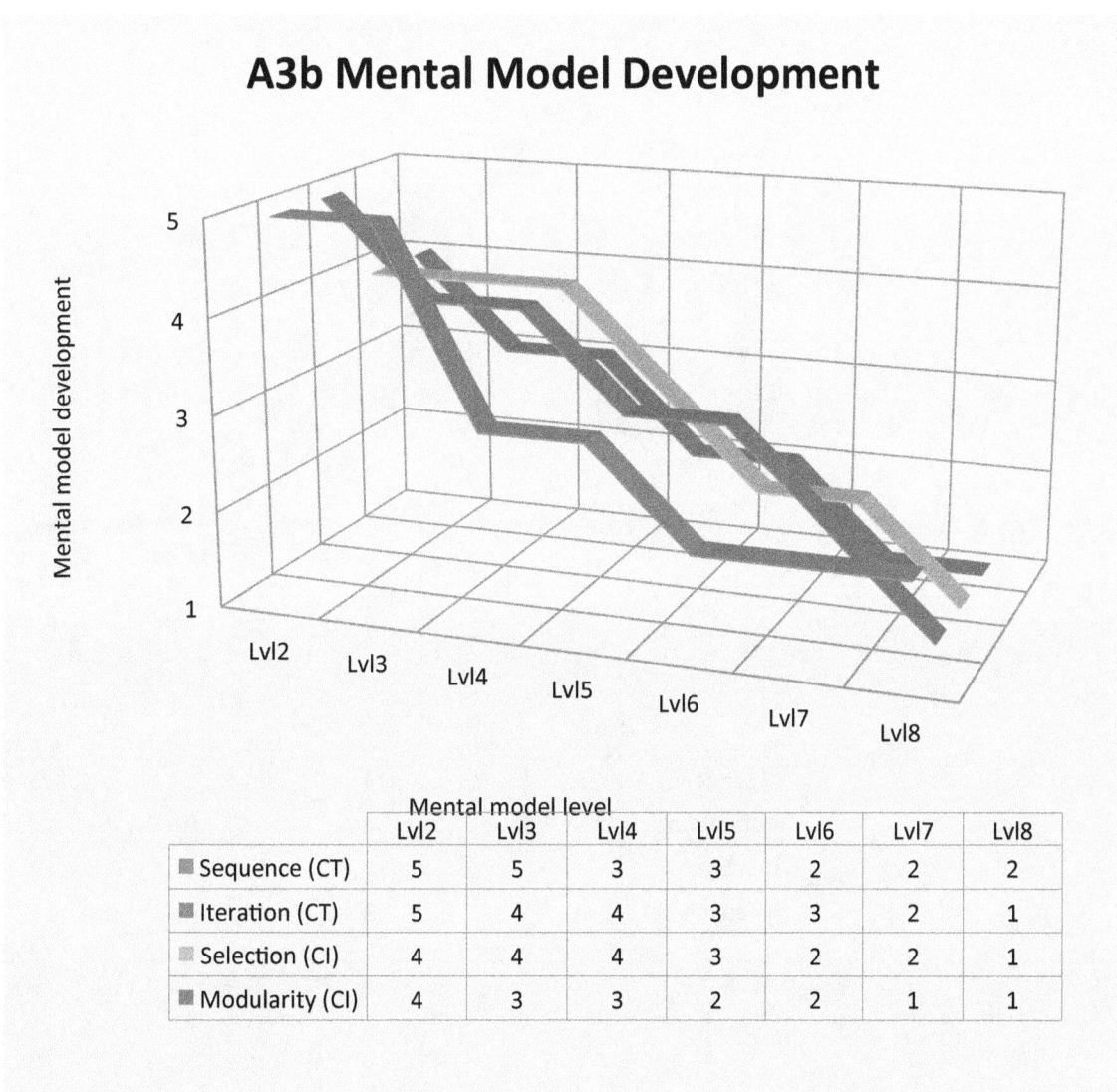

	Mental model level						
	Lvl2	Lvl3	Lvl4	Lvl5	Lvl6	Lvl7	Lvl8
Sequence (CT)	5	5	3	3	2	2	2
Iteration (CT)	5	4	4	3	3	2	1
Selection (CI)	4	4	4	3	2	2	1
Modularity (CI)	4	3	3	2	2	1	1

Figure 5.6   Student A3b concept development

5.1.1.7   Student A4a

Figure 5.7 shows A4a's very rapidly increasing difficulty as the degree of conceptual difficulty (Level) increased. She also showed rapidly increasing difficulty as the complexity of the concept (sequence to modularity) increased. A3a was one of the students (*n*=20) who were interviewed and whose mental model tracing is presented (see Section 5.3.4).

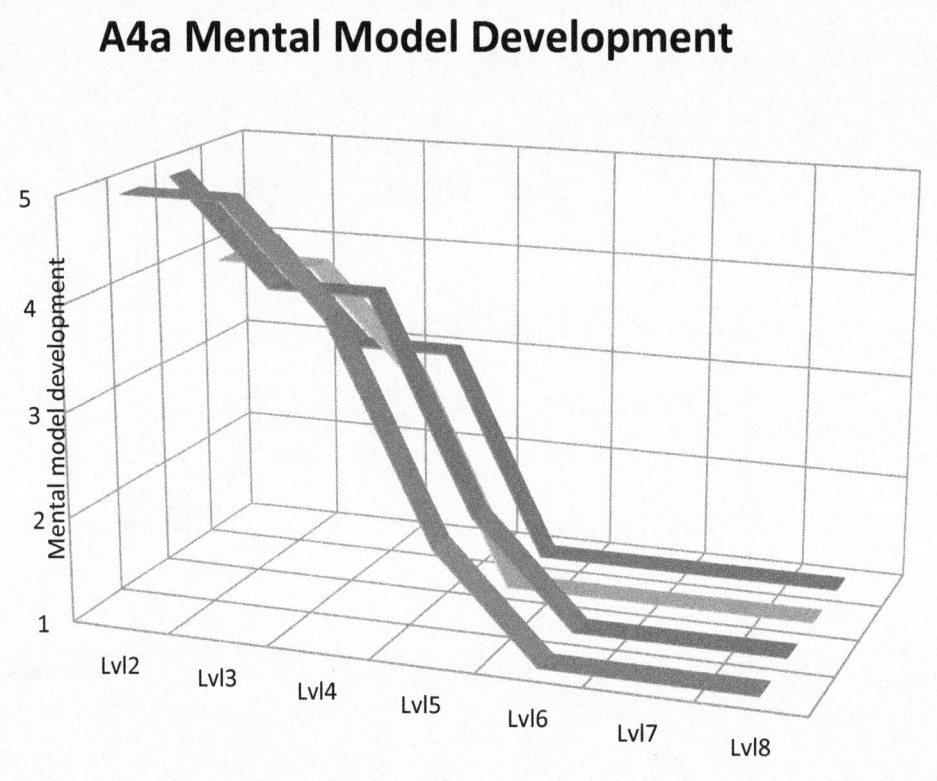

	Mental model level						
	Lvl2	Lvl3	Lvl4	Lvl5	Lvl6	Lvl7	Lvl8
Sequence	5	5	4	2	1	1	1
Iteration	5	4	4	2	1	1	1
Selection	4	4	3	1	1	1	1
Modularity	4	3	3	1	1	1	1

Figure 5.7   Student A4a concept development

5.1.1.8   Student A4b

Figure 5.8 shows A4b's initial difficulty with all concepts and increasing difficulty as the degree of conceptual difficulty (Level) increased. She also showed consistent results as the complexity of the concept (sequence to modularity) increased with some improvement in the selection concept.

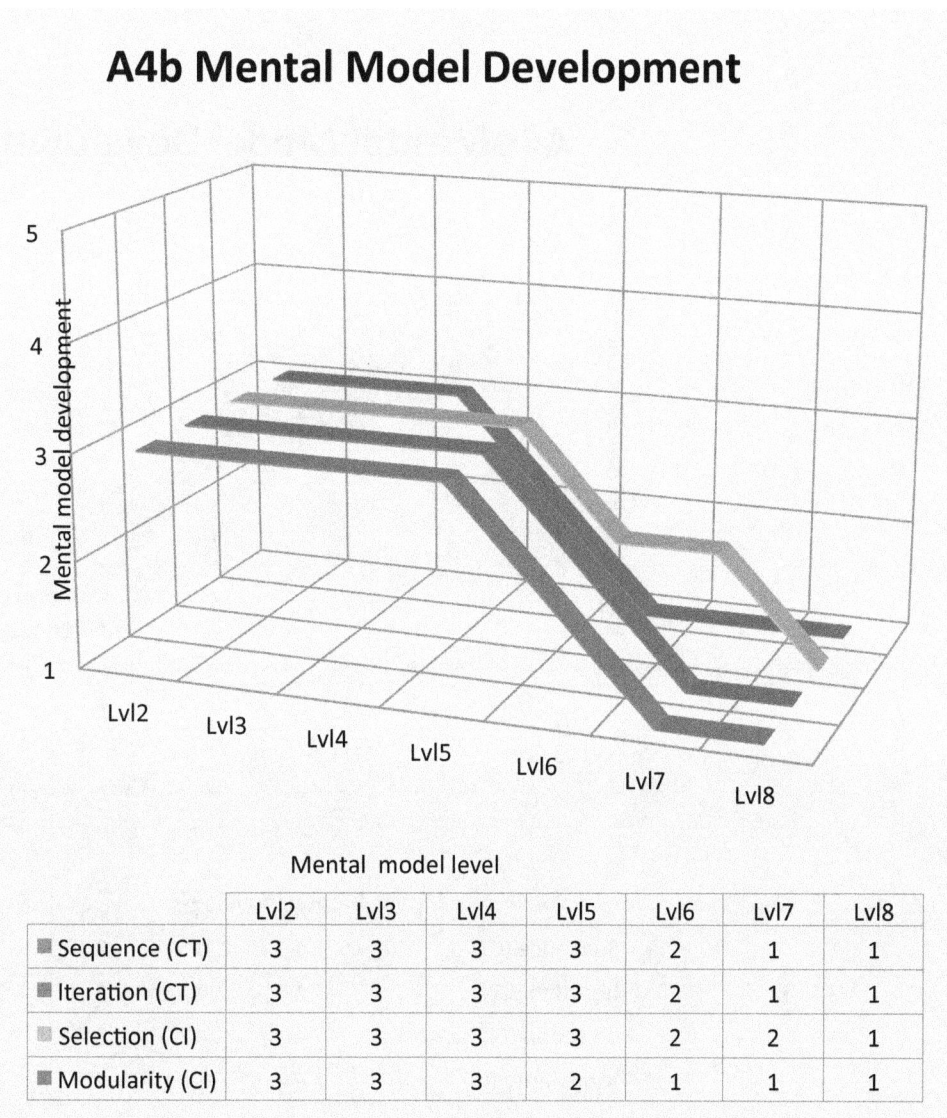

Figure 5.8   Student A4b concept development

5.1.1.9   Student A4c

Figure 5.9 shows A4c's increasing difficulty as the degree of conceptual difficulty (Level) increased. She also showed some increasing difficulty as the complexity of the concept (sequence to modularity) increased. A4c was one of the students (*n*=20) who were interviewed and whose mental model tracing is presented (see Section 5.3.5). She was also one of nine students included as a narrative (*Frodo*, Section 6.1).

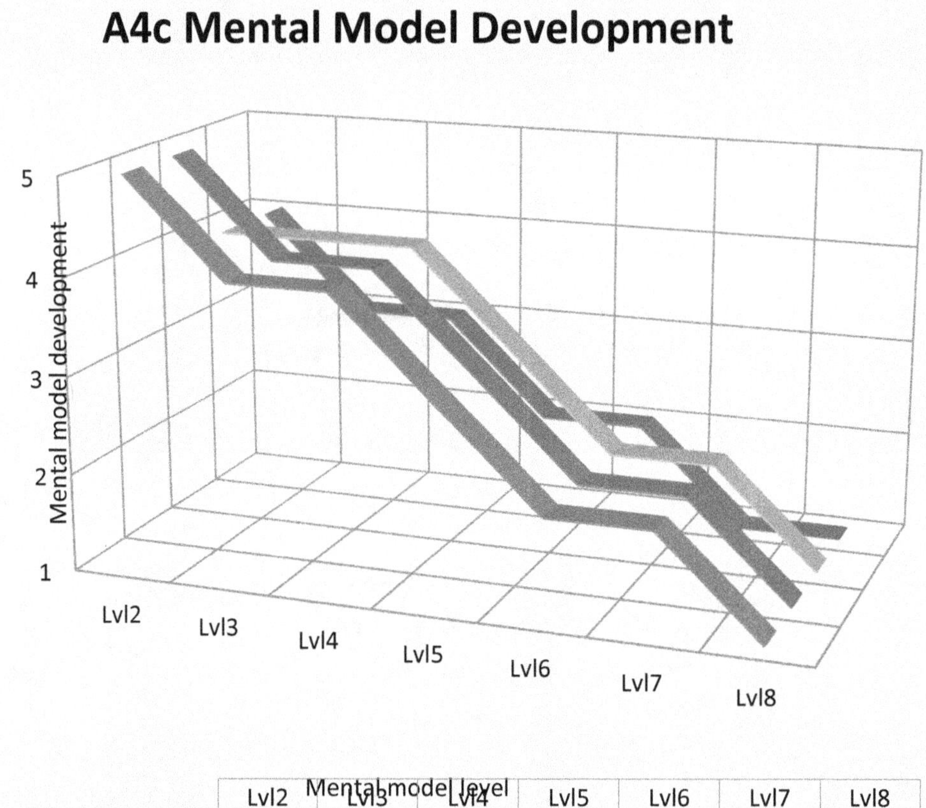

A4c Mental Model Development

	Lvl2	Lvl3	Lvl4	Lvl5	Lvl6	Lvl7	Lvl8
Sequence (CT)	5	4	4	3	2	2	1
Iteration (CT)	5	4	4	3	2	2	1
Selection (CI)	4	4	4	3	2	2	1
Modularity (CI)	4	3	3	2	2	1	1

Figure 5.9   Student A4c concept development

5.1.2 Cohort B

The students in Cohort B ($n=12$) developed mental models of three concepts: sequence, iteration and selection. They studied all three using an Unconstrained Icon visualisation tool (*RoboLab*). The students in Cohort B, organised in six pairs, were B1a, B1b, B2a, B2b, B3a, B3b, B4a, B4b, B5a, B5b, B6a and B6b. Their concept development is discussed respectively in Sections 5.1.2.1-5.1.2.12.

5.1.2.1   Student B1a

Figure 5.10 shows B1a's increasing difficulty as the degree of conceptual difficulty (Level) increased. She also showed rapidly increasing difficulty beyond mental storyboarding (Level 5) as the complexity of the concept (sequence to modularity) increased. B1a showed consistent results as the complexity of the concept (sequence to selection) increased.

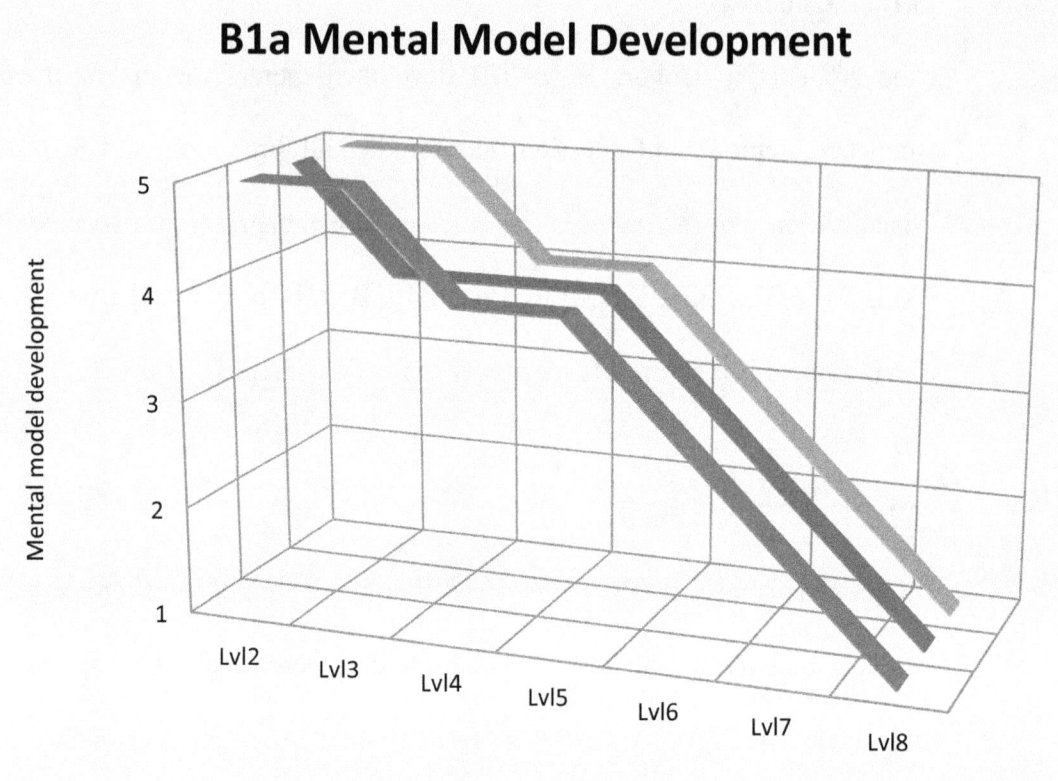

Figure 5.10 Student B1a concept development

5.1.2.2   Student B1b

B1b also showed an inability to progress beyond mental storyboarding (Level 5) as the degree of conceptual difficulty (Level) increased. She showed consistent results as the complexity of the concept (sequence to selection) increased. B1b was one of the students (*n*=20) who was interviewed and whose mental model tracing is presented (see Section 5.3.6). She was also one of nine students included as a narrative (*Gimli*, Section 4.3.7 and 6.4). Figure 5.11 shows her increasing difficulty as the degree of conceptual difficulty (Level) increased.

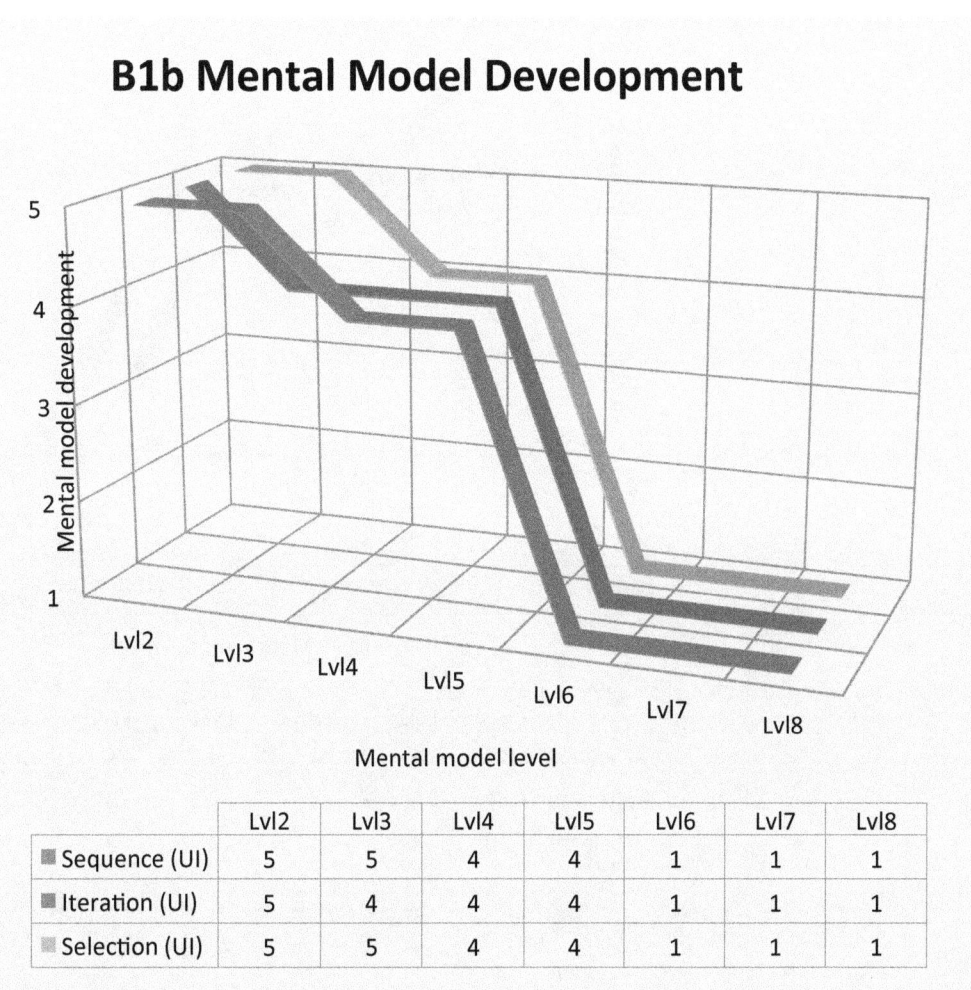

Figure 5.11   Student B1b concept development

5.1.2.3   Student B2a

Figure 5.12 shows increasing difficulty as the degree of conceptual difficulty (Level) increased. She also showed rapidly increasing difficulty beyond mental storyboarding (Level 5) as the complexity of the concept (sequence to modularity) increased. B2a showed consistent results as the complexity of the concept (sequence to selection) increased. A3a was one of the students (n=20) who was interviewed and whose mental model tracing is presented (see Section 5.3.7).

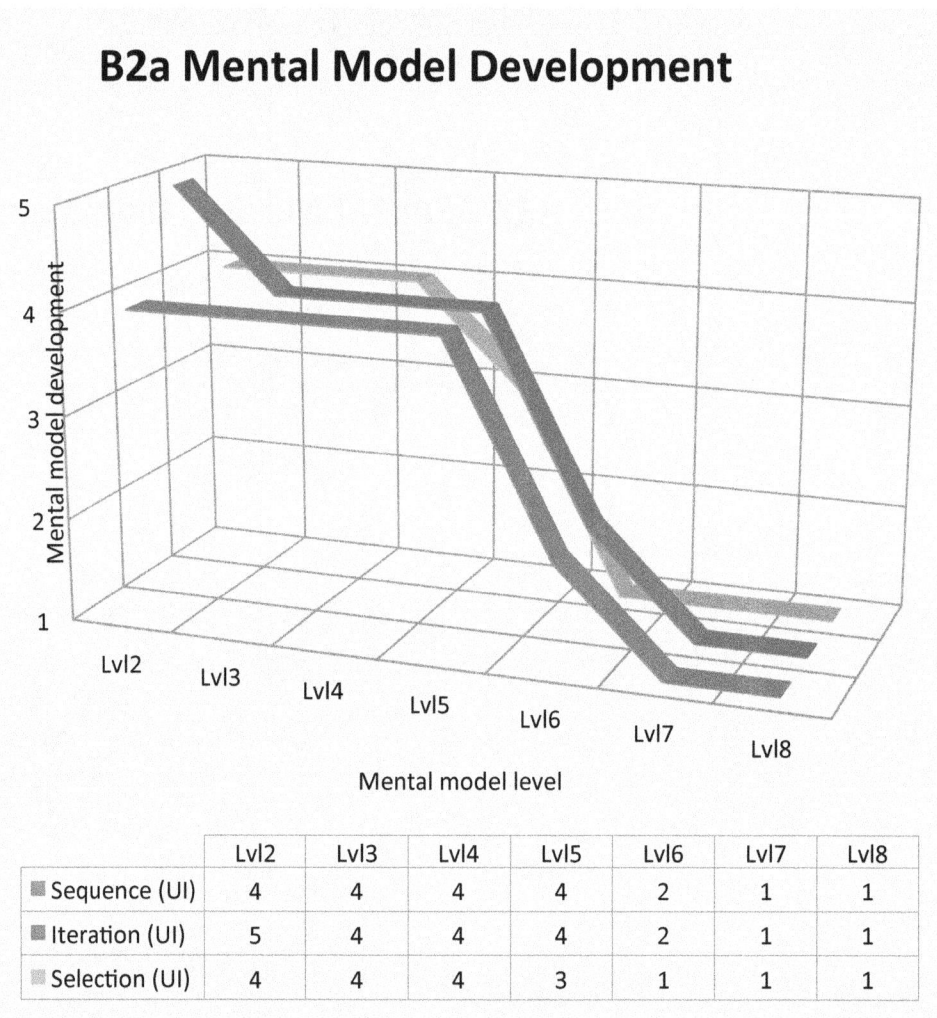

	Lvl2	Lvl3	Lvl4	Lvl5	Lvl6	Lvl7	Lvl8
Sequence (UI)	4	4	4	4	2	1	1
Iteration (UI)	5	4	4	4	2	1	1
Selection (UI)	4	4	4	3	1	1	1

Figure 5.12   Student B2a concept development

5.1.2.4   Student B2b

Figure 5.13 shows B2b's increasing difficulty as the degree of conceptual difficulty (Level) increased. She also showed an inability to progress beyond mental storyboarding (Level 5) as the degree of conceptual difficulty (Level) increased. She showed consistent results as the complexity of the concept (sequence to selection) increased. B2b was one of the students (*n*=20) who were interviewed and whose mental model tracing is presented (see Section 5.3.8).

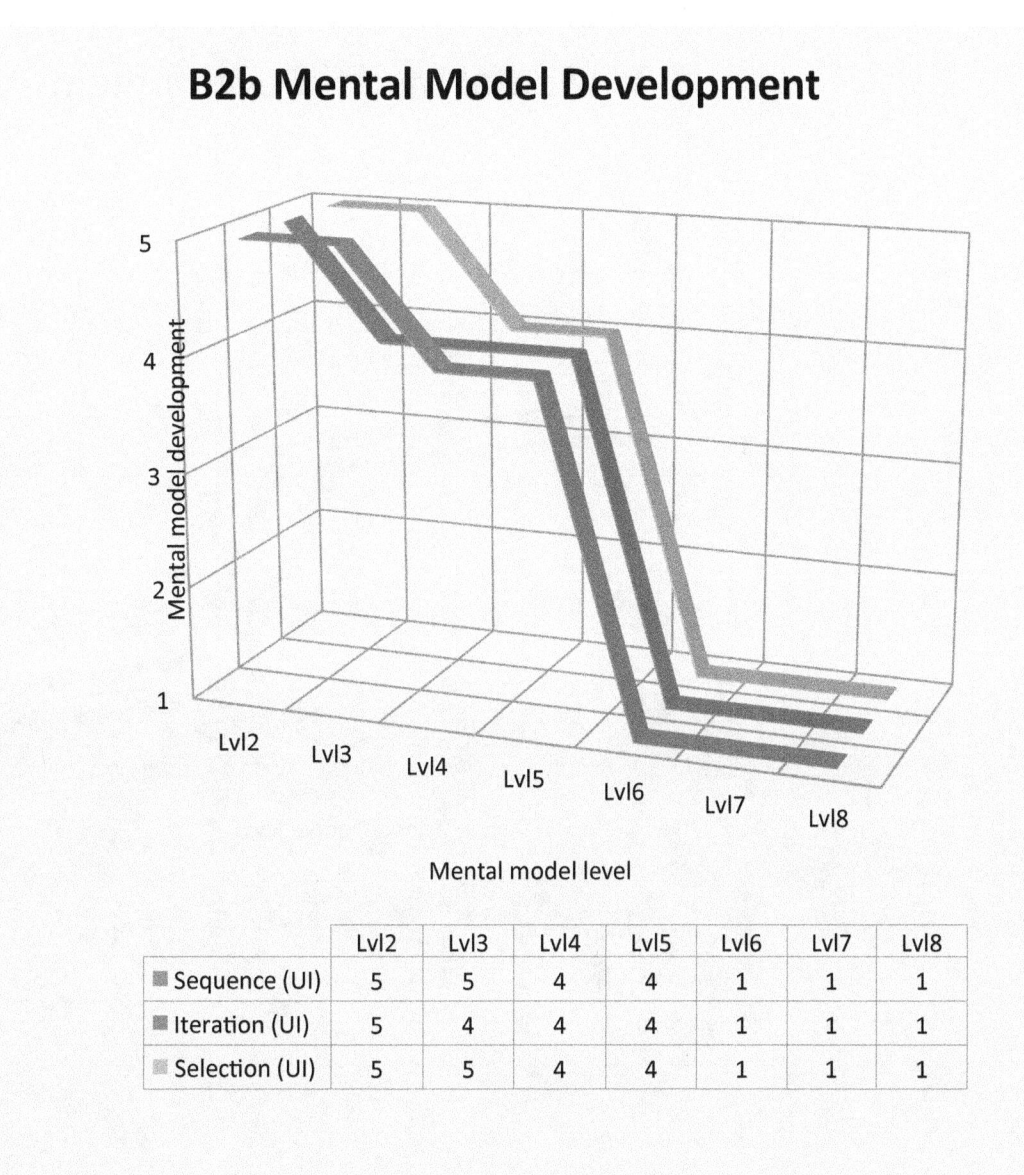

Figure 5.13   Student B3a concept development

5.1.2.5   Student B3a

Figure 5.14 shows B3a's initial but consistent difficulty with all concepts and was unable to progress beyond mental storyboarding (Level 5) as the degree of conceptual difficulty (Level) increased. She showed consistent results as the complexity of the concept (sequence to selection) increased. B3a was one of the students (*n*=20) who were interviewed and whose mental model tracing is presented (see Section 5.3.9).

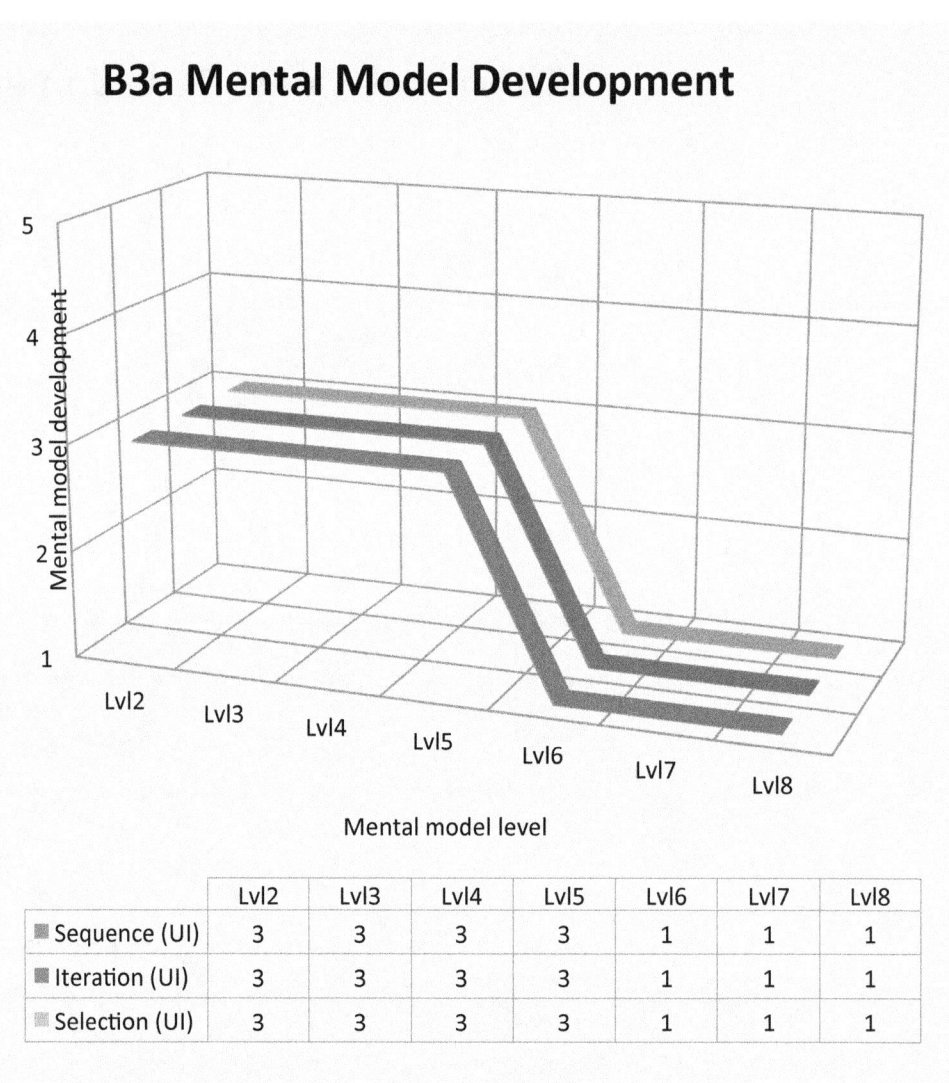

Figure 5.14   Student B3a concept development

5.1.2.6   Student B3b

Figure 5.15 shows B3b's increasing difficulty as the degree of conceptual difficulty (Level) increased but she was unable to progress beyond mental storyboarding (Level 5). She showed consistent results as the complexity of the concept (sequence to selection) increased.

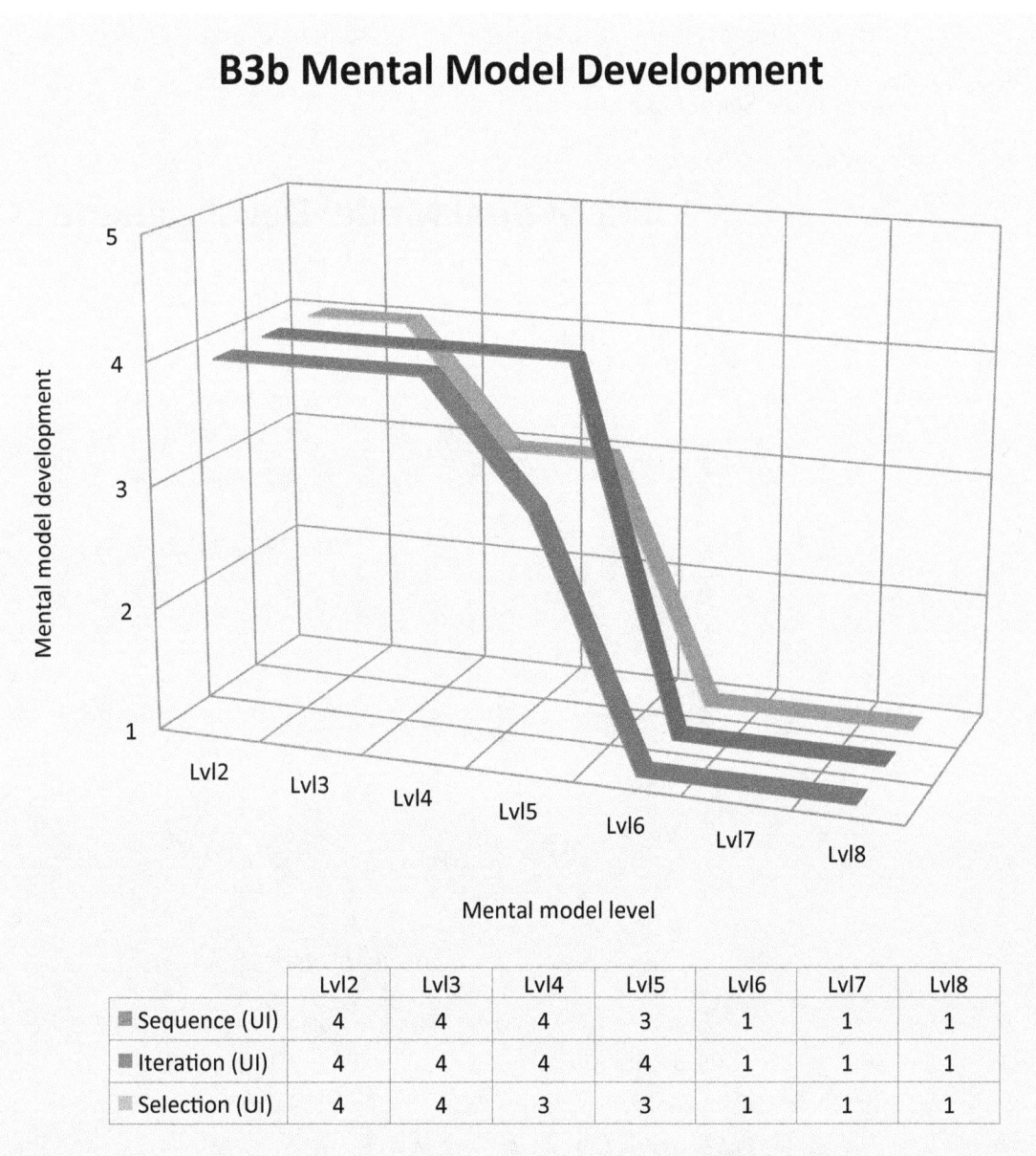

Figure 5.15   Student B3b concept development

5.1.2.7   Student B4a

Figure 5.16 shows B4a's gradually increasing difficulty as the degree of conceptual difficulty (Level) increased. B4a was one of the students ($n=20$) who were interviewed and whose mental model tracing is presented (see Section 5.3.10). She was also one of nine students included as a narrative (*Gandalf*, Section 6.5). B4a did not participate in the development of the sequence and iteration concepts due to illness (see Section 6.5).

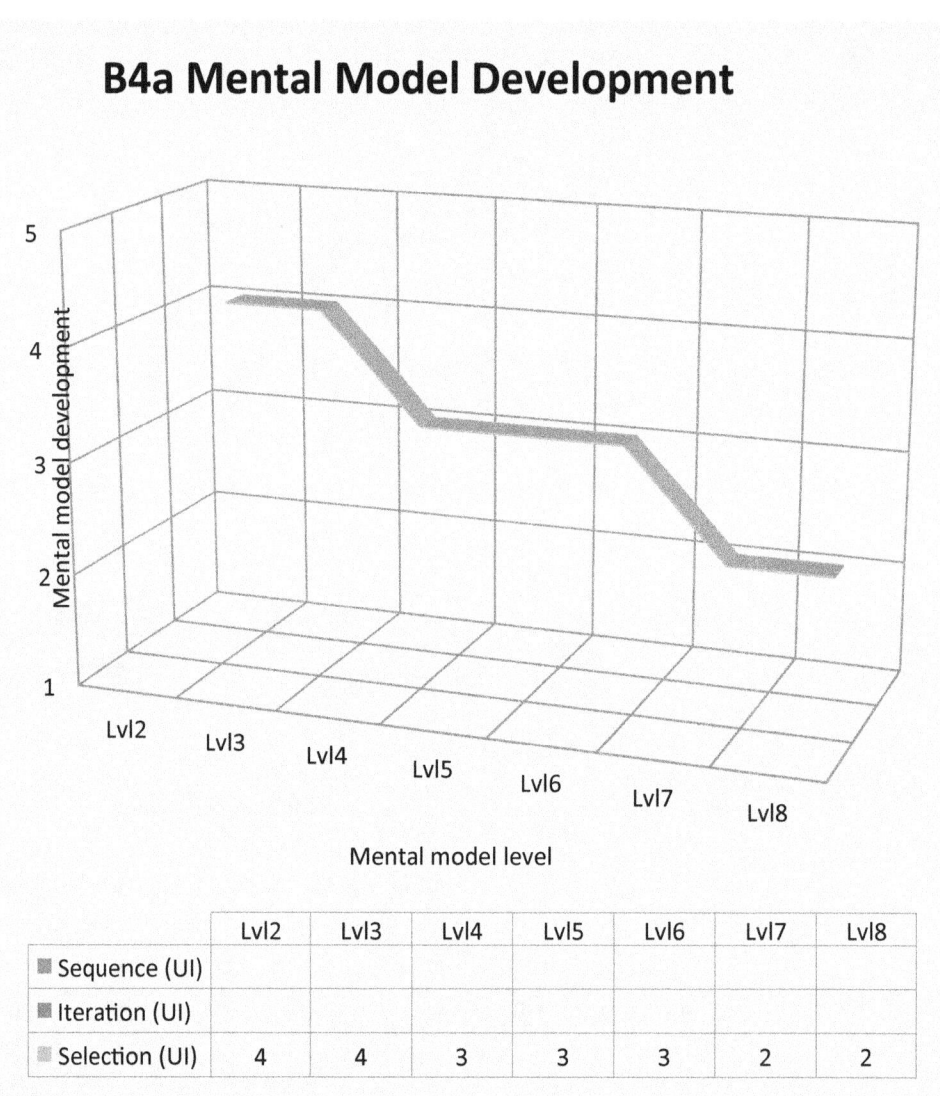

	Lvl2	Lvl3	Lvl4	Lvl5	Lvl6	Lvl7	Lvl8
Sequence (UI)							
Iteration (UI)							
Selection (UI)	4	4	3	3	3	2	2

Figure 5.16   Student B4a concept development

5.1.2.8   Student B4b

Figure 5.17 shows B4b's increasing difficulty as the degree of conceptual difficulty (Level) increased. She also showed increasing difficulty as the complexity of the concept (sequence to selection) increased. B4b was one of the students ($n=20$) who was interviewed and whose mental model tracing is presented (see Section 5.3.11).

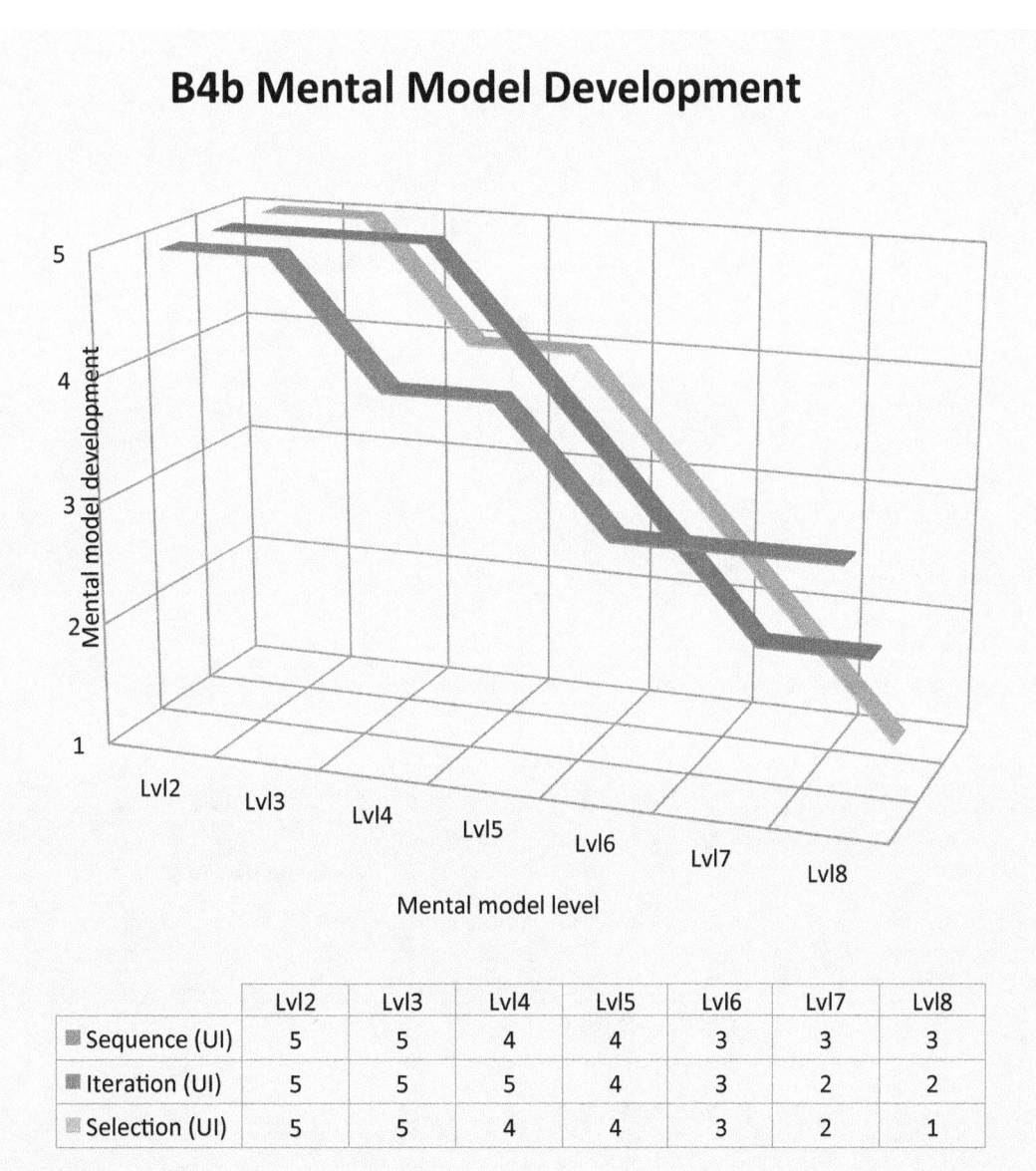

	Lvl2	Lvl3	Lvl4	Lvl5	Lvl6	Lvl7	Lvl8
Sequence (UI)	5	5	4	4	3	3	3
Iteration (UI)	5	5	5	4	3	2	2
Selection (UI)	5	5	4	4	3	2	1

Figure 5.17   Student B4b concept development

5.1.2.9   Student B5a

Figure 5.18 shows B5a's increasing difficulty as the degree of conceptual difficulty (Level) increased. She also showed some increasing difficulty as the complexity of the concept (sequence to selection) increased.

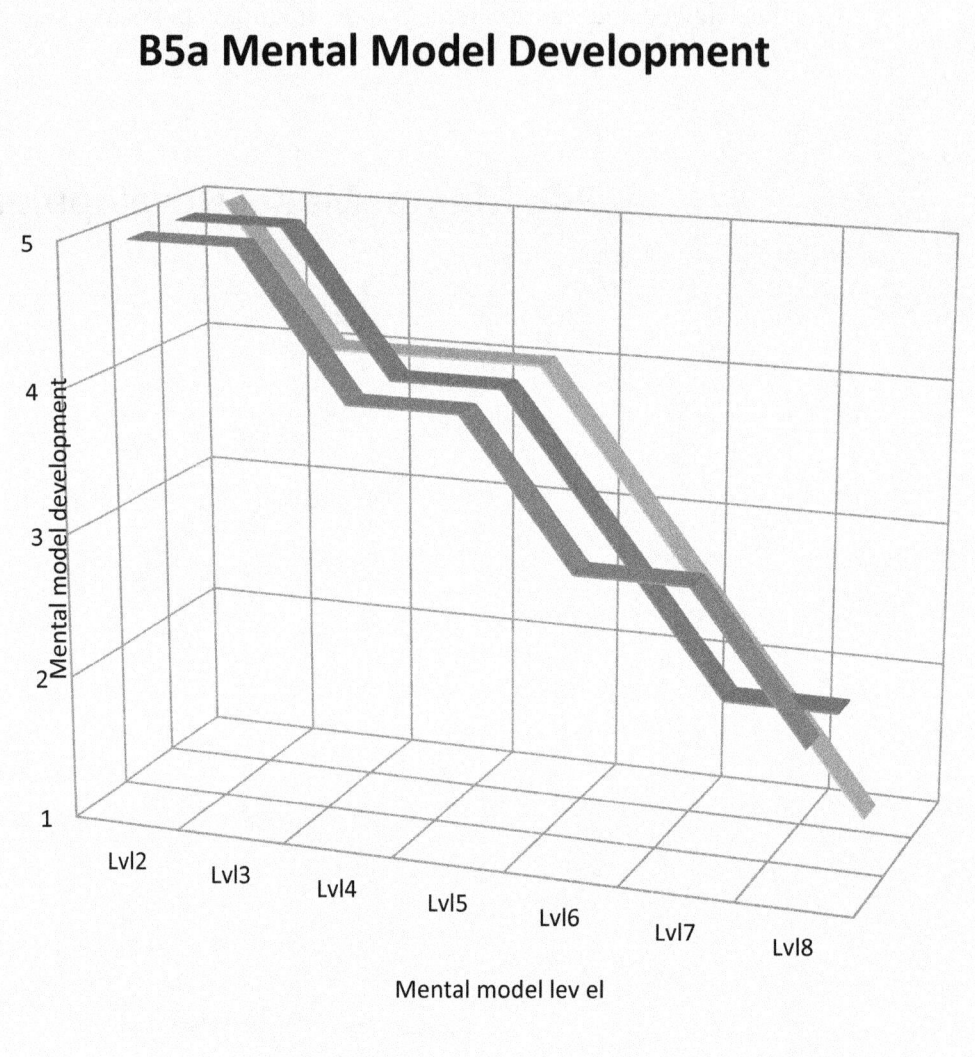

	Lvl2	Lvl3	Lvl4	Lvl5	Lvl6	Lvl7	Lvl8
■ Sequence (UI)	5	5	4	4	3	3	2
■ Iteration (UI)	5	5	4	4	3	2	2
■ Selection (UI)	5	4	4	4	3	2	1

Figure 5.18   Student B5a concept development

5.1.2.10   Student B5b

B5b showed generally consistent results as the complexity of the concept (sequence to selection) increased. A3a was one of the students (*n*=20) who was interviewed and whose mental model tracing is presented (see Section 5.3.12). Figure 5.19 shows B5b's increasing difficulty as the degree of conceptual difficulty (Level) increased, rapidly increasing beyond mental storyboarding (Level 5).

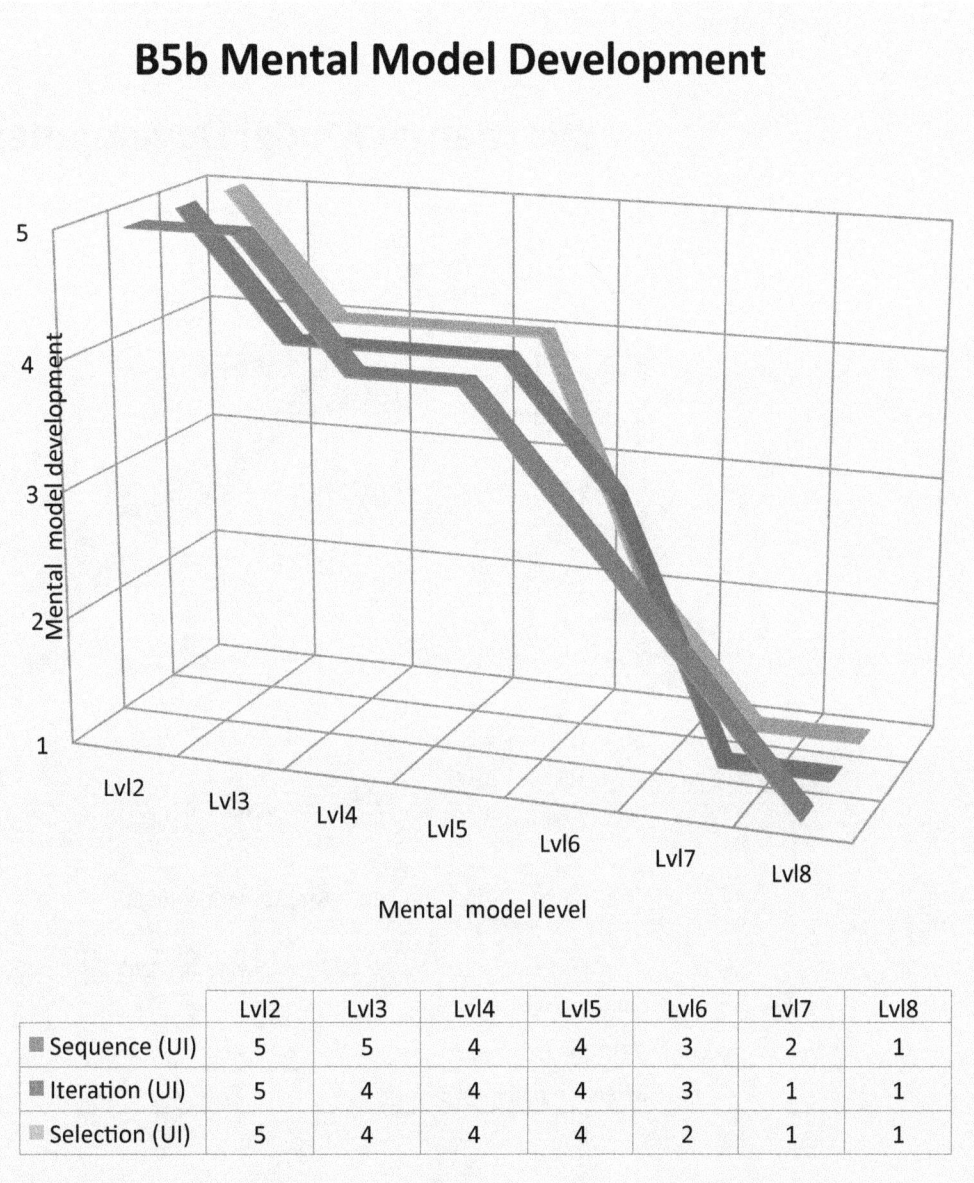

	Lvl2	Lvl3	Lvl4	Lvl5	Lvl6	Lvl7	Lvl8
■ Sequence (UI)	5	5	4	4	3	2	1
■ Iteration (UI)	5	4	4	4	3	1	1
■ Selection (UI)	5	4	4	4	2	1	1

Figure 5.19   Student B5b concept development

5.1.2.11   Student B6a

Figure 5.20 shows B6a's increasing difficulty as the degree of conceptual difficulty (Level) increased, rapidly increasing beyond mental storyboarding (Level 5) and while generally consistent (sequence to selection), progress at storyboarding (Level 5) decreased as the complexity of the concept increased. A3a was one of the students (*n*=20) who were interviewed and whose mental model tracing is presented (see Section 5.3.13).

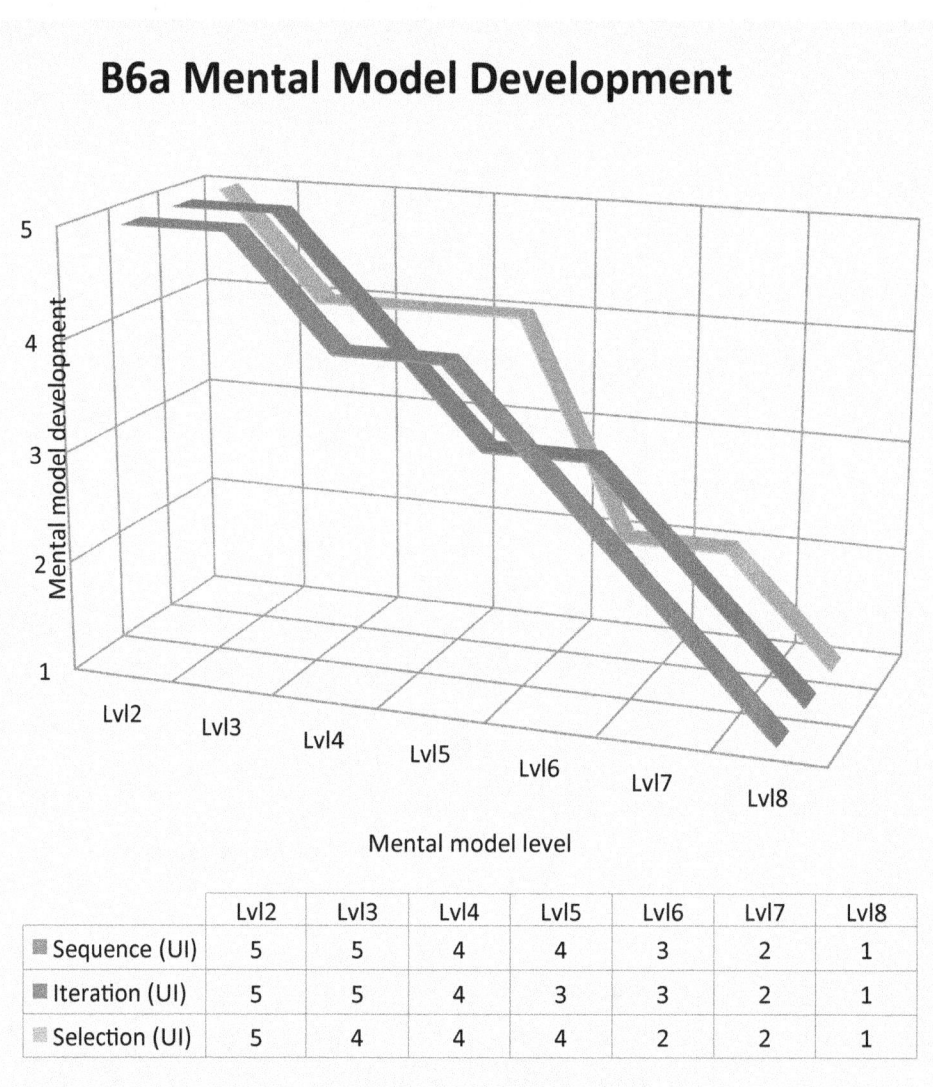

	Lvl2	Lvl3	Lvl4	Lvl5	Lvl6	Lvl7	Lvl8
Sequence (UI)	5	5	4	4	3	2	1
Iteration (UI)	5	5	4	3	3	2	1
Selection (UI)	5	4	4	4	2	2	1

Figure 5.20   Student B6a concept development

5.1.2.12   Student B6b

Figure 5.21 shows increasing difficulty as the degree of conceptual difficulty (Level) increased and while generally consistent (sequence to selection), B6b improved at Inventising (Level 8) as the complexity of the concept increased.

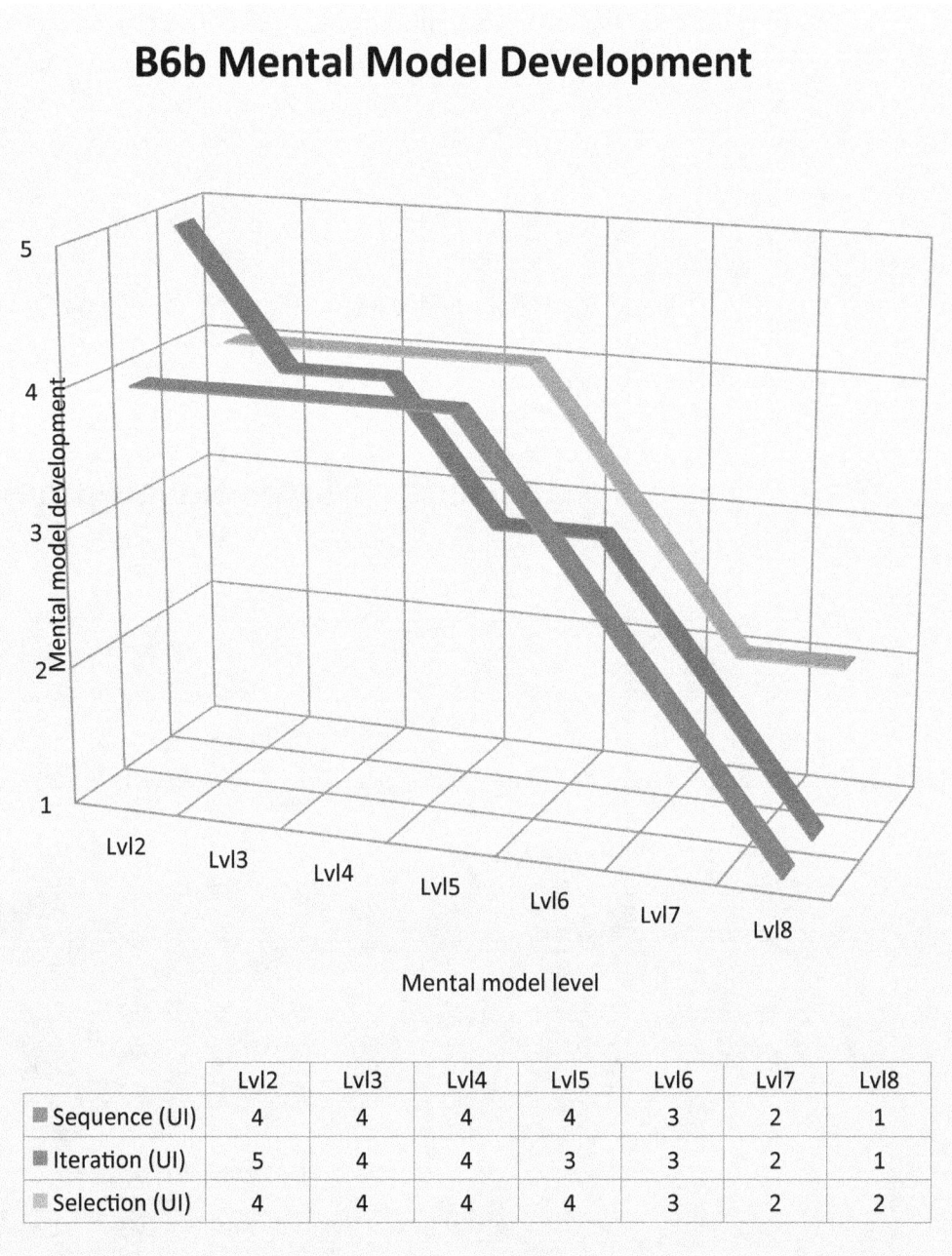

	Lvl2	Lvl3	Lvl4	Lvl5	Lvl6	Lvl7	Lvl8
Sequence (UI)	4	4	4	4	3	2	1
Iteration (UI)	5	4	4	3	3	2	1
Selection (UI)	4	4	4	4	3	2	2

Figure 5.21   Student B6b concept development

5.1.3 Cohort C

The students in Cohort C (*n=8*) developed mental models of a single concept during the study, that is, sequence using an Unconstrained Text visualisation tool (*PHP*). The students in Cohort C, organised in three pairs, were C1a, C1b, C2a, C2b, C3a, C3b, C4a and C4b. Their concept development is discussed respectively in Sections 5.1.3.1-5.1.3.6.

5.1.3.1   Student C1a

Figure 5.22 shows C1a's gradually increasing difficulty as the degree of conceptual difficulty (Level) increased.

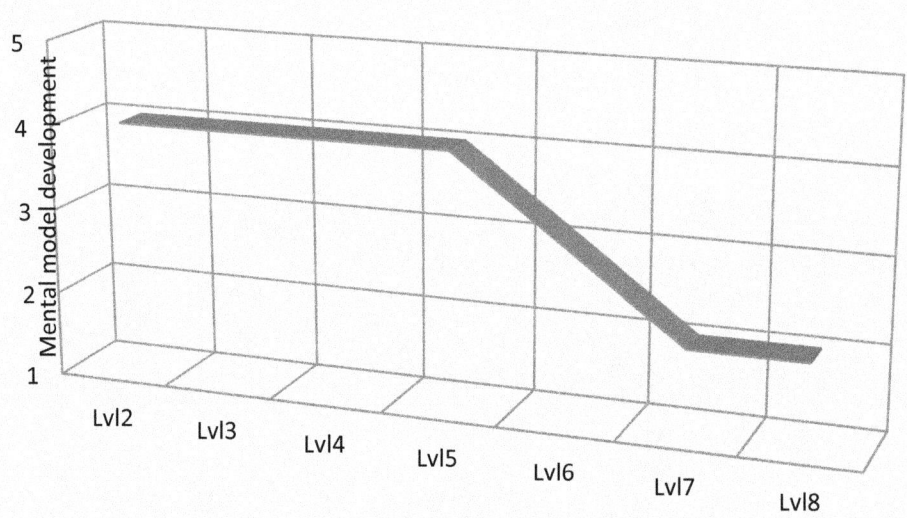

Figure 5.22 Student C1a concept development

5.1.3.2   Student C1b

Figure 5.23 shows C1b's rapidly increasing difficulty as the degree of conceptual difficulty (Level) increased with no progress made from Formalising (Level 5). C1b was one of the students (*n*=20) who were interviewed and whose mental model tracing is presented (see Section 5.3.15).

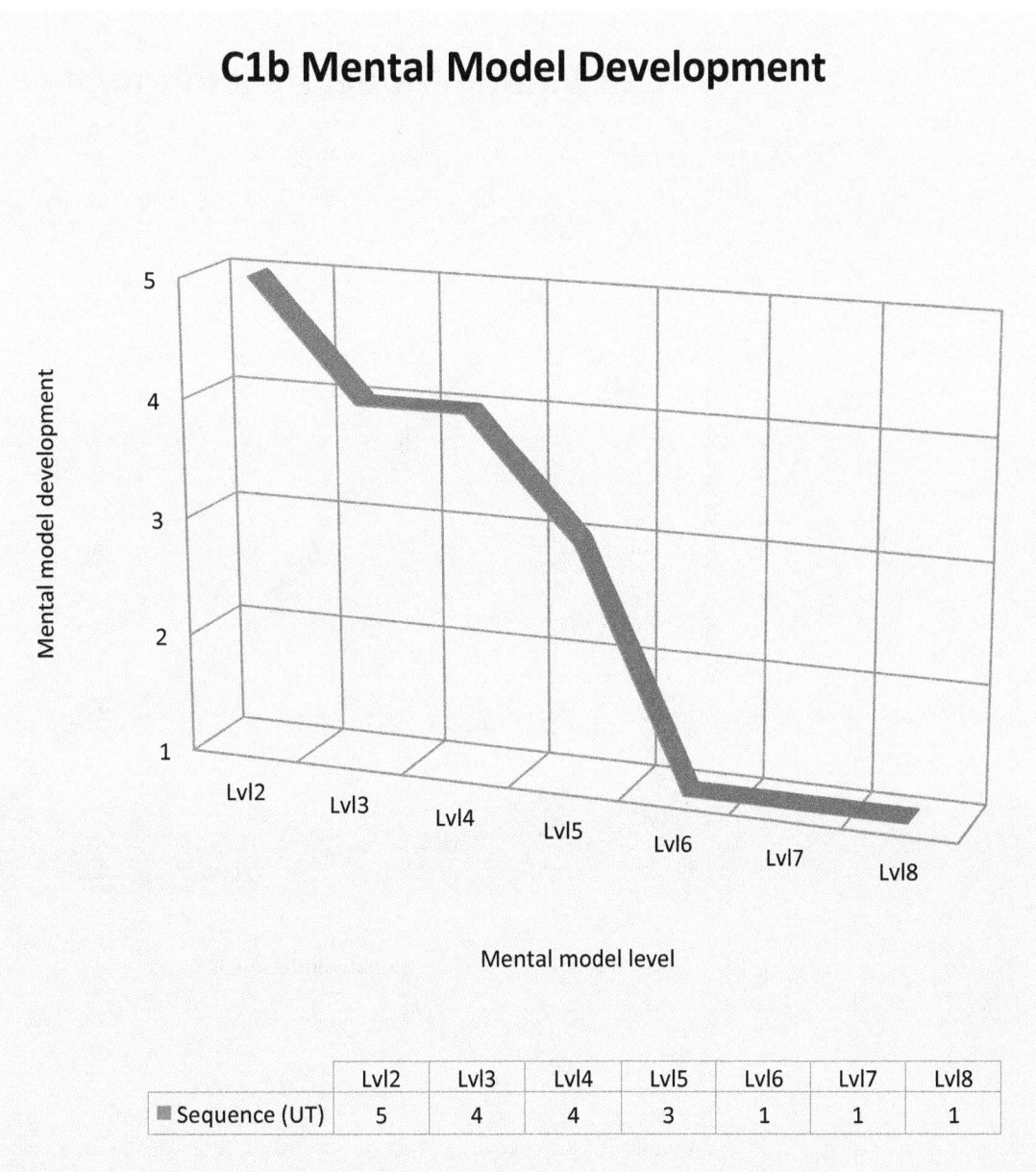

Figure 5.23   Student C1b concept development

5.1.3.3   Student C2a

Figure 5.24 shows C2a's initial improvement followed by gradually increasing difficulty as the degree of conceptual difficulty (Level) increased. C2a was one of the students (*n*=20) who were interviewed and whose mental model tracing is presented (see Section 5.3.16).

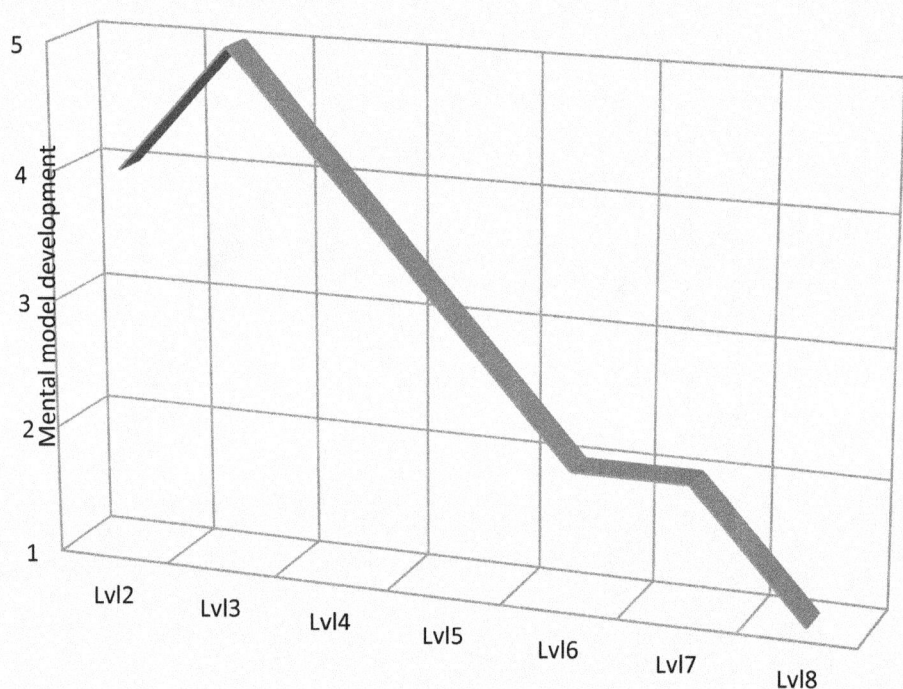

Figure 5.24   Student C2a concept development

5.1.3.4   Student C2b

Figure 5.25 shows C2b's very gradual increasing difficulty as the degree of conceptual difficulty (Level) increased.

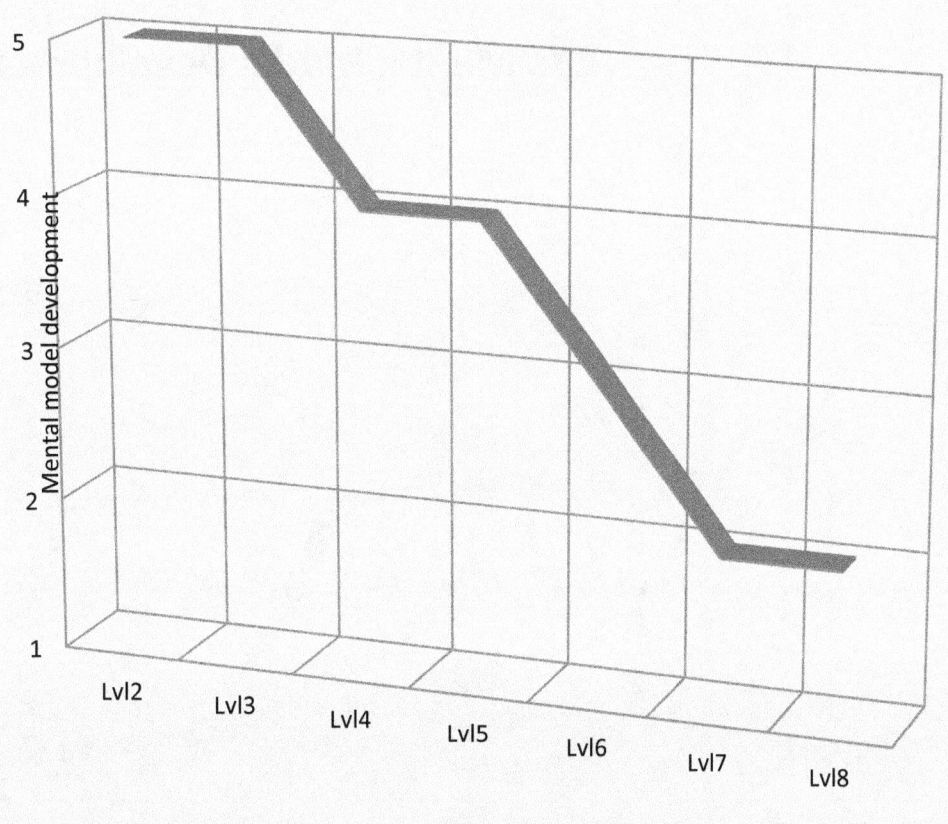

Figure 5.25   Student C2b concept development

5.1.3.5 *Student C3a*

Figure 5.26 shows C3a's initial difficulties and at Formalising (Level 5) was unable to demonstrate progress in development of her mental model. C3a was one of the students (*n*=20) who was interviewed and whose mental model tracing is presented (see Section 5.3.17). She was also one of nine students included as a narrative (*Boromir*, Section 6.7).

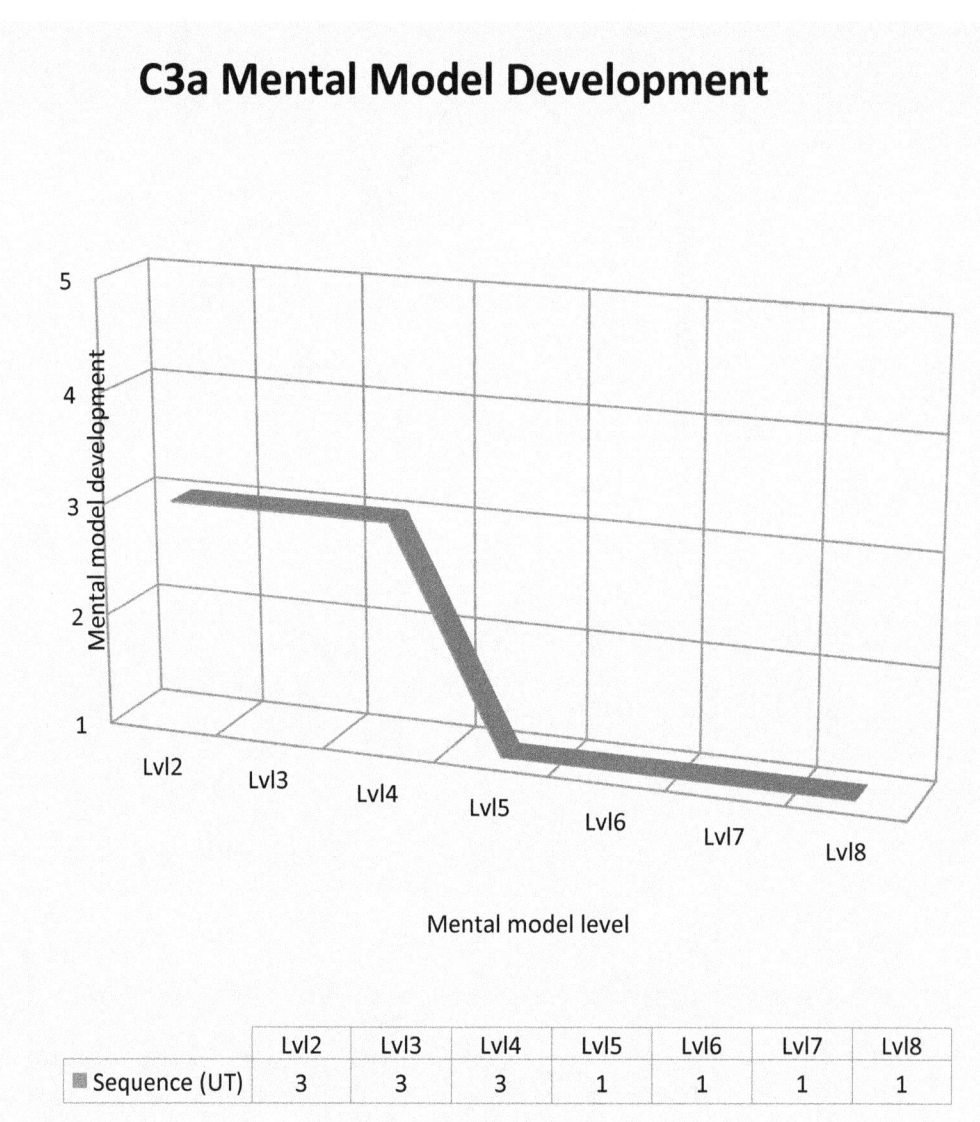

	Lvl2	Lvl3	Lvl4	Lvl5	Lvl6	Lvl7	Lvl8
■ Sequence (UT)	3	3	3	1	1	1	1

Figure 5.26   Student C3a concept development

5.1.3.6   Student C3b

Figure 5.27 shows C3b's consistent ability to Property Noticing (Level 4) followed by gradually increasing difficulty as the degree of conceptual difficulty (Level) increased.

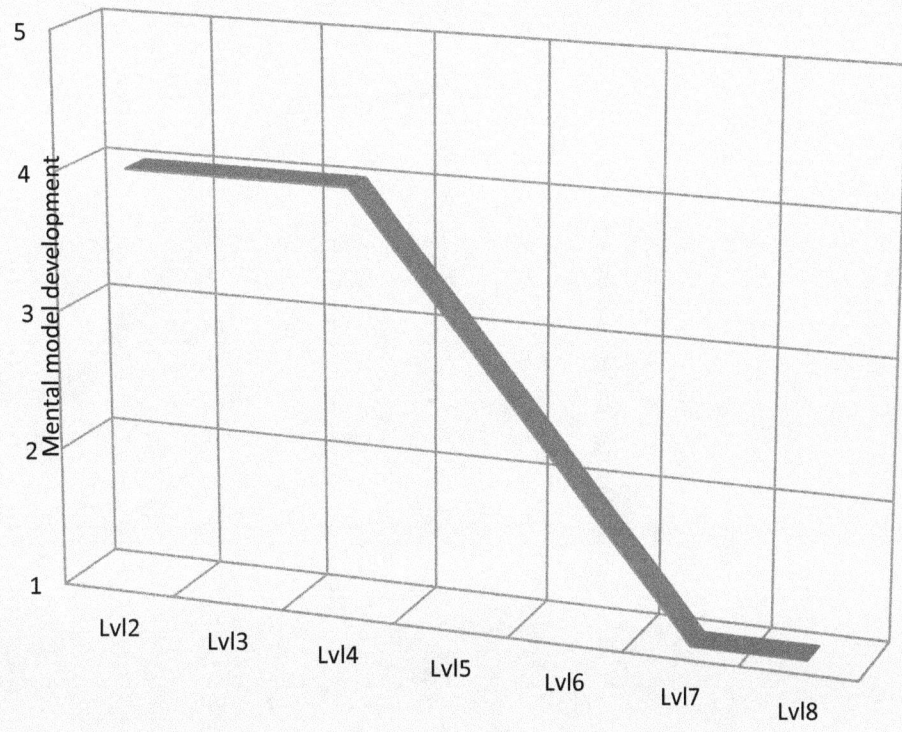

Figure 5.27   Student C3b concept development

5.1.3.7   Student C4a

Figure 5.28 shows C4a's consistently high ability to Property Noticing (Level 4) followed by a gradually increasing difficulty to Observing (Level 6) with consistent ability thereafter through to Inventising (Level 8) as the degree of conceptual difficulty (Level) increased.

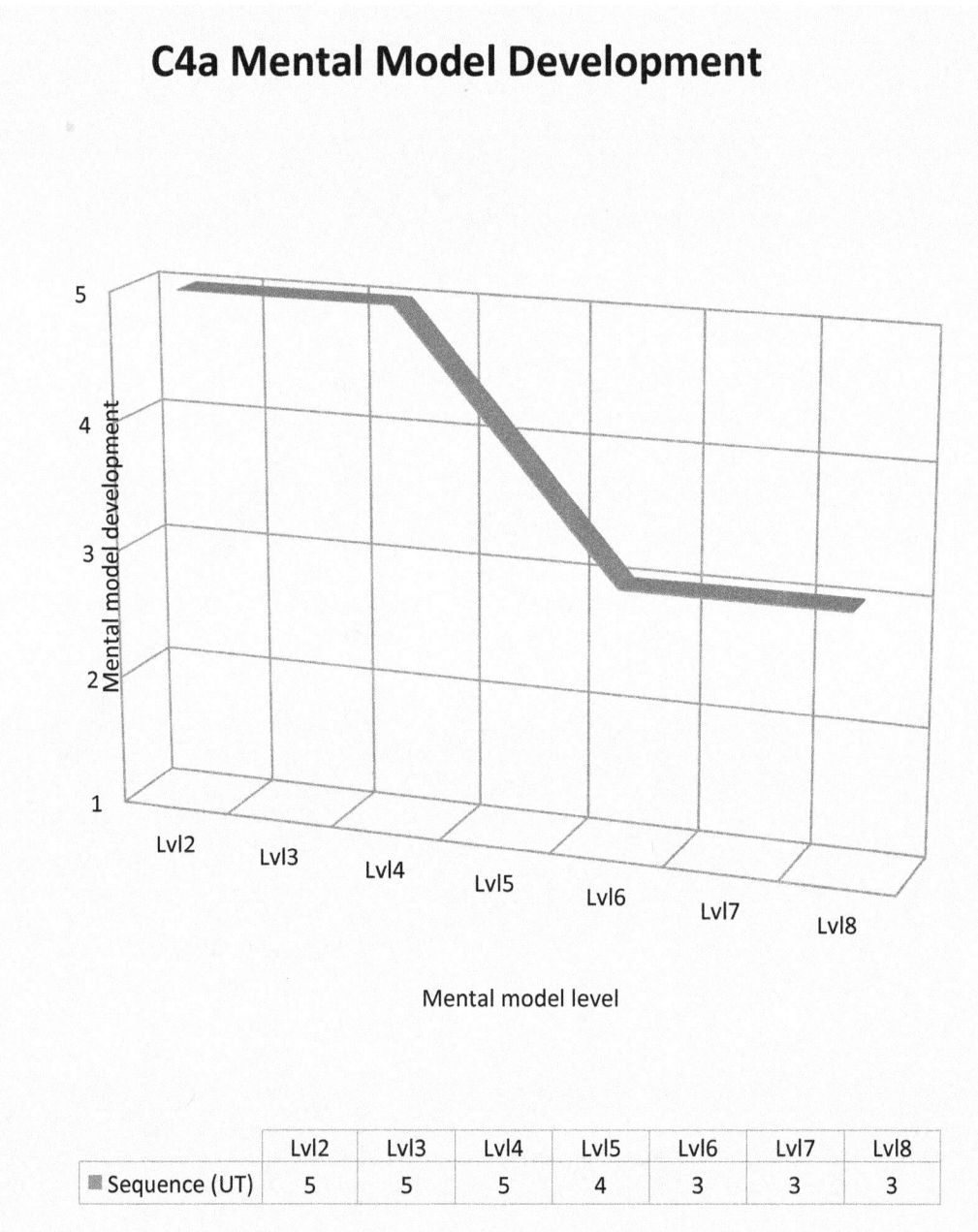

Figure 5.28   Student C4a concept development

5.1.3.8   Student C4b

Figure 5.29 shows C4b's gradually increasing difficulty as the degree of conceptual difficulty (Level) increased. C4b was one of the students ($n=20$) who was interviewed and whose mental model tracing is presented (see Section 5.3.18). She was also one of nine students included as a narrative (*Aragorn*, Section 6.6).

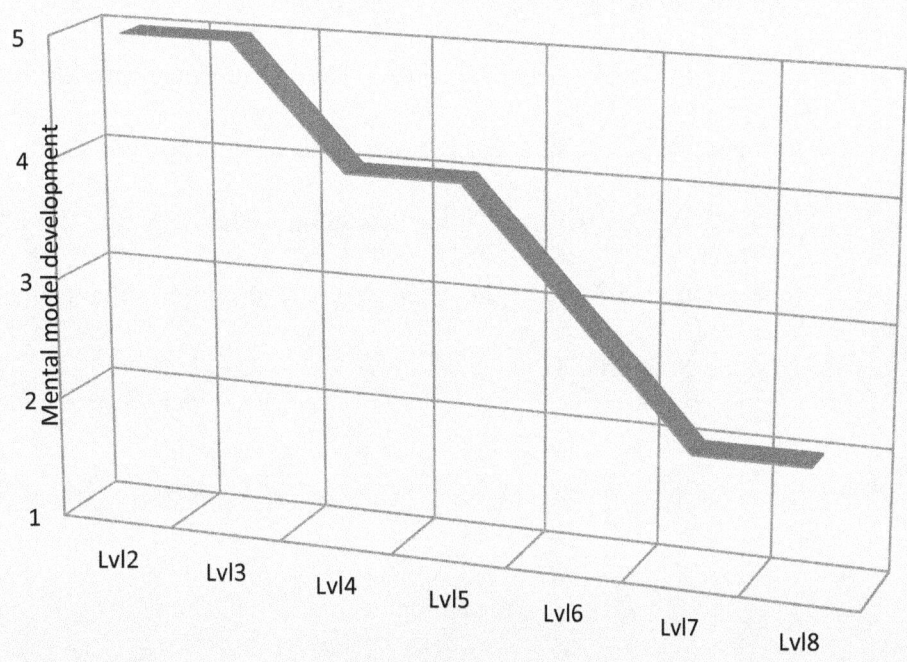

Figure 5.29   Student C4b concept development

5.1.4 Cohort D

The students in Cohort D (*n=2*) developed mental models of four concepts (sequence, iteration, selection and modularity) during the study. These students D1a and D1b used differing visualisation tools. Their progress is discussed in 5.1.4.1 and 5.1.4.2.

5.1.4.1 Student D1a

D1a studied the four concepts using a Constrained Text visualisation tool (*Alice*). Figure 5.30 shows D1a's erratic but increasing difficulty as the degree of conceptual difficulty (Level) increased. She also experienced some increasing difficulty as the complexity of the concept (sequence to selection) increased. D1a was one of the students (*n=20*) who was interviewed and whose mental model tracing is presented (see Section 5.3.19). She was also one of nine students included as a narrative (*Pippin*, Section 6.8).

D1a Mental Model Development

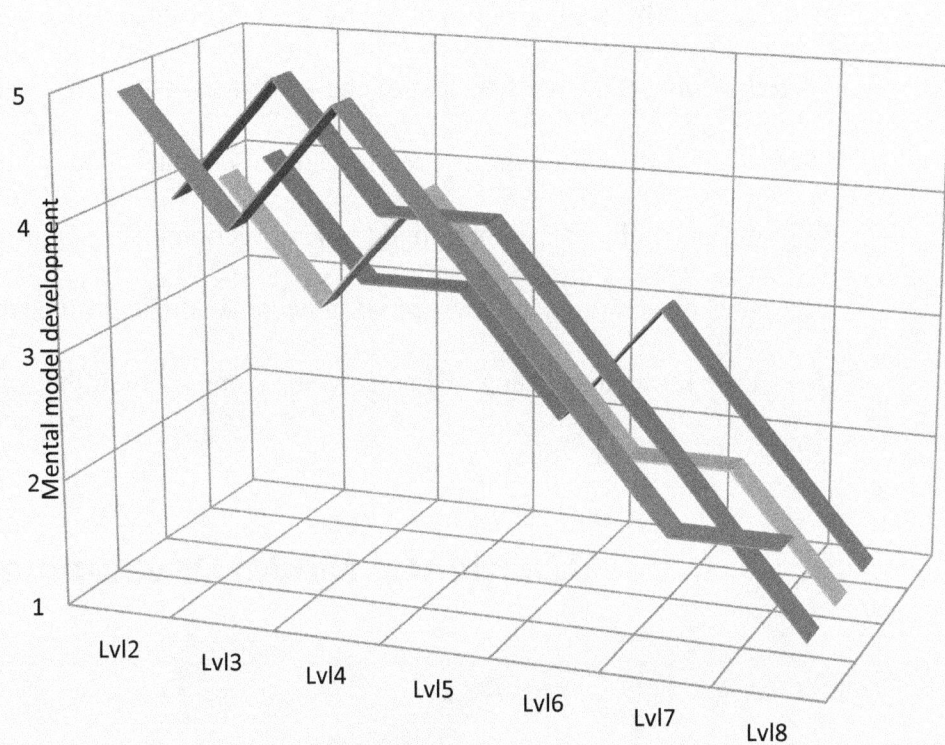

	Lvl2	Lvl3	Lvl4	Lvl5	Lvl6	Lvl7	Lvl8
■ Sequence (CT)	5	4	5	4	3	2	2
■ Iteration (CT)	4	5	4	4	3	2	1
■ Selection (CT)	4	3	4	3	2	2	1
■ Modularity (CT)	4	3	3	2	3	2	1

Figure 5.30   Student D1a concept development

5.1.4.2   Student D2a

D2a developed mental models of four concepts (sequence, iteration, selection and modularity). She studied all four using an Unconstrained Text visualisation tool (*Visual Basic*). D2a was the last of the students (*n*=20) who was interviewed and whose mental model tracing is presented (see Section 5.3.20). She was also one of nine students included as a narrative (*Merry*, Section 6.9). Figure 5.31 shows D2a's increasing difficulty as the degree of conceptual difficulty (Level) increased. She also showed some increasing difficulty as the complexity of the concept (sequence to selection) increased.

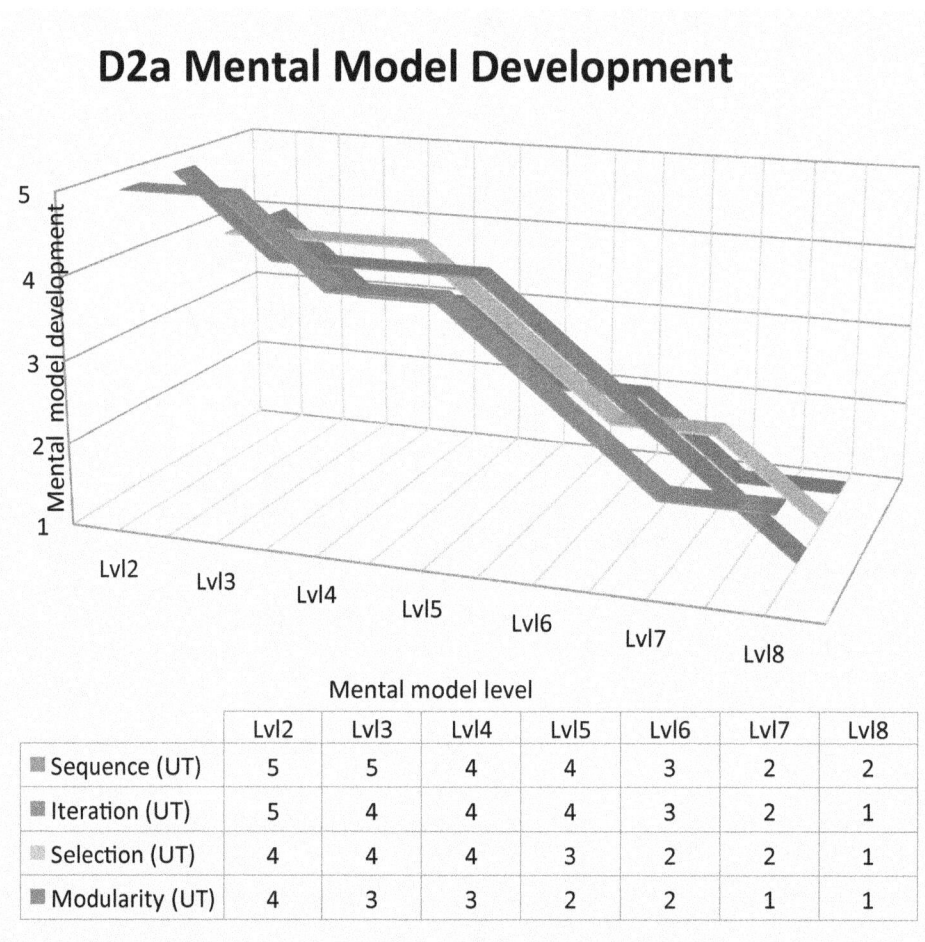

	Lvl2	Lvl3	Lvl4	Lvl5	Lvl6	Lvl7	Lvl8
Sequence (UT)	5	5	4	4	3	2	2
Iteration (UT)	5	4	4	4	3	2	1
Selection (UT)	4	4	4	3	2	2	1
Modularity (UT)	4	3	3	2	2	1	1

Figure 5.31   Student D2a concept development

5.1.5 Concept development comparison

Each student ($N=31$) produced an individual concept development graph (see Section 5.1.1) of each concept they developed. The following graph averages this development for each of the four concepts studied (see Chapter 4.4.1), that is sequence (S), iteration (I), selection (D), and modularity (M).

The graph (Figure 5.3.2) summarises student mental model development for each concept developed in this study. A rating was given (from "1" to "5") against a range (see Section 4.4.1 and Appendix 2) of mental model development performance measures. In each case, the higher the number, the more effective the student was at developing that level of her mental model using that visualisation tool. Levels 1 to 8 refer to mental model levels (Pirie & Kieren, 1992).

Mental Model Development Comparison

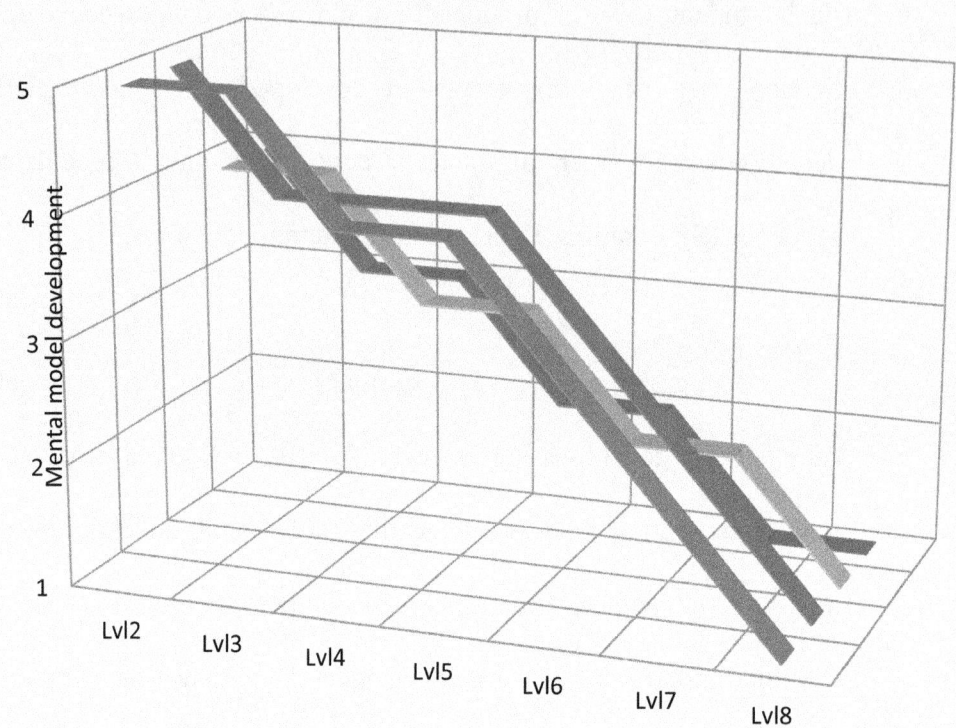

	Lvl2	Lvl3	Lvl4	Lvl5	Lvl6	Lvl7	Lvl8
■ Sequence	5	5	4	4	3	2	1
■ Iteration	5	4	4	4	3	2	1
■ Selection	4	4	3	3	2	2	1
■ Modularity	4	3	3	2	2	1	1

Figure 5.32 Overall concept development effectiveness

5.1.6 Visualisation tool comparison

Each student ($N=31$) produced an individual concept development graph (see Section 5.1.1) for each of the concepts they developed. The following summarises this development for each of the four types of visualisation tools (see Chapter 3) with the Visual Basic and PHP programming languages combined as representative of the Unconstrained Text visualisation tool (PHP/VB (UT), Alice (CT), GameMaker (CI), RoboLab (UI)).

Each graph summarises student mental model development for each visualisation tool used in this study. A rating was given (from "1" to "5") against a range (see Section 4.4.1 and Appendix 2) of mental model development performance measures. In each case, the higher the number, the more effective the student was at developing that level of her mental model using that visualisation tool. Levels 1 to 8 refer to mental model levels (Pirie & Kieren, 1992).

The overall effectiveness of each visualisation tool is shown for each of the four concepts developed in this study (see Figures 5.33 – 5.36). The following collective graph (see Figure 5.37) records overall development of all four concepts for each visualisation tool.

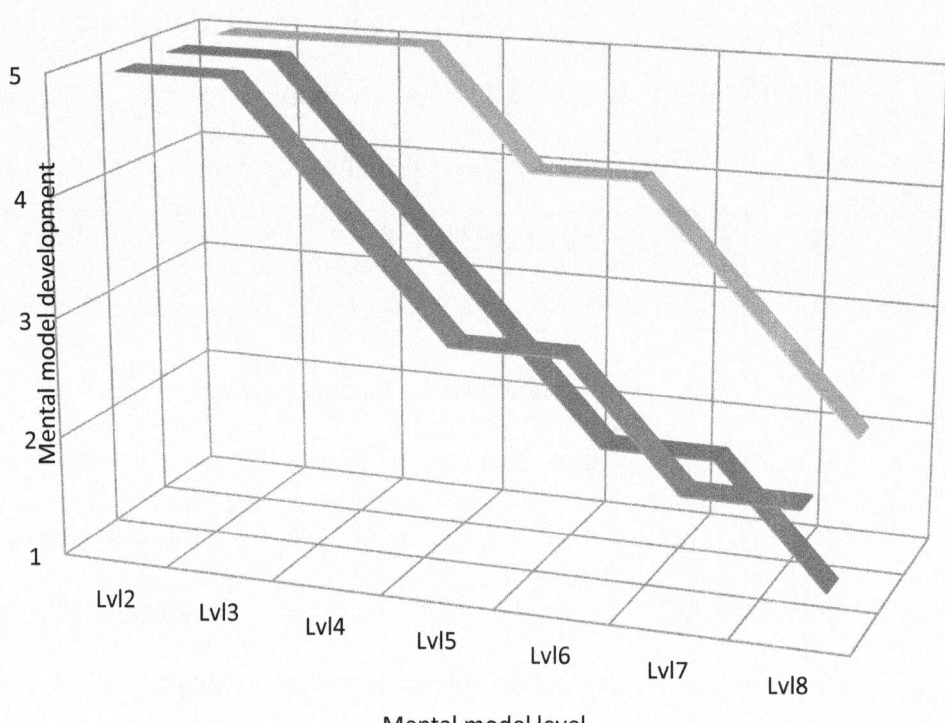

	Lvl2	Lvl3	Lvl4	Lvl5	Lvl6	Lvl7	Lvl8
■ PhP,VB (UT)	5	5	4	3	3	2	2
■ Alice (CT)	5	5	4	3	2	2	1
■ RoboLab (UI)	5	5	5	4	4	3	2

Figure 5.33   Overall visualisation tool effectiveness – Sequence

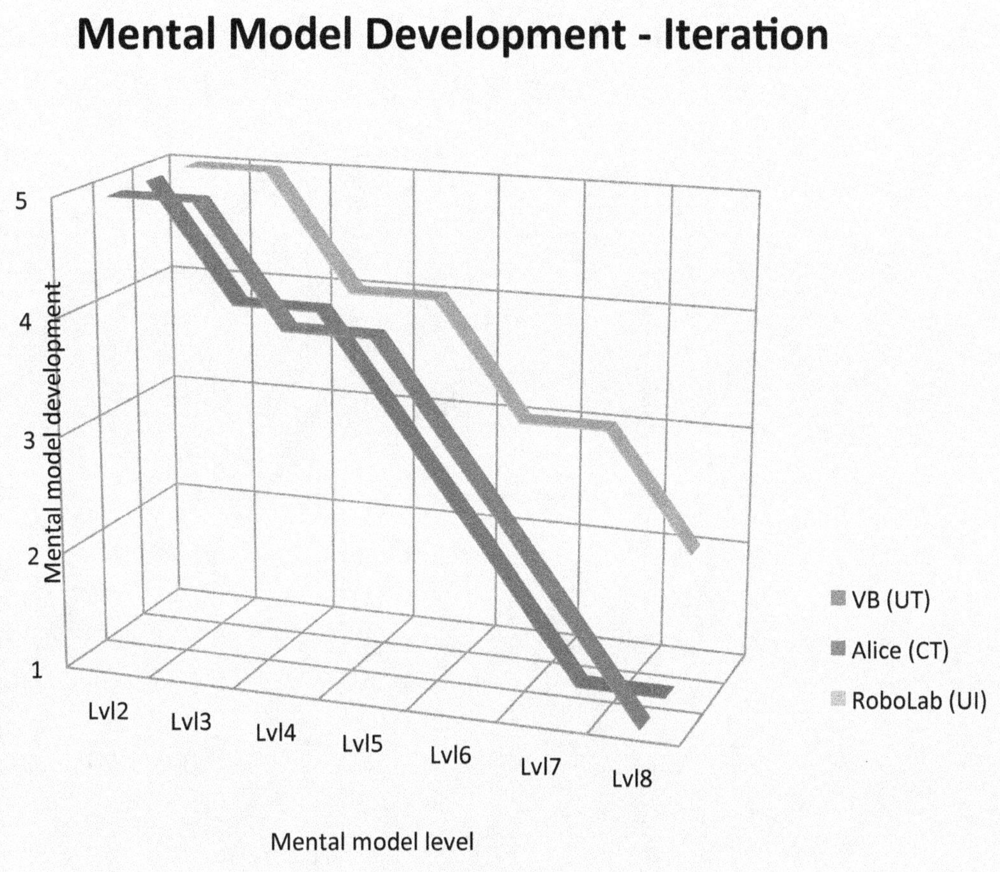

Mental Model Development - Iteration
5
4
3
2
1
Mental model development
Lvl2
Lvl3
Lvl4
Lvl5
Lvl6
Lvl7
Lvl8
Mental model level
VB (UT)
Alice (CT)
RoboLab (UI)

	Lvl2	Lvl3	Lvl4	Lvl5	Lvl6	Lvl7	Lvl8
VB (UT)	5	5	4	4	3	2	1
Alice (CT)	5	4	4	3	2	1	1
RoboLab (UI)	5	5	4	4	3	3	2

Figure 5.34 Overall visualisation tool effectiveness - Iteration

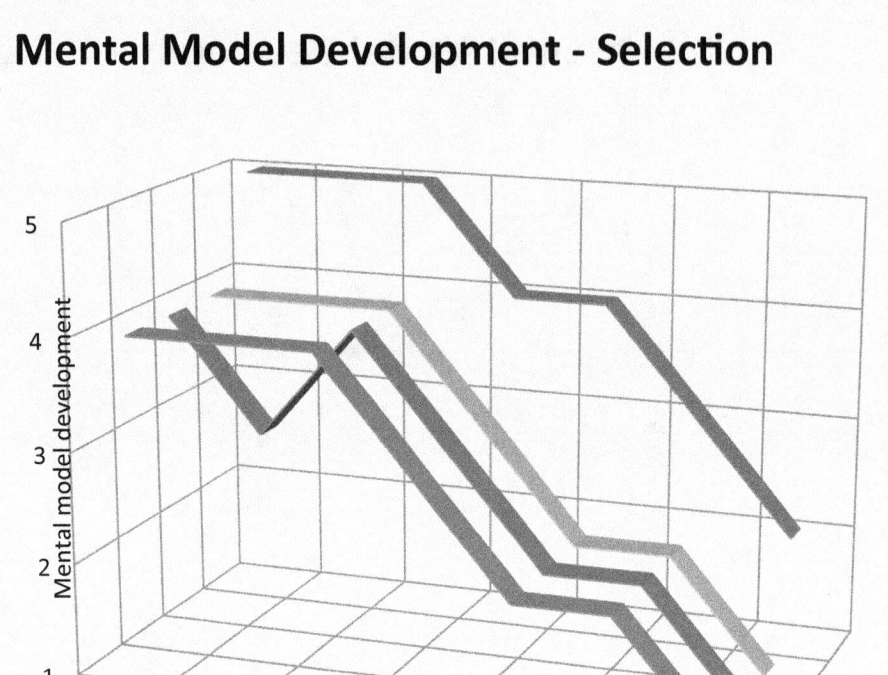

Figure 5.35 Overall visualisation tool effectiveness – Selection

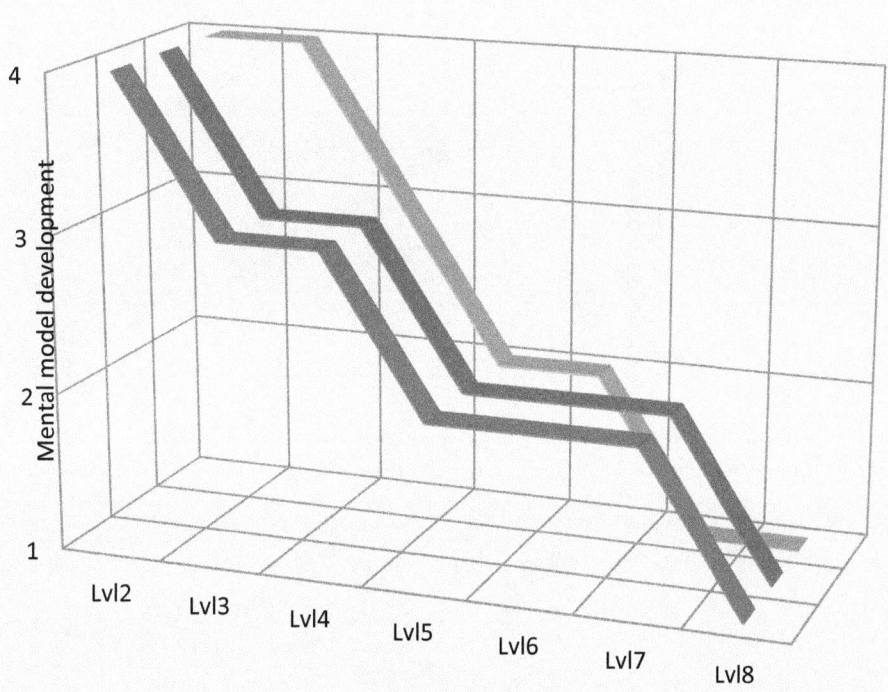

Figure 5.36   Overall visualisation tool effectiveness - Modularity

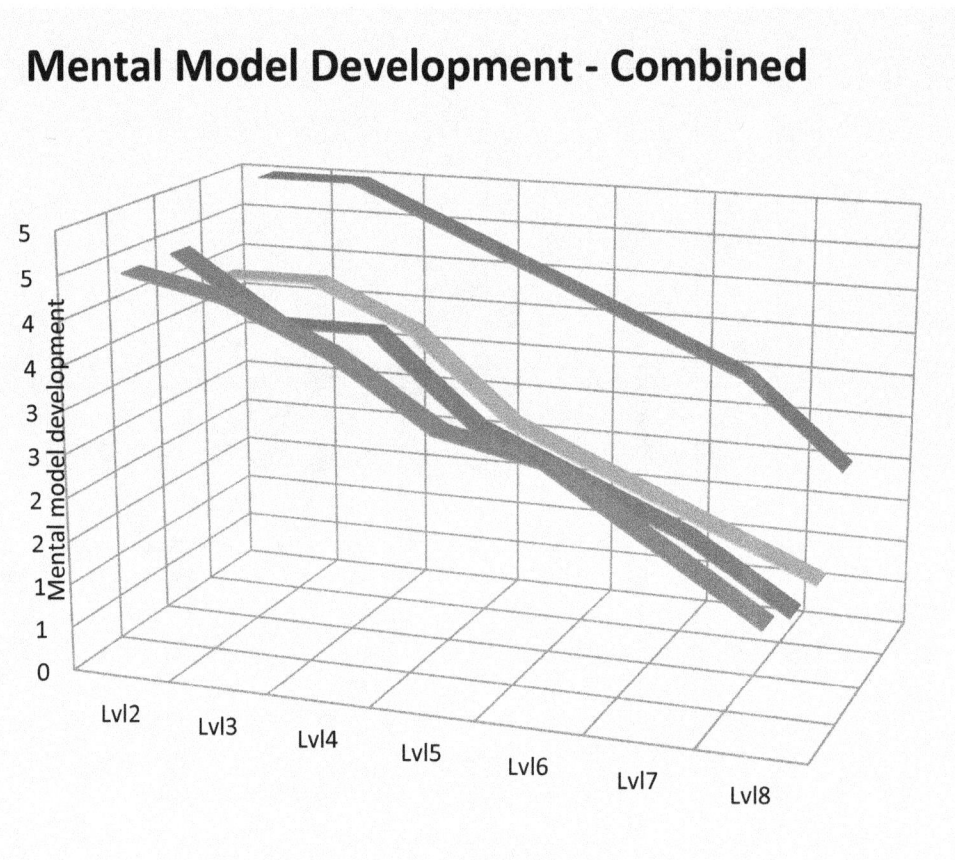

	Mental model level						
	Lvl2	Lvl3	Lvl4	Lvl5	Lvl6	Lvl7	Lvl8
PhP,VB (UT)	4.50	4.25	3.75	3.00	2.75	2.00	1.25
Alice (CT)	4.50	3.75	3.75	2.75	2.25	1.75	1.00
GameMaker (CI)	4.00	4.00	3.50	2.50	2.00	1.50	1.00
RoboLab (UI)	5.00	5.00	4.50	4.00	3.50	3.00	2.00

Figure 5.37 Overall visualisation tool effectiveness - Combined

Interpretation and analysis of the collective graphs is developed in the discussion and conclusions chapter (see Section 7.5).

5.2 Effectiveness surveys

Students were administered surveys (see Section 4.3.4 and 4.3.5) to determine their satisfaction with the effectiveness of each visualisation tool to assist their learning. Two survey instruments (Survey 1 (described in Section 4.4.4.1) and Survey 2 (described in Section 4.4.4.2)) were administered. Each question was completed against a Likert (1932) scale (1-5) and presented in a stacked column graph (see Sections 4.9.2 and 4.9.3) to demonstrate the comparative response of cohorts of varying sizes. The surveys are presented in full in Appendix A. The higher the number on the horizontal axis, the more positive the cohort response is to the question.

5.2.1 Survey 1

Survey 1 was administered to all students for each concept they studied. It provided student perceptions on (a) the effectiveness of the visualisation to help them learn the concept, (b) how enjoyable the tool was to use for that concept, and (c) the effect of the tool on how quickly they learnt the concept.

a. the first question addressed students' perception (see Figures 5.38 – 5.41) of the effectiveness of the visualisation tool in helping them to learn about a specific concept.

For the concept of sequence (see Figure 5.38), students perceived that the RoboLab (UI) and Alice (CT) visualisation tools were the most effective in assisting them learn about the concept of sequence. PHP (UT) was not perceived as particularly effective though Visual Basic (UT) was considered effective by the small cohort involved. GameMaker (CI) was not used to develop the concept of sequence in this study.

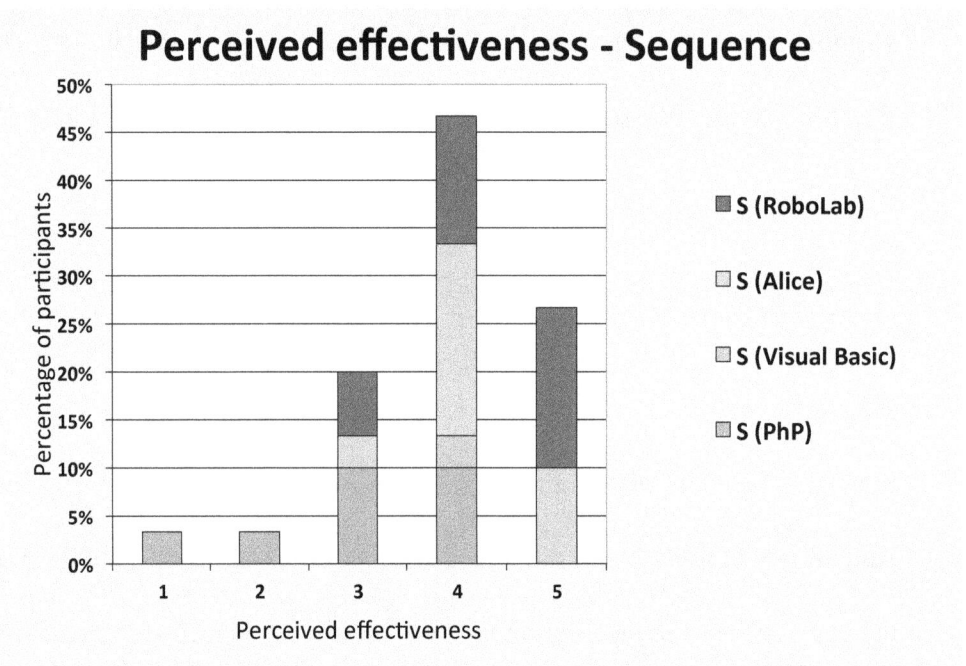

Figure 5.38   Student perception of tool effectiveness in learning – Sequence

For the concept of iteration (see Figure 5.39), students perceived that the RoboLab (UI) visualisation tool was very effective in assisting them learn about the concept of iteration. The Alice (CT) tool was also considered to be effective as was Visual Basic (UT). PHP (UT) and GameMaker (CI) were not used to develop the concept of iteration in this study.

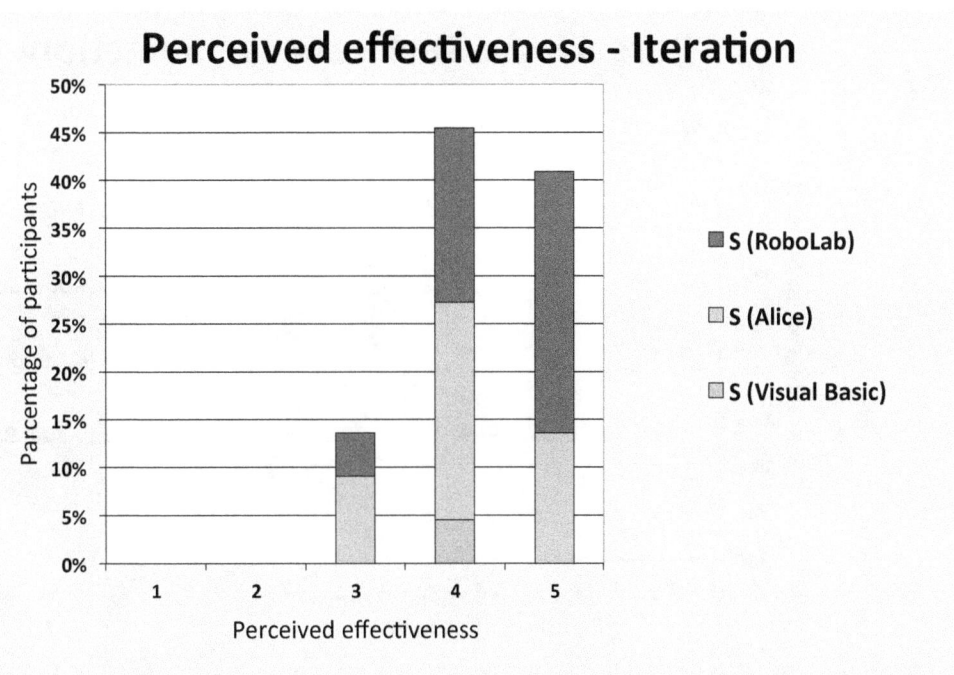

Figure 5.39 Student perception of tool effectiveness in learning - Iteration

For the concept of selection (see Figure 5.40), students perceived that the RoboLab (UI) visualisation tool was very effective in assisting them learn about the concept of selection. The Alice (CT) tool was also considered to be very effective for the small cohort involved. GameMaker (CI) was considered effective as was Visual Basic (UT). PHP (UT) was not used to develop the concept of selection in this study.

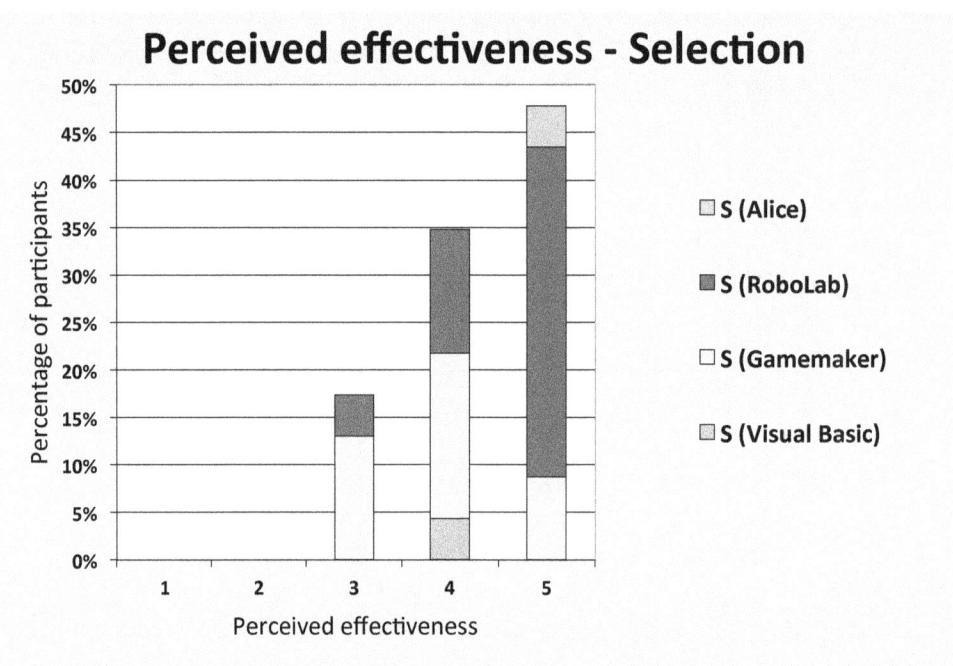

Figure 5.40 Student perception of tool effectiveness in learning - Selection

For the concept of modularity (see Figure 5.41), students perceived that the Alice (CT) and Visual Basic (UT) visualisation tools were very effective in assisting them learn about the concept of modularity. The GameMaker (CI) tool was considered to be effective. PHP (UT) and Robolab (UI) were not used to develop the concept of modularity in this study.

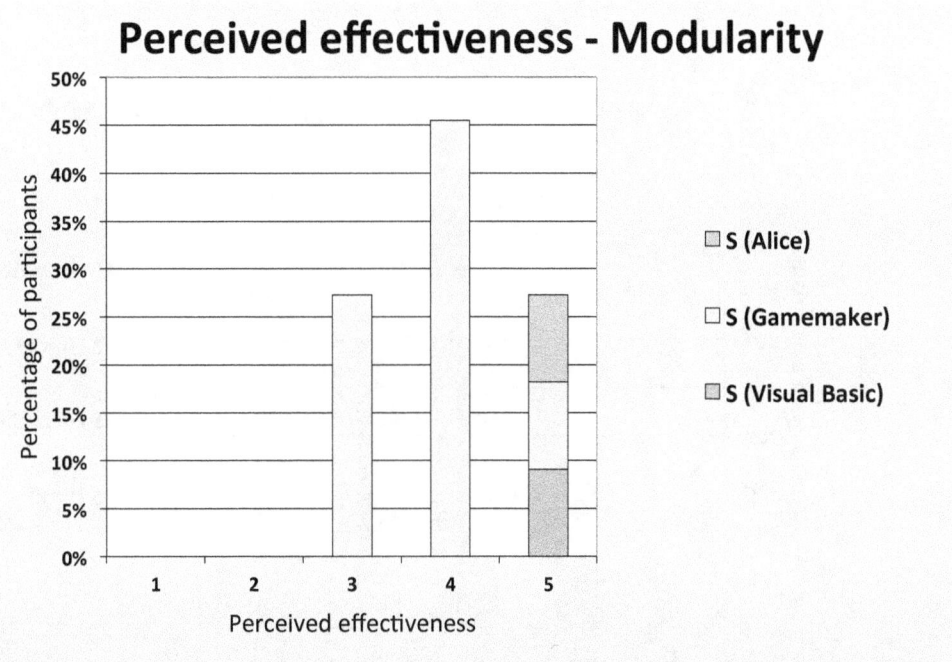

Figure 5.41   Student perception of tool effectiveness in learning - Modularity

b. the second question addressed students perceived' enjoyment (see Figures 5.42 – 5.45) in using the visualisation tool for specific concepts. For the concept of sequence (see Figure 5.42), students perceived that their use of the Alice (CT) visualisation tool was very enjoyable. RoboLab (UI) was considered enjoyable. PHP (UT) was not perceived as enjoyable while Visual Basic (UT) was considered neither enjoyable nor not enjoyable by the small cohort involved. GameMaker (CI) was not used to develop the concept of sequence in this study.

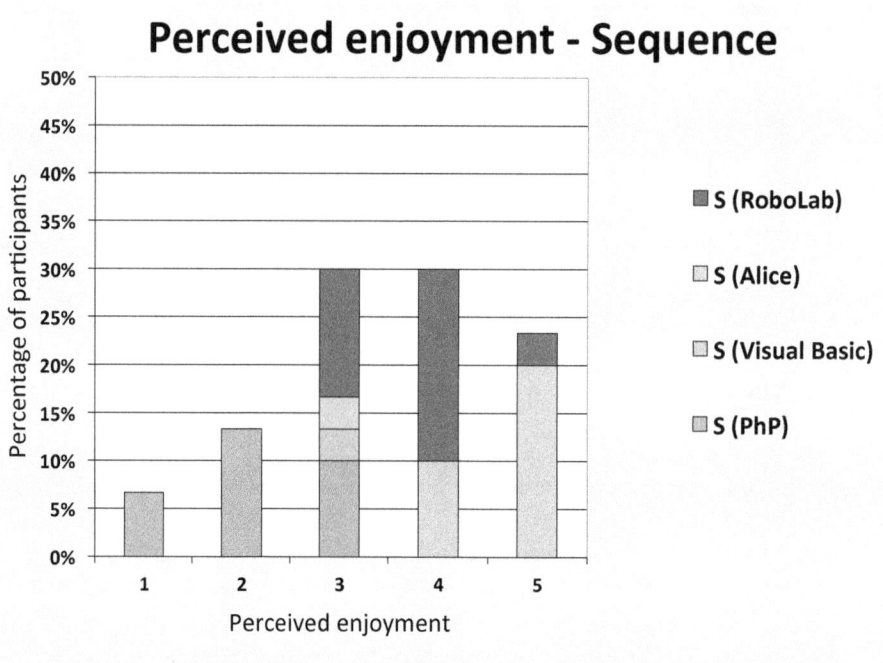

Figure 5.42   Student perception of enjoyment – Sequence

For the concept of iteration (see Figure 5.43), students perceived that using the RoboLab (UI) and Alice (CT) visualisation tools was very enjoyable. The Visual Basic (UT) tool was considered enjoyable. PHP (UT) and GameMaker (CI) were not used to develop the concept of iteration in this study.

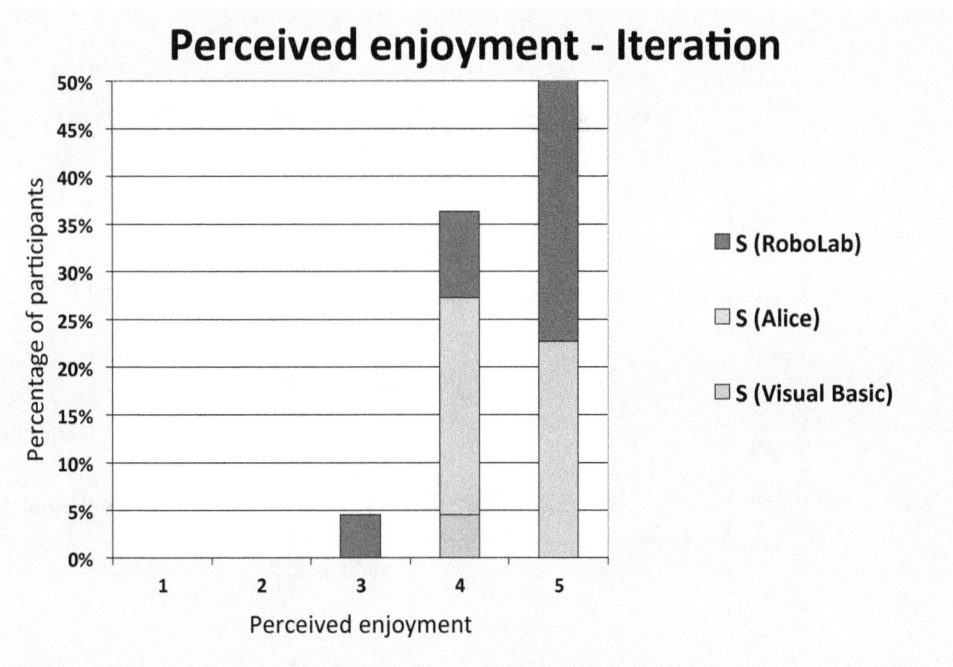

Figure 5.43   Student perception of enjoyment - Iteration

For the concept of selection (see Figure 5.44), students perceived that learning using the RoboLab (UI) visualisation tool was very enjoyable as was Visual Basic (UT). The Alice (CT) tool was considered enjoyable by the small cohort involved as was GameMaker (CI). PHP (UT) was not used to develop the concept of selection in this study.

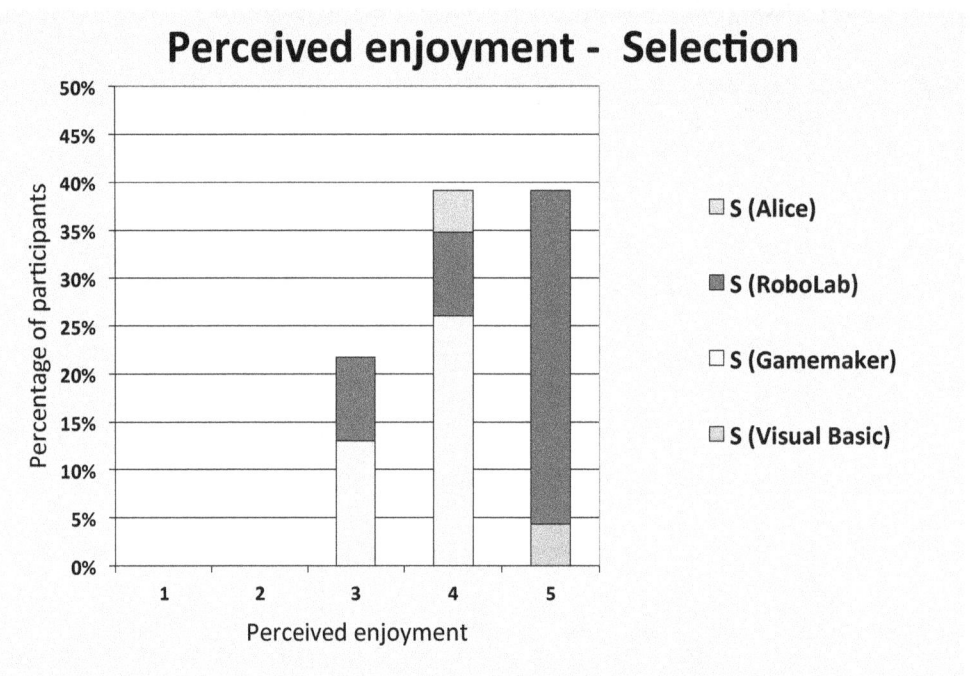

Figure 5.44 Student perception of enjoyment - Selection

For the concept of modularity (see Figure 5.45), the small cohort using Visual Basic (UT) found it enjoyable. The GameMaker (CI) tool received mixed responses and learning the concept of modularity using the Alice (CT) tool was not considered enjoyable. PHP (UT) and Robolab (UI) were not used to develop the concept of modularity in this study.

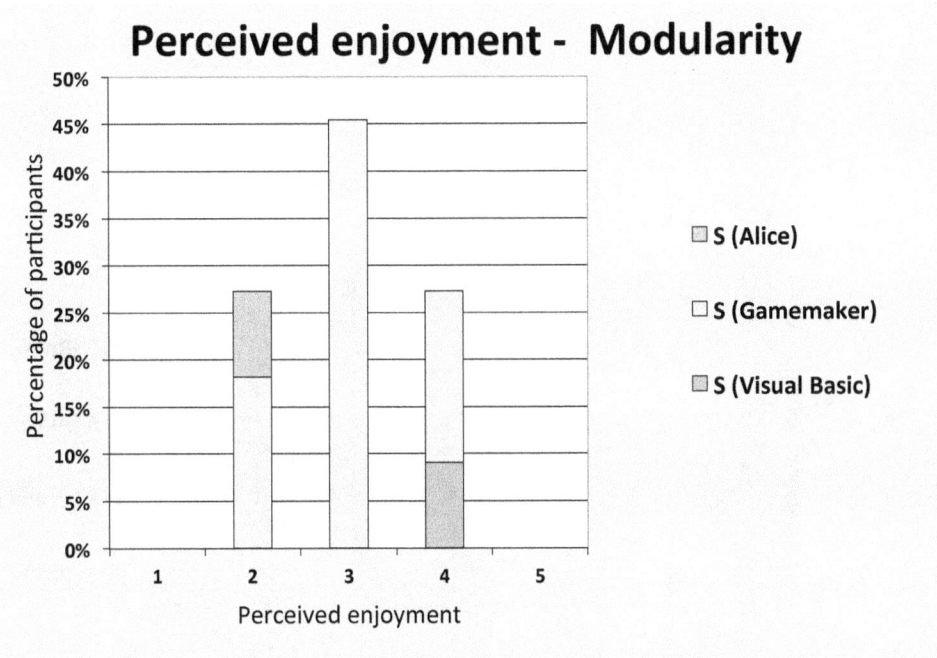

Figure 5.45   Student perception of enjoyment - Modularity

c. the third question addressed student perception on how quickly they learnt the concept using the tool (see Figures 5.46 – 5.49) for specific concepts. For the concept of sequence (see Figure 5.40), students' perceived that their use of the Alice (CT) and RoboLab (UI) assisted in learning the concept more quickly than they would have without using the tool. PHP (UT) was not perceived as assisting by some students while Visual Basic (UT) was considered no more or less effective than not using the tool. GameMaker (CI) was not used to develop the concept of sequence in this study.

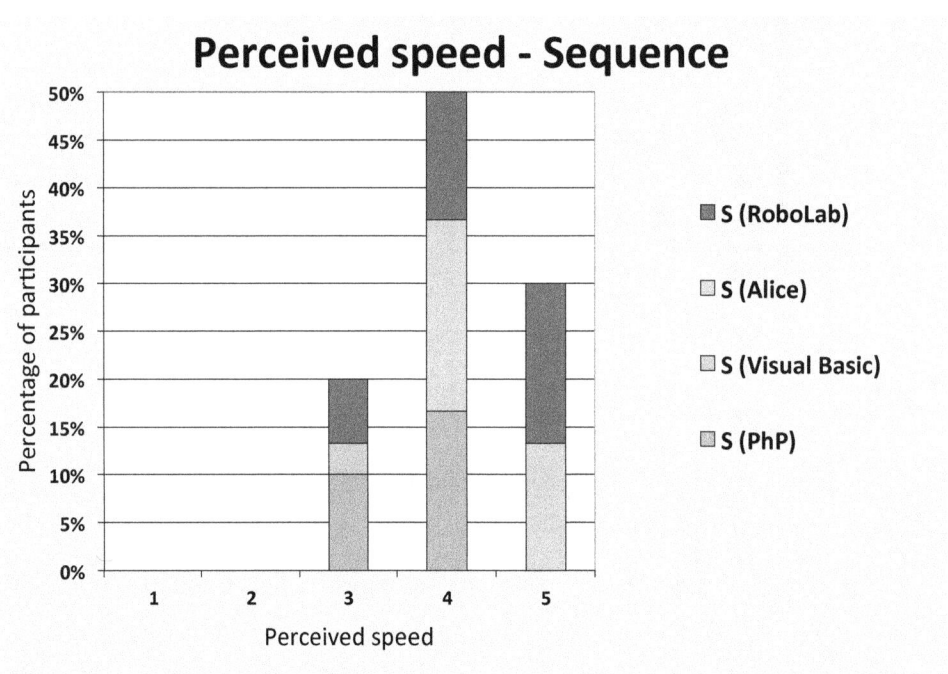

Figure 5.46 Student perception of speed of learning – Sequence

For the concept of iteration (see Figure 5.47), students perceived that using the RoboLab (UI), Alice (CT) and Visual Basic (UT) visualisation tools assisted in learning the concept more quickly. PHP (UT) and GameMaker (CI) were not used to develop the concept of iteration in this study.

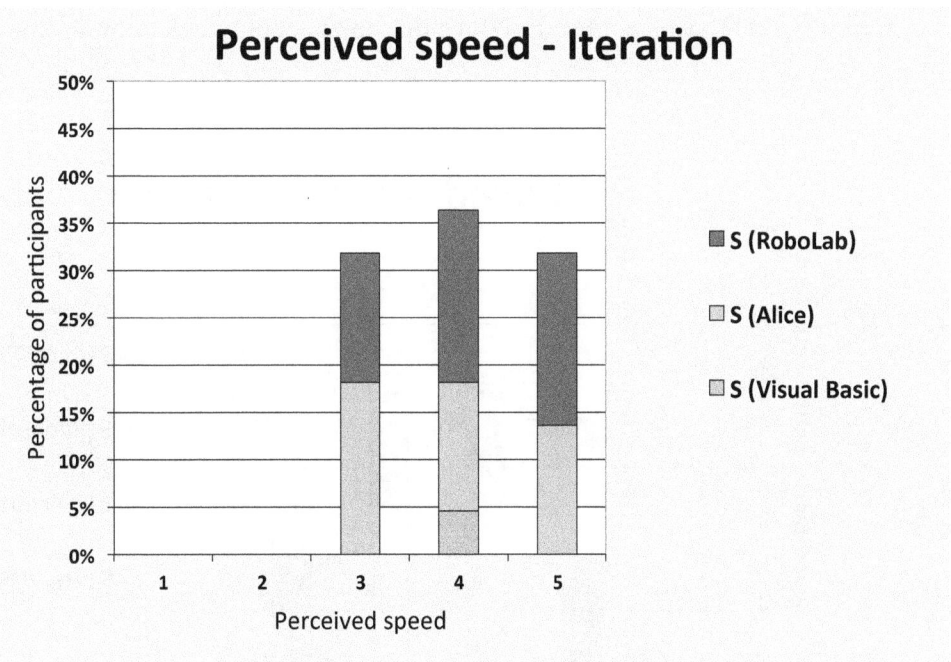

Figure 5.47   Student perception of speed of learning - Iteration

For the concept of selection (see Figure 5.48), students perceived that learning using the Alice (CT) visualisation tool helped them learn the concept very quickly. The RoboLab (UI) and GameMaker (CI) visualisation tools were perceived as assisting them to learn the concept more quickly by slightly more students than perceived they would have learnt the concept less quickly without using the tool. The small cohort using the Visual Basic (UT) perceived no speed advantage from the tool. PHP (UT) was not used to develop the concept of selection in this study.

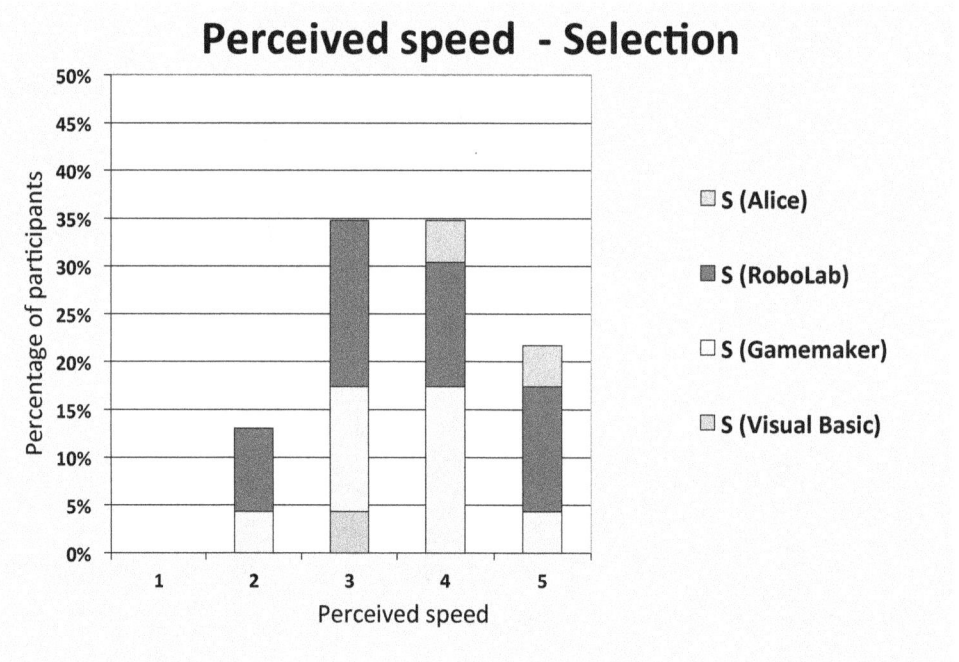

Figure 5.48   Student perception of speed of learning - Selection

For the concept of modularity (see Figure 5.49), the small cohort using Alice (CT) found the tool helped them learn the concept very quickly. The small cohort using Visual Basic (UT) found it helped them learn the concept quickly. The GameMaker (CI) tool received very mixed responses, with equal numbers of students finding it made learning the concept slower, faster than, or just as quickly as they would have otherwise. PHP (UT) and Robolab (UI) were not used to develop the concept of modularity in this study.

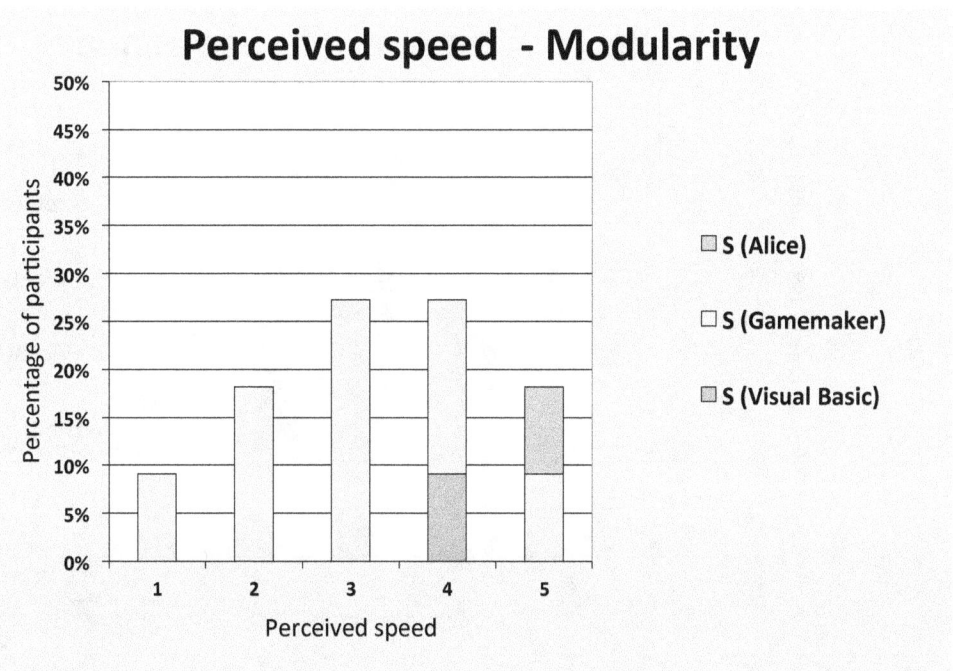

Figure 5.49 Student perception of speed of learning - Modularity

d. an overall scaled ranking of student perceptions is provided by combination of survey responses (see Figures 5.50 to 5.43).

For the concept of sequence (see Figure 5.50), the RoboLab (UI) and Alice (CT) visualisation tools were perceived as the most effective software visualisation tools. Visual Basic (UT) was considered a generally effective tool but PHP (UT) was not perceived by students as an effective tool for the concept of sequence. GameMaker (CI) was not used to develop the concept of sequence in this study.

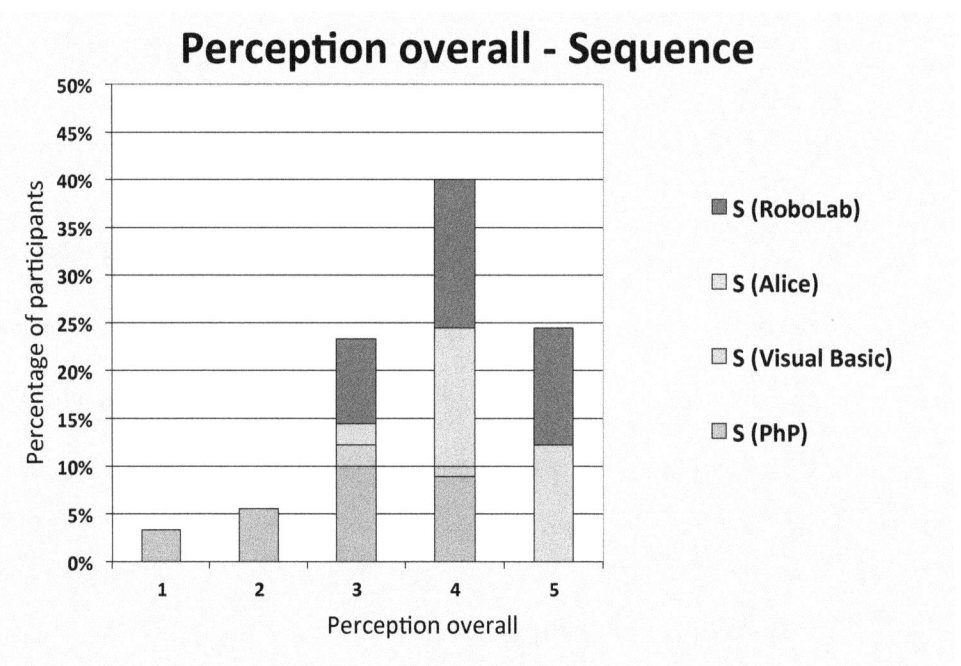

Figure 5.50   Student perception overall – Sequence

For the concept of iteration (see Figure 5.51), the RoboLab (UI) visualisation tool was perceived as a very effective tool. The Alice (CT) tool was considered an effective tool as was Visual Basic (UT). PHP (UT) and GameMaker (CI) were not used to develop the concept of iteration in this study.

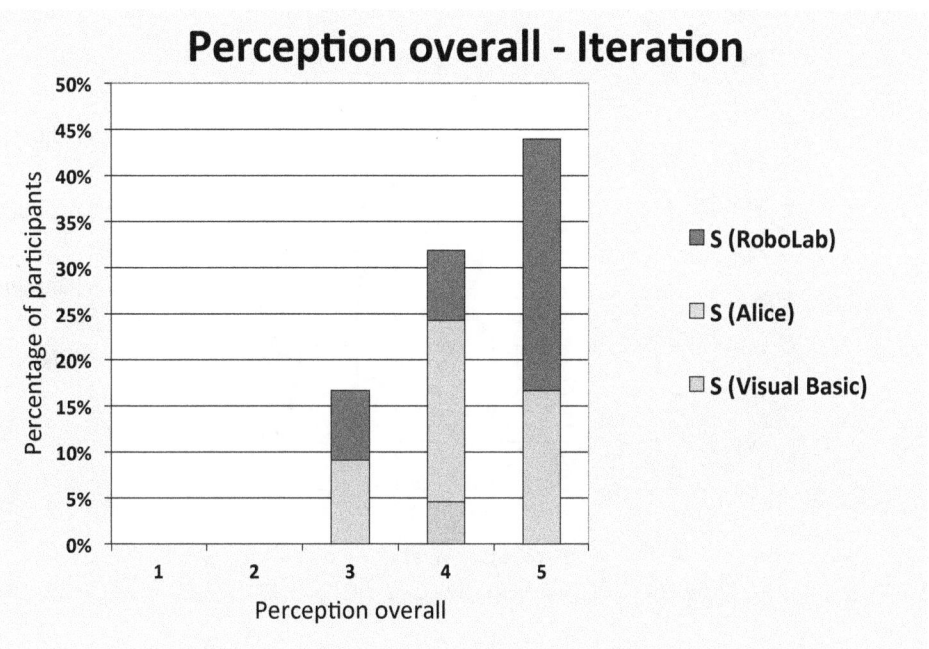

Figure 5.51   Student perception overall - Iteration

For the concept of selection (see Figure 5.52), the RoboLab (UI) visualisation tool was perceived a very effective tool as was the Alice (CT) tool. GameMaker (CI) was considered effective as was Visual Basic (UT). PHP (UT) was not used to develop the concept of selection in this study.

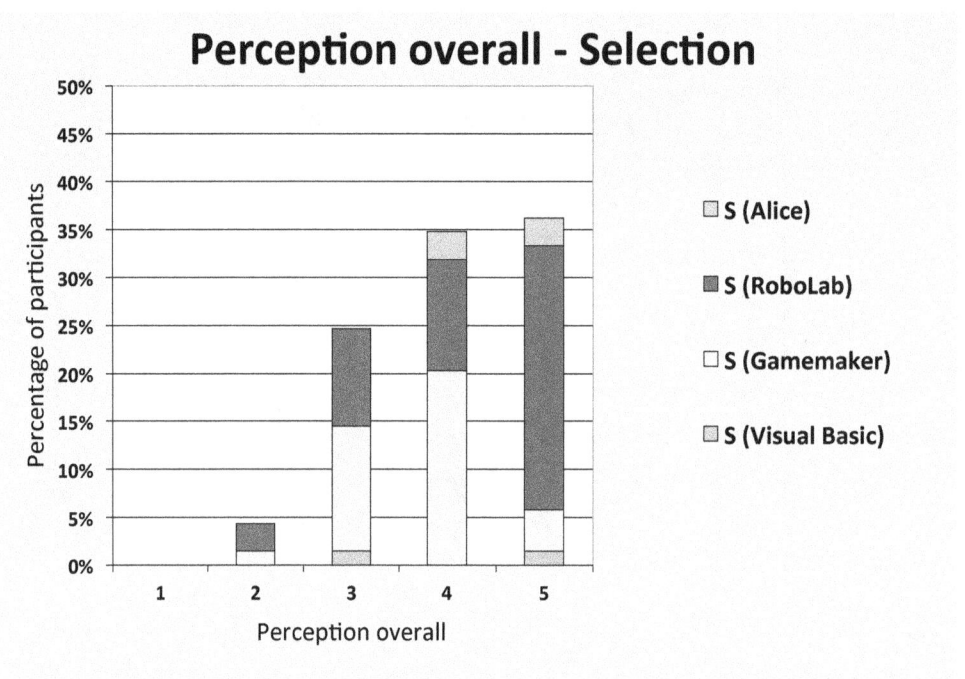

Figure 5.52   Student perception overall - Selection

For the concept of modularity (see Figure 5.53), students' perceived that the Visual Basic (UT) visualisation tool was very effective, Alice (CT) was perceived as helping learn the concept very quickly but was not perceived as enjoyable or particularly effective in developing the concept of modularity. The GameMaker (CI) tool was considered to be an effective tool by some students, but was perceived by others as ineffective or detrimental. PHP (UT) and Robolab (UI) were not used to develop the concept of modularity in this study.

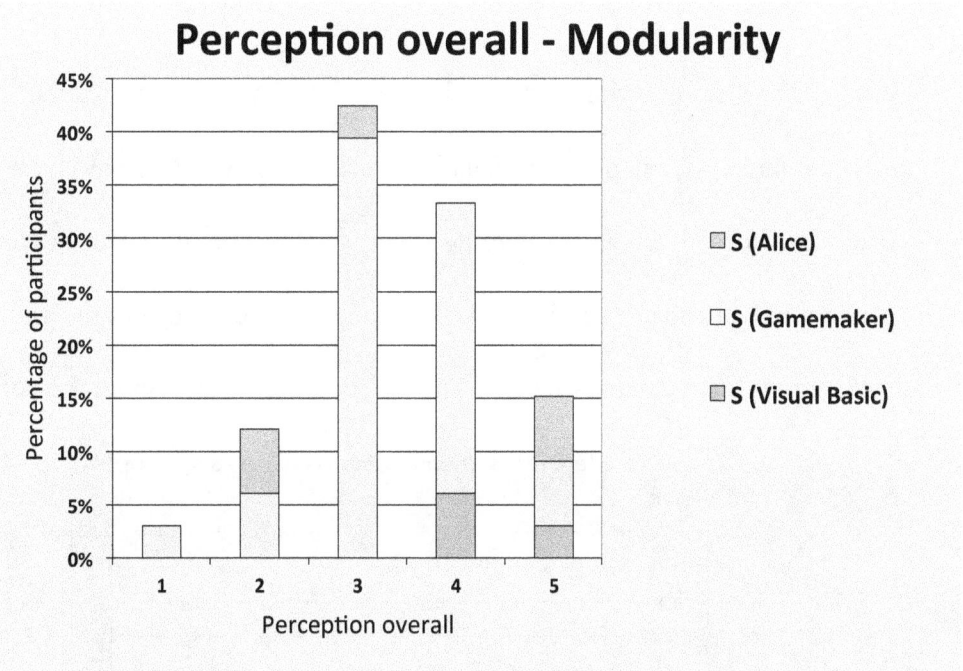

Figure 5.53   Student perception overall - Modularity

5.2.2 Survey 2

Survey 2 was administered to nine students who used more than one visualisation tool (Cohort A). This provided an opportunity to compare students' perceived differences in visualisation tools. Survey 2 provided student perceptions on (a) the difference in effectiveness of the visualisation tool to help them learn the concept, (b) the difference in how enjoyable the tools were to use for that concept, and (c) the difference in how quickly they learnt the concept with each tool. The higher the number on the horizontal axis, the more positive the cohort response is to the visualisation tool 1, GameMaker. The lower the number, the more positive the cohort response is to visualisation tool 2, Alice (Appendices A and B).

a. The first question addressed the students' perceived difference between the effectiveness of Gamemaker (Visualisation Tool 1) over Alice (Visualisation Tool 2) (see Figures 5.54 – 5.57) in helping them to learn about a specific concept. For the concept of sequence (see Figure 5.54), students perceived that the GameMaker (CI) was more effective than Alice (CT) in assisting them learn about the concept.

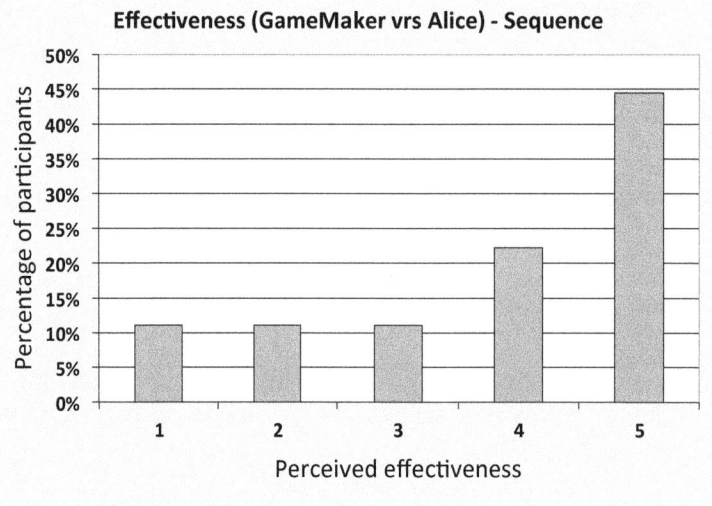

Figure 5.54   Effectiveness of GameMaker over Alice – Sequence

For the concept of iteration (see Figure 5.55), students' perceived that the GameMaker (CI) was much more effective than Alice (CT) in assisting them learn about the concept of iteration.

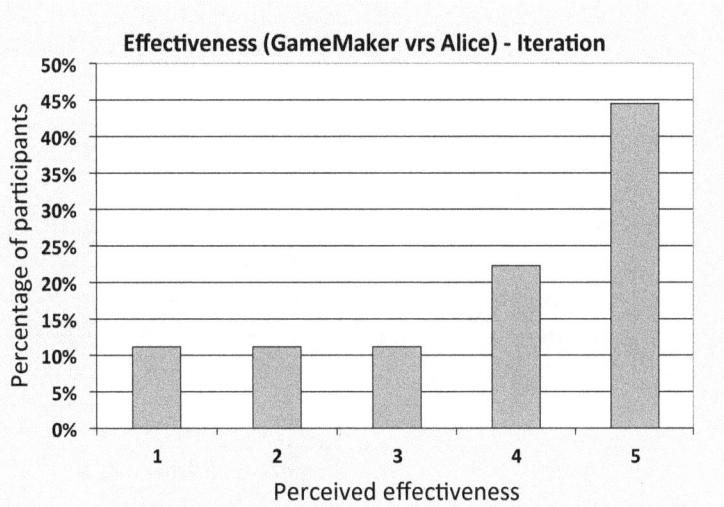

Figure 5.55   Effectiveness of GameMaker over Alice - Iteration

For the concept of selection (see Figure 5.56), students perceived that the GameMaker (CI) was less effective than Alice (CT) in assisting them learn about the concept of selection.

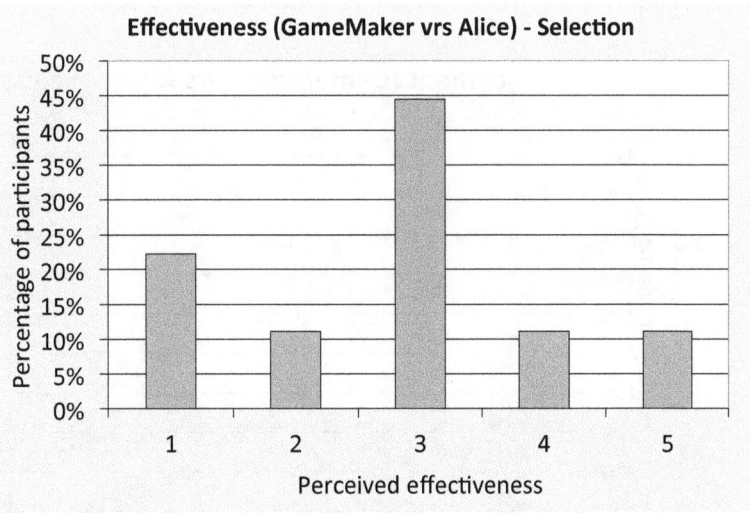

Figure 5.56   Effectiveness of GameMaker over Alice - Selection

For the concept of modularity (see Figure 5.57), students perceived that the GameMaker (CI) was much less effective than Alice (CT) in assisting them learn about the concept of modularity.

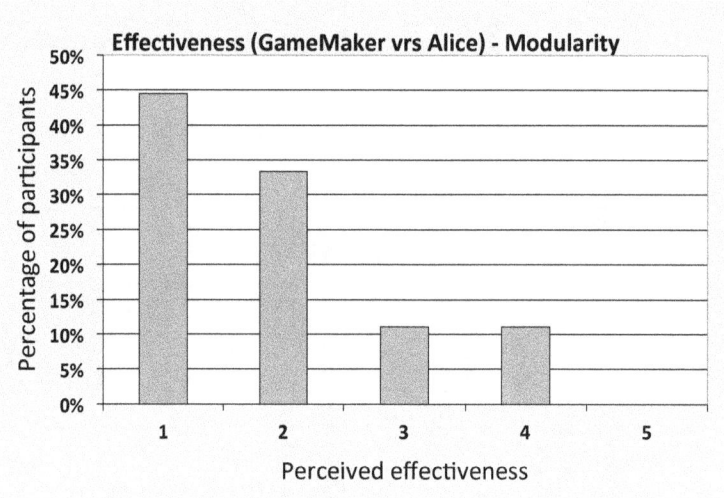

Figure 5.57   Effectiveness of GameMaker over Alice - Modularity

b.   The second question addressed the students perceived enjoyment of GameMaker (Visualisation Tool 1) over Alice (Visualisation Tool 2) (see Figures 5.58 – 5.61). For the concept of sequence (see Figure 5.58), students perceived that the GameMaker (CI) was more enjoyable than Alice (CT).

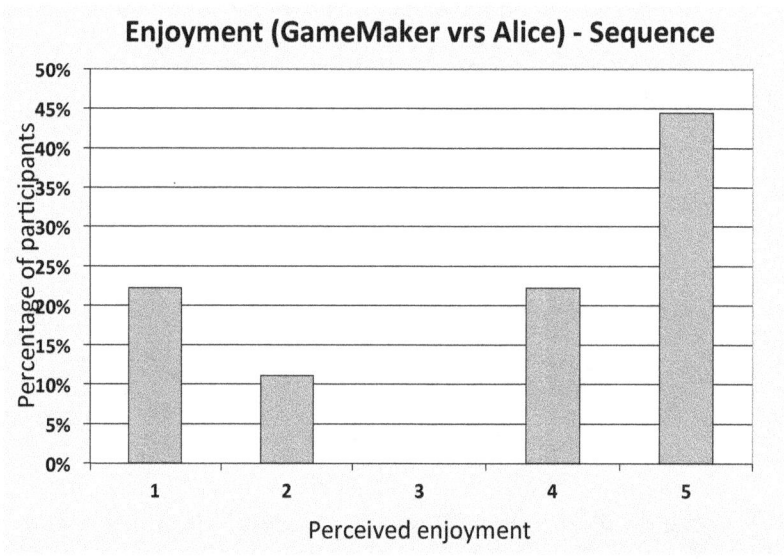

Figure 5.58   Enjoyment of GameMaker over Alice – Sequence

For the concept of iteration (see Figure 5.59), students perceived that the GameMaker (CI) was much more enjoyable than Alice (CT).

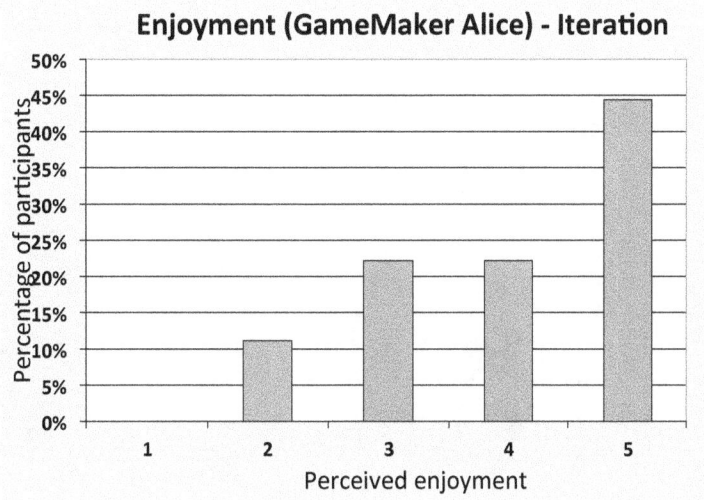

Figure 5.59   Enjoyment of GameMaker over Alice – Iteration

For the concept of selection (see Figure 5.60), students perceived that the GameMaker (CI) was less enjoyable than Alice (CT).

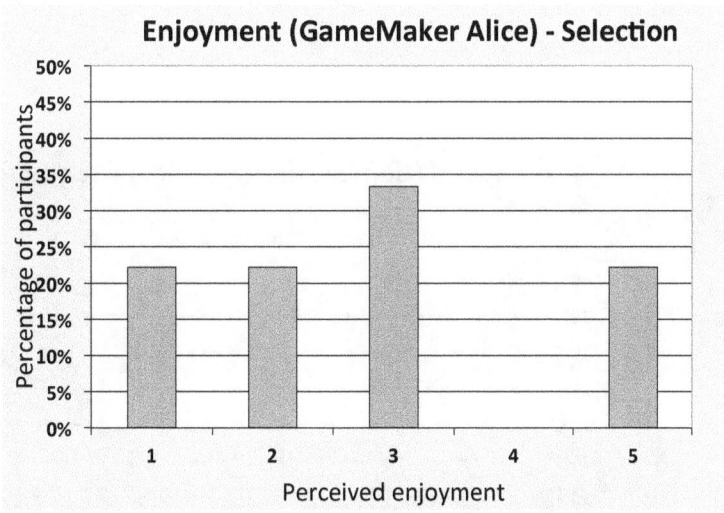

Figure 5.60   Enjoyment of GameMaker over Alice - Selection

For the concept of modularity (see Figure 5.61), students perceived that the GameMaker (CI) was much less enjoyable than Alice (CT).

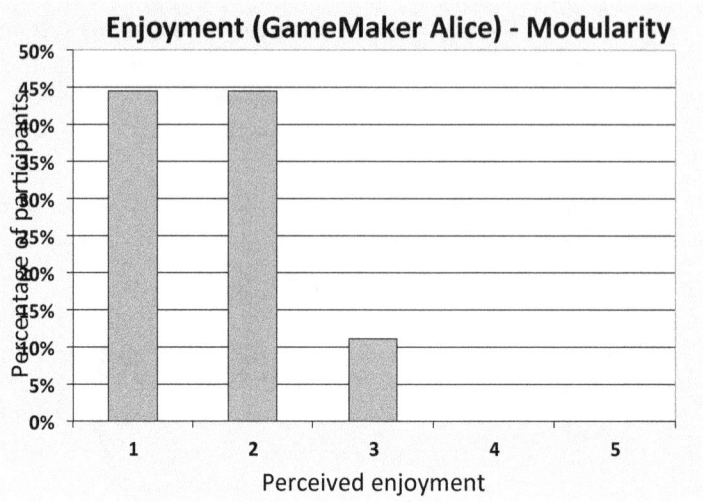

Figure 5.61   Enjoyment of GameMaker over Alice - Modularity

c. The third question addressed student perceived speed of learning GameMaker (Visualisation Tool 1) over Alice (Visualisation Tool 2) (see Figures 5.62 – 5.65). For the concept of sequence (see Figure 5.62), students perceived that the GameMaker (CI) was quicker to learn with than Alice (CT).

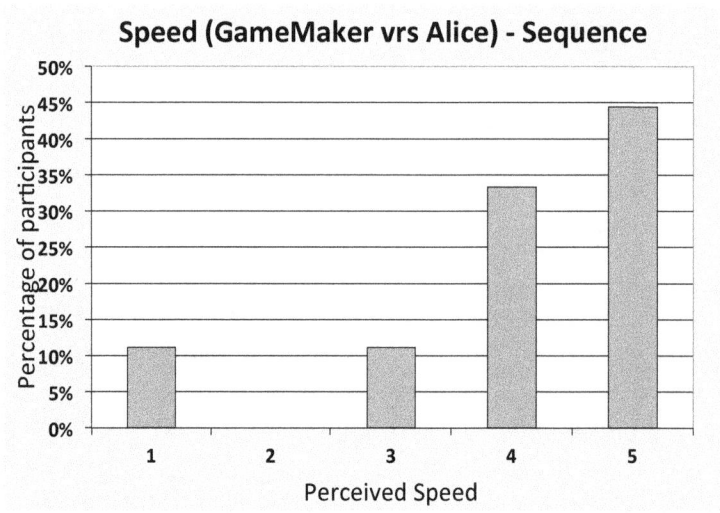

Figure 5.62   Learning speed of GameMaker over Alice – Sequence

For the concept of iteration (see Figure 5.63), students' perceived that the GameMaker (CI) was much quicker to learn with than Alice (CT).

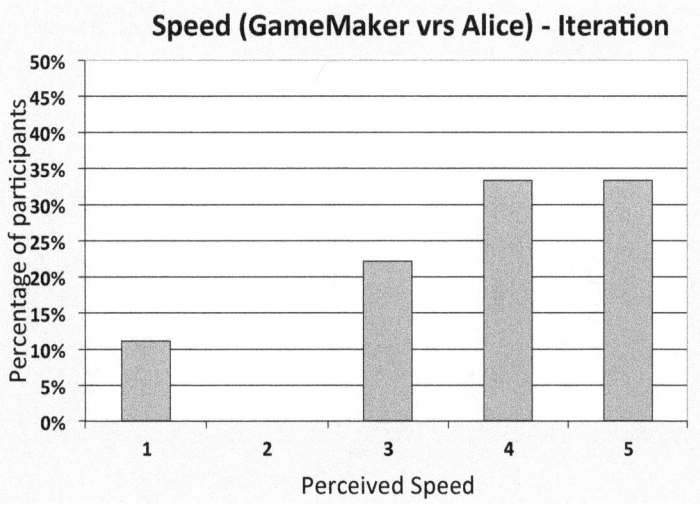

Figure 5.63 Learning speed of GameMaker over Alice - Iteration

For the concept of selection (see Figure 5.64), students perceived that the GameMaker (CI) was slower to learn with than Alice (CT).

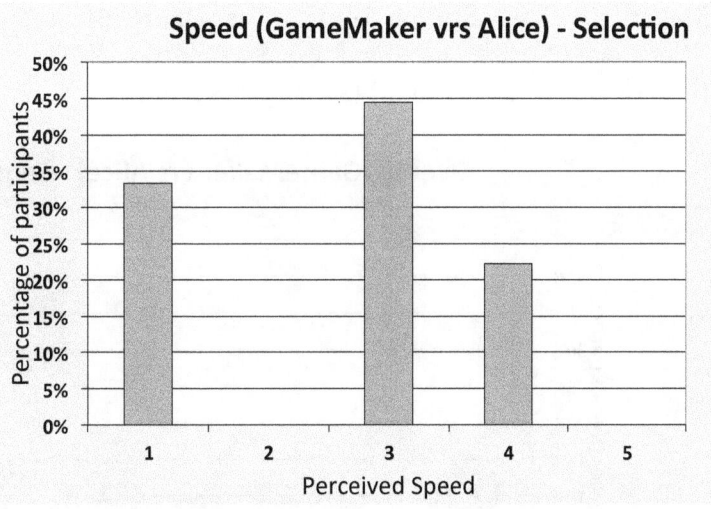

Figure 5.64 Learning speed of GameMaker over Alice - Selection

For the concept of modularity (see Figure 5.65), students perceived that the GameMaker (CI) was much slower to learn with than Alice (CT).

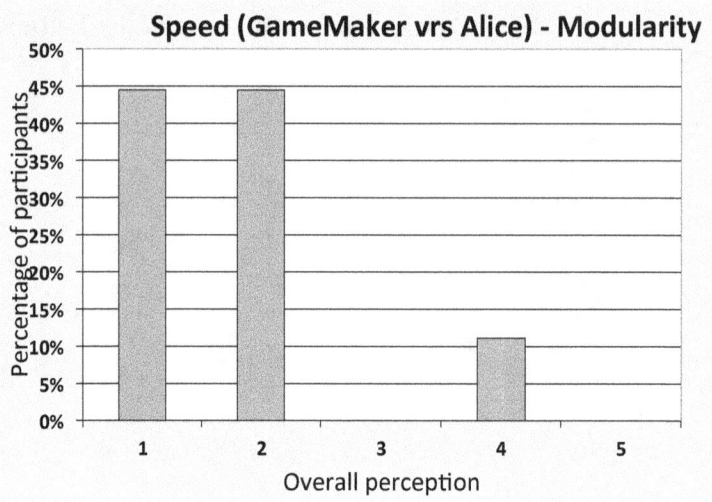

Figure 5.65   Learning speed of GameMaker over Alice - Modularity

d.   Student perceived overall effectiveness of GameMaker (Visualisation Tool 1) over Alice (Visualisation Tool 2) was produced by averaging survey responses (see Figures 5.66 to 5.70). For the concept of sequence, students perceived that overall, GameMaker (CI) (Visualisation Tool 1) was a more effective visualisation tool than Alice (CT) (Visualisation Tool 2) (see Figures 5.66).

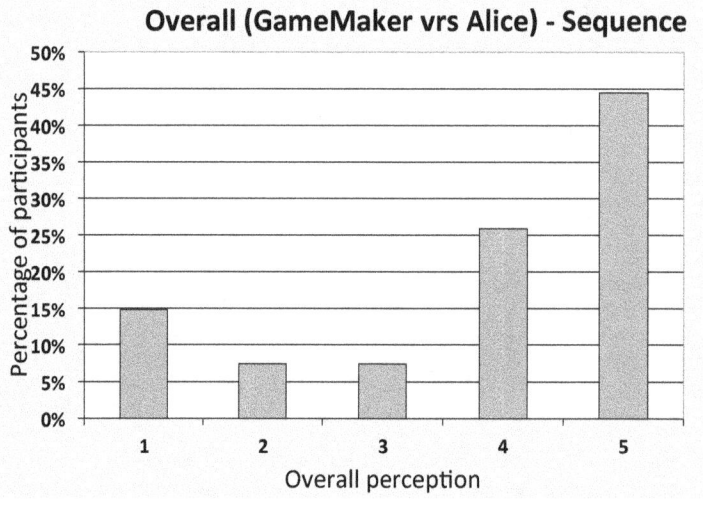

Figure 5.66   Overall effectiveness of GameMaker over Alice – Sequence

For the concept of iteration, students perceived that overall, GameMaker (CI) (Visualisation Tool 1) was a much more effective visualisation tool than Alice (CT) (Visualisation Tool 2) (see Figures 5.67).

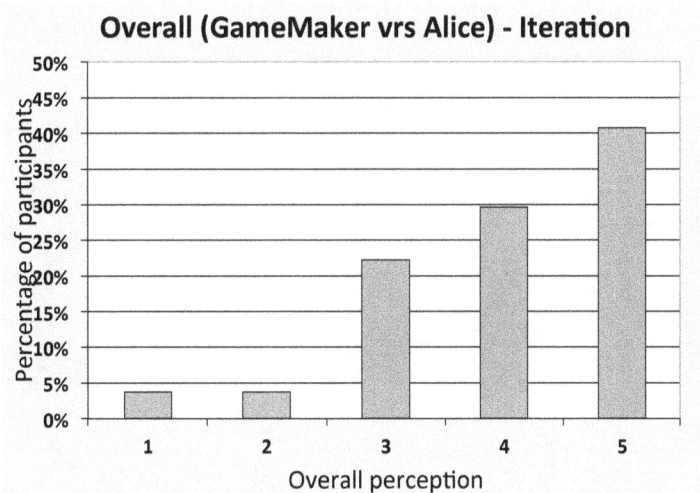

Figure 5.67   Overall effectiveness of GameMaker over Alice - Iteration

For the concept of iteration, students perceived that overall, GameMaker (CI) (Visualisation Tool 1) was a less effective visualisation tool than Alice (CT) (Visualisation Tool 2) (see Figures 5.68).

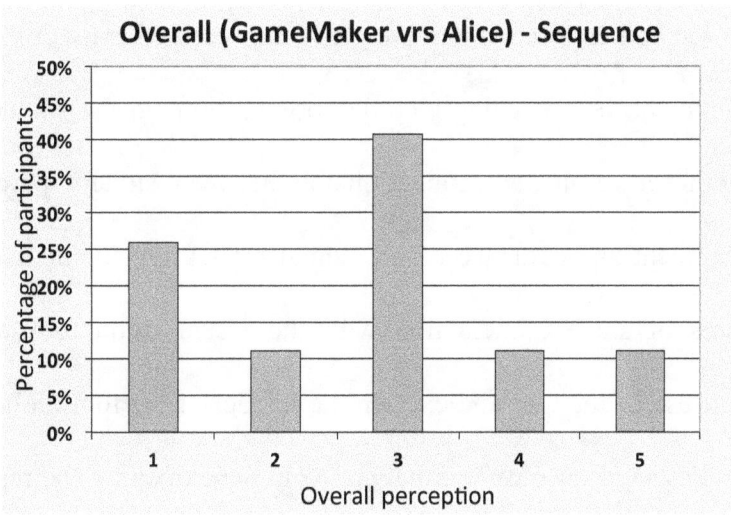

Figure 5.68   Overall effectiveness of GameMaker over Alice - Selection

For the concept of modularity, students perceived that overall, GameMaker (CI) (Visualisation Tool 1) was a much less effective visualisation tool than Alice (CT) (Visualisation Tool 2) (see Figures 5.69).

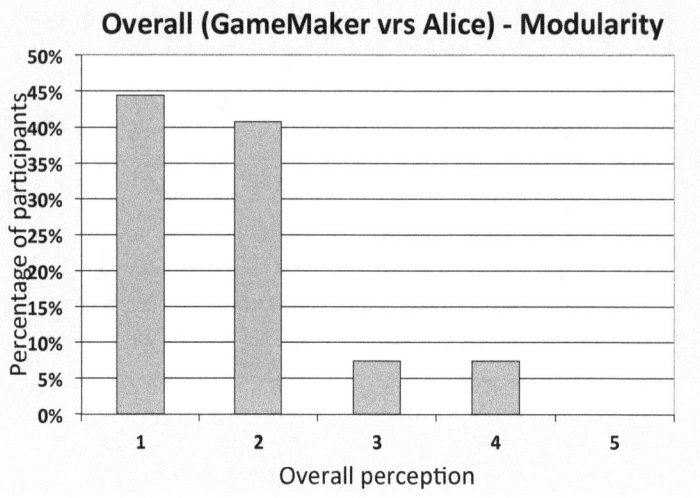

Figure 5.69   Overall effectiveness of GameMaker over Alice - Modularity

5.3   Mental Model Traces

Selected students (*n*=20) were interviewed and mental model development traces verified. Stimulated recall interviews used speak-aloud and peer discussion from video recordings to collaboratively develop verified traces of student mental model development. By matching recorded observations to the student recorded trace and problem set results, a detailed match between student perceived mental model development and evidence based mental model development was achieved. Screen captures of student interaction with the visualisation tool was used to describe student use of the tool and explain the impact of the tool on her learning processes. The following traces were collaboratively developed by the researcher and subjects, with each point discussed and verified by available evidence. While scaled measurements (see Section 5.1) were used in discussions, these formed only one factor in determining trace placements. In all cases, however, agreement of traces was achieved and matched the evidence provided by scaled measurements.

Figures 5.70 to 5.91 trace student mental model development for each concept studied. The traces have been scaled to the same five point scale as used to graph concept development by individual students. In each case, the higher the number, the more effective the student was at developing that level of her mental model. Mental model development for each concept is traced in a different quarter of the radar graph. For each concept, trace points are recorded for each mental model level 1 to 8 (Pirie & Kieren, 1992). The resulting radar graphs provide comparative traces of the concepts developed by the student. Each trace includes selected comments related to points drawn from the trace in Chapters 6 and 7. Comments were recorded by students in their student journals (see Section 4.3.3.5) or transcribed from speak aloud, peer discussion or stimulated recall interviews (see Chapter 4) (see Section 4.9.4 for an explanation of how to interpret radar plot graphs).

The following collective trace (see Figure 5.70) records traces for all twenty of the students selected for trace development. The collective trace radar graph (see Section 4.9.4) provides a comparative overview of mental model development for these students. In particular it highlights the difficulties students overall experienced with the selection and modularity concepts, and the similarities in response spreads for the four concepts.

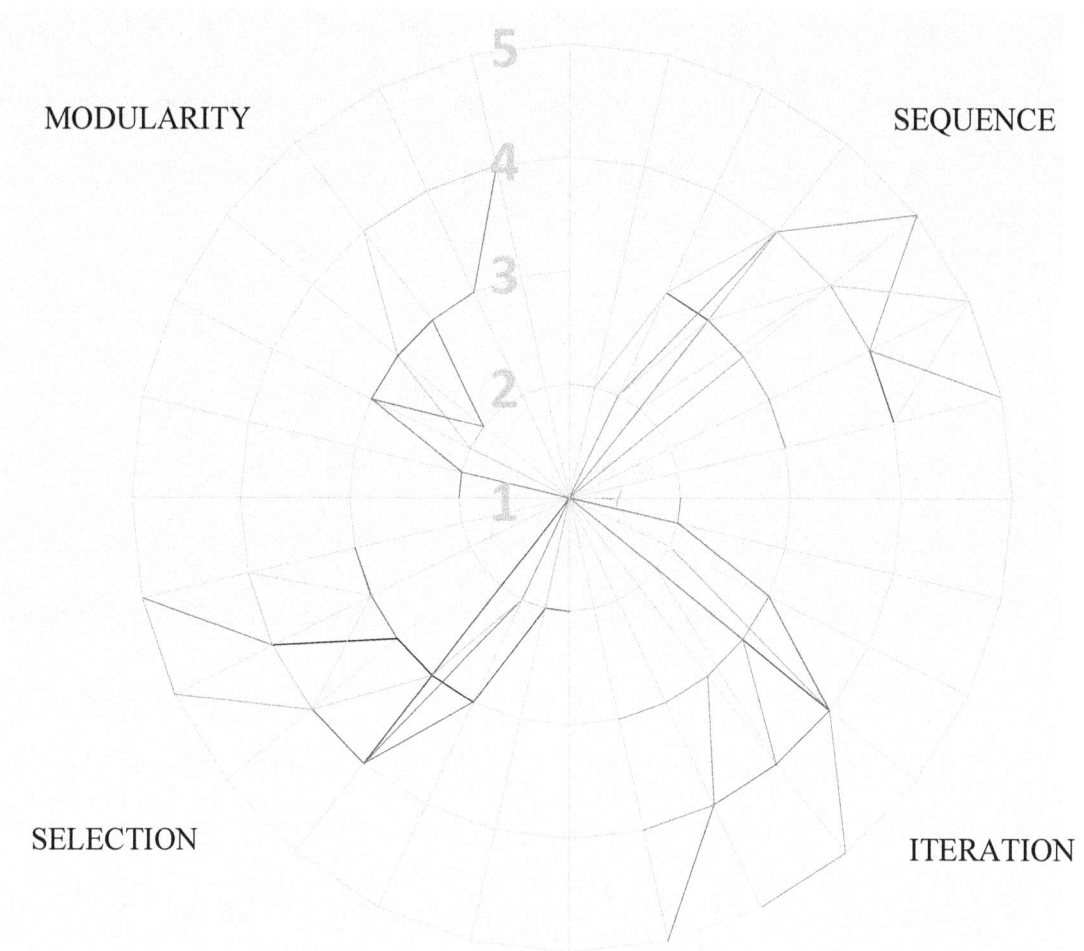

Figure 5.70   Collective Trace

5.3.1   Student A1a

During the study student A1a developed mental models of four concepts (sequence, iteration, selection and modularity). She studied sequence and iteration using a Constrained Text visualisation tool (*Alice*) and selection and modularity using a Constrained Icon visualisation tool (*GameMaker*). Her cognitive development is summarised in Section 5.1.1.1 and Figure 5.71 shows her concept development traces.

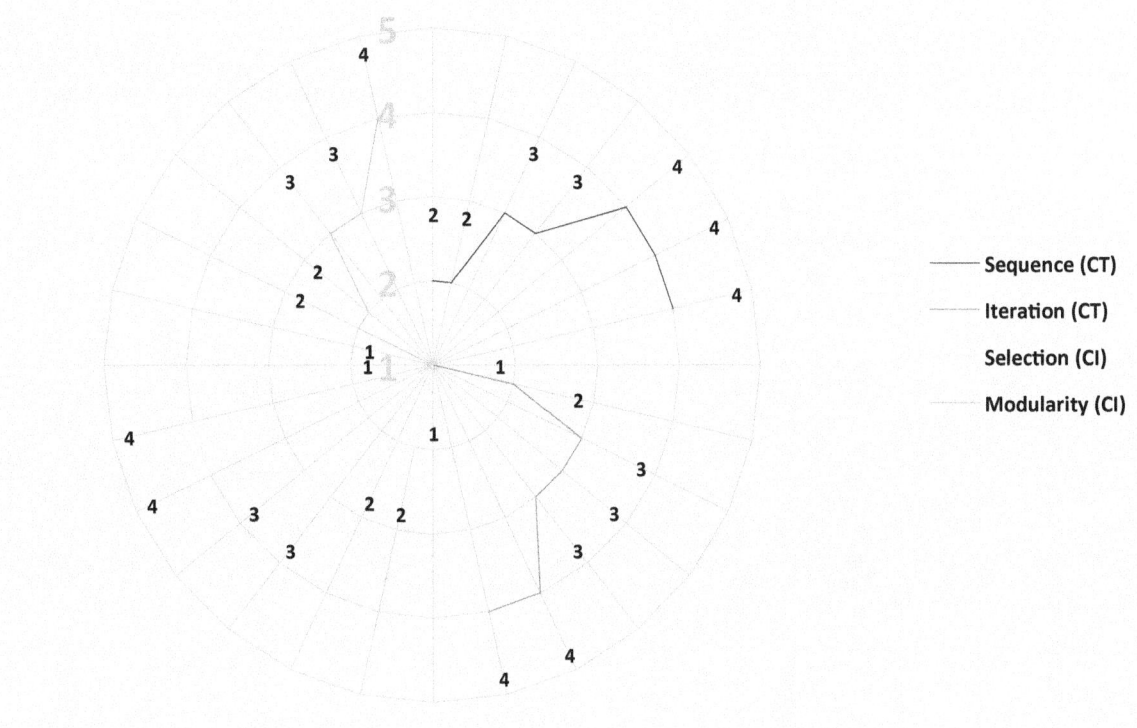

Figure 5.71   Student A1a Trace

Selected comments:

"I liked storyboarding, it helped me understand what was going to happen and when." (sequence, Level 2)

"Thinking about all of the different options there were in letting the program make selections was hard to keep in my head all at once." (selection, Level 4)

"Putting everything into a flowchart helped me understand what bits would run when and how they would effect each other, it was hard trying to remember all this and drawing it helped." (modularity, Level 7)

5.3.2   Student A2b

During the study student A2b developed mental models of four concepts (sequence, iteration, selection and modularity). She studied sequence and iteration using a Constrained Text visualisation tool (*Alice*) and selection and modularity using a Constrained Icon visualisation tool (*GameMaker*). Her cognitive development is summarised in Section 5.1.1.4 and Figure 5.72 shows her concept development traces.

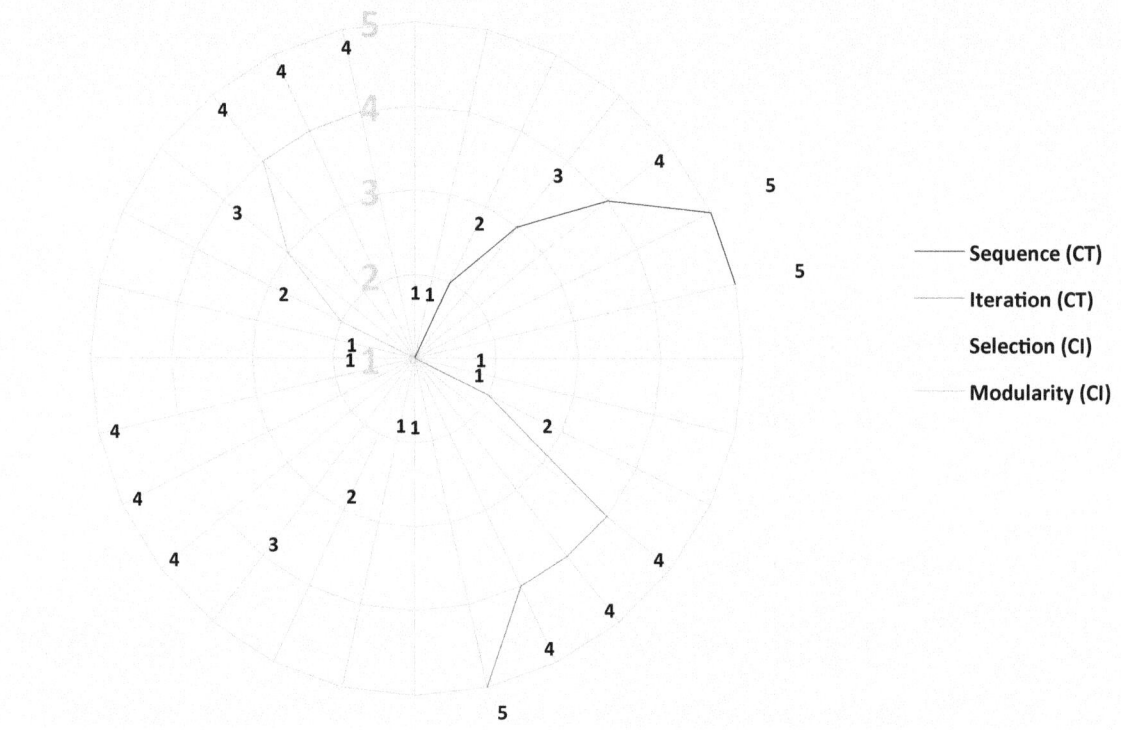

Figure 5.72   Student A2b Trace

Selected comments:

"I found it difficult to solve problems without examples. I can do them when I know what to do, but working out how to do problems I haven't done before is hard for me." (modularity, Level 5)

5.3.3 Student A3a

During the study student A3a developed mental models of four concepts (sequence, iteration, selection and modularity). She studied sequence and iteration using a Constrained Text visualisation tool (*Alice*) and selection and modularity using a Constrained Icon visualisation tool (*GameMaker*). Her cognitive development is summarised in Section 5.1.1.5. She was also one of nine students included as a narrative (*Sam*, Section 6.2). Figure 5.73 shows her concept development traces.

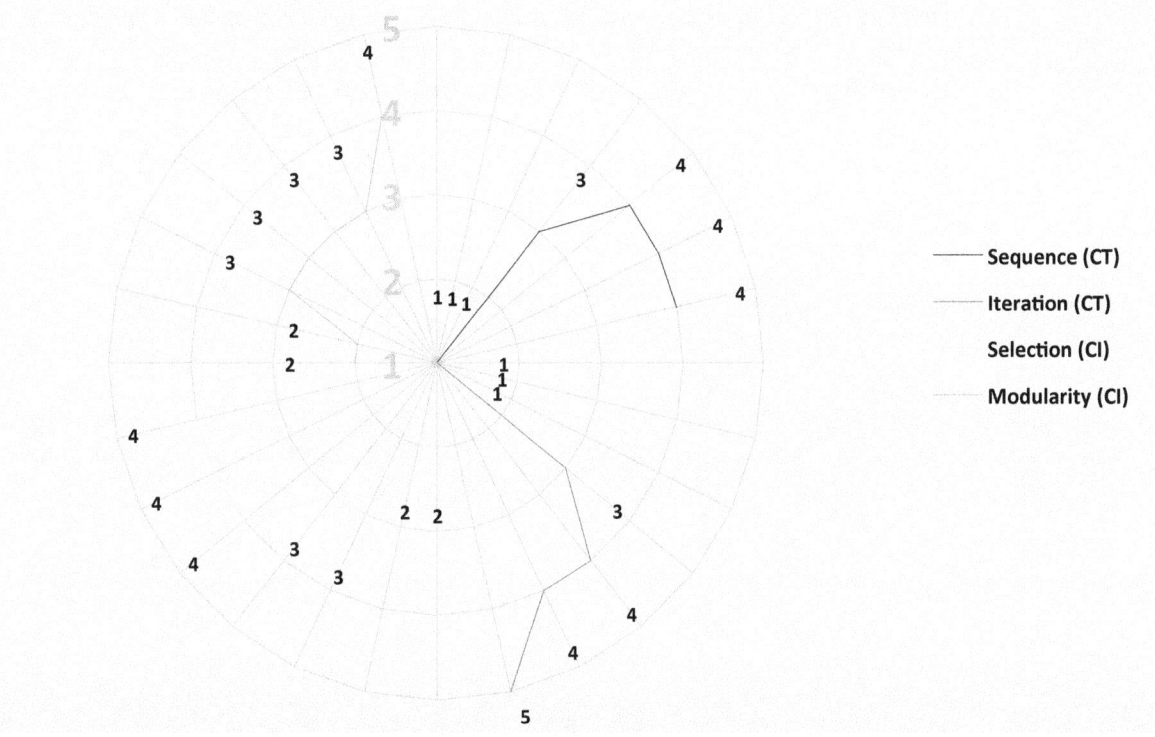

Figure 5.73   Student A3a Trace

Selected comments:

"Mental storyboarding was harder that drawing a storyboard at first, but once I knew how to do it, it was much quicker and easier than drawing it and I could make changes without having to draw it again." (selection, Level 5)

"Coming up with new ideas is hard, you have to think through everything you know and try and work out what you don't know." (modularity, Level 8)

"...ignored the commands and used the pictures to think about how the program would work, I arranged them in groups so they could work as a module or go off down different paths depending on which choice the player makes." (modularity, Level 8)

5.3.4 Student A4a

During the study student A4a developed mental models of four concepts (sequence, iteration, selection and modularity). She studied sequence and iteration using a Constrained Text visualisation tool (*Alice*) and selection and modularity using a Constrained Icon visualisation tool (*GameMaker*). Her cognitive development is summarised in Section 5.1.1.7 and Figure 5.74 shows her concept development traces.

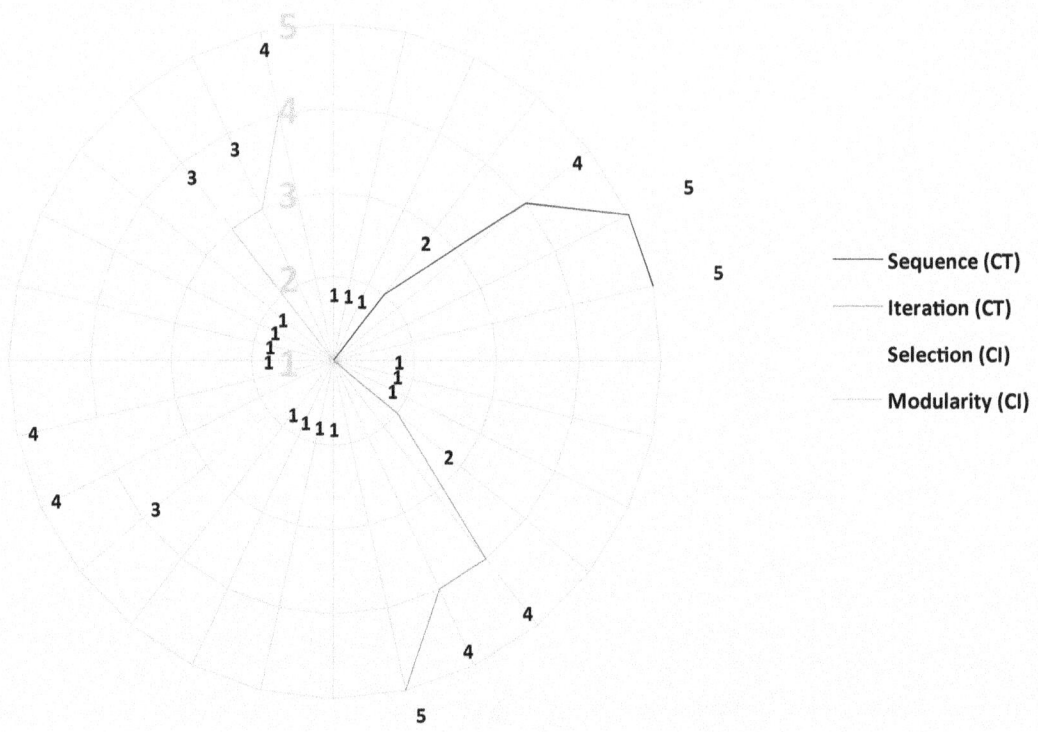

Figure 5.74   Student A4a Trace

Selected comments:

"It was hard to think about lots of different things at once and work out which was the best answer". (iteration, Level 5)

"It was hard to work out what to do when I hadn't seen how to do it before. Working it out for myself was hard." (sequence, Level 6)

"It was easier to do the hard problems using GameMaker, I could understand more how to come up with different ways of solving them." (modularity, Level 6)

"Thinking through the problem and explaining it was easier with GameMaker. It let me see what was happening, Alice was a lot of fun but it was harder to work things out." (modularity, Level 7)

5.3.5 Student A4c

During the study student A4c developed mental models of four concepts (sequence, iteration, selection and modularity). She studied sequence and iteration using a Constrained Text visualisation tool (*Alice*) and selection and modularity using a Constrained Icon visualisation tool (*GameMaker*). Her cognitive development is summarised in Section 5.1.1.9. She was also one of nine students included as a narrative (*Frodo*, Section 6.1). Figure 5.75 shows her concept development traces.

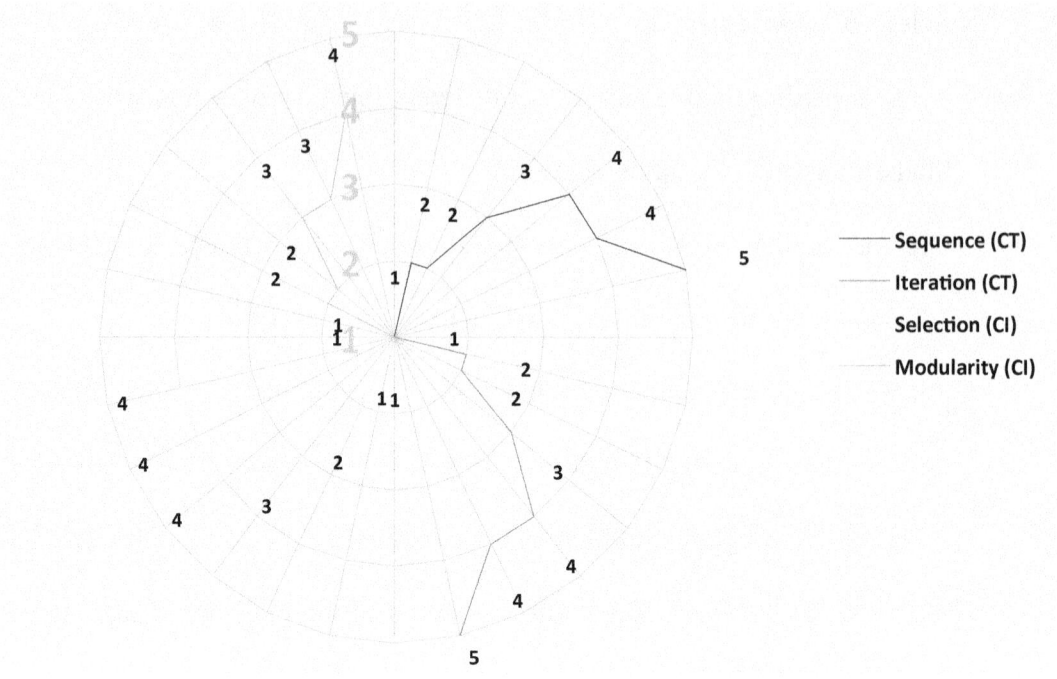

Figure 5.75   Student A4c Trace

Selected comments:

"When I had to not use drawings, I could think through the steps by seeing the drawing in my head. It was easier using Alice as I could then see the Alice screen and my head." (iteration, Level 3)

"I was stuck here and could not think it through so I worked it out on paper – this was folding back?" (sequence, Level 3)

"Sometimes I would just try out lots of ideas on the computer until I got one that worked. Then I worked it out on paper." (selection, Level 4)

"When doing the flowcharts, I remembered back to how I made the storyboard and thought through the steps that we used then" (iteration, Level 6)

"When I finished all the problems for level five I had problems with doing the ones we hadn't done before. You had to think a lot more about how they would work." (selection, Level 6)

"It was easy to make flowcharts, you could just turn your storyboard so that they went down instead of across." (sequence, Level 5)

"I got stuck trying to do my flowchart. I couldn't work out how to show my loops. They work on the computer but kept getting messed up on paper." (iteration, Level 8)

"It was easier to explain how things worked using GameMaker. It made things easier to understand and explain because I could see how it worked on screen." (modularity, Level 8)

5.3.6 Student B1b

During the study student B1b developed mental models of three concepts (sequence, iteration and selection). She studied all three using an Unconstrained Icon visualisation tool (*Robolab*). Her cognitive development is summarised in Section 5.71. She was also one of nine students included as a narrative (*Gimli*, Section 6.4). Figure 5.1.2.2 shows her concept development traces.

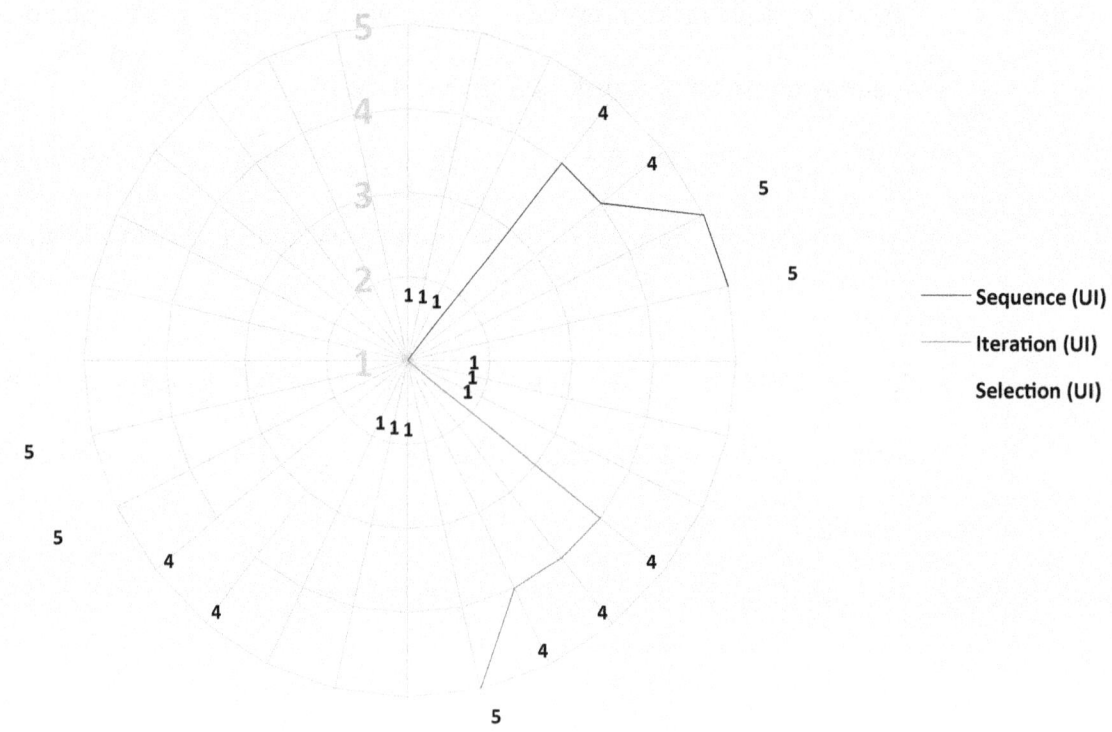

Figure 5.76   Student B1b Trace

Selected comments:

"It is easy to draw flowcharts by making them the same as on RoboLab. I could find mistakes by seeing where the mistakes were in RoboLab." (iteration, Level 4)

"Loops within loops was confusing, it was hard to remember what was happening." (iteration, Level 5)

"I had some problems with the harder problems, I could get some correct answers but I wasn't sure why." (selection, Level 6)

"Could not get my animations to work together. One would always start slow or too quickly or not start or not stop." (sequence, Level 6)

"[another student] was able to help me solve some problems but I still couldn't explain how to solve them." (selection, Level 8)

"Folding back did not help much – I was still stuck until Mr Z [Researcher] gave me more problems to do." (iteration, Level 8)

5.3.7 Student B2a

During the study student B2a developed mental models of three concepts (sequence, iteration and selection). She studied all three using an Unconstrained Icon visualisation tool (*Robolab*). Her cognitive development is summarised in Section 5.1.2.3 and Figure 5.77 shows her concept development traces.

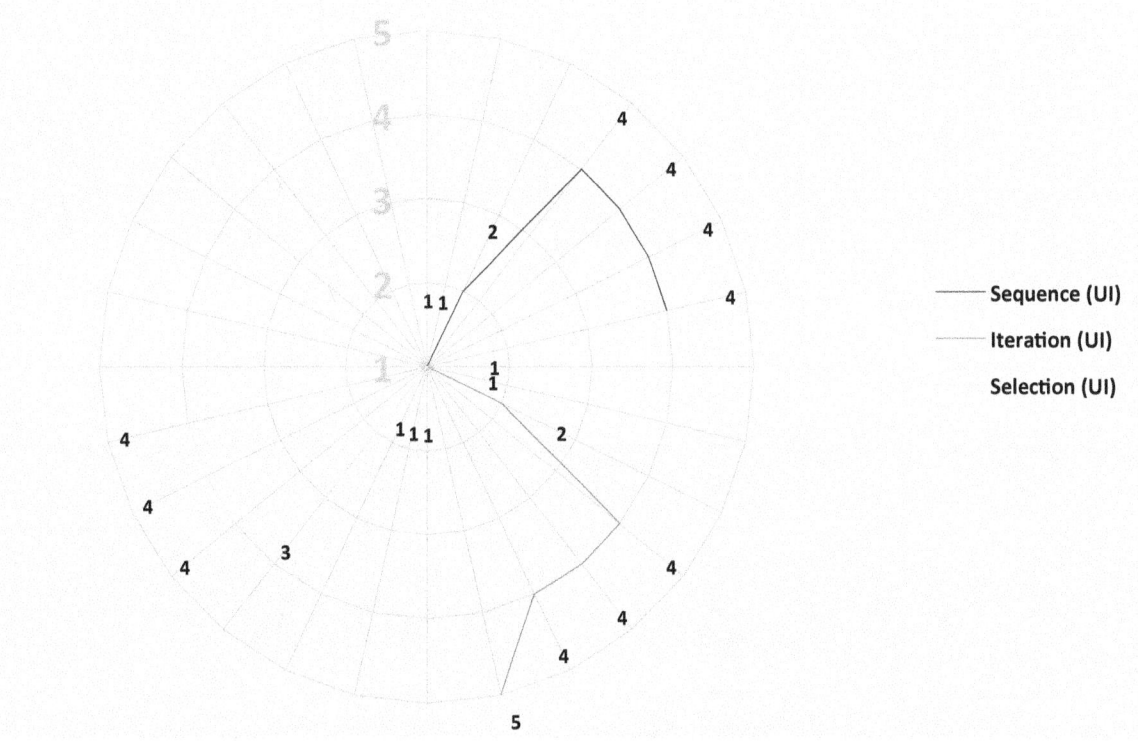

Figure 5.77   Student B2a Trace

Selected comments:

"Doing things without putting them down on paper first really made me think about what I was doing." (sequence, Level 5)

"Having to work things out in my head and then explain it helped me learn about RoboLab. Just doing it, I would just do it and not think about why it was the right thing to do." (iteration, Level 5)

5.3.8 Student B2b

During the study student B2b developed mental models of three concepts (sequence, iteration and selection). She studied all three using an Unconstrained Icon visualisation tool (*RoboLab*). Her cognitive development is summarised in Section 5.1.2.4 and Figure 5.78 shows her concept development traces.

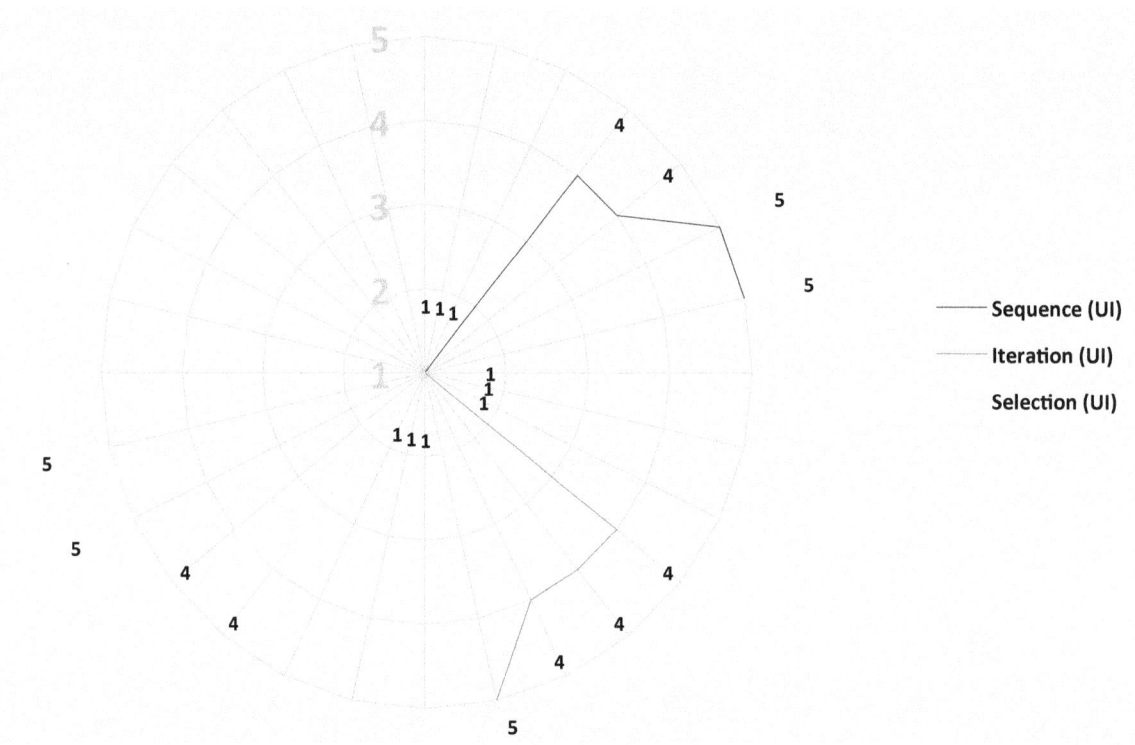

Figure 5.78   Student B2b Trace

Selected comments:

"Doing the mental model was good but when I was stuck it didn't help me much. I still couldn't work out how to do the problems." (iteration, Level 5)

"I tried to do easier problems but this didn't help." (selection, Level 5)

5.3.9 Student B3a

During the study student B3a developed mental models of three concepts (sequence, iteration and selection). She studied all three using an Unconstrained Icon visualisation tool (*RoboLab*). Her cognitive development is summarised in Section 5.1.2.5 and Figure 5.79 shows her concept development traces.

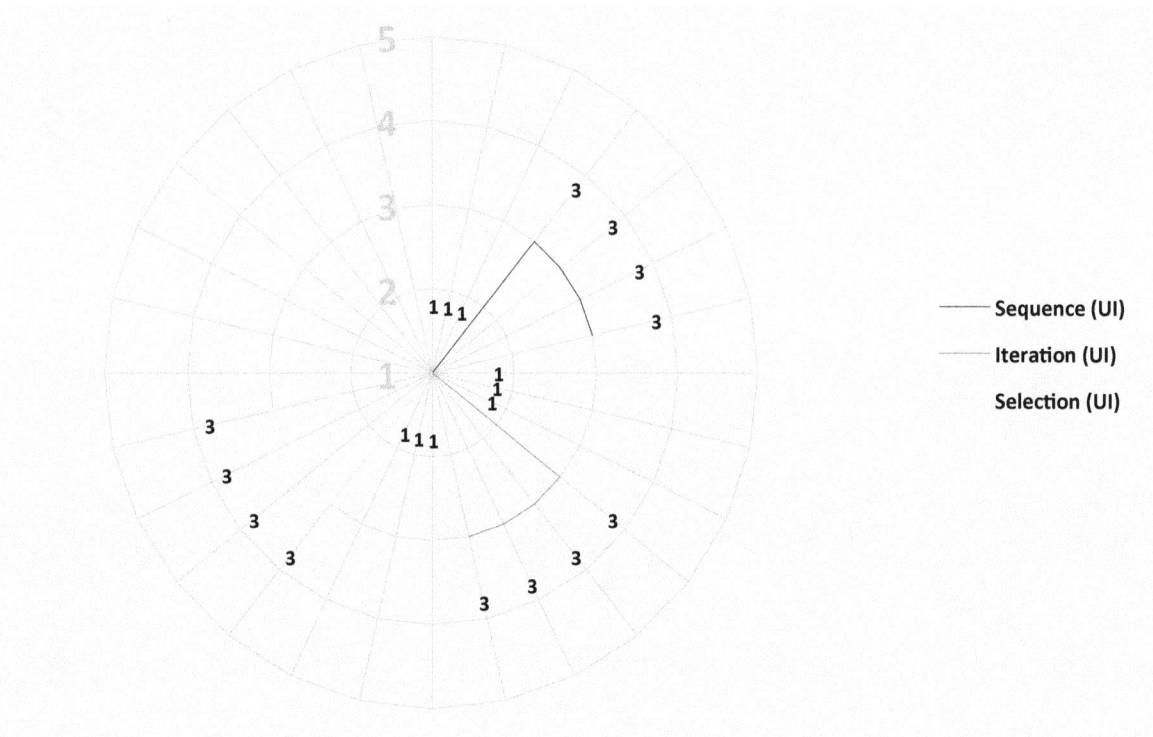

Figure 5.79   Student B3a Trace

Selected comments:

"I found putting my ideas on a storyboard hard to do, I wanted my robot to do things I could not put on paper." (sequence, Level 2)

"I find it hard to think through all the things I want my program to do. It would be better if i could just tell it what to do so I wouldn't have to explain it." (iteration, Level 4)

5.3.10 Student B4a

During the study student B4a developed mental models of a single concept (selection). She studied this using an Unconstrained Icon visualisation tool (*RoboLab*). Her cognitive development is summarised in Section 5.1.2.7. She was also one of nine students included as a narrative (*Gandalf*, Section 6.5). Figure 5.80 shows her concept development traces.

Figure 5.80   Student B4a Trace

Selected comments:

"Mr Zagami [Researcher] taught me to program a robot in year 5, I remembered some of the things we did to get it to dance... this helped me." (selection, Level 3)

"I don't really get how to do my MM [Mental Model] trace. I just do it. Having to explain takes too long." (selection, Level 4)

"I was away when we did loops and it was confusing when we had to use loops for the hard problems" (selection, Level 6)

5.3.11 Student B4b

During the study student B4b developed mental models of three concepts (sequence, iteration and selection). She studied all three using an Unconstrained Icon visualisation tool (*RoboLab*). Her cognitive development is summarised in Section 5.1.2.8 and Figure 5.81 shows her concept development trace.

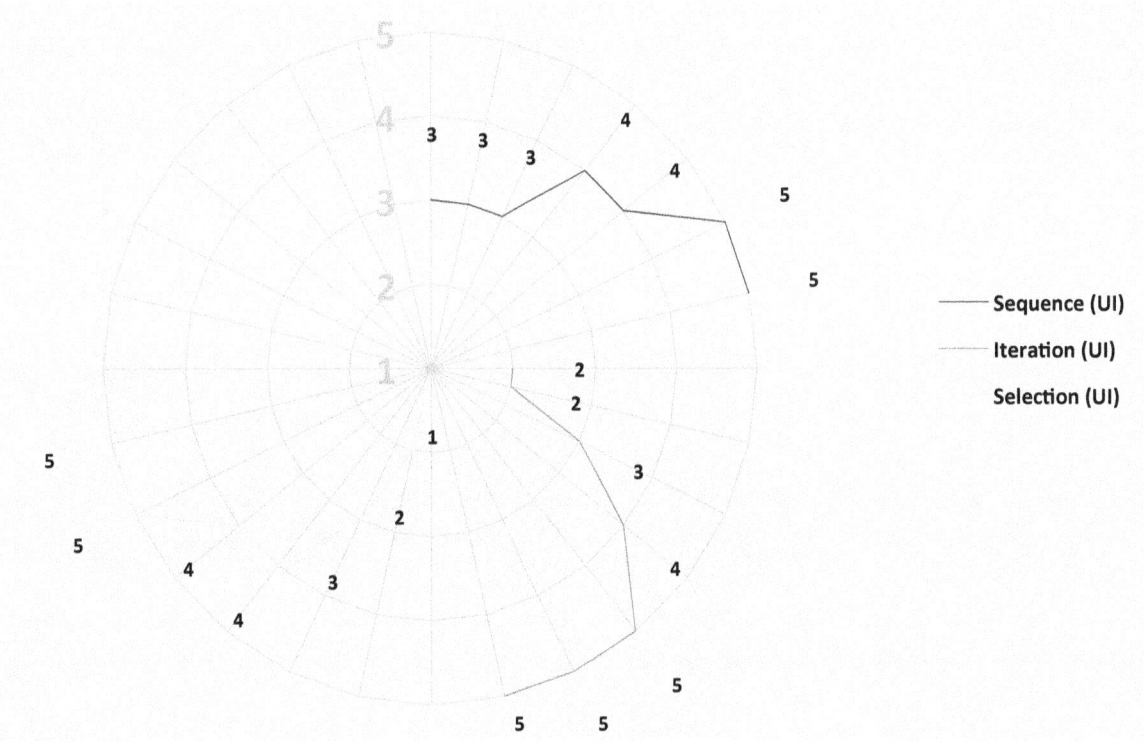

Figure 5.81   Student B4b Trace

Selected comments:

"I think that having to work things out in your head and explain them was a good idea. It helped me think through and organise my thoughts." (selection, Level 3)

"Sometimes I wanted my program to do things but could not work out which icon to use or where it should go. I would then think about how I did it in another problem and then think about how to use it to solve the problem. Sometimes it still didn't work though, then I was stuck." (selection, Level 7)

5.3.12 Student B5b

During the study student B5b developed mental models of three concepts (sequence, iteration and selection). She studied all three using an Unconstrained Icon visualisation tool (*RoboLab*). Her cognitive development is summarised in Section 5.1.2.10 and Figure 5.82 shows her concept development traces.

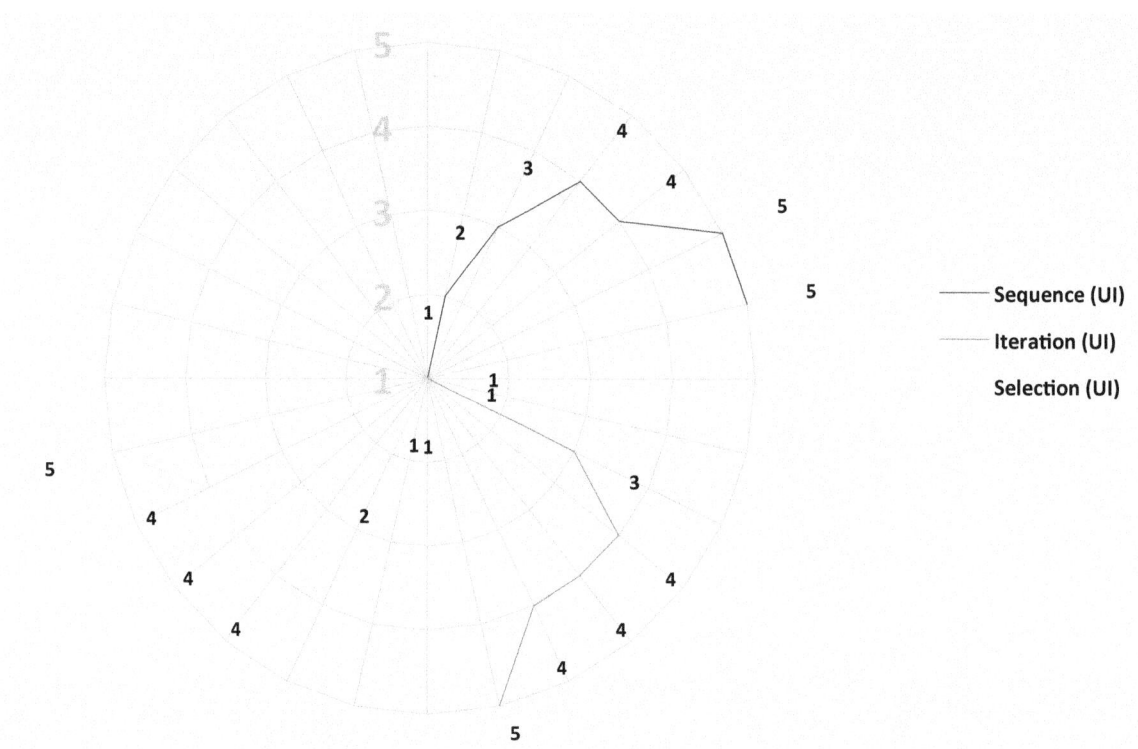

Figure 5.82   Student B5b Trace

Selected comments:

"Doing the loops was a good way of understanding them. Having to think about what was going on with lots of loops really made me learn about loops." (iteration, Level 6)

5.3.13 Student B6a

During the study student B6a developed mental models of three concepts (sequence, iteration and selection). She studied all three using an Unconstrained Icon visualisation tool (*RoboLab*). Her cognitive development is summarised in Section 5.1.2.11. She was also one of nine students included as a narrative (*Legolas*, Section 6.3). Figure 5.83 shows her concept development traces.

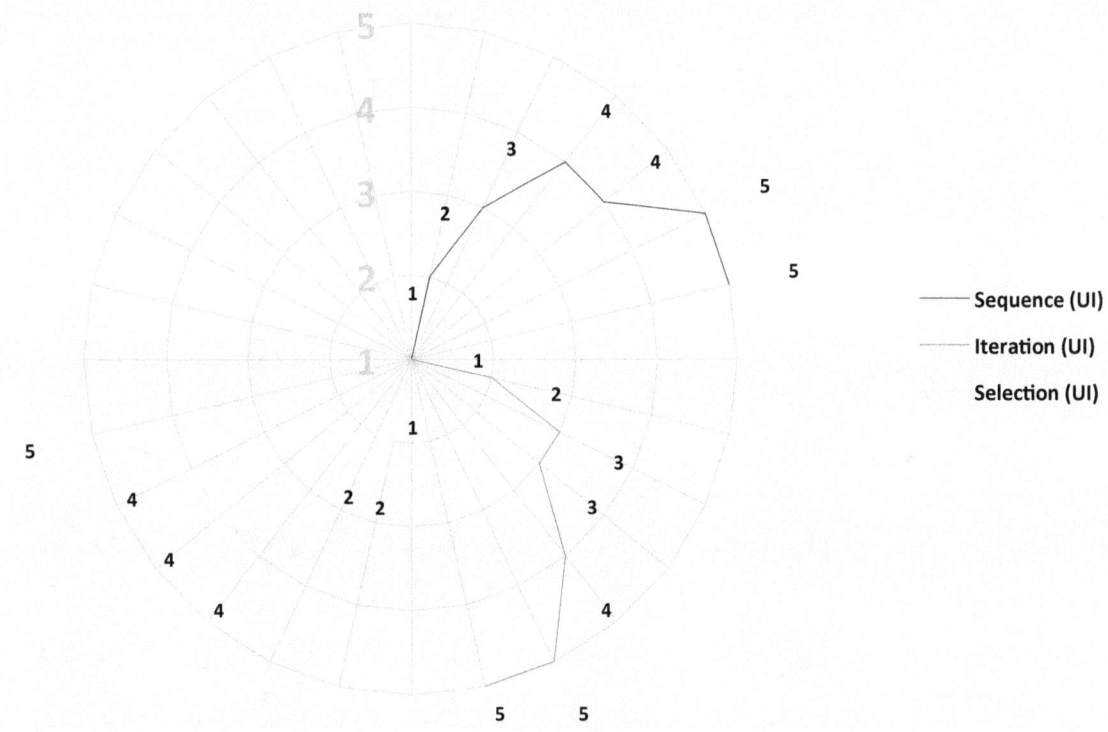

Figure 5.83   Student B6a Trace

Selected comments:

"I did not need to write down all the steps all of the time, I used RoboLab to help me work it out" (selection, Level 2)

"It was harder to keep all the steps in mind at once. Loops inside loops was very difficult to think through" (iteration, Level 3)

"could not work this out so drew it down on paper then used this to redraw it on the screen" (selection, Level 4-5)

"I visualised what the pictures would look like on the screen and the different ways of linking them together so it would work" (sequence, Level 6)

"I did not really understand the flowchart so just used what I knew was working on screen and turned this into my flowchart" (iteration, Level 8)

5.3.14 Student B6b

During the study student B6b developed mental models of three concepts (sequence, iteration and selection). She studied all three using an Unconstrained Icon visualisation tool (*RoboLab*). Her cognitive development is summarised in Section 5.1.2.12 and Figure 5.84 shows her concept development traces.

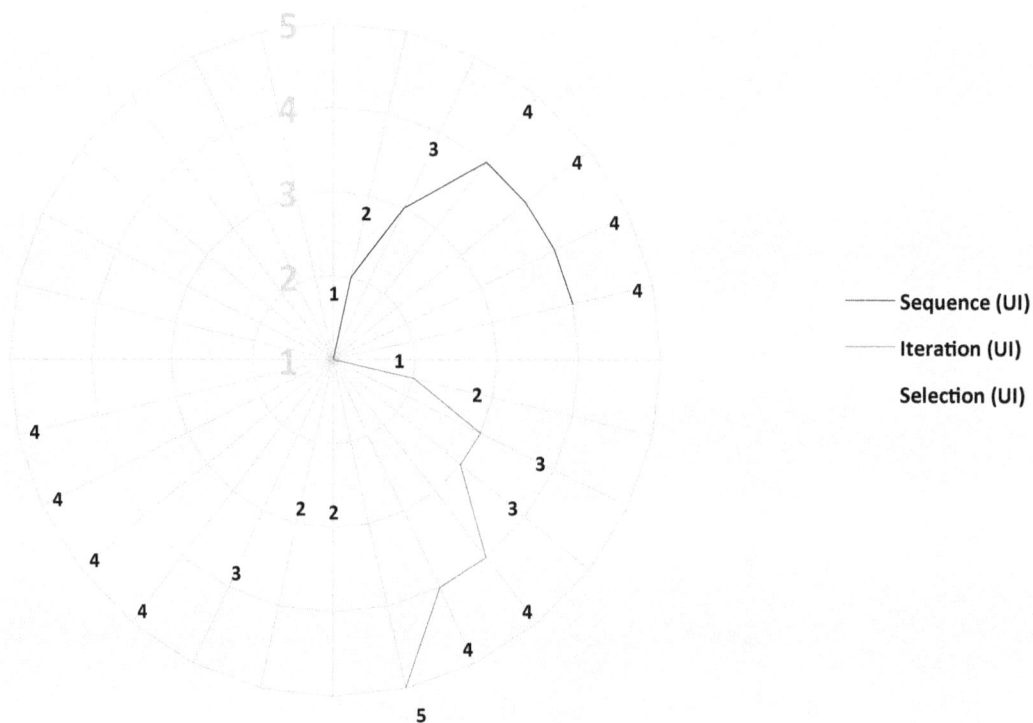

Figure 5.84   Student B6b Trace

Selected comments:

"Drawing storyboards takes too long, it is easier for me to do it first and then explain it." (selection, Level 2)

"Working out how to put in all the choice icons was hard in my head. RoboLab did make it easier as I could think about how they would go on the computer." (sequence, Level 4)

5.3.15 Student C1b

During the study student C1b developed mental models of a single concept (sequence). She studied sequence using an Unconstrained Text visualisation tool (*PHP*). Her cognitive development is summarised in Section 5.1.3.2 and Figure 5.85 shows her concept development trace.

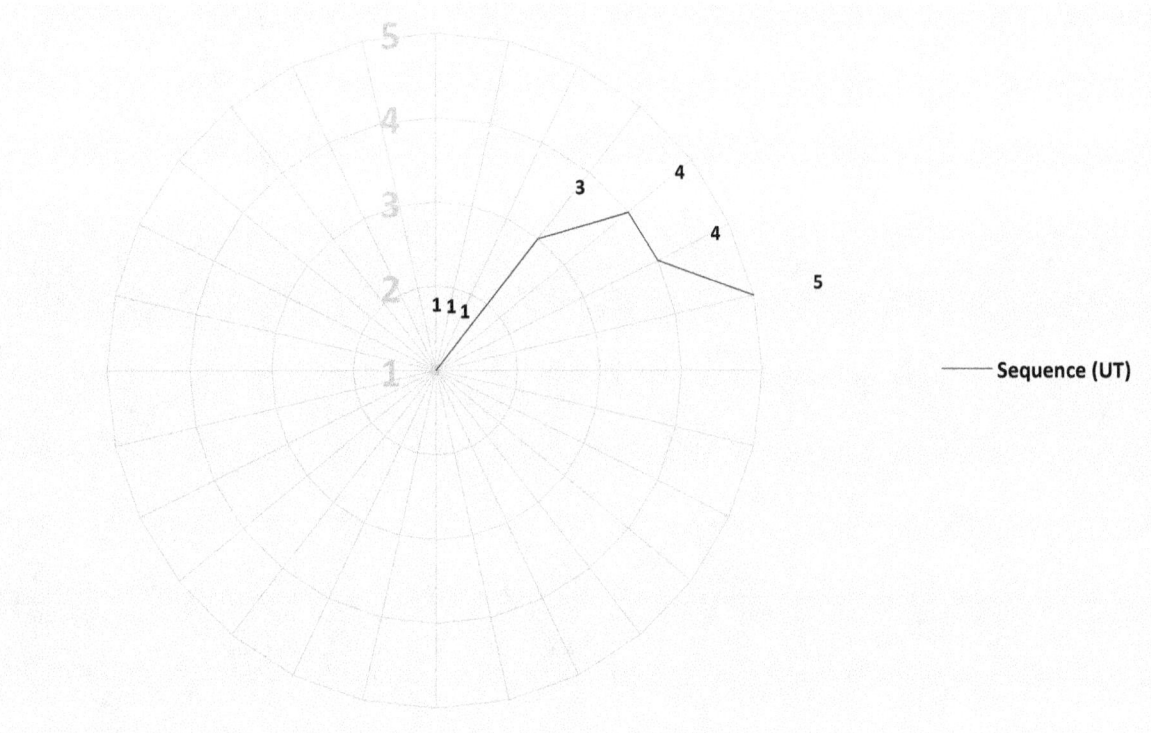

Figure 5.85   Student C1b Trace

Selected comments:

"The storyboards helped me work out what should go first and think about how to arrange my steps." (sequence, Level 2)

5.3.16 Student C2a

During the study student C2a developed mental models of a single concept (sequence) during the study. She studied sequence using an Unconstrained Text visualisation tool (*PHP*). Her cognitive development is summarised in Section 5.1.3.3. and Figure 5.86 shows her concept development trace.

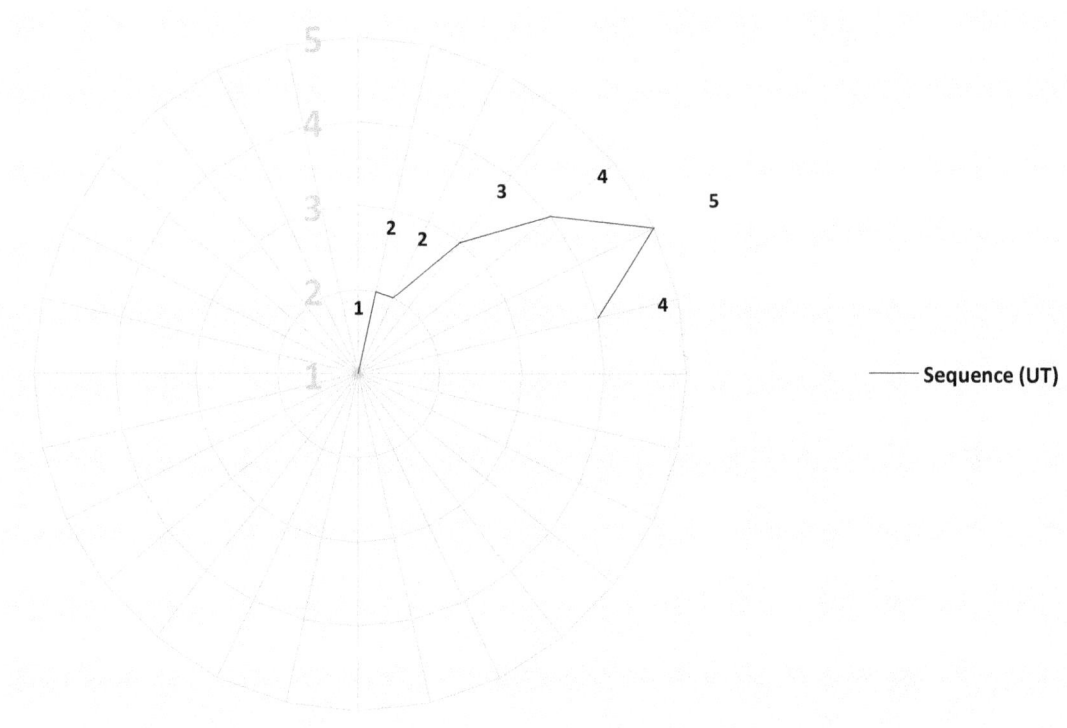

Figure 5.86   Student C2a Trace

Selected comments:

"I found it easier to think about the problem and then try out solutions rather than write it down or draw it. Having to explain it takes too long and I learn more easily by doing than explaining." (sequence, Level 4)

5.3.17 Student C3a

During the study student C3a developed mental models of a single concept (sequence). She studied sequence using an Unconstrained Text visualisation tool (*PHP*). Her cognitive development is summarised in Section 5.1.3.5. She was also one of nine students included as a narrative (*Boromir*, Section 6.7). Figure 5.87 shows her concept development trace.

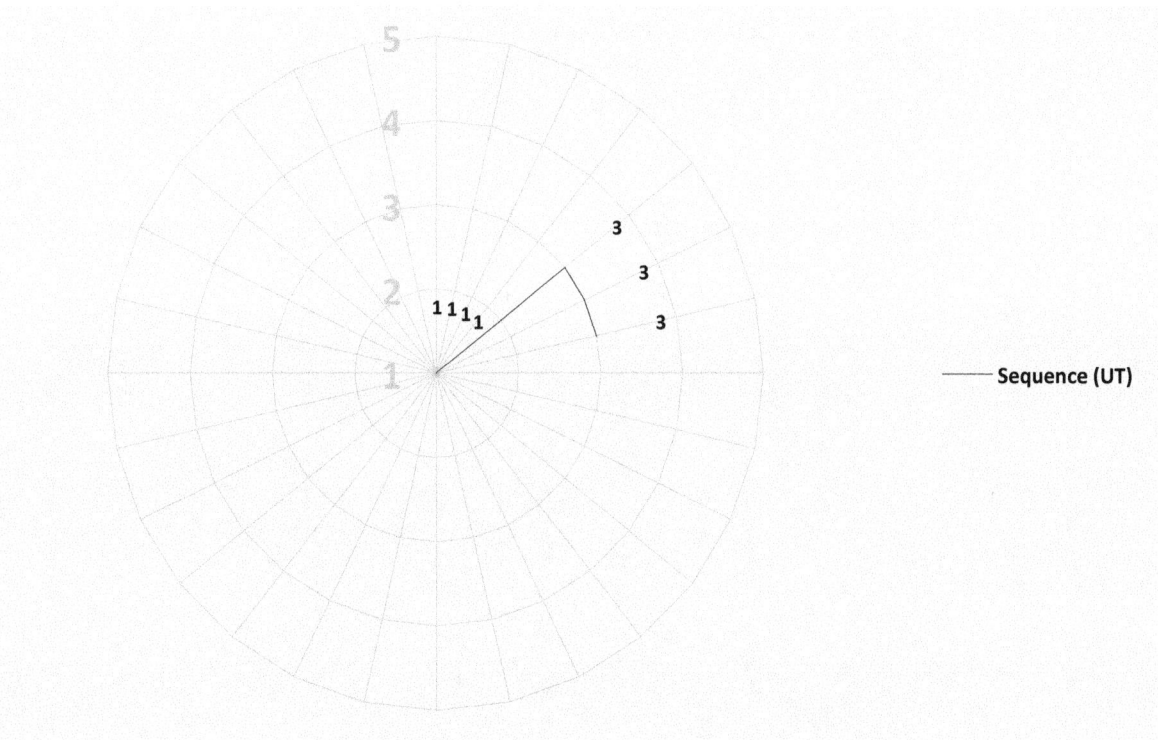

Figure 5.87   Student C3a Trace

Selected comments:

"I found it hard to remember all the PHP words." (sequence, Level 2)

"getting all the words correct took a long time. If you spell it wrong it doesn't work." (sequence, Level 3)

"I got my name to show but could not get my age to work out. It always said I was born today". (sequence, Level 5)

5.3.18 Student C4b

During the study student C4b developed mental models of a single concept (sequence). She studied sequence using an Unconstrained Text visualisation tool (*PHP*). Her cognitive development is summarised in Section 5.1.3.8. She was also one of nine students included as a narrative (*Aragorn*, Section 6.6). Figure 5.88 shows her concept development trace.

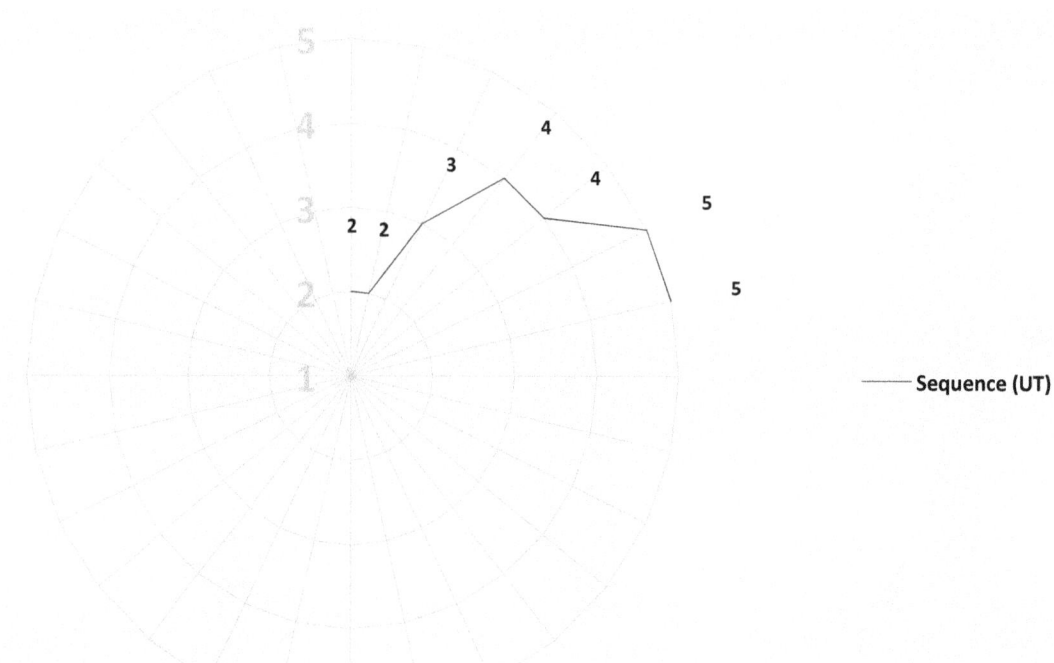

Figure 5.88   Student C4b Trace

Selected comments:

"Storyboarding helped me work out how everything was going to work and fixed a lot of problems before I had to program" (sequence, Level 2)

"I found it hard choosing which bits of a program to use. Any of them might work. It was hard to make the best choice until after I had made them." (sequence, Level 4)

"Explaining how things work in the step by step way is hard." (sequence, Level 6)

"Flow drawings made explaining things easier, you could see what was meant to happen." (sequence, Level 7)

5.3.19 Student D1a

During the study student D1a developed mental models of four concepts (sequence, iteration, selection and modularity). She studied all four using a Constrained Text visualisation tool (*Alice*). Her cognitive development is summarised in Section 5.1.4.1. She was also one of nine students included as a narrative (*Pippin*, Section 6.8). Figure 5.89 shows her concept development trace.

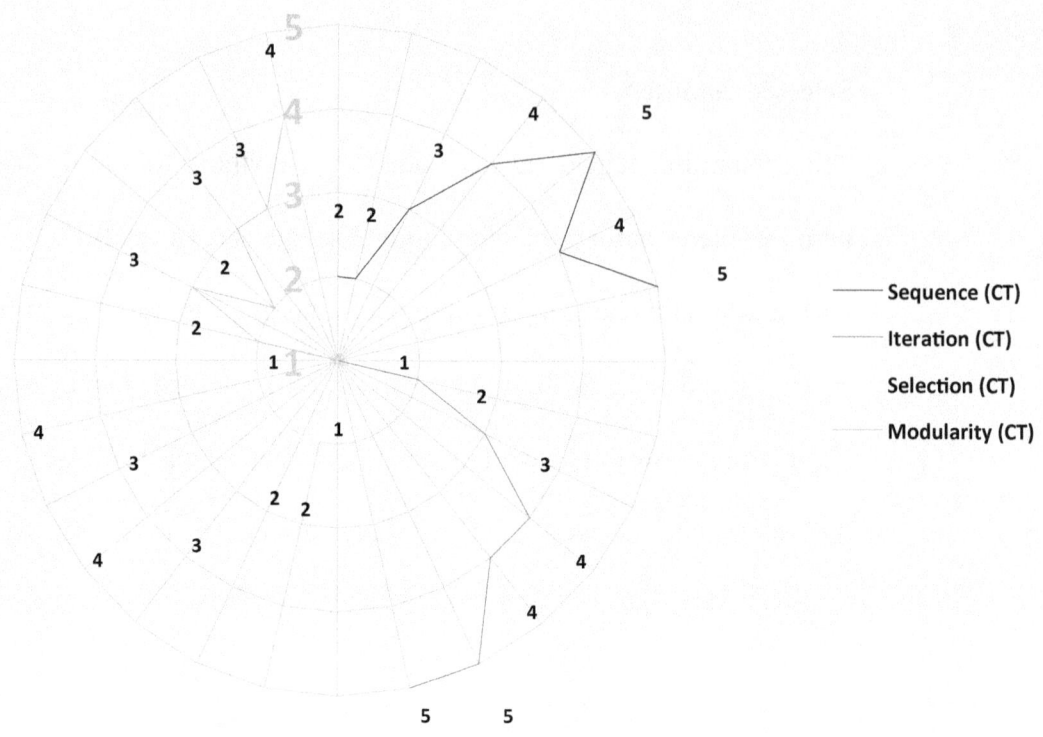

Figure 5.89   Student D1a Trace

Selected comments:

"I kept overlooking things I know I know how to do." (modularity, Level 5)

"Making the program repeat itself and not having to make long programs was challenging and fun." (iteration, Level 6)

"Trying to get the smallest program was a challenge." (iteration, Level 8)

5.3.20 Student D2a

During the study student D2a developed mental models of four concepts (sequence, iteration, selection and modularity). She studied four using an Unconstrained Text visualisation tool (*Visual Basic*). Her cognitive development is summarised in Section 5.1.4.2. She was also one of nine students included as a narrative (*Merry*, Section 6.9). Figure 5.90 shows her concept development traces.

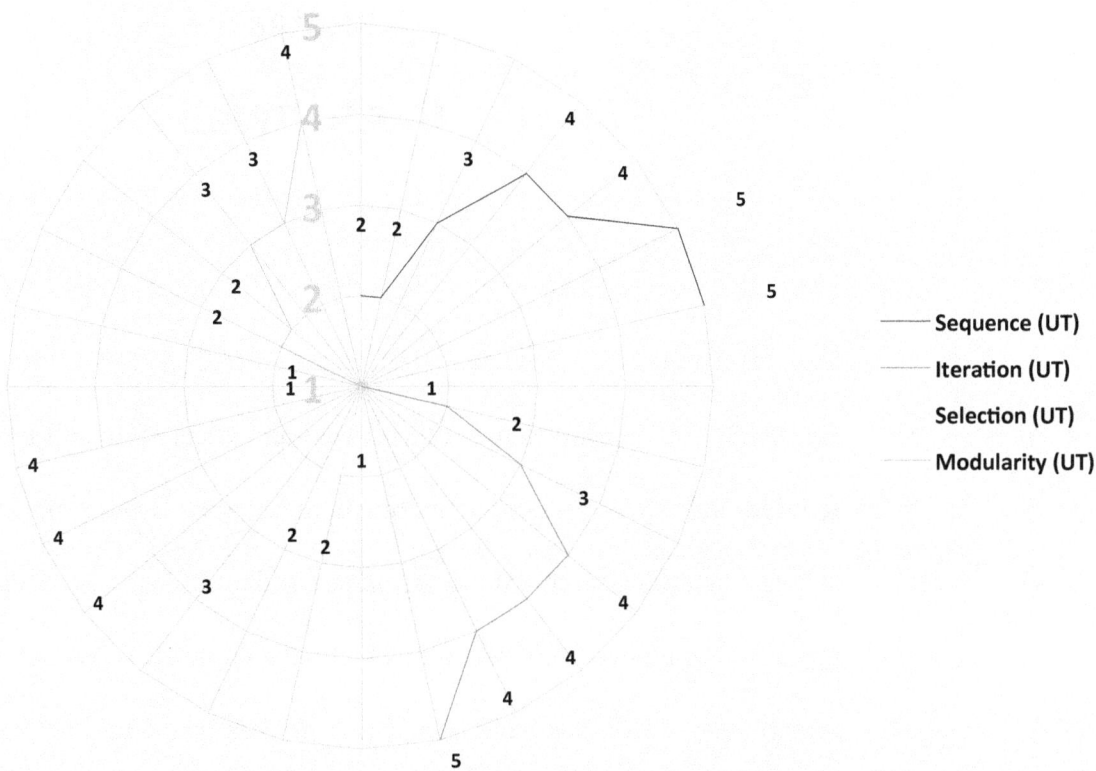

Figure 5.90 Student D2a Trace

Selected comments:

"Storyboarding helped" (sequence, Level 3)

"It was complicated learning the commands but when I had them learnt, in my memory, I was able to think things through much quicker than when I had to keep looking them up." (selection, Level 7)

The following chapter draws up these finding to generate a series of nine narratives that seek to explain what has occurred and the theoretical propositions arising from the data.

Chapter 6

NARRATIVES

From the twenty students (*n*=20) selected for trace analysis (Chapter 5), nine students (*n*=9) were selected (see Sections 4.2 and 4.3) for development as narratives. The narratives use a theoretical-analytical style and a mix of sequential-focused and category-focused narrative report (see Section 4.1). They present an analysis of the research data in an understandable format and detail the theoretical propositions arising from the study. Due to the complexity of some linkages between narratives, pseudonyms have been drawn from a well known work of fiction to aid comprehension, providing cognitive hooks in comparing and contrasting selected students and the groupings represented in discussion of the research (Chapter 7). Figures 6.1 and 6.20 summarise the students selected for narratives.

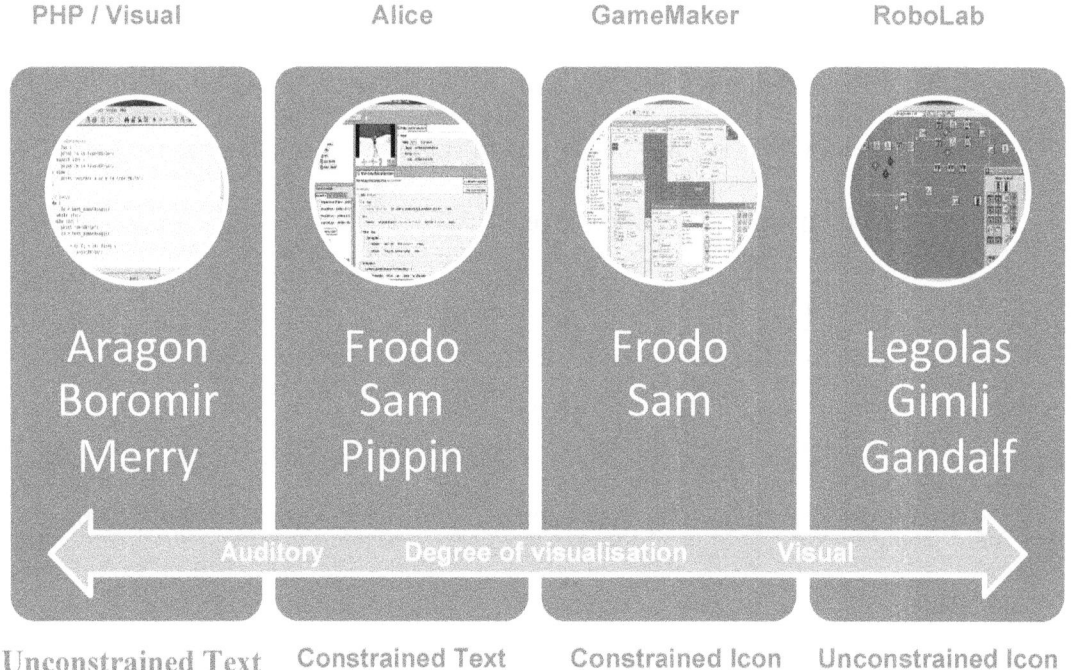

Figure 6.1   Narratives summary by degree of visualisation

6.1 Frodo

A4c, who we will call Frodo (see Section 5.1.1.9 and Section 5.3.5), is representative of nine (*N*=31) or 29% of the population who studied four concepts using multiple visualisation tools and is generally indicative of their collective responses. Generally, Frodo is representative of 22 (*N*=31) or 71% of students who developed mental models with increasing difficulty within each concept. Frodo completed four ICT courses (see Section 4.2) involved in the study across the full range of concepts (Sequence, Iteration, Selection, and Modularity). The first two concepts Frodo developed, used a Constrained Text tool (*Alice*) while the last two concepts used a Constrained Icon tool (*GameMaker*) (see Figures 6.2 and 6.3).

Frodo's initial concept maps (see Section 4.4.1) identified between two and three concepts. They included some linkage between concepts but very little structured grouping of concepts. Initially Frodo progressed rapidly through the mental model development levels. She quickly developed an understanding of sequence to the extent that she could articulate the concept on paper as storyboards (Level 2) and effectively implemented her designs using a Constrained Text tool. The Constrained Text tool assisted this translation with Frodo designing her solutions as flowcharts and replicating these using the Constrained Text tool which provided a similar digital representation to a flowchart. As Frodo's mental model developed she was able to dispense with writing down her initial design and progressed to mentally manipulating the solution steps and translating these to the Constrained Text tool using a process of mental storyboarding (Level 3).

As the concepts became more complex, Frodo experienced increasing difficulty in moving from Property Noticing (Level 4) to Formalising (Level 5) (see Figure 6.2). Frodo became reliant on the rapid prototyping capabilities of the tool to guess and check possible solutions without fully developing the concept mentally. At this point some folding back was evident with Frodo returning to identifying the intermediary steps involved (Level 4) and articulating her designs on paper before translation to the tool. Frodo experienced difficulties taking her understanding of each concept from familiar (Level 4) to unfamiliar situations (level5) but eventually consolidated her mental model sufficiently in Property Noticing (Level 4) to progress her mental model to Formalising (Level 5). Frodo continued developing her models with some difficulty, though less so for the selection concept, formalising and organising her observations (Level 6) to develop formal descriptions of her conceptual understanding. She then structured this thinking into logical structures (Level 7) in the form of formal flowcharts, for all concepts except iteration. Frodo was unable to advance effectively to the inventising (Level 8) stage in her study of sequence and iteration, but was able to develop her mental models of selection and modularity to the point of identifying several new concepts.

Frodo's final concept maps identified between two and four concepts, they included substantial linkage between concepts, and from few to substantial grouping of concepts. Her final concept maps for selection and modularity were significantly more advanced than her final concept maps for selection and iteration.

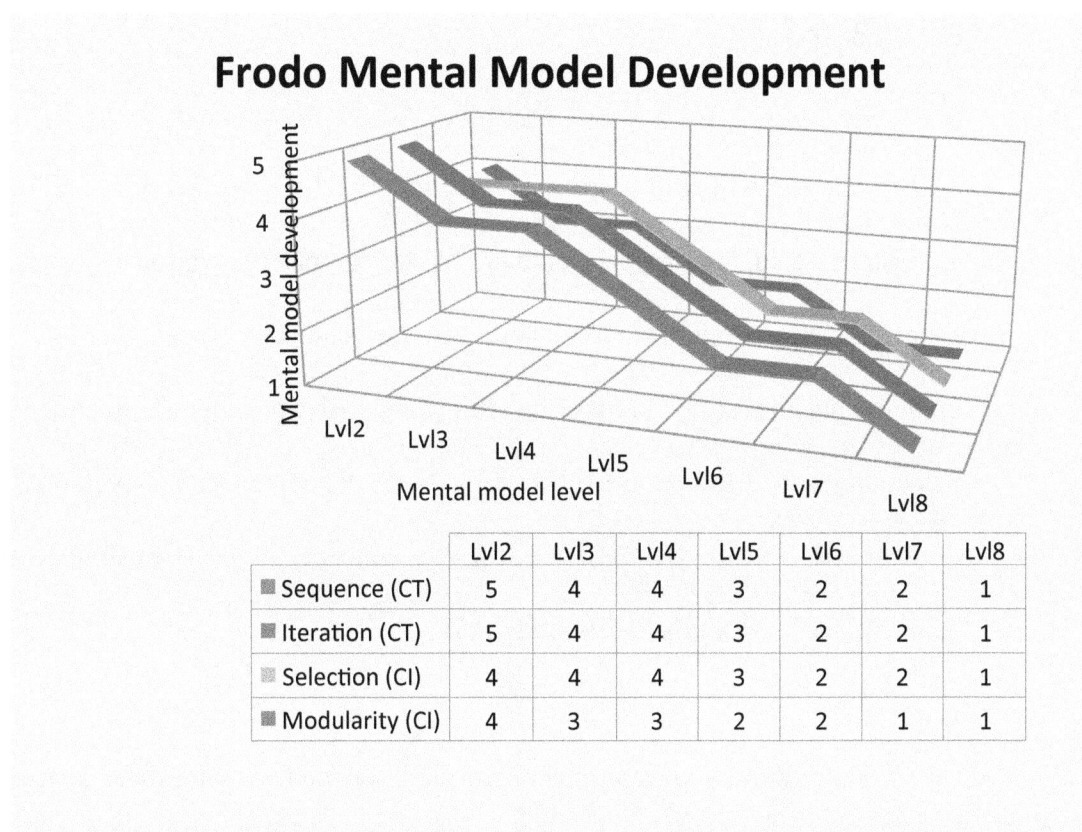

Figure 6.2   Frodo Trace (repeated from Figure 5.9)

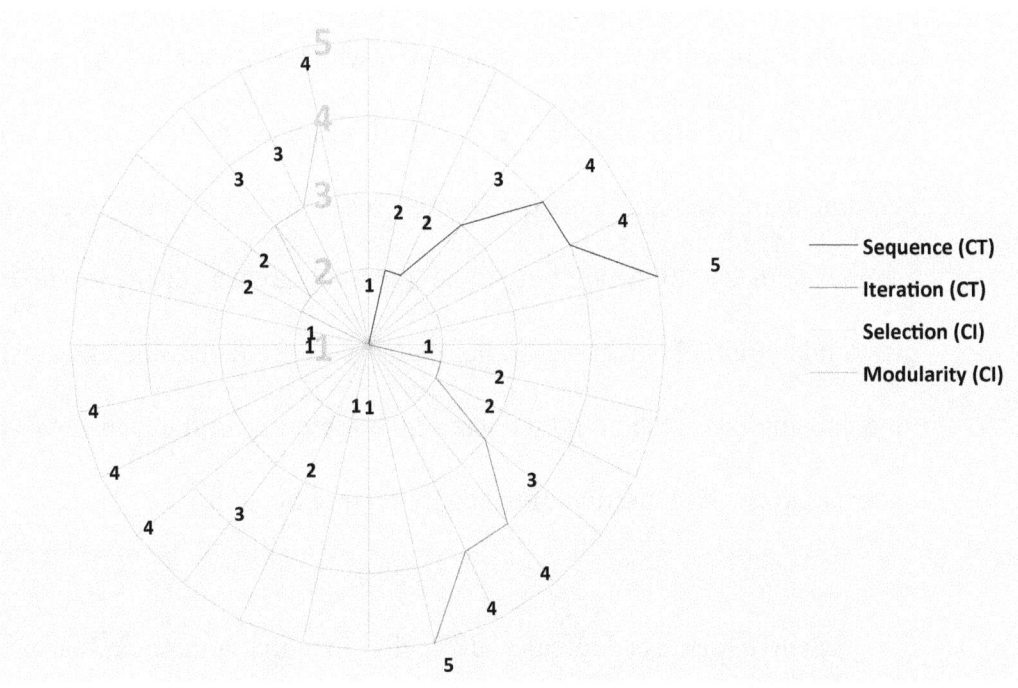

Figure 6.3   Frodo Trace (repeated from Figure 5.74)

6.2 Sam

A3a, who we will call Sam (see Section 5.1.1.5 and Section 5.3.3), is also representative of nine ($N=31$) or 29% of the sample population who studied four concepts using multiple visualisation tools. Sam completed four ICT courses involved in the study across the full range of concepts (Sequence, Iteration, Selection, and Modularity). The first two concepts Sam developed, used a Constrained Text tool (*Alice*); the last two concepts used a Constrained Icon tool (*GameMaker*) (see Figures 6.14 and 6.15).

Sam's initial concept maps identified between two and three concepts. They included some linkage between concepts and some structured grouping of concepts. Sam developed to Image Making (Level 2) with little difficulty, experiencing slightly greater success with the iteration concept, developing complex storyboards to the problems presented. Sam progressed with equal ease to Image Having (Level 3) and Property Noticing (Level 4) in developing mental models of sequence, iteration and selection. Sam experienced greater difficulties in developing the more complex concept of Modularity. She reported greater difficulty in concurrently maintaining multiple processes in her memory as she determined the best solution to modularising tasks. Sam reported a strong preference for the GameMaker tool based on its aid to her visualisation of the concepts (see Section 5.3.3).

Sam experienced greater difficulty in solving non-similar problems and progressing her mental models for the sequence and iteration concepts to Formalising (Level 5). She was unable in progress these concepts beyond

Formalising (Level 5) and despite several folding back attempts was unable to further develop her mental models for sequence and iteration. Sam was, however, able to further develop her mental models for selection and modularity. While she continued to experience some difficulties, Sam was able to develop both concepts to Inventising (Level 8) and generate nascent aspects of new concepts. Sam's final concept maps identified between one and four concepts, they included substantial linkage between concepts, and substantial grouping of concepts (in selection and modularity).

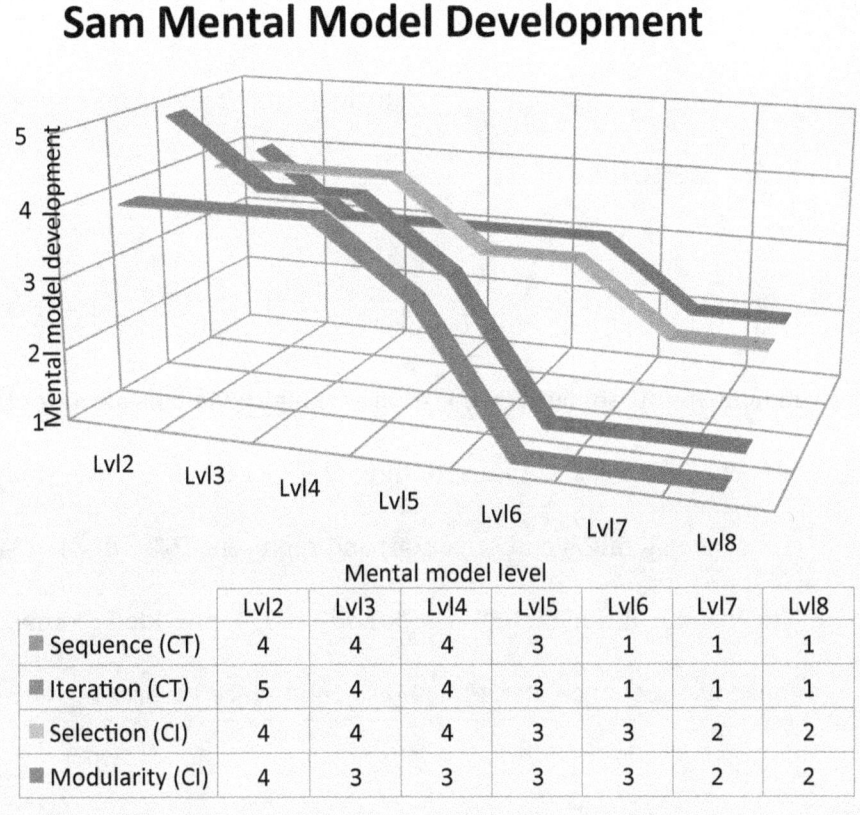

	Lvl2	Lvl3	Lvl4	Lvl5	Lvl6	Lvl7	Lvl8
Sequence (CT)	4	4	4	3	1	1	1
Iteration (CT)	5	4	4	3	1	1	1
Selection (CI)	4	4	4	3	3	2	2
Modularity (CI)	4	3	3	3	3	2	2

Figure 6.4 Sam Trace (repeated from Figure 5.5)

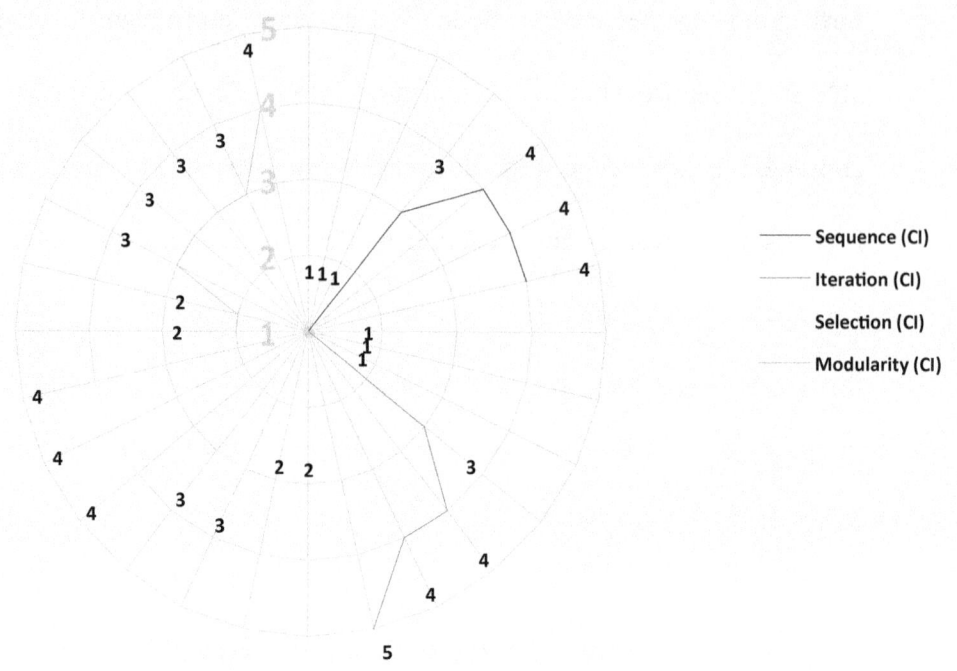

Figure 6.5   Sam Trace (repeated from Figure 5.73)

6.3 Legolas

B6a, who we will call Legolas (see Section 5.1.2.11 and Section 5.3.11), is indicative of students who used a single visualisation tool to develop several concepts. Legolas completed three ICT courses in the study of three concepts (sequence, iteration and selection) and represent 26% ($n=8$) of students who used the Unconstrained Icons tool (*RoboLab*). This provided comparison between three concepts - sequence, iteration and selection (see Figures 6.6 and 6.7).

Legolas's initial concept maps identified between two and three concepts. They included some linkage between concepts but very little structured grouping of concepts. Legolas progressed similarly to Frodo, progressing rapidly through the initial mental model levels with a gradually increasing difficulty as the complexity of each concept increased. She quickly developed a comprehensive understanding of all three concepts to the extent that she could articulate the concept as a physical representation on paper (Level 2). The Unconstrained Icon tool assisted her translation with Legolas designing her solutions as flowcharts and replicating these using the Unconstrained Icon tool which provided a similar digital representation of a flowchart. As Legolas's mental model developed, she was able to dispense with writing down her initial design and progressed to mentally manipulating the solution steps and translating these to the Unconstrained Icon tool (Level 3). She reported that this manipulation was aided by mental visualisation of the "pictures" (Icons) used by the visualisation tool (*RoboLab*).

Legolas was slightly less effective in developing the selection concept to Image Having (Level 3) with the mental retention and manipulation of intermediate steps reported as more difficult in the more complex selection concept, particularly with respect to nested selections and selections with more than three nodes (Branches). As the concepts became more complex, Legolas experienced increasing difficulty. In moving from Property Noticing (Level 4) to Formalising (Level 5) some folding back was evident (as with Frodo) when studying the iteration concept with Legolas returning to and articulating her designs on paper (Level 3) before translation to the tool. In developing Property Noticing (Level 4) and Formalising (Level 5), Legolas experienced greater difficulty with the iteration concept, reporting increasing difficulties in the mental manipulation of intermediary steps where the process involved retention of previous steps and the determination of options based on these previous steps. This became increasing difficult for the selection concept in Formalising (Level 5) problems sets in non-similar situations.

Legolas was also increasingly unable to formalise and organise her observations (Level 6) as the complexity of the concept increased. While she was able to explain her thinking in terms of logically structured flowcharts (Level 8) at a basic level, this was assisted by the visualisation tool (*RoboLab*) which provided a linear translation for correct solutions. Legolas was unable to advance effectively to the inventising (Level 8) stage in any of her mental models. Legolas's final concept maps identified between three and four concepts, they included substantial linkage between concepts, and substantial grouping of concepts.

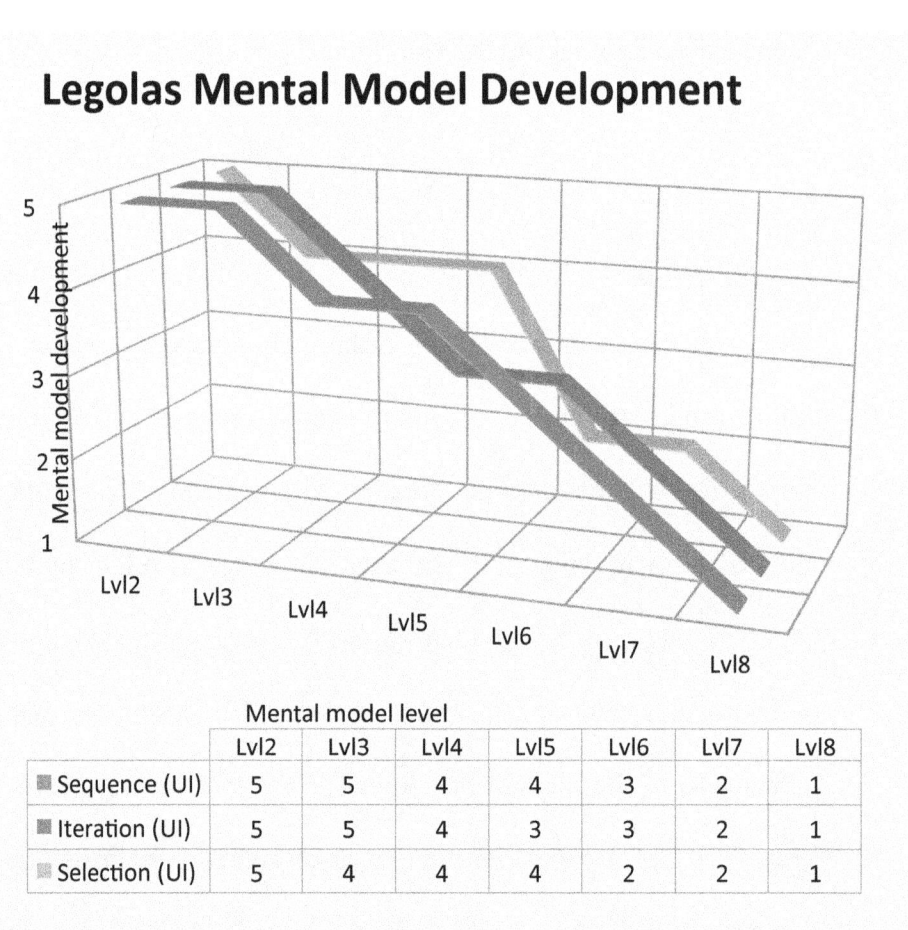

Legolas Mental Model Development

	Mental model level						
	Lvl2	Lvl3	Lvl4	Lvl5	Lvl6	Lvl7	Lvl8
■ Sequence (UI)	5	5	4	4	3	2	1
■ Iteration (UI)	5	5	4	3	3	2	1
■ Selection (UI)	5	4	4	4	2	2	1

Figure 6.6   Legolas Trace (repeated from Figure 5.20)

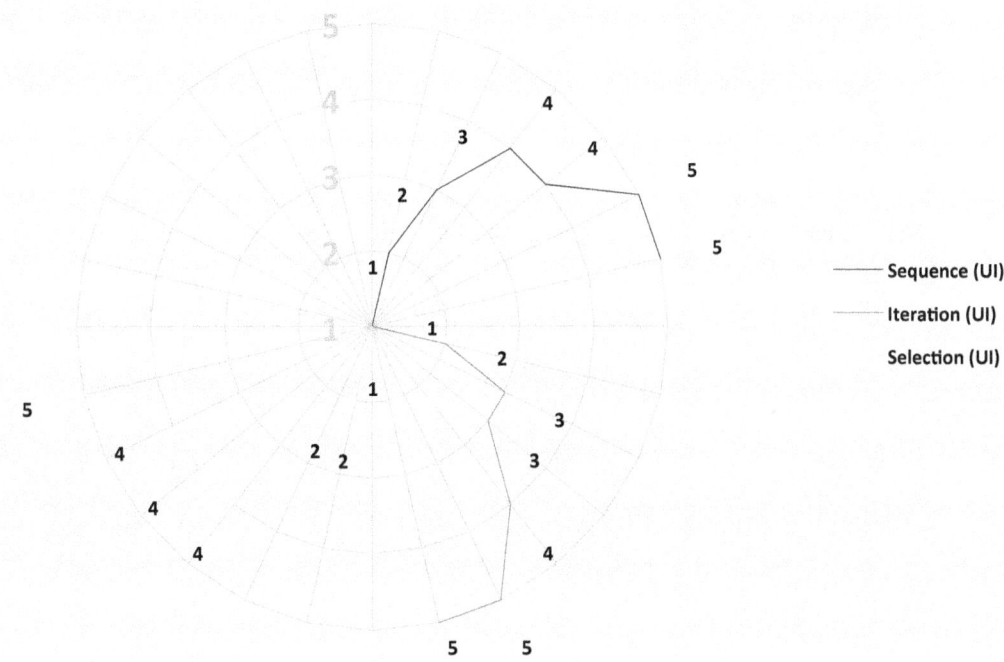

Figure 6.7   Legolas Trace (repeated from Figure 5.83)

6.4   Gimli

B1b, who we will call Gimli (see Section 5.1.2.2 and Section 5.3.6), is representative of students who used a single visualisation tool to develop several concepts. Gimli completed three ICT courses in the study of three concepts (sequence, iteration and selection). Gimli represent 26% (*n*=8) of students who used the Unconstrained Icons tool (*RoboLab*). This provided comparison between three concepts - sequence, iteration and selection (see Figures 6. 8 and 6. 9).

Gimli's initial concept maps identified between two and three concepts. They included some linkage between concepts but very little structured grouping of concepts. Gimli progressed typically as compared to Frodo, progressing rapidly through the initial mental model levels with a gradually increasing difficulty as the complexity of each concept increased. She quickly developed a comprehensive understanding of all three concepts to the extent that she could articulate the concept as a physical representation on paper (Level 2). The Unconstrained Icon tool assisted her translation with Gimli designing her solutions as flowcharts and replicating these using the Unconstrained Icon tool which provided a similar digital representation of a flowchart. As Gimli's mental model of the concept developed, she was able to dispense with writing down her initial design and progressed to mentally manipulating the solution steps and translating these to the Unconstrained Icon tool (Level 3).

Gimli was slightly less effective in developing the iteration concept to Image Having (Level 3) with the mental retention and manipulation of intermediate steps reported as more difficult in the more complex iteration concept, particularly with respect to nested iterations. This difficulty with the iteration concept continued to Property Noticing (Level 4) with the determination of intermediary steps identified within the context of the overall problem identified as the main difficulty.

Gimli did not experience similar problems with the more complex selection concept, reporting that similarities to the iteration concepts assisted in developing this concept. She was able to progress from similar to non-similar situations - Formalising (Level 5) with little difficulty but was then unable to progress her mental model in any of the three concepts studied. Gimli was unable to formalise and organise her observations (Level 6) during these problem sets. While she was able to storyboard her concepts (Level 2), Gimli was unable to explain her problem set solutions in a form that demonstrated a mental model of the concepts that was organised and included a logical structure. Despite several folding back process to Formalising (Level 5), Property Noticing (Level 4), and even Image Making (Level 2), Gimli was unable to progress her mental model beyond Formalising (Level 5). Gimli's final concept maps identified between one and two concepts, they included some linkage between concepts, and some grouping of concepts. This is reflected in the difficulties Gimli experienced in progressing her mental models beyond Formalising (Level 5).

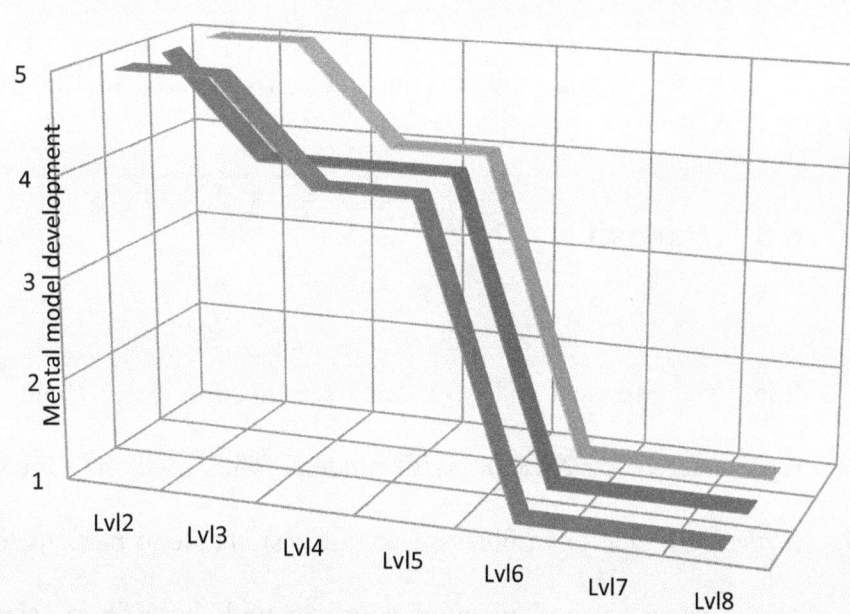

	Lvl2	Lvl3	Lvl4	Lvl5	Lvl6	Lvl7	Lvl8
Sequence (UI)	5	5	4	4	1	1	1
Iteration (UI)	5	4	4	4	1	1	1
Selection (UI)	5	5	4	4	1	1	1

Figure 6.8   Gimli Trace (repeated from Figure 5.11)

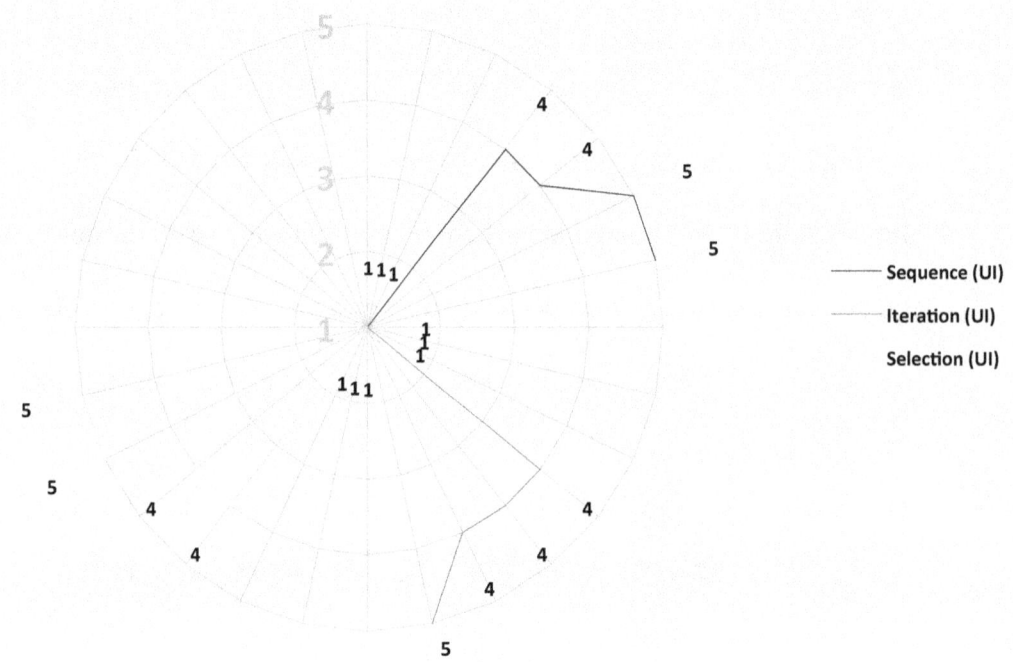

Figure 6.9   Gimli Trace (repeated from Figure 5.76)

6.5 Gandalf

B4a, who we will call Gandalf (see Section 5.1.2.7 and Section 5.3.10), is representative of 26% (n=8) of students who used the Unconstrained Icons tool (*RoboLab*). Due to an illness, Gandalf was unable to participate in the development of the sequence and iteration concepts with her cohort. Her study of selection however, provided comparison with students with prior experience in the mental model development of concepts (see Figures 6.10 and 6.11).

Gandalf's initial concept map identified four concepts. They included substantial linkage between concepts and some structured grouping of concepts. Gandalf progressed typically as compared to Frodo, progressing rapidly through the initial mental model levels with a gradually increasing difficulty as the complexity of each concept increased. She developed detailed physical storyboards (Level 2) and was able to progress to mental storyboarding (Level 3) with little difficulty.

She had greater difficulty in identifying properties in similar situations (Level 4) and reported some confusion where problem sets drew on concepts of sequence and iteration. She was however, able to progress to organising her observations (Level 6) and maintained some capacity to develop basic formal flowcharts (Level 7) and inventising (Level 8). Gandalf's final concept map identified three concepts, they included substantial linkage between concepts, and some grouping of concepts.

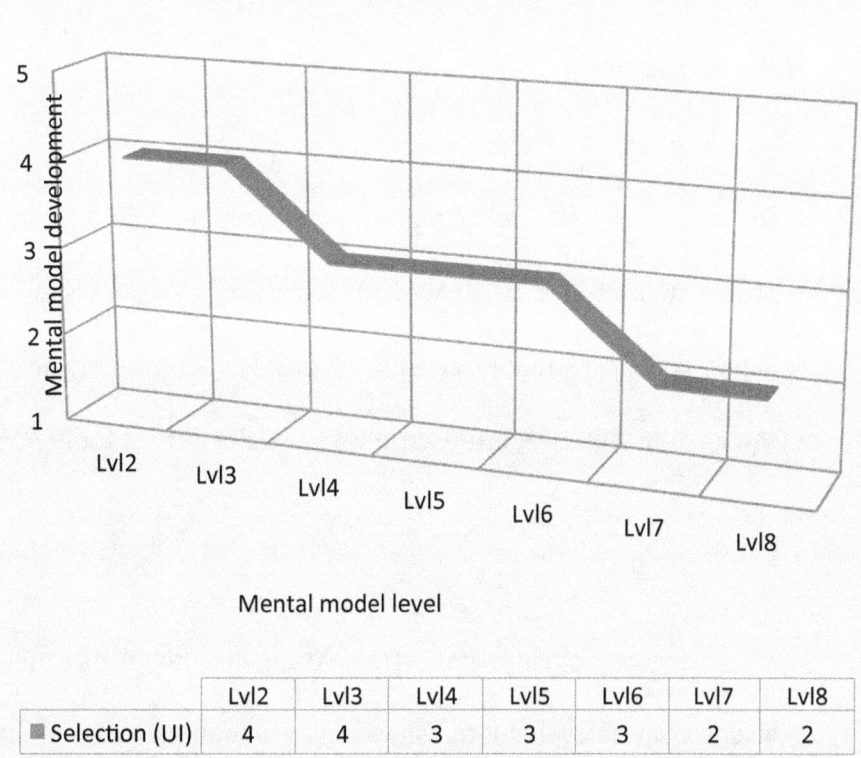

Figure 6.10   Gandalf Trace (repeated from Figure 5.16)

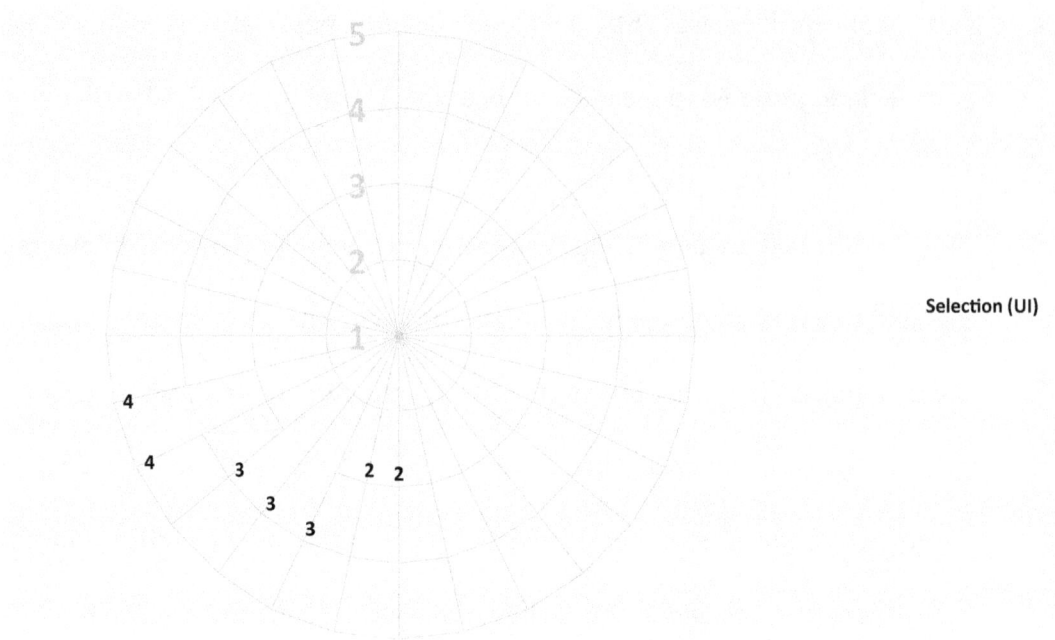

Figure 6.11   Gandalf Trace (repeated from Figure 5.80)

6.6 Aragorn

C4b, who we will call Aragorn (see Section 5.1.3.8 and Section 5.3.18), is representative of 26% (*n*=8) students who used a single visualisation tool to develop a single concept. Aragorn completed one ICT course in the study of one concept (sequence) in this Aragorn used the Constrained Text tool (*PHP*) (see Figures 6.12 and 6.13).

Aragorn developed an effective mental model of sequence, with a detailed concept map (Level 1) translated into a comprehensive storyboard (Level 2). Effective use of mental storyboarding (Level 3) to solve the problem sets provided, a detailed understanding of the commonalities of the concept in similar situations (Level 4). She has some difficulty in solving non-similar problems (Level 5) with most difficulty reported in retaining complex intermediary steps while considering the range of possible alternative solutions.

Aragorn had increasing difficulty in formalising and organising (Level 6) her mental model with particular difficulty in articulating the interactions between command properties in determining their correct sequencing. While experiencing some increasing difficulties formalising her thinking into structured flowcharts (Level 7), Aragorn was able to produce effective flowchart representations despite the use of a purely textual tool that provided minimal graphical cuing. She was able to develop several new concepts (Level 8) from her mental model. Aragorn's final concept map identified four concepts; they included substantial linkage between concepts, and substantial grouping of concepts.

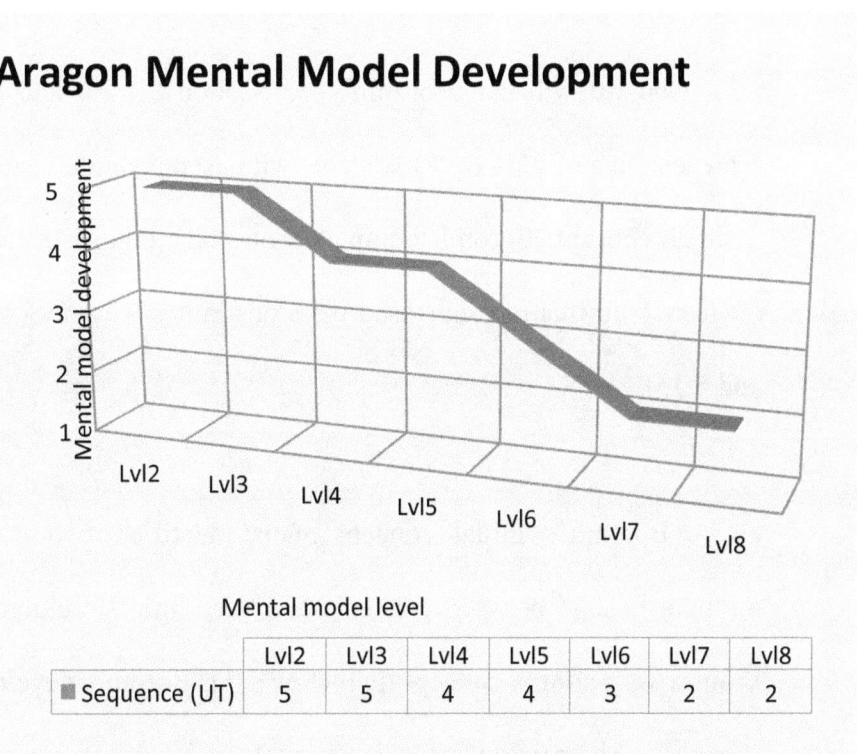

Figure 6.12   Aragorn Trace (repeated from Figure 5.29)

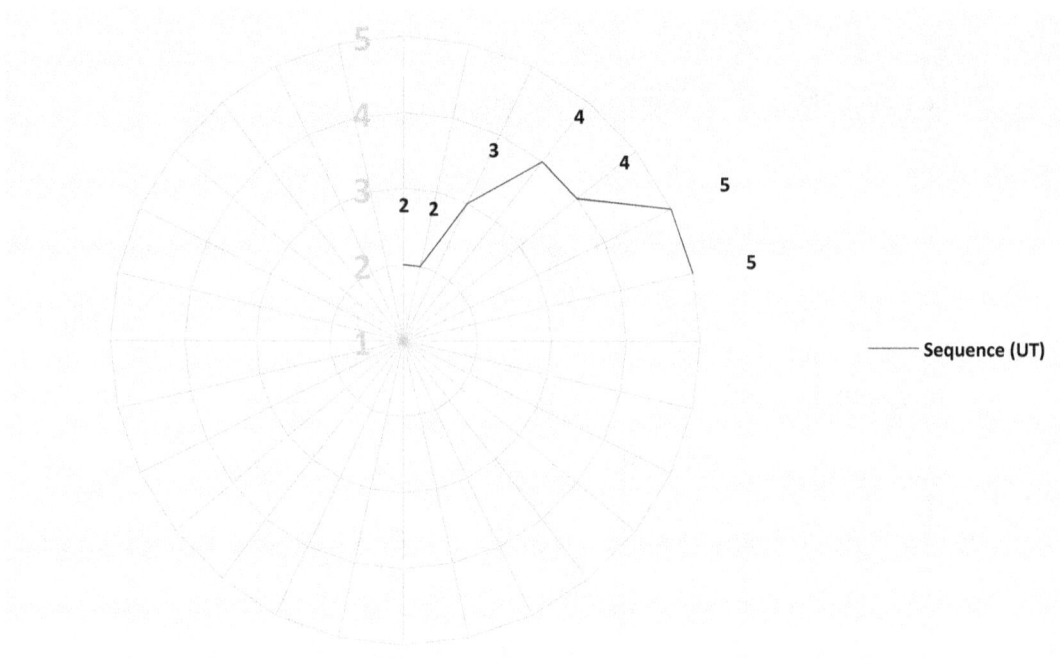

Figure 6.13   Aragorn Trace (repeated from Figure 5.88)

6.7   Boromir

C3a, who we will call Boromir (see Section 5.1.3.6 and Section 5.3.17), is also representative of 26% (*n*=8) students who used a single visualisation tool to develop a single concept. Boromir completed one ICT course in the study of one concept (sequence) in this Boromir used the Constrained Text tool (*PHP*) (see Figures 6.14 and 6.15).

Boromir's initial concept maps identified two concepts. They included minimal linkage between concepts and very little structured grouping of concepts. From a very simple concept map (Level 1), Boromir developed a basic storyboard (Level 2). She reported that her mental model development was constrained by a need to learn the syntax of the unconstrained text visualisation tool before being able to think through the processes involved in the problem sets. Difficulties in learning this syntax again hampered her mental storyboarding (Level 3) with errors in syntax dominating her thought processes despite the abstraction of storyboarding and the relative unimportance of syntax to effective solutions.

Boromir was able to develop her mental model of sequence to Property Noticing (Level 4) in which she completed tasks in familiar contexts, particularly when the number of intermediary steps was small. She was unable however to progress her model to Formalising (Level 5) and complete problem sets in non-similar situations. Despite folding back attempts to previous levels, lack of success in developing the initial levels of her mental model was reported as a significant factor in subsequent difficulties. Boromir's final concept maps identified few concepts; they included no linkage between concepts, and no grouping of concepts. This is reflected in the difficulties Boromir experienced in progressing her mental models beyond Property Noticing (Level 4).

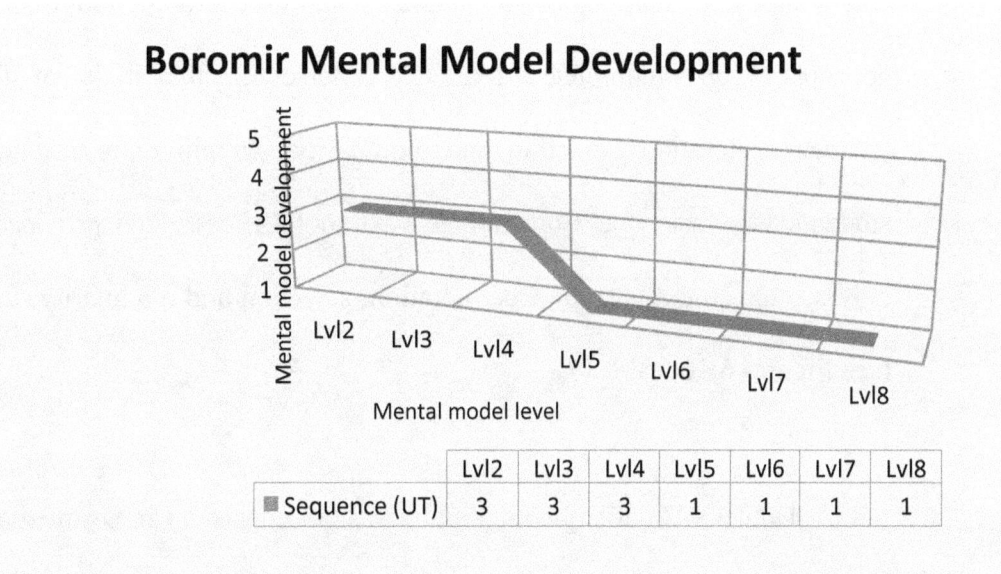

Figure 6.14   Boromir Trace (repeated from Figure 5.26)

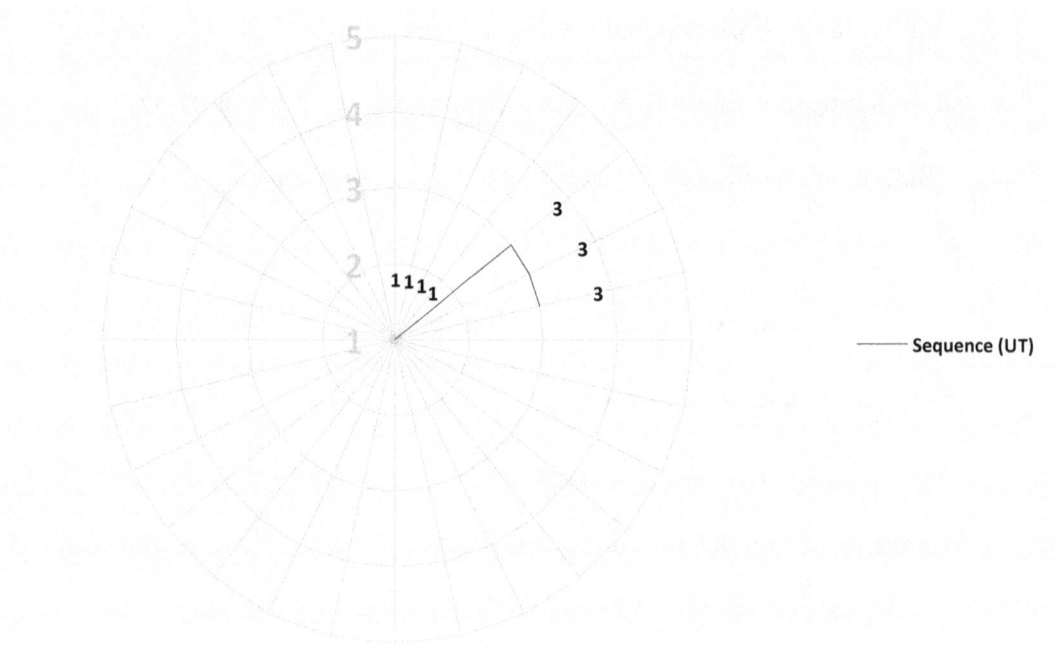

Figure 6.15   Boromir Trace (repeated from Figure 5.87)

6.8 Pippin

D1a who we will call Pippin (see Section 5.1.4.1 and Section 5.3.19) is representative of fourteen (*N*=31) students who used a single tool to develop several concepts. Pippin completed four ICT courses in the study of four concepts (sequence, iteration, selection and modularity). Pippin represent the ten (*N*=31) students who used the Constrained Text tool (*Alice*). This provided comparison between the concepts (sequence, iteration, selection and modularity) using this tool. (see Figures 6.16 and 6.17)

Unlike 94% of students, Pippin was not consistent in her mental model level development. Pippin initially progressed similarly to Frodo. She would several times, however, achieve greater success in higher complexity levels of her mental model. Pippin attributed this inconsistency to 'overlooked' insights but detailed analysis shows that the inconsistencies could more readily be attributed to a lack of attention and focus on the problem sets at those points in time. Pippin's initial concept map identified between two and four concepts. They included some linkage between concepts and some structured grouping of concepts. Pippin had difficulty in developing storyboards (Level 2) for her problem sets in all concepts except iteration.

Pippin reported engagement with the iteration problem set and this additional focus assisted her mental model development at this level. Pippin's development of mental storyboards (Level 3) decreased as the complexity of the concept increased. She showed an understanding of the commonalities of concepts in similar situations (Level 4) but had difficulty in solving non-similar problems (Level 5) with difficulty with complex intermediary steps, particularly in solving problems sets for modularity.

Pippin had increasing difficulty in formalising and organising (Level 6) her mental model with particular difficulty in articulating the interactions for all concepts except selection. She reported increased understanding of the selection problem set at this facilitated the structured visualisations possible with the Alice syntax display. This understanding was carried forward to her development of the concept of modularity and in both cases, assisted her subsequent thinking and capacity to develop structured flowcharts (Level 7) and develop new concepts (Level 8). Pippin's final concept maps identified three to four concepts; they included substantial linkage between concepts, and some grouping of concepts. Her concept maps for selection and modularity were superior to those for sequence and iteration.

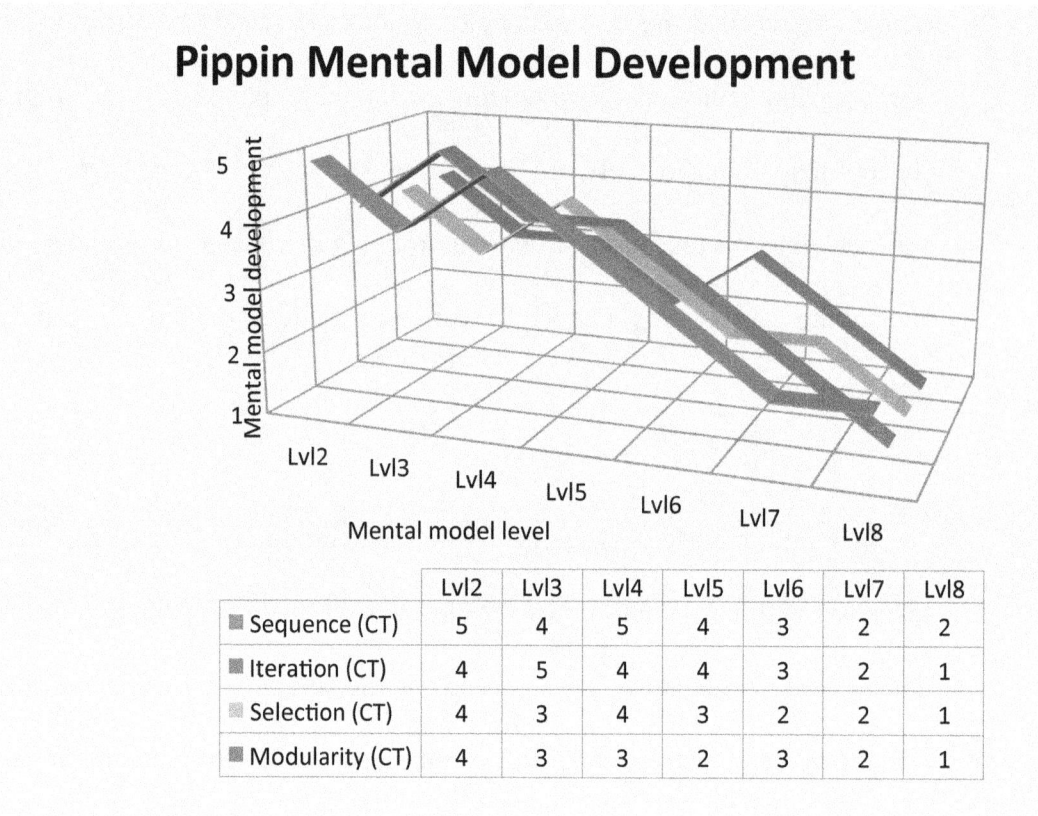

Figure 6.16 Pippin Trace (repeated from Figure 5.30)

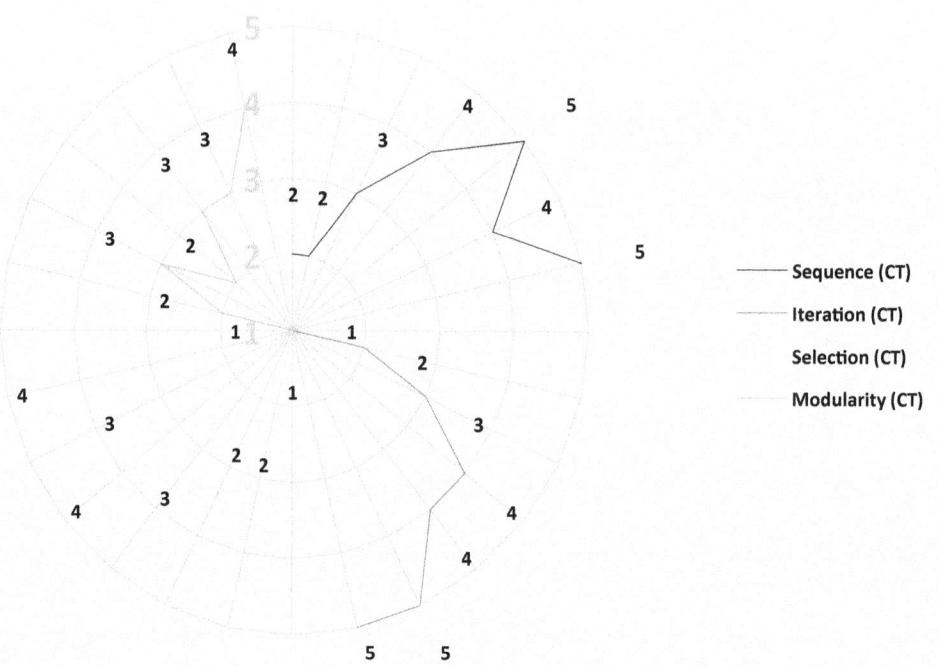

Figure 6.17 Pippin Trace (repeated from Figure 5.89)

6.9 Merry

D2a, who we will call Merry (see Section 5.1.4.1 and Section 5.3.19), is representative of fourteen ($N=31$) students who used a single visualisation tool to develop several concepts. Merry completed four ICT courses in the study of four concepts (sequence, iteration, selection and modularity). Merry represents the only student who used the Unconstrained Text tool (*Visual Basic*). This provided comparison between the concepts (sequence, iteration, selection and modularity) using this tool (see Figures 6.18 and 6.19).

Merry developed a very good mental model of sequence, but decreasing capacity as the complexity of the concept increased. She developed concept maps (Level 1) and translated them into a storyboard (Level 2), effective use of mental storyboarding (Level 3) to solve the problem sets provided, but again had increasing difficulty with more complex concepts of selection and modularity. She showed an understanding of the commonalities of concepts in similar situations (Level 4) but she had difficulty in solving non-similar problems (Level 5) with difficulty with complex intermediary steps, particularly in solving problems sets for modularity.

Merry had increasing difficulty in formalising and organising (Level 6) her mental model with particular difficulty in articulating the interactions between Visual Basic command properties in determining their correct sequencing, particularly where this impacted on the required syntax. While experiencing significant difficulties formalising her thinking into structured flowcharts (Level 7) she was able to produce some flowchart representations for sequence, iteration and selection, but not modularity. She was able to develop several new concepts (Level

8) from her mental model of sequence but not for iteration, selection or modularity. Merry's final concept map identified four concepts; they included substantial linkage between concepts, and some grouping of concepts.

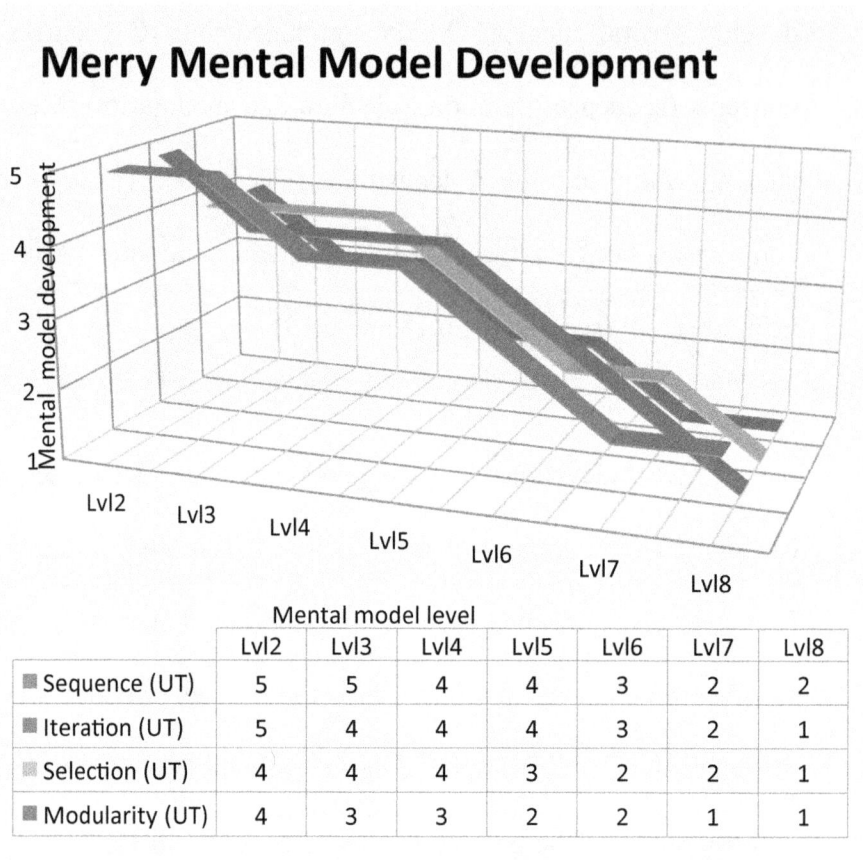

	Lvl2	Lvl3	Lvl4	Lvl5	Lvl6	Lvl7	Lvl8
Sequence (UT)	5	5	4	4	3	2	2
Iteration (UT)	5	4	4	4	3	2	1
Selection (UT)	4	4	4	3	2	2	1
Modularity (UT)	4	3	3	2	2	1	1

Figure 6.18   Merry Trace (repeated from Figure 5.31)

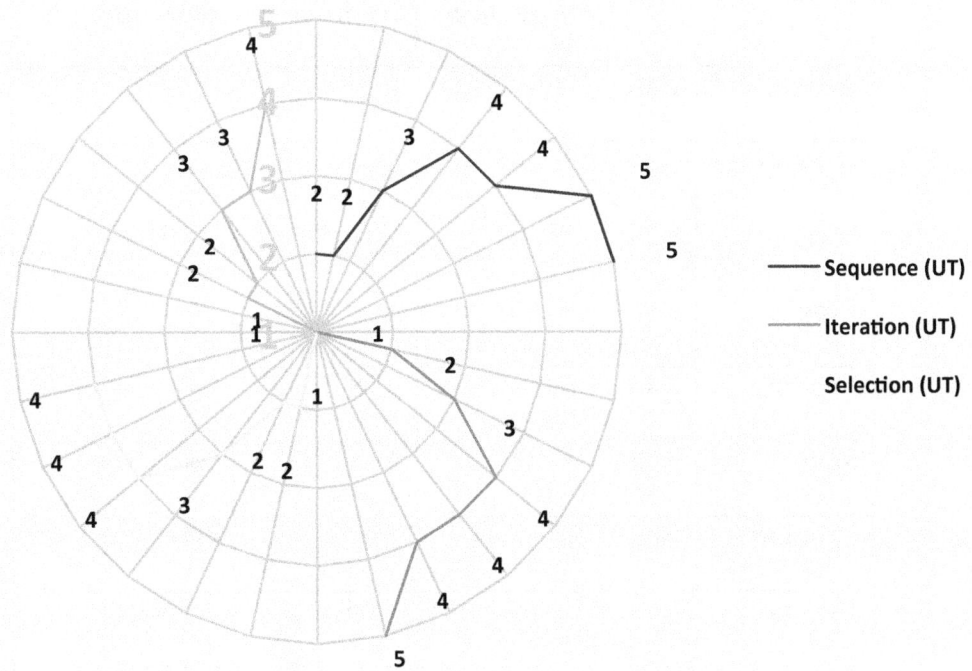

Figure 6.19 Merry Trace (repeated from Figure 5.90)

While each narrative provides an insight into individual processes, collectively the narratives contribute to categorisation and overall analysis of the effect of visualisation on learning in the domain of programming. The following narrative summary is grouped according to the visualisation tool (Figure 6.20) used, and provides a context for comparing narratives against the degree of visualisation provided by the software visualisation tool (see Section 7.5).

		Sequence	Iteration	Selection	Modularity
Aragorn	C4b	PHP (UT)			
Boromir	C3a	PHP (UT)			
Merry	D2a	VB (UT)	VB (UT)	VB (UT)	VB (UT)
Pippin	D1a	Alice (CT)	Alice (CT)	Alice (CT)	Alice (CT)
Frodo	A4c	Alice (CT)	Alice (CT)	GameMaker (CI)	GameMaker (CI)
Sam	A3a	Alice (CT)	Alice (CT)	GameMaker (CI)	GameMaker (CI)
Gandalf	B4a			RoboLab (UI)	
Legolas	B6a	RoboLab (UI)	RoboLab (UI)	RoboLab (UI)	
Gimli	B1b	RoboLab (UI)	RoboLab (UI)	RoboLab (UI)	

Figure 6.20 Narratives summary by tool

In the following chapter, this analysis is structured into examples through which individual narratives are combined with comparative data (See Figures 5.32) and surveys of perceived effectiveness to develop a greater understanding of the effect of visualisation on the learning process (see Chapter 7).

Chapter 7

DISCUSSION

From the nine narratives developed in Chapter 6 and from analysis of the data in Chapter 5, a number of findings have been derived by comparing and contrasting individual narratives and the results of the study overall. Firstly, an overview of archetypical response is examined and general trends for the population identified (see Section 7.1). This is followed by an examination of occurrences of plateauing (see Section 7.2) and the effect of prior learning on mental model development (see Section 7.3). The discussion section closes by examining the degree of visualisation of the software visualisation tools used in the study, and the effect they have had on student learning. This is contained in two sections, through the focused examination of a specific case studies (see Section 7.4) and through the overall effect the degree of visualisation of various tools has had for the population of the study as a whole (see Section 7.5).

Seventeen conclusions are made in three categories that address the aims of the study (see Section 1.2). The first (general) aim relates to the effect of visualisation on the learning process (Section 8.1), the second (operational) aim relates to the use of mental model theory to track the learning process (Section 8.2), and the third (emerging) aim relates to the reasons why previous studies have failed (Section 8.3). This is followed by a summary of the four significant contributions this study makes (Section 8.4), and ends with directions for future research (Section 8.5).

7.1 Everyman – the archetypal response

Frodo (see Sections 5.1.1.8, 5.3.5 and 6.1) is representative of the majority of the population sampled 22 ($N=31$) and a basis against which to compare more complex narratives. Frodo engaged with a range of visualisation technologies and used these to develop a number of mental models. In this, Frodo consciously used mental model theory to track her cognitive development and actively identified points at which she experienced difficulty in progressing her learning (see Section 1.4).

Mental model theory (see Section 2.3) proved to be an effective framework to assist Frodo to identify her degree of understanding of concepts against a scaled continuum (see Section 5.3.5). This provided a reference aid to metacognitive understanding, and detailed tracking of her learning processes (see Finding 10, Section 8.2).

Frodo displayed little difficulty with the initial stages of concept development in any of the four programming processes. But in each case, as the concept was developed, it became increasingly difficult for Frodo to progress to subsequent stages.

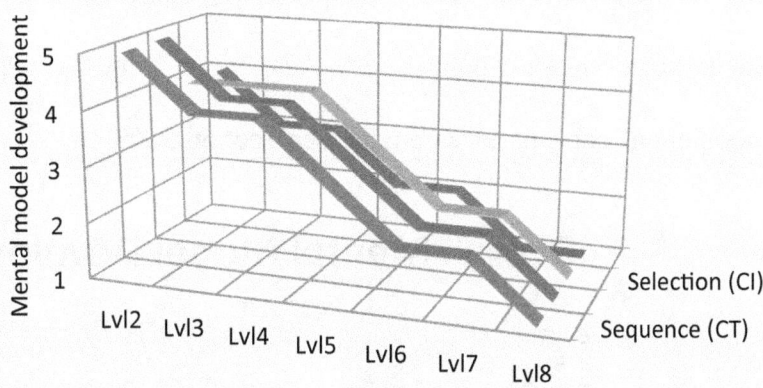

Figure 7.1   Frodo's archetypal trace

Frodo's progress is archetypically what could logically be expected from cognitive load theory (see Section 2.5). As the difficulty and degree of complexity of the concept increased, it became harder for Frodo to refine her mental model to that new level of complexity. Initially, as the complexity of the concept (sequence – iteration – selection – modularity) increased, Frodo found it increasingly difficult to develop her mental model of the concept to previous degrees (see 5.1.1.9). With respect to visualisation, Frodo found Constrained Text and Constrained Icons equally effective at some levels, particularly at the lower levels of complexity. However, Constrained Icons were found to be more effective for her in moving from observing to structuring (Level 6 to 7) and from structuring to inventising (Level 7 to 8). This differentiation between the results of the visualisation tool showed that beyond property noticing (Level 4), while both continued to show increasing difficulty as the concept complexity increased, this was markedly less difficult using the constrained icon tool (see Section 8.2).

Frodo provides an archetypal profile on which to compare the remaining narratives. Her mental model development graph (Figure 7.1) can be compared with the population as a whole (Figure 7.2), drawn from the overall effectiveness of the populations concept development (see Section 5.1.5).

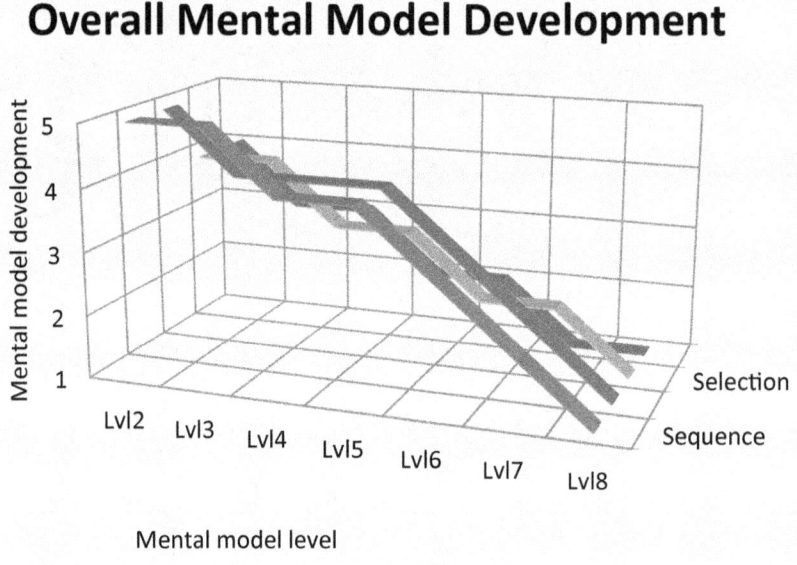

Figure 7.2   Overall concept development effectiveness

7.2   Plateauing

Plateauing of student mental model development occurred when little of no further progress occurred for that concept. Two forms of plateauing were identified in this study. The first with respect to development of the learners mental model development (see Section 2.4), and the second with regard to the complexity of a concept (see Section 2.5).

Rumelhart and Norman (1981) (see Section 2.4) suggested that a lack of metacognitive skill may impose limits on concept development. This lack of learned automation of cognitive processes can subsequently reduce available working memory (Schneider & Shiffrin, 1977). Mental model theory (Pirie & Kieren, 1992) also notes delineation between Levels 1 to 4 and Levels 5 to 8. Formalising (Level 5) marks a de-contextualised shift to where concepts are free from the context from which they were derived (see Section 2.4).

Gimli (see Sections 5.1.1.2, 5.3.6 and 6.4) is representative of a proportion of the population ($n=8$ or 26%), who experienced difficulties progressing beyond a specific level of complexity of their mental model. Regardless of the complexity of the concept or the visualisation tool in use, these students plateaued at a consistent level. For Gimli, this was from property noticing to formalising (Levels 4 to 5). She progressed typically (as compared with Frodo) but was unable to develop her mental model of a concept beyond property noticing (Level 4) (see Figure 7.3).

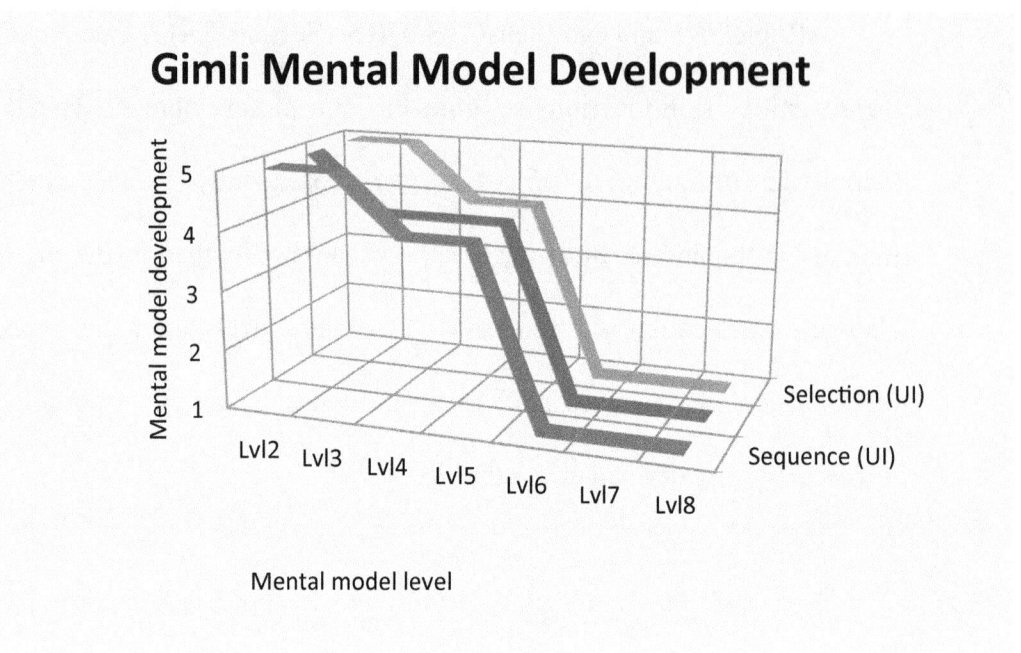

Figure 7.3   Gimli plateuing

Gimli had great difficulty in noting properties and abstracting commonalities. In the case of sequence, Gimli was unable to take a sequence developed for one task and incorporate it into the solution of other tasks. In developing the concept of iteration, Gimli was unable to take individual iterative processes and run several in parallel such that they were synchronised. In developing the concept of selection, Gimli was unable to combine smaller selections to generate complex nested selections. These difficulties are representative of a change from activities in which the context was generally well defined, to one that is generally free of specific context.

In addition to a contextual shift from Level 4 to 5, Pirie and Kieren (1992) identified boundary levels from levels 2 to 3, 4 to 5, and 6 to 7. All occurrences of plateauing in this study occurred at one of these levels. In six of the eight cases, it occurred from Levels 4 to 5; the remaining two cases occurred from Levels 6 to 7. While folding back (Pirie & Kieren, 1992) occurred in all such cases, it did not result in continued progression. In each case, Gimli identified the point where she experienced difficulty in progressing from one mental model level to the next. In order to more fully understand the concept, she utilised folding back to return to learning activities at Level 4, and in one case to Level 2. Gimli had a very clear mental model of each concept up to and including Level 4 and was able to demonstrate this understanding in her activities, learning log, interviews and speak aloud sessions (see Section 4.4.2).

Despite spending considerable time on progressing from Level 4 to 5, she was unable to further develop her mental model in any of the three concepts. The process confirmed the progressive nature of the mental model process (see Section 2.4) with Gimli being unable to develop levels beyond Level 5 despite attempts to bypass this level. Interview and trace analysis suggested that Gimli (see Sections 5.3.6 and 6.4) lacked an understanding of the metacognitive processes involved and that this lack of understanding inhibited her in addressing levels that required abstraction and consideration of the concept beyond a given context to a generalisable solution (see Finding 10, Section 8.2).

Legolas (see Sections 5.1.2.11, 5.3.6 and 6.3) on the other hand, mirrored the concepts and visualisations tools used by Gimli. In comparing Legolas and Gimli, there is almost no difference in their mental model development up to the plateau point (Level 4) (see Figure 7.4).

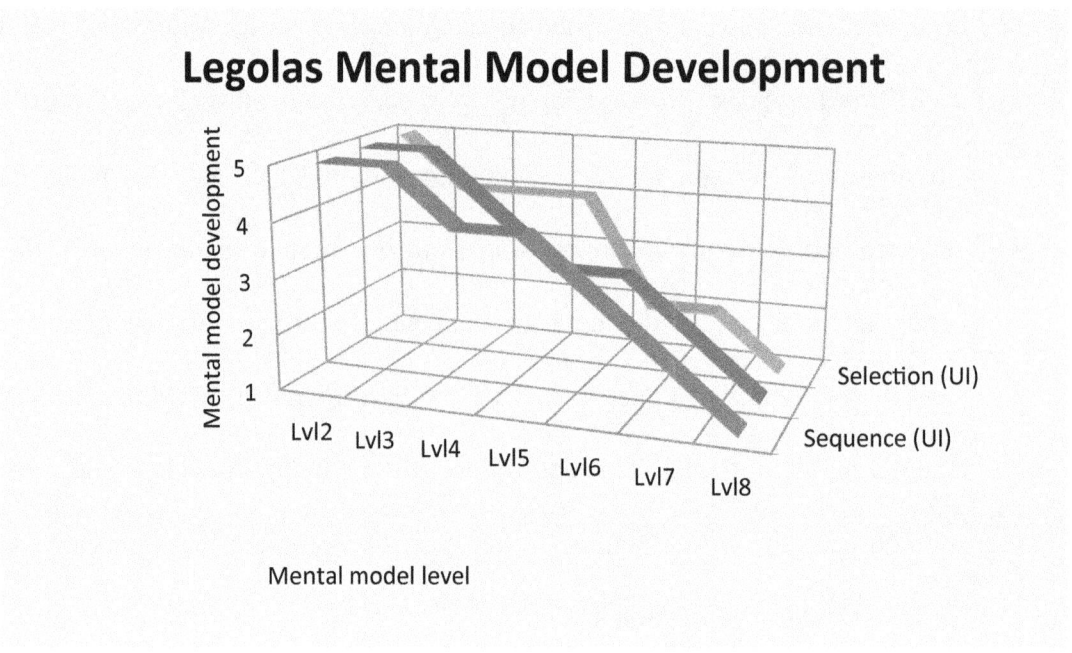

Figure 7.4   Legolas Trace

Legolas reported none of the difficulties experienced by Gimli in developing her mental model of a concept beyond property noticing (Level 4). While she does progressively experience difficulty as the level of her mental model develops, she does not plateau at any point. Interview and trace analysis (see Section 6.3) showed that Legolas had a well developed understanding of the metacognitive processes involved. These processes were automatic except when she was focused on describing and understanding her learning processes (see Section 2.5). This understanding may have assisted her in addressing levels that required abstraction and without specific context as suggested by Rumelhart and Norman (1981). It also reduced her cognitive load as she was able to focus on problem solving and not on the learning processes (see Section 8.4).

7.3 Effect of prior learning

While Legolas was able to outperform Gimli because of her greater understanding of the learning processes involved (see Section 7.2), Gandalf (see Sections 5.1.2.7, 5.3.10, and 6.5) provided another perspective, the effect of prior knowledge (Tuovinen, 2000) on mental model development.

Gandalf missed developing the lower complexity concepts of sequence and iteration due to an illness. Her first experience with the use of mental model theory to track her learning was in studying the concept of selection. This provided a significantly increased cognitive load as she was required to develop solutions to complex problems without prior experience in developing similar problems for lower complexity concepts. In addition she had to develop an understanding of the metacognitive processes involved in tracking and articulating her mental model development.

Despite these impediments, Gandalf did not demonstrate difficulty in developing her mental model of selection to an above average, compared to Frodo, mental model (see Figure 7.5). Gandalf did describe initial difficulties in understanding the metacognitive processes involved and a significant proportion of her cognitive processing was initially used on this aspect (see Section 2.5). Unlike most (92%) students however, Gandalf had prior experience with computer programming (see Section 6.5). This experience provided a framework to associate new learning and significantly reduced her cognitive load when it would have otherwise been expected to be exceeded as demonstrated by Gimli (see Section 7.2).

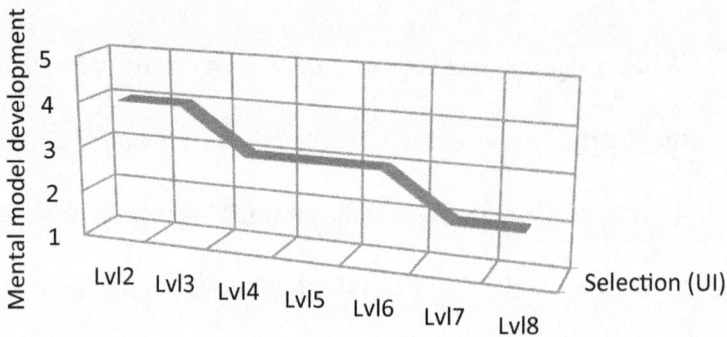

Figure 7.5   Gandalf Trace

The process of scaffolding pervious experiences to support new learning is well established (Maybin et al., 1992; Reiser, 2004; Vygotsky, 1978) and the automating of prior knowledge (Tuovinen, 2000) and procedural processes (see Section 4.6) can reduce cognitive load, freeing working memory for problem solving and further developing the mental model (see Finding 12, Section 8.2).

The influence of prior knowledge is also shown in comparing the mental model development of Aragorn (see Sections 5.1.3.8, 5.3.18 and 6.6) and Boromir (see Sections 5.1.3.1, 5.3.17, and 6.7). Aragorn had initial success in developing a detailed mental model of the concept of sequence (see Figure 7.6) and this enabled subsequent stages to fully develop. Boromir did not experience initial success in developing her mental model (see Figure 7.7) and as a result, her subsequent development was limited by gaps in her knowledge and poorly developed processes. Limitations in her initial mental model produced a ceiling to which subsequent stages could not exceed. This demonstrated the importance of developing strong foundational understanding and the reliance of subsequent mental model development on prior stages (see Finding 11, Section 8.2). Student comments and trace (see Section 5.3.17) suggest the reduced initial mental model on which to develop associations was not sufficient for subsequent mental model development.

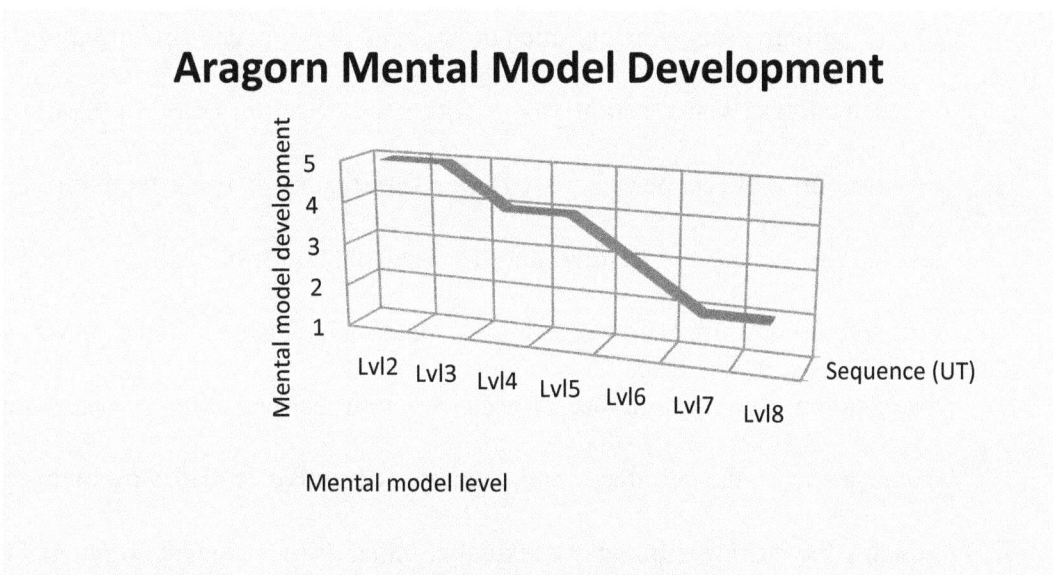

Figure 7.6   Aragorn Trace

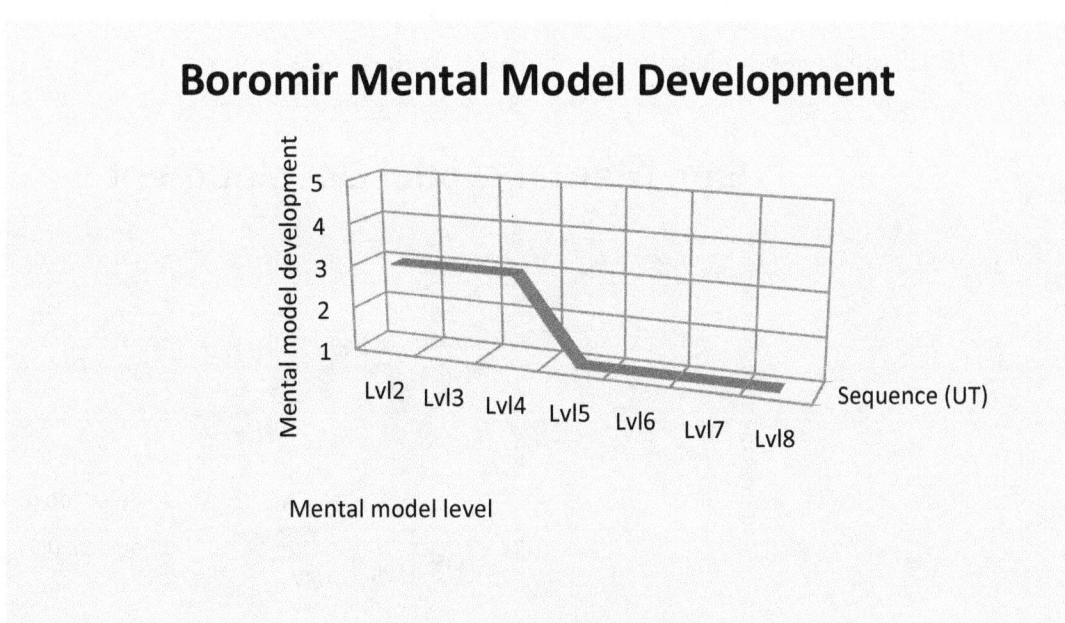

Figure 7.7   Boromir Trace

7.4 Effect of degree of visualisation

Sam (see Sections 5.1.1.5, 5.5.3 and 6.2), using the constrained icon visualisation tool (GameMaker) (see Section 3.3) was able to develop a complex mental model of selection and modularity through to inventising (Level 8) but was unable (see Figure 7.8) to similarly develop her mental models of sequence and iteration using the constrained text visualisation tool (Alice) (see Section 3.2). In Sam's case, one visualisation tool (GameMaker - CI) was significantly more effective in helping her develop her mental model than another visualisation tool (Alice - CT). While both tools required a mix of textual and visual processing, the more successful visualisation tool (GameMaker) was reported as providing greater support for visualisation of the problems and reducing cognitive load for problem solving by reducing the need to think about textual commands (see student comments in Section 5.3.3). This is supported by analysis of student perceived effectiveness (see Section 5.2.2) and overall visualisation tool effectiveness (see Figure 7.12).

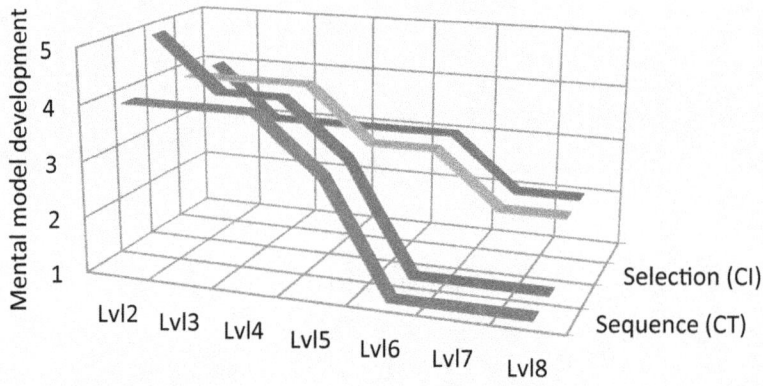

Figure 7.8   Sam Trace

7.5 Overall effect of degree of visualisation

While narratives (see Chapter 6) provide insight into the cognitive development processes of individual students, collectively the students in this study compared the effectiveness of the visualisation tools used (see Section 5.1.5). This range of visualisation tools form a continuum (see Figure 7.9) describing the degree of visualisation they support from predominantly auditory processing, through a mix of visual and auditory processing, to tools that predominantly support visual processing (see Chapter 3).

Figure 7.9   Processing continuum

The range of software visualisation tools used in this study (see Figure 7.10 and Table 6.2) relate to this processing continuum (see Figure 7.9) as verified in trace analyses (see Section 4.4 and 5.3).

Figure 7.10   Programming Languages continuum

This, in turn, provides a continuum depicting the degree of visualisation used by a software visualisation tool (see Figure 7.11) and can be related to the effectiveness of the tool as assessed in this study (see Chapter 5).

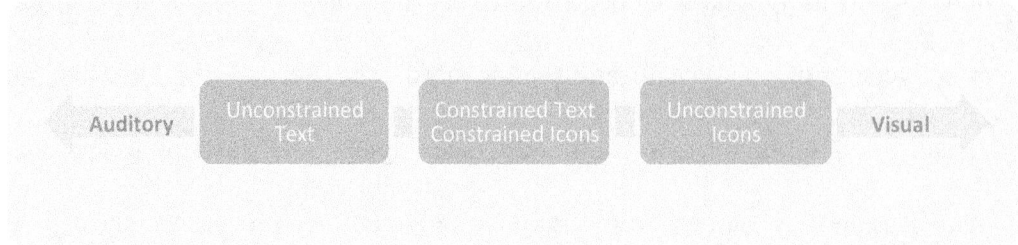

Figure 7.11   Visualisation continuum

Analysis of student concept development (Section 5.1.5 and Figure 7.12) shows that the degree of visualisation does not relate directly to the effectiveness of the visualisation tools along the continuum described (see Figures 7.9, 7.10 and 7.11).

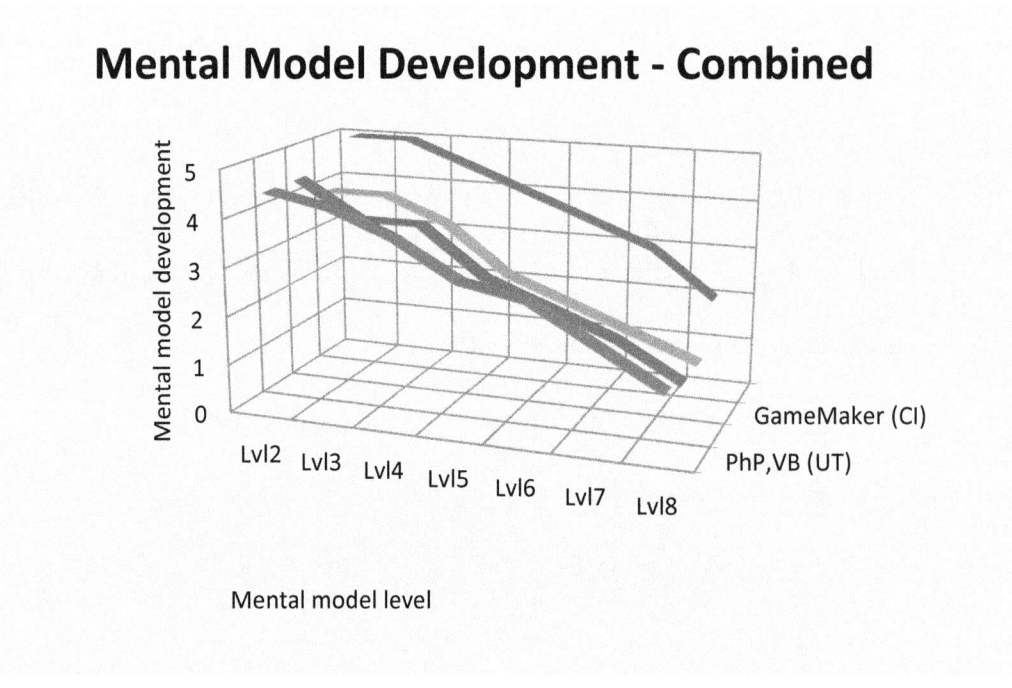

Figure 7.12   Overall visualisation tool effectiveness - Combined

The combined, overall visualisation tool effectiveness graph (Figure 7.12), shows that the RoboLab visualisation tool was the most effective in developing the concepts examined in this study. The RoboLab programming language (Unconstrained Icons) used predominantly visual processing to reduce cognitive load (see Section 7.1) and promote cognitive development.

The combined, overall visualisation tool effectiveness graph (Figure 7.12), shows that the Alice and GameMaker visualisation tools were the least effective overall in developing the concepts examined in this study. The Alice (Constrained Text) and GameMaker (Constrained Icons) programming languages used a mix of visual and auditory processing, that increased cognitive load and had a positive or negative effect on cognitive development depending on the complexity of the concept (see Section 7.4).

The combined graph (Figure 7.12), also shows that the Visual Basic and PHP visualisation tools were initially effective in developing the concepts examined in this study but were not as effective as the RoboLab visualisation tool in developing a complex understanding of the concepts using these tools. The Visual Basic (UT) and PHP (UT) programming languages used predominantly auditory processing and did not necessarily promote cognitive development to the same extent as programming languages that are predominantly visual.

To understand the role of the degree of visualisation on the effectiveness of student learning, it is necessary to examine the development of individual concepts. In the overall development of the concept of sequence (see Figure 7.13), a low complexity concept in relation to the other concepts developed in this study, there is was minimal difference in effectiveness between the degrees of visualisation.

Student trace analysis (see Section 4.5.2) demonstrate that for concepts with low cognitive demand, where the use of predominately visual, auditory or a mixture of the two does not exceed working memory capacity, there is minimal difference in the effectiveness of the visualisation tools to develop the concept (see Section 7.4). The GameMaker (CI) visualisation tool was not used in the development of the concept of sequence.

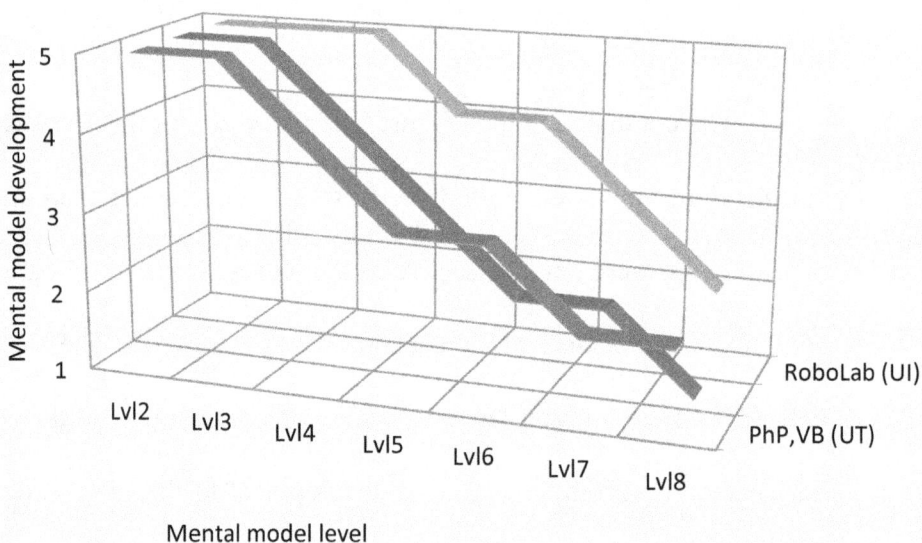

Figure 7.13 Overall visualisation tool effectiveness – Sequence

The next most complex concept was iteration (see Figure 7.14), the Alice (CT) visualisation tool, relying on auditory processing but including some visual processing, is less effective at developing the concept of iteration than tools relying predominately on either auditory or visual processing. The GameMaker (CI) visualisation tool was again not used in the development of this concept.

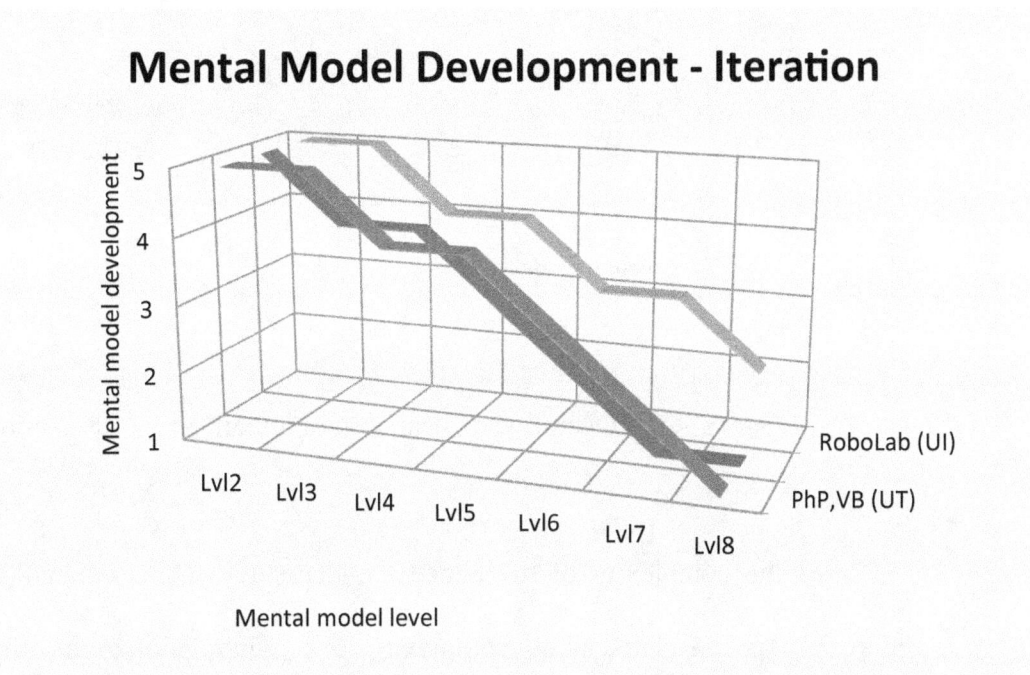

Figure 7.14 Overall visualisation tool effectiveness - Iteration

This can also be seen in the overall development of the next most complex concept, selection (see Figure 7.15). Both GameMaker (relying on visual processing but including some auditory processing) and Alice (relying on auditory processing but including some visual processing) are less effective at developing the concept of selection than tools relying predominately on either auditory or visual processing.

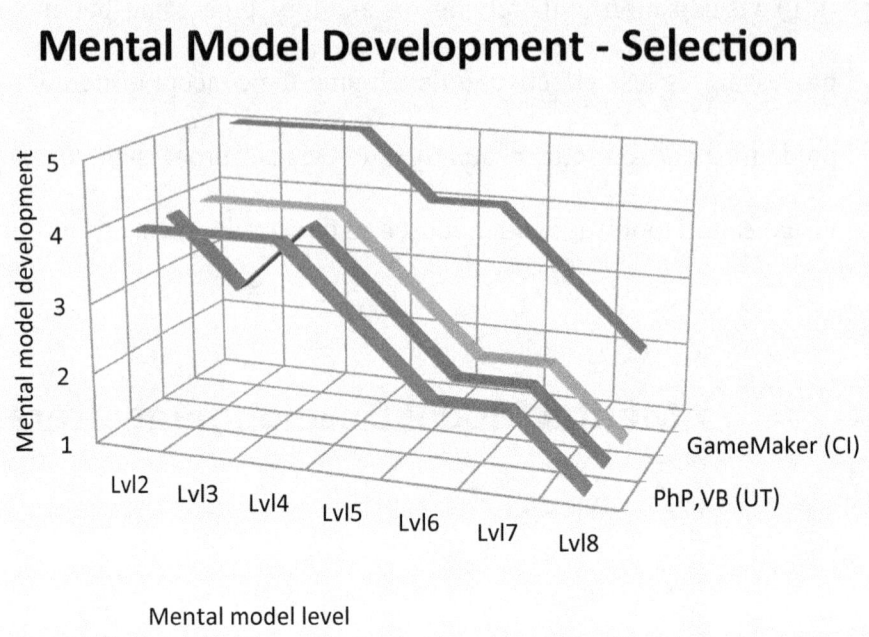

Figure 7.15   Overall visualisation tool effectiveness – Selection

As the complexity of the concept under study increased, modularity (see Figure 7.16) is considered a high complexity concept in relation to the other concepts developed in this study, there was again considerable difference in the effectiveness of tools using a single mode of processing, in this case auditory, and those using a mix of auditory and visual processing. The RoboLab (UI) visualisation tool was not used in the development of this concept.

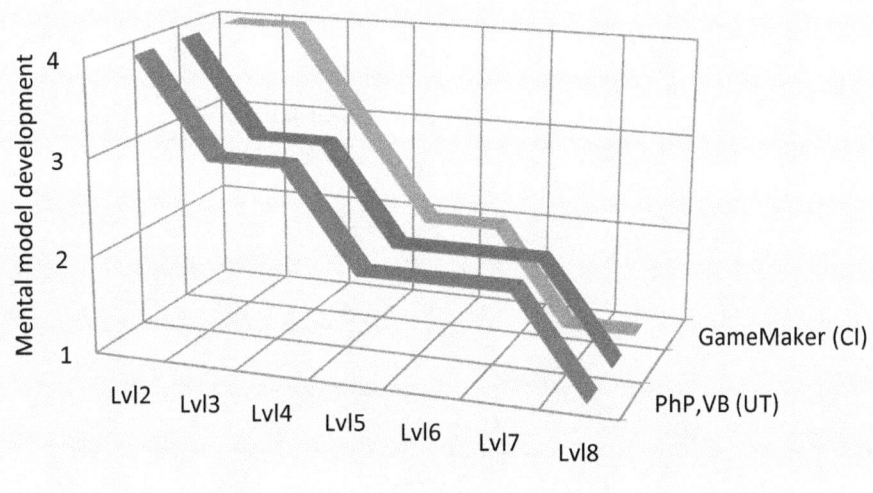

Figure 7.16 Overall visualisation tool effectiveness – Modularity

When examined as a whole (see Figure 7.17), including concept development effectiveness (see Section 5.1), perceived effectiveness (see Section 5.2), and mental model traces (see Section 5.3) the Unconstrained Icon visualisation tool RoboLab was the most successful in teaching fundamental programming concepts. RoboLab relies to the greatest degree on visual processing and the least on auditory processing (see Section 3.4).

The study has also shown (see Sections 7.1, 7.2, 7.4 and 7.5) the cognitive impact of combining visual and auditory processing (Findings 1, 2 and 3), and that while effective at low levels of concept complexity (see Section 7.4), can impede cognitive development of complex concepts.

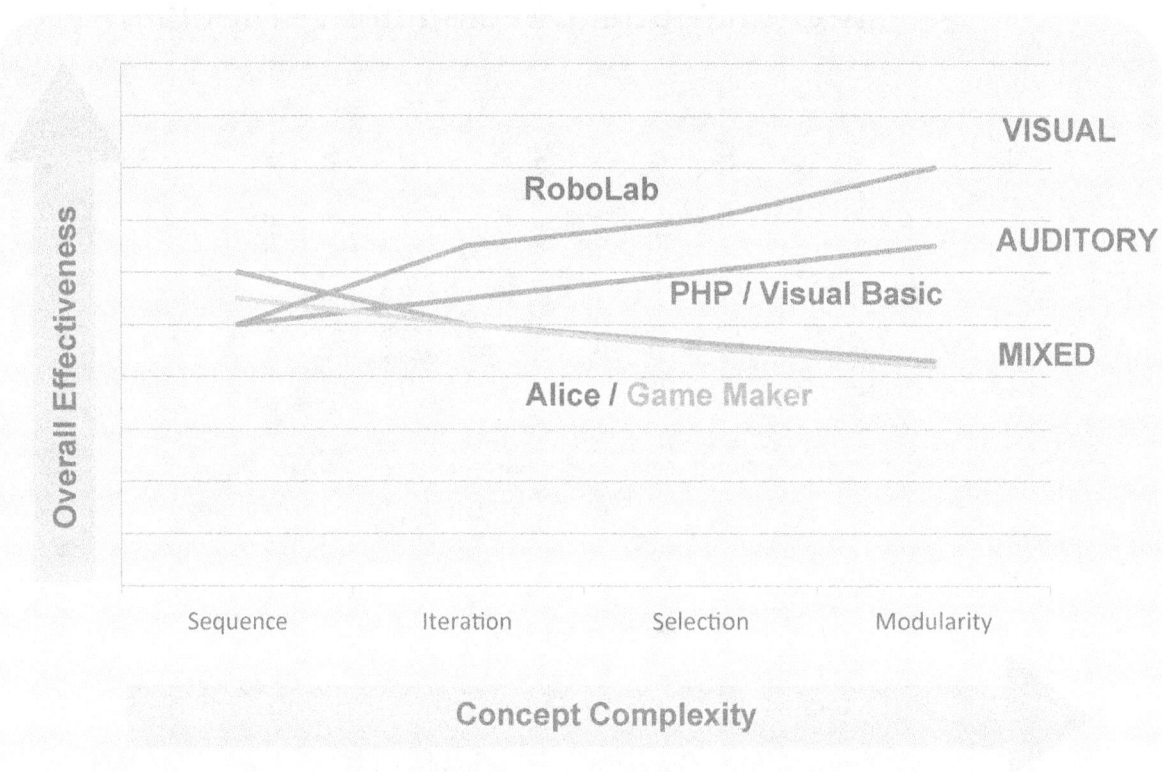

Figure 7.17   Overall effectiveness

In examining the effect of visualisation on the learning process through collective case studies exploring the effectiveness of various software visualisation tools, a number of conclusions can be drawn and are presented in the following and final chapter (Chapter 8).

Chapter 8

CONCLUSIONS

At its simplest, this study was concerned with how and why visualisation could support the learning of programming concepts. The three aims of the qualitative instrumental collective case study described in this study were:

1. to increase understanding of the effect of visualisation on the learning process with a focus on the effect of software visualisations on learning in the domain of programming;

2. to extend the use of mental model theory to track learning processes and incorporate metacognitive self analysis; and

3. to forward an explanation of the failure of software visualisation to improve educational outcomes in quantitative research studies through the use of a qualitative approach.

Seventeen conclusions have been derived from the study. These can be organised in three categories with each category analogous to an aim of study (see Section 1.2). These are:

1. Conclusions 1-9 relate to the first or overarching aim, that is, the effect of visualisation on the learning process (Section 8.1).

2. Conclusions 10-15 relate to the second or operational, aim, that is the use of mental model theory to track the learning process (Section 8.2),

3. Conclusions 16-17 relate to the third or emergent aim, that is, the reasons why previous studies have failed (Section 8.3).

The study has added to the domain of knowledge in this field through four significant contributions (Section 8.4). This chapter will conclude with directions for future research (Section 8.5).

8.1 The effect of visualisation on the learning process

The first nine conclusions of the study relate to the first or overarching aim (Section 1.2). These can be further divided into conclusions related (a) generally to levels of concept complexity (Conclusions 1-3) and (b) specifically to differing programming languages in terms of their effectiveness as visualisation tools to support the learning of fundamental programming concepts (Conclusions 4-9).

Conclusion 1. The study finds that for the cohorts investigated (see Section 4.2), those programming languages that are predominantly visual (see Section 7.5), reduce cognitive load (see Section 7.4) and promote cognitive development (see Section 7.5).

Conclusion 2. The study finds that for the cohorts investigated (see Section 4.2), those programming languages that mix visual and auditory processing (see Section 7.5), increase cognitive load (see Section 7.4) and can have a positive or negative effect on cognitive development depending on the complexity of the concept (see Section 7.5).

Conclusion 3. The study finds that for the cohorts investigated (see Section 4.2), those programming languages that are predominantly auditory processing (see Section 7.5), reduce cognitive load (see Section 7.4) but do not necessarily promote cognitive development to the same extent as programming languages that are predominantly visual (see Section 7.5).

Conclusion 4. The study finds that the PHP and Visual Basic programming languages (see Sections 3.1 and 3.4) rely predominantly on auditory cognitive processing (see Section 7.5).

Conclusion 5. The study finds that the Alice and GameMaker programming languages (see Section 4) rely on both visual and auditory cognitive processing (see Section 7.5).

Conclusion 6. The study finds that the RoboLab programming language (see Section 4) relies predominantly on visual cognitive processing (see Section 7.5).

Conclusion 7. The study finds that for low complexity concept development (see Section 2.5), programming languages that rely on both visual and auditory cognitive processing (Alice and GameMaker) are more effective in supporting learning of fundamental programming concepts (see Section 7.5) than those that rely on either visual or auditory (but not both) cognitive processes (PHP, Visual Basic, and RoboLab). The study finds that for the cohorts investigated, this was primarily due to the cognitive reinforcement resulting from simultaneous processing of both visual and auditory elements providing greater resources for problem solving and mental model development (see Section 7.5).

Conclusion 8. The study finds that for high complexity concept development (see Section 2.5), programming languages that rely on either visual or auditory (but not both) cognitive processing (PHP, Visual Basic, and RoboLab) are more effective in supporting the learning of fundamental programming concepts(see Section 7.5) than those that rely on both visual and auditory cognitive processing (Alice and GameMaker). The study finds that for the cohorts investigated this was primarily due to the cognitive load resulting from simultaneous processing of both visual and auditory elements reducing working memory capacity for problem solving (see Section 7.5).

Conclusion 9. The study finds that for high complexity concept development (see Section 2.5), programming languages that rely predominantly on visual cognitive processes (RoboLab) are more effective in supporting learning of fundamental programming concepts(see Section 7.5) than those that rely on auditory cognitive processes (PHP and Visual Basic). The study finds that for the cohorts investigated this was primarily due to the cognitive reinforcement resulting from visual elements providing greater resources for problem solving and mental model development (see Section 7.4).

8.2 Mental model theory to track the learning process

The study made use of mental model theory to track cognitive development of programming concepts. This resulted in six Conclusions (Conclusions 10-15), which relate to the second or operational aim of the study (Section 1.2).

Conclusion 10. The study finds that mental model theory provided an effective framework to track the learning processes occurring for the cohorts investigated (see Section 7.1).

Conclusion 11. The study finds that mental model theory provides an effective framework to track the degree to which learning of programming concepts are supported by visualisations (see Section 7.2).

Conclusion 12. The study finds that scaffolding (see Section 7.3) the use of visualisation tools provides an automation of procedural processes (see Section 4.6) and maximises the capacity of working memory for problem solving.

Conclusion 13. The study has verified difficulties at level boundaries (see Section 2.4) and between contextual and decontextualised (see Section 4.5.1) levels predicted by mental model theory. These points and plateauing at the contextual-decontextual boundary were supported by observations in this study (see Section 7.2).

Conclusion 14. Student self identification of mental model development (see Section 1.4 and 4.2) was verified (see Section 4.4.2) as an effective means of identifying cognitive processes and tracing cognitive development (see Section 7.1).

Conclusion 15. A mental model development rubric (see Appendix C) developed to measure cognitive performance provided a consistent measurement of cognitive development for the cohorts studied(see Section 5.1). This consistency was confirmed by student self identified traces (see Section 5.3), verification interviews (see Section 4.4.2) and surveys (see Section 5.2).

8.3 Reasons for the failure of previous studies

The study identifies two probable reasons why previous studies on software visualisation (see Sections 7.1 and 8.1, Conclusions 7, 8 and 9) have shown minimal or negative educational benefit in teaching programming. These are related to the third or emergent aim of the study (Section 1.2).

Conclusion 16. Previous studies have invariably used software visualisation tools to teach very complex programming concepts (see Section 2.2) without consideration of the learning processes involved from either visualisation or cognitive perspectives. They have relied on a simplistic assumption that the use of visualisations will inherently improve the learning process without consideration of underlying cognitive processes or the previous failure rates of such studies.

As a result, previous studies have attempted to develop highly complex concepts without scaffolding the cognitive processing processes involved (see Sections 7.3 and 8.2Conclusion 12). This may have resulted in disproportionate cognitive processing being used on novel visual learning processes and reducing that available for problem solving. In effect, students may have spent the majority of their available cognitive processing capacity on the unfamiliar learning processes involved in these studies, leading to the inconclusive or reduced learning outcomes reported.

Conclusion 17. While purporting to be studies into visualisation, previous studies have invariably developed and used visualisation tools that rely on both visual and auditory cognitive processing (where textual processing is equated to auditory processing (see Section 2.1). Combined with high complexity concepts, the resulting cognitive load from simultaneous processing of visual and auditory elements may have reduced working memory capacity for problem solving and impeded learning in these studies (see Section 7.2).

8.4 Summary of contributions

This study presents four original and significant contributions to this field of research and highlights impact factors on the educational application of the research.

Contribution 1. The study has integrated visualisation theories and cognitive theories of memory to produce a greater understanding of the influences of both sets of theory on the processes involved in learning fundamental computer programming concepts. The resultant framework provides guidance to educators in using cognitive tools to take advantage of visualisations to support students in learning programming languages. In particular, it highlights the educational impact of mixing auditory (or text) and visual elements in which the resulting processing load, depending on the complexity of the programming concept, can enhance or degrade cognitive development. This contribution is placed within a broader research field on the instructional impact of multimedia resources (Kalyuga, 2000).

Contribution 2. The study has categorised and compared a range of programming languages and provided a framework for determining the effectiveness of a programming language to develop a particular concept depending on the complexity of the concept and the degree of visualisation supported by the programming language. This provides guidance to educators in determining the most effective programming language to employ for the development of specific concepts and to where the development of particular concepts will not be supported or will be impeded by a particular programming language.

Contribution 3. This study has provided an explanation, supported by theory, as to the lack of positive educational outcomes from previous studies into the use of software visualisations to teach computer programming. Conclusions from this study may inform future studies in software visualisation theory to support the learning of programming languages and improve the success rate of studies in this field.

Contribution 4. This study has shown that mental model theory can be used in an applied manner to accurately track student learning of fundamental programming concepts. The involvement of students in self directed metacognitive tracking was a key determiner of the successful application of mental model theory on the scale and fidelity required for this study. As such, the study provides an example and model for research based educational practice in which student metacognitive analysis of their individual cognitive processes can inform individual and classroom curriculum and pedagogy decisions.

8.5 Future Research

Five areas in which future research could be developed from this study are described: development of a quantitative study supporting the findings of this research; qualitative research to address limitations in this study; qualitative research to refine the finding of this study; application of this research to other domains; and, research into the involvement of students in this study.

The first suggestion for future research involves using the findings from this study to inform a quantitative research study (see Section 2.2) to fully develop the scope of research, both the qualitative how and why, and the quantitative what, where and when. This could be specifically targeted at more fully understanding the reasons for previous quantitative failures established by this study (see Section 8.3) and increasing the generalisability of this studies result. The application of direct measurement of cognitive activity using non-invasive electroencephalography (EEG) headsets may provide measurement of auditory and visual pre-processing and provide a measurable indication of processing load and overload events. Where low cost portable devices can be deployed in classroom environments, the capacity of students and their teachers to act as co-researchers to track and modify individual learning processes would be enhanced and increase the classroom application of approaches to improving the learning processes identified in this study.

Secondly, further qualitative study could aim to overcome the identified limitations of this study, in particular by addressing individual differences in subject prior ability in both their existing mental model of the subject matter and their existing higher order thinking skills such as analysis, synthesis and evaluation. By incorporating these factors (see Section 4.8) into future studies, a more detailed understanding may be made of the role of memory and visualisation in individual learning differences, particularly in the identification and remediation of factors that impede mental model development that are external but necessary to presented learning and teaching approaches. For example, a student's ability to evaluate may be insufficient to permit them to develop a mental model beyond a particular point where such development is predicated on such ability.

Thirdly, further study could aim at increasing the resolution of the study. While the present study explored the role of memory in visualisation, further refinement of the processes involved could be explored such as the role of Gestalt principles in the structure of visualisations and generated cognitive views (see Section 2.3), or the effectiveness of software visualisations to support cognitive chunking and the degree to which chunking improves mental model development beyond that addressed in this study.

Fourthly, the seventeen conclusions of this study could be applied to other domains. These may include studies into the effectiveness of visualisations on the learning of other subject matter, the applicability of mental model theory to track the learning process of different subject populations, or the applicability of mental model theory to track learning processes in other domains of knowledge.

Fifth and finally, student involvement as co-researchers in this study could be explored (see Section 1.3) and research conducted into the educational outcomes of such involvement. This could lead to the development and validation of a teaching approach incorporating visualisation, cognitive memory, and mental model theories.

References

Adams, J. (1967). *Human memory*. New York: McGraw-Hill.

Alabastro, M. S., Beckmann, G., Gifford, G., Massey, A. P., & Wallace, W. A. (1995). The use of visualisation modelling in designing a manufacturing process for advanced composite structures. *IEEE Transactions on Engineering Management, 42*(3), 223-242.

Alice (Version 2.0) [Computer Software]. Carnegie Mellon University: Stage3 Research Group. Retrieved October 27, 2007, from www.alice.org

Anderson, J. (1983). *The architecture of cognition*. Cambridge, MA: Harvard University Press.

Ausubel, D. (1963). *The psychology of meaningful verbal learning*. New York: Grune & Stratton.

Baddeley, A. & Hitch, G. (1974). Working memory. In G. A. Bower (Ed.), *Recent advances in learning and motivation,* (Vol.9, pp. 47-90). New York: Academic Press.

Baddeley, A. (1992). Working memory. *Science*, 255, 556-559

Baecker, R. M. (1975). Two systems which produce animated representations of the execution of computer programs. *ACM SIGCSE Bulletin*, 7, 158-167.

Baecker, R. M., & Marcus, A. (1990). *Human factors and typography for more readable programs*. Reading, MA: Addison-Wesley.

Baker, J., Cruz, I., Liotta, G., & Tamassia, R. (1996). Algorithm animation over the World Wide Web. *Proceedings of the workshop on Advanced Visual Interfaces, May 27-29, 1996, Gubbio, Italy.*

Baker, J., Cruz, I., Liotta, J., & Tamassia, R. (1995). A new model for algorithm animation over the WWW. *ACM Computing Surveys (CSUR), 27*(4), 568-572.

Bartlett, F.C. (1932). *Remembering: An experimental and social study*. Cambridge: Cambridge University Press.

Bartlett, F.C. (1958). *Thinking*. New York: Basic Books.

Bassil, S. & Keller, R. (2001). Software visualization tools: survey and analysis. *Proceedings of 9th International Workshop on Program Comprehension, pp. 7-17, May 12-13, 2001, Toronto, Canada.*

Becker, B. W. (2007). *Java: Learning to program with robots*. Boston, MA: Thomson Course Technology.

Boroni , C., Goosey, F., Grinder, M., & Ross, R. (1998). A paradigm shift! The internet, the web, browsers, java and the future of computer science education. *ACM SIGCSE Bulletin, 30*(1), 145-152.

Bottorff, J. L. (1994). Using videotaped recordings in qualitative research. In J. M. Morse (Ed.), *Critical issues in qualitative research methods,* (pp. 244-261). Thousand Oaks, CA: Sage.

Brown, M. H., & Sedgewick, R. (1984). A system for algorithm animation. *Proceedings of ACM SIGGRAPH `84, pp. 177-186, New York: ACM.*

Bruner, J. (1960). *The process of education*. Cambridge, MA: Harvard University Press.

Brusilovsky, P., Eduardo, C., Hvorecky, J, Kouchnirenko, A, & Miller, P. (1997). Mini-languages: a way to learn programming principles. *Education and Information Technologies, 2*(1), 65-83.

Bucciarelli, M. (2007). How the construction of mental models improves learning. *Mind and Society, 6*(1), 67-89.

Buckner, R. & Carroll, D. (2007). Self projection and the brain. *Trends in Cognitive Sciences, 11*(2), 49-57.

Bull, S., & Brna, P. (1997). 'What does Susan know that Paul doesn't? (and vice-versa): contributing to each other's student model. *Proceedings of International Conference on Artificial Intelligence in Education, pp. 568 – 570, June 1997, Amsterdam, Netherlands.*

Bull, S., Brna, P., & Pain, H. (1995). Extending the scope of the student model. *User Modeling and User-Adapted Interaction, 5*(1), 44-65.

Capozolli, P. & Rogers, C. (2005). RoboLab. (Version 2.5) [Computer Software]. Tufts University: Centre for Engineering Educational outreach. Retrieved October 27, 2005, from http://www.ceeo.tufts.edu/robolabatceeo/

Card, S. K., Mackinlay, J. D., & Schniedermann, B. (1999). *Readings in Information Visualization: Using Vision to Think.* San Francisco, CA: Morgan Kaufmann Publishers.

Card, S., Moran, T. & Newell, A. (1983). The psychology of human-computer interaction. Hillsdale, NJ: Lawrence Erlbaum Associates, Inc.

Carnegie Mellon University: Stage3 Research Group (2008). *What is Alice?* Retrieved April 20, 2008, from http://www.alice.org/whatIsAlice.htm

Cermak, L. & Craik, F. (1979). *Levels of Processing in Human Memory.* Hillsdale, NJ: Erlbaum.

Chandler, P., & Sweller, J. (1991). Cognitive load theory and the format of instruction. *Cognition and Instruction, 8*, 293-332.

Cimolino, L., & Kay, J. (2002). Verified concept mapping for eliciting conceptual understanding. *Proceedings ICCE Workshop on Concepts and Ontologies in Web-based Educational Systems, International Conference on Computers in Education, CS-Report 02-15, 2002, Technische Universiteit, Eindhoven.*

Cimolino, L., Kay, J. & Miller, A. (2002). Verified concept mapping for eliciting conceptual understanding. Retrieved July 12, 2005, from http://www.cs.usyd.edu.au/~judy/Homec/Ronto.html

Cimolino, L., Kay, J., & Miller, A. (2003). Incremental student modelling and reflection by verified concept-mapping. *Proceedings of the 11th International Conference on Artificial Intelligence in Education, July 20 – 22, 2003, Sydney, Australia.*

Cimolino, L., Kay, J., & Miller, A. (2004). Concept mapping for eliciting verified personal ontologies. *International Journal of Continuing Engineering Education and Lifelong Learning, 14*(3), 56-61.

Clark, J. M., & Paivio, A. (1991). Dual coding theory and education. *Educational Psychology Review, 3*, 149-210.

Cobb, P., & Whitenack, J. W. (1996). A method for conducting longitudinal analysis of classroom videorecordings and transcripts. *Educational Studies in Mathematics, 30*, 213-228.

Collins, A., & Gentner, D. (1987). How people construct mental models. In D. Holland & N. Quinn (Eds.), *Cultural Models in Thought and Language*. Cambridge: Cambridge University Press.

Conrow, K., & Smith, R. G. (1970). NEATER2: A PL/I Source statement reformatter. *Communications of the ACM, 13*(11), 669-675.

Cooper, S., Dann, W., & Pausch, R. (2003). Teaching objects-first in introductory computer science. Paper presented at the 34th SIGCSE Technical Symposium on Computer Science Education, Reno, NV.

Craik, F. & Lockhart, R. (1972). Levels of processing: A framework for memory research. *Journal of Verbal Learning & Verbal Behavior, 11*, 671-684.

Crapo, A. (2002). A cognitive-theoretical approach to the visual representation of modelling context. (Doctoral dissertation, Rensselaer Polytechnic Institute, 2002). Dissertation.

Crapo, A., Waisel, L., Wallace, W., & Willemain, T. (2000). Visualization and the process of modeling: a cognitive-theoretic view. *Proceedings of the 6th ACM SIGKDD International Conference on Knowledge Discovery and Data Mining, August 2000, Boston, United States.*

Creswell, J. (1998). *Qualitative inquiry and research design: Choosing among five traditions.* Thousand Oaks, CA: Sage Publications, Inc.

D'Agostino, P. R., O'Neill, B. J., & Paivio, A. (1977). Memory for pictures and words as a function of level of processing: Depth or dual coding? *Memory & Cognition, 5*, 252-256.

Dann, W., Cooper, S., & Pausch, R. (2005). *Learning to program with Alice.* New York: Prentice Hall.

Davis, G. E. (1989). Children talking about children's mathematics. *Mathematics Education Research Journal, 1*(2), 35-42.

Davis, R. B., Maher, C., & Martino, A. (1992). Using videotapes to study the construction of mathematical knowledge of individual children working in groups. *Journal of Science, Education, and Technology, 1*(3), 177-189.

deKleer, J. & Brown, J.S. (1981). Mental models of physical mechanisms and their acquisition. In J.R. Anderson (ed.), *Cognitive Skills and their Acquistion*. Hillsdale, NJ: Erlbaum.

Dimopoulos, K., Koulaidis, V. & Sklaveniti, S. (2003). Towards an analysis of visual images in school science textbooks and press articles about science and technology. *Research in Science Education, 33*, 189-216.

Douglas, S.A. (1993). Using conversational analysis to discover breakdown in the design of user interfaces. *Proceedings of the CSCW Workshop on Ethnographic Methods and Design, June 1993, London, UK.*

Dunn, R., Dunn, K., & Price, G. E. (1975). *Learning style inventory*. Chappaqua, NY: Rita Dunn and Associates.

Erickson, F. (1992). The interface between ethnography and microanalysis. In M. D. LeCompte, W. L. Millroy, & J. Preissle (Eds.), *The handbook of qualitative research in education,* (pp. 201-225). San Diego, CA: Academic Press.

Ezell, C. (1990). Creating pedagogical programming environments. *Communications of the ACM, 22*(2), 42-46.

Fernandez M., & Mackie, I. (2006). Developments in computational models. *Mathematical structures in computer science, 16*, 553-555.

Finke, R. (1990). *Creative imagery: Discoveries and inventions in visualization*. Hillsdale, NJ: Lawrence Erlbaum Associates.

Francisco, J. S., Nicoll, G., & Trautmann, M. (1998). Integrating multiple teaching methods into a general chemistry classroom. *Journal of Chemical Education, 75(*2), 210-213.

Fuster, J. (1995). *Memory in the cerebral cortex*. MIT Press. Boston, MA.

Gardner, H. (1985). *The Mind's New Science*. New York: Basic Books, Inc.

Gathercole, S. E., & Baddeley, A. D. (1993). *Working memory and language*. Hove, UK: Lawrence Erlbaum Associates.

Gentner, D. & Stevens, A. (1983). *Mental Models*. Hillsdale, NJ: Erlbaum.

Goldstine, Herman H.; Goldstine, A. [1946] (1982). The Electronic Numerical Integrator and Computer (ENIAC), *The Origins of Digital Computers: Selected Papers*. New York: Springer-Verlag, 359-373.

Goldstein, H. H., & von Neumann, J. (1947). Planning and coding problems of an electronic computing instrument. In A. H. Taub (Eds.), *von Neumann, J., Collected works,* (pp. 80-151). New York: McMillan.

Götschi, T., Sanders, I., & Galpin, V. (2003). Mental models of recursion. *Proceedings of the 34th SIGCSE Technical Symposium on Computer Science Education, February 19-23, 2003, Reno, Navada, USA.*

Green, T. & Petrie, M. (1996). Usability analysis of visual programming languages: A cognitive dimensions' framework. *Journal of Visual Programming Languages, 7*(2), 131-174.

Grissom, S., McNally, M., & Naps, T. (2003). Algorithm visualization in CS education: comparing levels of student engagement. *Proceedings of the 2003 ACM symposium on Software visualization, June 11-13, 2003,* San Diego, California.

Guba, E. G., & Lincoln, Y. S. (1981). *Effective evaluation: Improving the usefulness of evaluation results through responsive an naturalistic approaches*. San Francisco: Jossey-Bass.

Guba, E.. G., & Lincoln, Y. S. (1989). *Fourth Generation Evaluation*. Beverly Hills, CA: Sage

Guthrie, E.R. (1935). *The Psychology of Learning*. New York: Harper.

Haibt, L. M. (1959). A program to draw multi-level flow charts. *Proceedings of The Western Joint Computer Conference, June 15-16, 1959*, San Francisco, CA.

Hall, R. (2000). Videorecording as theory. In R. Lesh (Ed.), *Handbook of research data design in mathematics and science education.* (pp. 647-664). Mahwah, NJ: Lawrence Erblaum Associates.

Hasselmo, M. E. & McClelland, J. L. (1999). Neural models of memory. *Current Opinion Neurobiology, 9*, 184-188.

Healey, C. G., Booth, K. S., & Enns, J. T. (1996). High-speed visual estimation using preattentive processing. *ACM Transactions on Computer-Human Interaction, 3*(2), 107-135.

Henderson, L., Putt, I., & Coombs, G. (2002). Mental models of teaching and learning with the WWW. *Proceedings of the 8th ASCILITE conference on Computers in Learning in Tertiary Education, December 2002, Auckland, New Zealand.*

Holland, J.H., Holyoak, K.J., Nisbett, R.E., Thagard, P.R. (1986). *Induction: Processes of Inference, Learning and Discovery*. Cambridge, MA: MIT Press.

Horwitz, P. (2005). GenScope project. Retrieved October 20, 2006, from http://genscope.concord.org/about/staff.html.

Howard, R., Carver, C., & Lane, W. (1996). Felder's learning styles, Bloom's taxonomy, and the Kolb learning cycle: Tying it all together in the CS2 course. *Proceedings of the 27th SIGCSE Technical Symposium on Computer Science education, pp. 227-231, February 15-17, 1996, Philadelphia, United States of America.*

Hsi, S., & Hoadley, C. M. (1997). Productive discussion in science: Gender equity through electronic discourse. *Journal of Science Education and Technology, 10*(1).

Hull, C. (1943). *Principles of Behavior*. New York: Appleton-Century-Crofts.

Hundhausen, C. D., Douglas, S. A., & Stasko, J. T. (2002). A meta-study of algorithm visualization effectiveness. *Journal of Visual Languages and Computing, 13*(3), 259-290.

Jensen, J., & Rodgers, R. (2001). Cumulating the intellectual gold of case study research. *Public Administration Review, 61*, 235-246.

Johnson-Laird, P. N. (1983). *Mental Models: Towards a Cognitive Science of Language, Inference, and Consciousness*. Cambridge, MA: Harvard University Press.

Jokinen, P., Pelkonen M, Voutilainen, U., & Meriläinen, P. (1998). Stimulated recall interview - a different data gathering method for studying perceptions and experiences in transcultural nursing. In: P. Meriläinen, K. Vehviläinen-Julkunen (Eds.), *Transcultural Nursing - Global Unifier of Care, Facing Diversity with Unity. Proceedings of the 23rd Annual Nursing Research Conference, pp.61-70, June 9-12, 1997, Kuopio, Finland.*

Jonassen, D. H., Wilson, B., Wang, S., & Grabinger, R. (1993). Constructivist uses of expert systems to support learning. *Journal of Computer-Based Instruction, 20*(3), 86-94.

Jonassen, D. H. (1994). Technology as cognitive tools: Learners as designers. Retrieved November 3, 2006, from http://itech1.coe.uga.edu/itforum/paper1/paper1.html.

Jonassen, D. H., & Reeves, T. C. (Ed.). (1996). *Learning with technology: Using computers as cognitive tools.* New York: Macmillan.

Jonassen, D. H. (1999). *Computers as mindtools for schools: Engaging critical thinking* (2nd ed.). New York: Prentice Hall.

Kalyuga, S. (2000). When using sound with a text or picture is not beneficial for learning. *Australian Journal of Educational Technology, 16*(2), 161-172.

Kastburg, S. E. (2001). Understanding mathematical concepts: the case of the logarithmic function. (Doctoral dissertation, University of Georgia, 2001). Dissertation.

Kienle, H. & Muller, H. (2001). Leveraging program analysis for web site reverse engineering. *Proceedings of the 3rd International Workshop on Web Site Evolution, pp. 117-125, November 10, 2001, Florence, Italy.*

Kieras, D. & Bovair, S. (1984). The role of mental models in learning to operate a device. *Cognitive Science, 8,* 255-273.

Kieras, D. E., & Myer, D. E. (1999). EPIC: A cognitive architecture for computational modelling of human performance. Retrieved July 6, 2005, from http://ai.eecs.umich.edu/people/kieras/epic.html

Kim, B., & Reeves, T. (2007). Reframing research on learning with technology: in search of the meaning of cognitive tools, *Instructional Science, 35*(3), 207-256.

Kintsch, W. (1974). *The Representation of Meaning in Memory.* Hillsdale, NJ: Erlbaum.

Kirriemuir, J., & McFarlane, A. (2004). Literature review in games and learning: A report for NESTA Futurelab. Retrieved November 3, 2006, from http://www.nestafuturelab.org/research/reviews/08_01.htm.

Klatzky, R.L. (1980). *Human Memory: Structures and Processes* (2nd Edition). San Francisco, CA: Freeman.

Klausmeier, H.J. (1980). *Learning and Teaching Concepts.* New York: Academic Press.

Klotz, E. (1991). Visualisation in geometry: a case study of multimedia mathematics education project. *In:* W. Zimmerman & S. Cunningham (Eds.), *Visualisation in teaching and learning mathematics.* (pp. 95-104). USA: Mathematics Association of America.

Knowlton, K. C. (1966). *L[6]: Bell Telephone Laboratories Low-Level Linked List Language.* 16 mm black and white sound film, 16 minutes. Murray Hill, NJ: Technical Information Libraries, Bell Laboratories.

Knuth, D. E. (1963). Computer-Drawn Flowcharts. *Communications of the ACM, 6*(9), 555-563.

Knuth, D. E. (1984). Literate Programming. *The Computer Journal, 27*(2), 97-111.

Kosslyn, S. M., Sukel, K. E., & Bly, B. M. (1999). Squinting with the mind's eye: Effects of stimulus resolution on imaginal and perceptual comparisons. *Memory and Cognition, 27*(2), 276-287.

Kulik, J. A. (Ed.). (1994). *Meta-analytic studies of findings on computer-based instruction.* Hillsdale, NJ: Lawrence Erlbaum.

Kushan, B. (1994). Preparing programming teachers, *ACM SIGCSE Bulletin, 26*(1), 248-252.

Laird, J.E., Newell, A., & P.S. Rosenbloom. (1987). Soar: An architecture for general intelligence. *Artificial Intelligence, 33,* 1-64.

Likert, R. (1932). A Technique for the Measurement of Attitudes. *Archives of Psychology, 140,* 1-55.

Lajoie, S. P., & Derry, S. J. (Eds.). (1993). *Computers as cognitive tools*. Hillsdale, NJ: Lawrence Erlbaum.

Larkin, J. H., & Simon, H. A. (1987).Why a diagram is (sometimes) worth ten thousand words. *Cognitive Science, 11*, 65-99.

Ledgard, H. F. (1975). *Programming proverbs*. Rochell Park, NJ: Hayden.

Lesh, R., & Lehrer, R. (2000). Iterative refinement cycles for videotape analysis of conceptual change. In R. Lesh (Ed.), *Handbook of research data design in mathematics and science education. (pp. 665-708). Mahway, NJ: Lawrence Erblaum Associates.*

Lindgren, E. & Sullivan, K. P. H. (2003). Stimulated recall as a trigger for increasing noticing and language awareness in the L2 writing classroom: A case study of two young female writers. *Language Awareness, 12*(3&4), 172-186.

Loftus, G. & Loftus, E. (1976). *Human Memory: The Processing of Information*. Hillsdale, NJ: Erlbaum.

Lum, A. (2003). Scrutable User Models in Decentralised Adaptive Systems. In P. Brusilovsky, A. Corbett, and F. Rosis (Eds.), *9th International Conference on User Modelling*, (pp. 426-428). Springer.

Mandler, J. (1984). *Stories, Scripts, and Scenes: Aspects of Schema Theory*. Hillsdale, NJ: Erlbaum.

Massey, A. P., & Wallace, W. A. (1996). Understanding and facilitating group problem structuring and formulation: Mental representations, interactions, and representation aids, *Decision Support Systems, 17*, 253-274.

Maybin, J., Mercer, N. and Stierer, B. (1992). 'Scaffolding' learning in the classroom. In K. Norman (ed.) *Thinking Voices*. London: Hodder and Stoughton.

Mayer, R. (1981). Psychology of Computer Programming for Novices. *Series in Learning and Cognition.* Report No. 81-2.

Mayer, R., Dyck, J. & Vilberg, W. (1986). Learning to program and learning to think: What's the connection? *Communications of the ACM, 29*(7), 605-610.

Mayer, R. E., & Wittrock, M. C. (1996). Problem-solving transfer. In R. Calfee & R. Berliner (Eds.), *Handbook of educational psychology.* (pp. 47-62). New York: Macmillan.

Mayer, R. E. (2001). *Multimedia learning.* New York: Cambridge University Press.

Mayer, R. E., Mautone, P. D., & Prothero, W. (2002). Pictorial aids for learning by doing in a multimedia geology simulation game. *Journal of Educational Psychology, 94*, 171-185.

Mayer, R. E., & Moreno, R. (2003). Nine ways to reduce cognitive load in multimedia learning. *Educational Psychologist, 38*, 43-52.

McQuillan, M. (2000). *The Narrative Reader.* New York, NY: Routledge.

Merriam, S. B. (1998). *Qualitative research and case study applications in education.* San Francisco, CA: Jossey-Bass.

Merrill, M. D., & Tennyson, R. (1977). *Teaching concepts: An instructional design guide* (1st ed.). Englewood Cliffs NJ: Educational Technology Publications.

Miller, G. A. (1956). The magical number seven, plus or minus two: Some limits on our capability for processing information. *Psychological Review, 63*, 81-97.

Miyake, N. (1986). Constructive interaction and the iterative process of understanding. *Cognitive Science, 10*, 151–177.

Moreno, Roxana & Richard Duran (2004). Do Multiple Representations Need Explanations? The Role of Verbal Guidance and Individual Differences in Multimedia Mathematics Learning. *Journal of Educational Psychology, 96*(3), 492-503.

Myers, B. A. (1990). Taxonomies of visual programming and program visualization. *Journal of Visual Languages and Computing, 1*(1), 97-123.

Naps, T., Roessling, G., Almstrum, V., Dann, W., Fleischer, R., Hundhausen, C., Korhonen, A., Malmi, L., Mchally, M., Rodger, S., & Valazquez-Iturbide, J. (2003). ITiCSE 2002 working group report: exploring the role of visualization and engagement in computer science education, *SIGCSE Bulletin, 35*,131–152.

Naps, T. (1996). Algorithm visualization served off the World Wide Web: Why and how. *ACM SIGCSE Bulletin, 28*(SI), 66-71.

Naps, T. (co-chair), Rößling, G. (co-chair), Almstrum, V., Dann, W., Fleischer, R., Hundhausen, C., Korhonen, A., Malmi, L., McNally, M., Roger, S., & Velazquesiturbide, J.A. (2003). "Exploring the Role of Visualization and Engagement in Computer Science Education." Report of the Working Group on "Improving the Educational Impact of Algorithm Visualization", *Communications of the ACM, 35*(2).

Naps, T., Eagan, J., & Norton, L. (2000) JHAVÉ — an environment to actively engage students in Web-based algorithm visualizations, *ACM SIGCSE Bulletin, 32*(1), 109-113.

Nassi, I. & Shneiderman, B. (1973). Flowchart technique for structured programming. *ACM SIGPLAN Notices, 8*(8), 12-26.

Newell, A. (1990). *Unified Theories of Cognition. Cambridge*, MA: Harvard University Press.

Norman, D. A. (1993). *Things That Make Us Smart: Defending Human Attributes in the Age of the Machine*. Reading, MA: Addison-Wesley Publishing Company.

Overmass, M. (2005). GameMaker (Version 6.1) [Computer Software]. Utrecht University: Institute of Information and Computing Sciences. Retrieved October 27, 2005, from www.gamemaker.nl

Paivio, A. (1986). *Mental Representations*. New York: Oxford University Press.

Papert, S. (1990). Introduction. In I. Herel (Ed.), *Constructionist learning.* (pp. 1-8). Cambridge, MA: Media Laboratory.

Pareja-Flores, C., & Velázquez-Iturbide, J. (2003). *Program execution and visualization on the web, Web-based education: learning from experience*. Hershey, PA: Idea Group Publishing.

Patton, M. (1990). *Qualitative Evaluation and Research Methods*. Newbury Park, CA: Sage Publications, Inc.

Pausch, R., & Conway, M. (2000). Alice: Lessons learned from building a 3D system for novices. Paper presented at the Conference on Human Factors in Computing Systems, The Hague, The Netherlands.

Pea, R. D., & Kurland, D. M. (1983). On the cognitive prerequisites of learning computer programming. Report to NIE (Contract #400-83-0016). Technical Report No. 18, Bank Street College, Center for Children and Technology.

Petre, M., Blackwell, A.F., & Green, T. R. G. (1996). *Cognitive questions in software visualisation.* Retrieved October 10, 2004, from http://www.cl.cam.ac.uk/users/afb21/publications/book-chapter.html

PHP. (2007, December 9). In *Wikipedia: The Free Encyclopedia*. Retrieved October 27, 2007, from http://en.wikipedia.org/wiki/php

Pinker, S. (1997). *How the mind works*. New York: W. W. Norton and Company.

Pirie, S. (1996a). Classroom video-Recording: When, why and how does it offer a valuable data source for qualitative research? *Proceedings of the 16th Annual Meeting of the North American Chapter of the International Group for the Psychology of Mathematics Education, October 14, 1996, Panama City, FL, United States.*

Pirie, S. (1996b). What are the data? An exploration of the use of video-recording as a data gathering tool in the mathematics classroom. *Proceedings of the 16th Annual Meeting of the North American Chapter of the International Group for the Psychology of Mathematics Education, October 14, 1996, Panama City, FL, United States.*

Pirie, S. (2001). Analysis, Lies, and videotape. *Proceedings of the 23rd Annual Meeting of the North American Chapter of the International Group for the Psychology of Mathematics Education, 2001, Snowbird, UH, United States.*

Pirie, S., & Kieren, T. (1989). A recursive theory of mathematical understanding. *For the Learning of Mathematics, 9*(4), 7-11.

Pirie, S., & Kieren, T. (1992). Watching Sandy's understanding grow. *The Journal of Mathematical Behavior, 11*(3), 243-257.

Powell, A. B., Francisco, J. M., & Maher, C. A. (2003). An analytical model for studying the development of learners' mathematical ideas and reasoning using videotape data. *Journal of Mathematical Behavior, 22*, 405-435.

Presmeg, N. (1997). Research on visualization in learning and teaching mathematics. In Gutierrez, A. & Boero, P. (Eds.). *Handbook of research on psychology of mathematics education: Past, present and future*, (pp. 205-235), Rotterdam/Taipei: Sense Publishers.

Price, B. A., Baecker, R. M. & Small, I. S. (1992). A principled taxonomy of software visualization. *Journal of Visual Languages and Computing*, *4*(3), 211-266.

Rader, C., Brand, C., & Lewis, C. (1997). Degrees of comprehension: Children's understanding of a visual programming environment. *Proceedings of the SIGCHI conference on human factors in computing systems, p.351-358, March 22-27, 1997, Atlanta, Georgia, United States.*

Reiber, L. (1995). A historical review of visualisation in human cognition. *Educational Technology, Research and Development*, *43*(1), 1042-1629.

Reigeluth, C. M. (Ed.). (1983). *Instructional-design theories and models: An overview of their current status*. Hillsdale, NJ: Erlbaum.

Reigeluth, C. M. (Ed.) (1987). *Instructional theories in action: Lessons illustrating selected theories and models*. Hillsdale, NJ: Erlbaum.

Reisburt, D., & Logie, R. (1993). The ins and outs of working memory: Overcoming the limits on learning from imagery. In B. Roskos-Edwoldsen, M. J. Inton-Peterson, & R. E. Anderson (Ed.), *Imagery, creativity, and discovery*, (pp. 39-76). Amsterdam: North-Holland Elsever Science Publishers.

Reiser, B. (2004). Scaffolding complex learning: The mechanisms of structuring and problematizing student work. *Journal of the Learning Sciences*, *13*(3), 273-304

Reiss, S., & Renieris, M. (2002). *The BLOOM Software Visualisation System.* Retrieved October 10, 2004, from http://www.cs.brown.edu/~spr/research/bllom/fullbloom.pdf

Reiss, S. (2005). The paradox of software visualization. *3rd IEEE International Workshop on Visualizing Software for Understanding and Analysis, pp. 19, September 25, 2005, Budapest, Hungary.*

Rieber, L. P. (2005). Multimedia learning in games, simulations, and microworlds. In R. E. Mayer (Ed.), *The Cambridge handbook of multimedia learning.* (pp. 549-567). Cambridge: Cambridge University Press.

Robertson, J., & Good, J. (2004). Interaction design and children. Paper presented at the Proceeding of the 2004 conference on Interaction Design and Children: Building a Community, Maryland.

Roschelle, J. (2000). Choosing and using video equipment for data collection. In R. Lesh (Ed.), *Handbook of research data design in mathematics and science education* (pp. 709-731). Mahway, NJ: Lawrence Erblaum Associates.

Roskos-Edwoldsen, B., Inton-Peterson, M. J., & Anderson, R. E. (1993). *Imagery, Creativity, and Discovery*. Amsterdam: North-Holland Elsever Science Publishers.

Roy, P., & St. Denis, R. (1976). Linear flowchart generator for structured language. *ACM SIGPLAN Notices, 11*(11), 58-64.

Rumelhart, D. & Norman, D. (1978). Accretion, tuning and restructuring: Three modes of learning. In J.W. Cotton & R. Klatzky (Eds.), *Semantic Factors in Cognition*. Hillsdale, NJ: Erlbaum.

Rumelhart, D.E. (1980). Schemata: The building blocks of cognition. In R.J. Spiro, B.Bruce, & W.F. Brewer (eds.), *Theoretical Issues in Reading and Comprehension*. Hillsdale, NJ: Erlbaum.

Rumelhart, D. & Norman, D. (1981). Analogical processes in learning. In J.R. Anderson (ed.), *Cognitive Skills and their Acquisition*. Hillsdale, NJ: Erlbaum.

Salomon G., Perkins D.N., Globerson T. (1991). Partners in cognition: extending human intelligence with intelligent technologies. *Educational Researcher, 20*(3), 2-9.

Sensalire, M. & Ogao, P. (2007). Tool user requirements classification: how software tools measure up. *Proceedings of the 5th International conference on Computer graphics, virtual reality, visualisation and interaction in Africa. pp.119-124. October, 29-31,2007, Grahamstown, SA.*

Shim, J. E., & Li, Y. (2006). Applications of Cognitive Tools in the Classroom. In M. Orey (Ed.), *Emerging perspectives on learning, teaching, and technology*. Retrieved January 6, 2008 from http://projects.coe.uga.edu/epltt/.

Schank, R.C. (1975). *Conceptual Information Processing*. New York: Elsevier.

Schank, R.C. (1982). *Dynamic Memory: A Theory of Reminding and Learning in Computers and People*. Boston, MA. Cambridge University Press.

Schneider, W. & Shiffrin, R.M. (1977). Controlled and automatic human information processing: I. Detection, Search, and Attention. *Psychological Review, 84,* 1-66.

Schnotz, W., & Bannert, M. (2003). Construction and interference in learning from multiple representation. *Learning and Instruction, 13*, 141–156.

Schumacher, R. & Czerwinski, M. (1992). Mental models and the acquisition of expert knowledge. In R. Hoffman (ed.), *The psychology of expertise*. New York: Springer-Verlag.

She☐edi, A. (2005). *Multiple Case Narrative: A Qualitative Approach to Studying Multiple Populations*. Philadelphia, PA: John Benjamins.

Shiffrin, R.M. & Schneider, W. (1977). Controlled and automatic human information processing: II. Perceptual learning, automatic attending, and a general theory. *Psychological Review, 84*, 127-190.

Shneiderman, B. (1985). When Children Learn Programming: Antecedents, concepts and outcomes. *Computing Teacher, 12*(5), 14-17.

Soloway, E. (1986). Learning to program = learning to construct mechanisms and explanations. *Communications of the ACM, 29*(9), 850-858.

Stake, R. (1995). *The art of case study research*. Thousand Oaks, CA: Sage Publications.

Stasko, J. (1997). Using student-built algorithm animation as learning aids. *ACM SIGCSE Bulletin, 29*(9), 25-29.

Stasko, J., & Lawrence, A. (1998). Empirically assessment algorithm animation as learning aids. *In* Stasko, J., Domingue, J., Brown, M. H., & Price, B. A. (Eds.), *Software Visualization,* (pp. 124-128). Boston, MA: MIT Press.

Stasko, J., Badre, A., & Lewis, C. (1993). Do algorithm animations assist learning?: An empirical study and analysis. *Proceedings of the SIGCHI conference on human factors in computing systems, pp.61-66, April 24-29, 1993, Amsterdam, The Netherlands.*

Sweller, J., (1998). Cognitive load during problem solving: Effects on learning, *Cognitive Science, 12*, 257-285.

Sweller, J. (1989). Cognitive technology: Some procedures for facilitating learning and problem solving in mathematics and science. *Journal of Educational Psychology, 81*(4), 457-466.

Sweller, J., & Cooper, G. A. (1985). The use of worked examples as a substitute for problem solving in learning algebra. *Cognition and Instruction, 2*(1), 59-89.

Sweller, J., & Chandler, P. (1994). Why some material is difficult to learn. *Cognition and Instruction, 12*(3), 185-233.

Sweller, J. (1999). *Instructional Design in Technical Areas, Australian Education Review, No. 43*. Camberwell, Victoria, Australia: Australian Council for Educational Research.

Tennyson, R.D. & Cocchiarella, M.J. (1986). An Empirically Based Instructional Design Theory for Teaching Concepts. *Review of Educational Research, 56*(1), 40-71.

The Brain, Cognition, and Action Laboratory: EPIC (2005). Retrieved October 30, 2004, from http://www.umich.edu/~bcalab/epic.html

Thorndike, E. (1913). *Educational Psychology: The Psychology of Learning*. New York: Teachers College Press.

Tolman, E.C. (1922). A new formula for behaviorism. *Psychological Review, 29*, 44-53.

Trow, M. (2000). Some Consequences of the new information and communication technologies for higher education. *Research and Occasional Paper Series: CSHE.5.00 University of California, Berkeley, CSHE.5.00*.

Tudoreanu, M. (2003). Designing effective program visualization tools for reducing user's cognitive effort. *Proceedings from the 2003 ACM symposium on software visualization, 2003, San Diego, United States.*

Tuovinen, J. (2000). Optimising student cognitive load in computer education. *Proceedings of the Fourth Annual Australasian Computing Education Conference, pp. 235-241, December 4-6, 2000, Melbourne, Australia.*

Tulving, E. & Donaldson, W. (1972). *Organization of Memory.* New York: Academic Press.

Turner, P., McGregor, I., Turner, S., & Carroll, F. (2003). Evaluating soundscapes as a means of creating a sense of place. *In* Brazil, E. & Shinn-Cunningham, B. (Eds.), *Proceedings of the 2003 International Conference on Auditory Display. pp.148-151, July 6-9, 2003, Boston, USA.*

Ursyn, A. & Sung, R. (2007). Learning science with art. *ACM SIGGRAPH 2007 educators program, Article No. 8, 2007, San Diego, USA.*

Van Der Veer, G. C. (1989). Individual differences and the user interface. *Ergonomics, 32*(11), 1431-1449.

Vygotsky, L. S. (1978). *Mind in society: The development of higher psychological processes.* Cambridge, MA: Harvard University Press.

Wade, N. J., & Swanston, M. (1991). *Visual perception.* London: Routledge.

Waisel, L. B. (1998). The cognitive role of visualization in modelling. (Doctoral dissertation, Rensselaer Polytechnic Institute, 1998). Dissertation.

Wang, M. C., Haertel, G. D., & Walberg, H. J. (1993). Toward a knowledge base for school learning. *Review of Educational Research, 63*(3), 249-294.

Ware, C. (2000). *Information Visualization: Perception for Design.* San Diego, CA: Academic Press.

White, B. & Frederiksen, J. (1985). Qualitative models and intelligent learning environments. In R. Lawler & M. Yazdani (Eds.), *Artifical Intelligence and Education*. Norwood, NJ: Ablex.

Yehezkel, C. (2002). A taxonomy of computer architecture visualizations. *Proceedings of the 7th Annual Conference on Innovation and Technology in Computer Science Education, June 24-28, 2002, Aarhus, Denmark.*

Yehezkel, C. (2003). Making program execution comprehensible one level above the machine language. *Proceedings of the 8th Annual Conference on Innovation and Technology in Computer Science Education, June 30 - July 2, 2003, Thessaloniki, Greece.*

Yin, R. (1984). *Case study research, design, and methods (3rd edition)*. Thousand Oaks, CA: Sage Publications.

APPENDIX A

SURVEY 1: Effectiveness survey (Visualisation tool)

In learning about (concept), I think:

5	the use of (Visualisation tool) greatly helped me learn about (concept)
4	the use of (Visualisation tool) helped me learn about (concept)
3	I would have learnt about (concept) just as well without using (Visualisation tool)
2	the use of (Visualisation tool) made it more difficult to learn about (concept)
1	the use of (Visualisation tool) made it much more difficult to learn about (concept)

In learning about (concept), I think:

5	the use of (Visualisation tool) made it much more enjoyable to learn about (concept)
4	the use of (Visualisation tool) made it more enjoyable to learn about (concept)
3	I would have enjoyed learning about (concept) just as well without using (Visualisation tool)
2	the use of (Visualisation tool) made it less enjoyable to learn about (concept)
1	the use of (Visualisation tool) made it much less enjoyable to learn about (concept)

In learning about (concept), I think:

5	the use of (Visualisation tool) made it much quicker to learn about (concept)
4	the use of (Visualisation tool) made it quicker to learn about (concept)
3	I would have learnt about (concept) just as quickly without using (Visualisation tool)
2	the use of (Visualisation tool) made it slower to learn about (concept)
1	the use of (Visualisation tool) made it much slower to learn about (concept)

APPENDIX B

SURVEY 2: Effectiveness survey (Multiple Visualisation tools)

In learning about (concept), I think:

5	the use of (Visualisation tool1) was much more effective than (Visualisation tools2) in helping me learn about (concept)
4	the use of (Visualisation tool1) was more effective than (Visualisation tools2) in helping me learn about (concept)
3	the use of (Visualisation tool1) was no more effective than (Visualisation tools2) in helping me learn about (concept)
2	the use of (Visualisation tool1) was less effective than (Visualisation tools2) in helping me learn about (concept)
1	the use of (Visualisation tool1) was much less effective than (Visualisation tools2) in helping me learn about (concept)

In learning about (concept), I think:

5	the use of (Visualisation tool1) made it much more enjoyable to learn about (concept) than (Visualisation tools2)
4	the use of (Visualisation tool1) made it more enjoyable to learn about (concept) than (Visualisation tools2)
3	I enjoyed learning about (concept) just as well using (Visualisation tool1) as (Visualisation tools2)
2	the use of (Visualisation tool1) made it less enjoyable to learn about (concept) than (Visualisation tools2)
1	the use of (Visualisation tool1) made it much less enjoyable to learn about (concept) than (Visualisation tools2)

In learning about (concept), I think:

5	the use of (Visualisation tool1) made it much quicker to learn about (concept) than (Visualisation tools2)
4	the use of (Visualisation tool1) made it quicker to learn about (concept) than

	(Visualisation tools2)
3	I would have learnt about (concept) just as quickly using (Visualisation tool1) as (Visualisation tools2)
2	the use of (Visualisation tool1) made it slower to learn about (concept) than (Visualisation tools2)
1	the use of (Visualisation tool1) made it much slower to learn about (concept) than (Visualisation tools2)

APPENDIX C

Mental Model Development Rubric

LEVEL 1: Primitive Knowing

Concepts

5	4	3	2	1
≥5 concepts	4 concepts	3 concepts	2 concepts	≤1 concept

Refinement of linkage between concepts

5	4	3	2	1
comprehensive (≥5) linkage	substantial (4) linkage	some (3) linkage	very little (2) linkage	no linkage

Complexity of grouping of concepts

5	4	3	2	1
comprehensive (≥5) structured grouping	substantial (4) structured grouping	some (3) structured grouping	very little (2) structured grouping	no structured grouping

LEVEL 2: Image Making

Time developing physical representations (Storyboards)

5	4	3	2	1
<10 minutes	≥10 minutes	≥15 minutes	≥20 minutes	≥30 minutes

Concepts developed from concept map into a storyboard

5	4	3	2	1
≥5 concepts	4 concepts	3 concepts	2 concepts	≤1 concept

Refinement to physical representation (storyboard) of mental model

5	4	3	2	1
comprehensive (≥5)	substantial (4)	some (3)	very little (2)	none

Complexity of concept development in alternative representations of the same concept

5	4	3	2	1
several (>3) physical representations	3 physical representations \	2 physical alternative representation	1 physical alternative representation	no alternative physical representations

LEVEL 3: Image Having

Time for refinement of mental model (Mental Storyboards)

5	4	3	2	1
<10 minutes	≥10 minutes	≥15 minutes	≥20 minutes	≥30 minutes

Concepts developed into a Mental Storyboard

5	4	3	2	1
≥5 concepts	4 concepts	3 concepts	2 concepts	≤1 concept

Refinement: Manipulation of mental objects to develop intermediary steps

5	4	3	2	1
manipulation of ≥4 mental objects	manipulation of 3 mental objects	manipulation of 2 mental objects	a manipulation of a mental object	no evidence of manipulation

Complexity: Mental steps developed between initial and final scene

5	4	3	2	1
≥5 mental steps developed	4 mental steps developed	3 mental steps	2 mental steps	a single mental step

LEVEL 4: Property Noticing (using Mental Storyboarding)

Time taking known properties and abstracting commonalities to similar situations

5	4	3	2	1
<10 minutes	≥10 minutes	≥15 minutes	≥20 minutes	≥30 minutes

Concept Transference to similar situations

5	4	3	2	1
≥5 properties transferred	4 properties transferred	3 properties transferred	2 properties transferred	≤1 property transferred

Refinement: Manipulation of mental objects to develop intermediary steps

5	4	3	2	1
manipulation of ≥4 mental objects	manipulation of 3 mental objects	manipulation of 2 mental objects	manipulation of a mental object	no evidence of manipulation

Complexity: Mental steps developed between initial and final scene

5	4	3	2	1
≥5 mental steps developed	4 mental steps developed	3 mental steps	2 mental steps	1 mental step

LEVEL 5: Formalising (using Mental Storyboarding)

Time taking known properties and abstracting commonalities to non- similar situations

5	4	3	2	1
<10 minutes	≥10 minutes	≥15 minutes	≥20 minutes	≥30 minutes

Concept Transference to non- similar situations

5	4	3	2	1
≥5 properties transferred	4 properties transferred	3 properties transferred	2 properties transferred	≤1 property transferred

Refinement: Manipulation of mental objects to develop intermediary steps

5	4	3	2	1
manipulation of ≥4 mental objects	manipulation of 3 mental objects	manipulation of 2 mental objects	manipulation of a mental object	no evidence of manipulation

Complexity: Mental steps developed between initial and final scene

5	4	3	2	1
≥5 mental steps developed	4 mental steps developed	3 mental steps	2 mental steps	1 mental step

LEVEL 6: Observing (using Storyboarding or Narrative)

Time to formalise and organise observations

5	4	3	2	1
<10 minutes	≥10 minutes	≥15 minutes	≥20 minutes	≥30 minutes

Concepts developed into a formal response

5	4	3	2	1
≥5 concepts developed	4 concepts developed	3 concepts developed	2 concepts developed	≤1 concepts developed

Refinement: Considerations or references to formal thinking

5	4	3	2	1
≥4 considerations or references	3 considerations or references	2 considerations or references	1 consideration or reference	No consideration or reference

Complexity: Interaction between considerations or references to formal thinking

5	4	3	2	1
complex interactions (≥5)	4 interactions	simple interaction (3)	very simple interaction (1-2)	no interaction

LEVEL 7: Structuring (using Flowcharts)

Time to develop explanation of formal thinking in terms of a logical structure

5	4	3	2	1
<10 minutes	≥10 minutes	≥15 minutes	≥20 minutes	≥30 minutes

Concepts included into a logical structure

5	4	3	2	1
≥5 concepts included	4 concepts included	3 concepts included	2 concepts included	≤1 concepts included

Refinement: Considerations or references to formal thinking

5	4	3	2	1
≥4 considerations or references	3 considerations or references	2 considerations or references	1 consideration or reference	No consideration or reference

Complexity: Assumptions made to logical structure

5	4	3	2	1
comprehensive (≥4)	substantial (3)	some (2)	very little (1)	no assumptions

LEVEL 8: Inventising

Time before going beyond structured understanding to generate new questions

5	4	3	2	1
<10 minutes	≥10 minutes	≥15 minutes	≥20 minutes	≥30 minutes

Concepts: questions generated from existing concept(s)

5	4	3	2	1
≥5 questions generated	4 questions generated	3 questions generated	2 questions generated	≤1 question generated

Refinement: Questions refined with reference to existing concept structure or assumptions

5	4	3	2	1
≥3 questions refined	2 questions refined	a question refined	a question refined to existing concept	little or no refinement

Complexity: Representations of the same question

5	4	3	2	1
several (>3) representations	three representations	two representations	a representation	no alternative representations

FINAL CONCEPT MAP

Concepts

5	4	3	2	1
≥5 concepts	4 concepts	3 concepts	2 concepts	≤1 concept

Refinement of linkage between concepts

5	4	3	2	1
comprehensive (≥5) linkage	substantial (4) linkage	some (3) linkage	very little (2) linkage	no linkage

Complexity of grouping of concepts

5	4	3	2	1
comprehensive (≥5) structured grouping	substantial (4) structured grouping	some (3) structured grouping	very little (2) structured grouping	no structured grouping

Appendix D

Student Workbook – Sequence (Alice) Cohort A & D1a

Advanced Information Technology — Sequence

SEQUENCE

1. The process of coming to an understanding of a concept starts with **primitive knowing**. This is your initial of understanding of the concept.

In the case of the concept of sequence, you will have various understandings of change and order of process, several derived from familiar curriculum areas including mathematics, music, science, sport and written structures. These are identified through brainstorming activities to develop an initial concept map of your understanding of sequence.

2. At the second level, **image making**, you will be asked, through specific tasks, to make distinctions in your previous abilities using them under new conditions or to new ends.

Through examples derived from your brainstorming activities, take these examples and in the ALICE programming environment, generate animations of objects moving, changing colour, changing size, etc. to visually represent these sequences. The ability to generate such sequences is used as a determiner that the second level has been achieved.

3. The third level, **image having**, involves refining the mental model to enable creation of views that can be manipulated, a "mental object" distinct from physical representations.

You will be asked to mentally generate animation sequences without the aid of storyboarding, running through complex sequences in your heads before trying them out in the programming environment. In particular the ability to visualise a series of movements or changes and determine the final position or state of an object is used as a determiner that the third level has been achieved.

4. The fourth level, **property noticing**, involves examining views for specific properties. By noting distinctions, combinations or connections between views, predictions of how they might be achieved can be made and such relationships recorded.

You are asked to combine smaller sequences to generate larger and more complex sequences. The ability to generate specific solutions utilising a correct sequencing of simpler sequences is used as a determiner that the fourth level has been achieved.

5. The fifth level, **formalising**, involves consciously thinking about the noted properties and abstracting commonalities. The mental model should now be class like and not dependent on example views.

Utilising the object oriented properties of objects in the ALICE programming environment, you will develop increasingly complex animations involving several body parts. The ability to utilise sequences developed for one body part e.g. an arm to animate other body parts e.g. a leg, is used as a determiner that the fifth level has been achieved.

6. The sixth level, **observing**, involves formalising and organising observations to an extent that they are considering and referencing their own formal thinking.

You will develop complex animations of several objects utilising a large set of sequences to develop animated movies. Your ability to describe the overall production sequence through the use of individual animated sequences is used as a determiner that the sixth level has been achieved.

7. The seventh level, **structuring**, involves being able to explain your formal thinking in terms of a logical structure and being aware of assumptions. An example is the creation of formal proofs.

You are required to represent their animated movies through the use of flow charts and storyboards. Your ability to describe the overall production sequence through the use of formal, logical diagrams is used as a determiner that the seventh level has been achieved.

8. The eighth and final level, **inventising**, is going "freely and imaginatively beyond structured understanding to create totally new questions that might develop into new concepts.

Your ability to identify where repeated sequences exist and postulate the advantage to be gained if the software could repeat these sequences is used as a determiner that the eighth and final level in development of this concept has been achieved.

SQEUENCE MENTAL MODEL

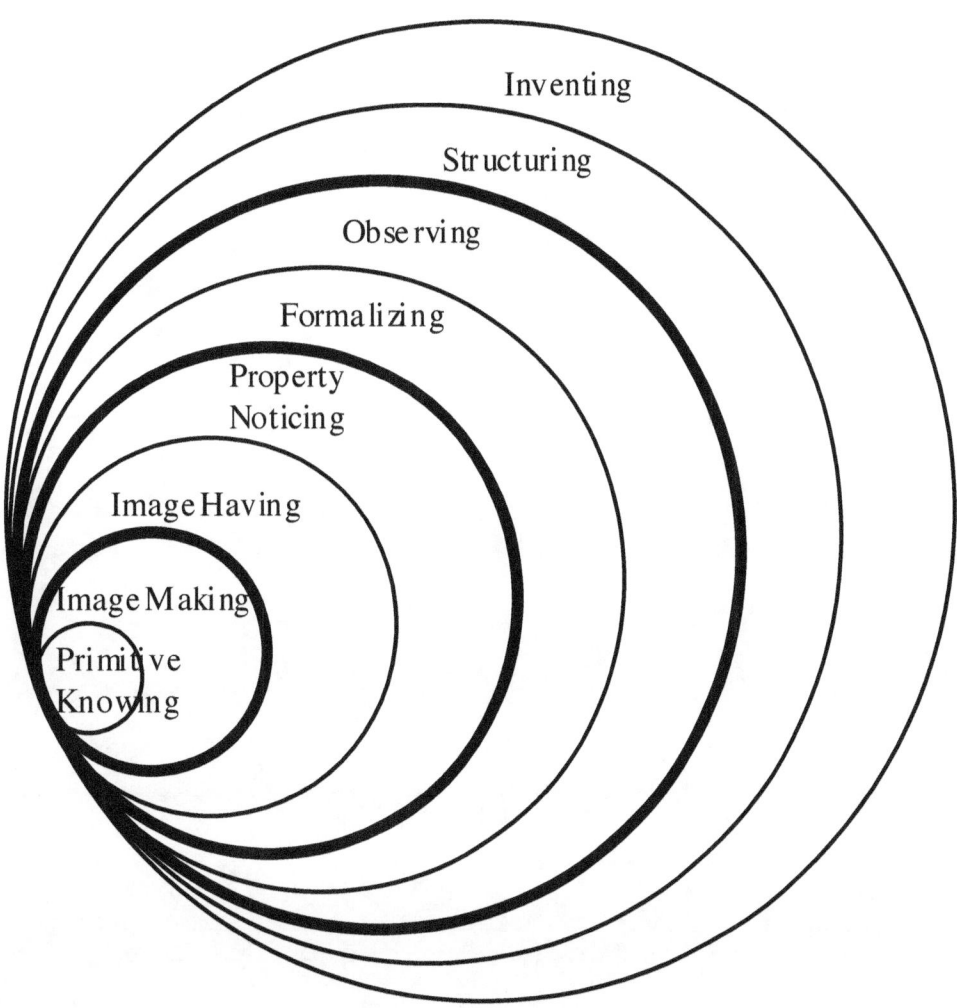

SEQUENCE (LEVEL 1) – Concept Map

SEQUENCE

SEQUENCE (LEVEL 2) – Animation Storyboards

Sequence:

[ ] [ ] [ ]

Notes

Sequence:

[ ] [ ] [ ]

Notes

Advanced Information Technology — Sequence

SEQUENCE (LEVEL 3) – Mental Storyboards

Describe your initial scene, describe your final scene, then describe the steps to get from one to another

Initial Scene	Final Scene	Steps

SEQUENCE (LEVEL 4) – Property Noticing

Create your own Methods by making a sequence for one object, and applying that sequence to other objects

Advanced Information Technology — Sequence

SEQUENCE (LEVEL 5) – Formalising

Develop a sequence to make one limb of a four legged animal move naturally, then apply this sequence to the other limbs

SEQUENCE (LEVEL 6) – Observing

Now develop several sequences to make a number of objects move together in one 'movie'

Advanced Information Technology — Sequence

SEQUENCE (LEVEL 7) – Structuring

Describe your 'movie' as a flowchart diagram

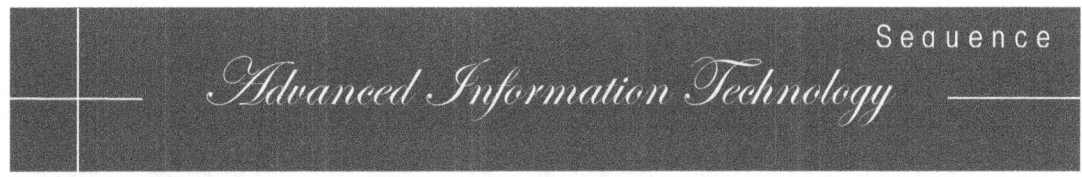

SEQUENCE (LEVEL 8) – Inventising

How can you utilise sequences in new and interesting ways:

Appendix E

Student Workbook (Part) – Iteration (Alice)

Advanced Information Technology — ITERATION

ITERATION

1. The process of coming to an understanding starts with **primitive knowing**. This is your initial of understanding of the concept.

    In the case of the concept of iteration, students will have some understanding of repetition, but an understanding that iteration comprises repeating blocks should be developed from the eighth inventising phase of their development of the concept of sequence. Examples of iterations should be identified through brainstorming activities to develop an initial concept map of their understanding of iteration.

2. At the second level, **image making**, you will be asked, through specific tasks, to make distinctions in your previous abilities using them under new conditions or to new ends.

    Through tasks derived from their brainstorming activities, take previous examples and in the ALICE programming environment, generate animations using simple repeated sets of instructions. The ability to generate such iterations is used as a determiner that the second level has been achieved.

3. The third level, **image having**, involves refining the mental model to enable creation of views that can be manipulated, a "mental object" distinct from physical representations.

    You will be asked to mentally run through animation iterations without the aid of storyboarding, running through complex iterations in your head before trying them out in the programming environment. In particular the ability to visualise a nested iteration(an iteration within an iteration) and determine the final position or state of an object is used as a determiner that the third level has been achieved.

4. The fourth level, **property noticing**, involves examining views for specific properties. By noting distinctions, combinations or connections between views, predictions of how they might be achieved can be made and such relationships recorded.

You are asked to combine iterations to generate complex nested iterations. The ability to generate specific solutions utilising a correct nesting of smaller iterations is used as a determiner that the fourth level has been achieved.

5. The fifth level, **formalising**, involves consciously thinking about the noted properties and abstracting commonalities. The mental model should now be class like and not dependent on example views.

Utilising the ability to parallel process sections of code in the ALICE programming environment, you will develop increasingly complex animations involving several iterations occurring at the same time. The ability to coordinate independent iterations on several objects is used as a determiner that the fifth level has been achieved.

6. The sixth level, **observing**, involves formalising and organising observations to an extent that they are considering and referencing their own formal thinking.

Utilising the ability to parallel process sections of code in the ALICE programming environment, you will develop increasingly complex animations involving several iterations occurring at the same time. The ability to coordinate independent iterations on several objects is used as a determiner that the sixth level has been achieved.

7. The seventh level, **structuring**, involves being able to explain your formal thinking in terms of a logical structure and being aware of assumptions. An example is the creation of formal proofs.

You are required to represent the use of iterations in their animated movies through the use of flow charts and storyboards. Your ability to describe the overall production sequence through the use of formal, logical diagrams is used as a determiner that the seventh level has been achieved.

8. The eighth and final level, **inventising**, is going "freely and imaginatively beyond structured understanding to create totally new questions that might develop into new concepts.

Your ability to identify where large sections of discrete code exist and postulate the advantage to be gained if the software could modularise these sections to facilitate their reuse is used as a determiner that the eighth and final level in the development of the concept of iteration has been achieved.

Appendix F

Student Workbook (Part) – Selection (Alice)

Advanced Information Technology — SELECTION

Selection

1. The process of coming to an understanding starts with **primitive knowing**. This is your initial of understanding of the concept.

    In the case of the concept of selection, you will have some understanding of choice, but an understanding that selection comprises a choice between sequence and iteration blocks should be developed from the eighth inventising phase of your development of the concept of iteration. Examples of selection should be identified through brainstorming activities to develop an initial concept map of your understanding of selection.

2. At the second level, **image making**, you will be asked, through specific tasks, to make distinctions in your previous abilities using them under new conditions or to new ends.

    Through tasks derived from their brainstorming activities, take previous examples and in the Gamemaker programming environment generate games by selecting between simple sets of instructions. The ability to generate such selection is used as a determiner that the second level has been achieved.

3. The third level, **image having**, involves refining the mental model to enable creation of views that can be manipulated, a "mental object" distinct from physical representations.

    You will be asked to mentally run through selection options without the aid of storyboarding, running through complex selections in your head before trying them out in the programming environment. In particular the ability to visualise a nested selection (a selection within a selection) and determine the final position or state of an object is used as a determiner that the third level has been achieved.

4. The fourth level, **property noticing**, involves examining views for specific properties. By noting distinctions, combinations or connections between views, predictions of how they might be achieved can be made and such relationships recorded.

You are asked to create selections to alter the properties of objects within your game. The ability to generate specific solutions utilising a series of selections is used as a determiner that the fourth level has been achieved.

5. The fifth level, **formalising**, involves consciously thinking about the noted properties and abstracting commonalities. The mental model should now be class like and not dependent on example views.

You are asked to combine selections to generate complex nested selections. The ability to generate specific solutions utilising a correct nesting of smaller selections is used as a determiner that the fourth level has been achieved.

6. The sixth level, **observing**, involves formalising and organising observations to an extent that they are considering and referencing their own formal thinking.

Utilising the ability to parallel process sections of code in the Gamemaker programming environment, you will develop increasingly complex games involving several activities occurring at the same time. The ability to coordinate independent activities on several objects is used as a determiner that the sixth level has been achieved.

7. The seventh level, **structuring**, involves being able to explain your formal thinking in terms of a logical structure and being aware of assumptions. An example is the creation of formal proofs.

You are required to represent the use of selection in your game through the use of flow charts and storyboards. Your ability to describe the overall sequence through the use of formal, logical diagrams is used as a determiner that the seventh level has been achieved.

8. The eighth and final level, **inventising**, is going "freely and imaginatively beyond structured understanding to create totally new questions that might develop into new concepts.

Your ability to identify where large sections of discrete code exist and postulate the advantage to be gained if choices can be made between these sections to increase complexity and facilitate their reuse is used as a determiner that the eighth and final level in the development of the concept of selection has been achieved.

www.ingramcontent.com/pod-product-compliance
Lightning Source LLC
Chambersburg PA
CBHW080857230426
43663CB00013B/2565